HISTORICAL DICTIONARIES OF RELIGIONS, PHILOSOPHIES, AND MOVEMENTS
Edited by Jon Woronoff

Historical Dictionary of the Holiness Movement

edited by William C. Kostlevy

Gari-Anne Patzwald
Associate Editor

Historical Dictionaries of Religions,
Philosophies, and Movements, No. 36

The Scarecrow Press, Inc.
Lanham, Maryland, and London
2001

SCARECROW PRESS, INC.

Published in the United States of America
by Scarecrow Press, Inc.
4720 Boston Way, Lanham, Maryland 20706
www.scarecrowpress.com

4 Pleydell Gardens, Folkestone
Kent CT20 2DN, England

British Library Cataloguing in Publication Information Available

Library of Congress Cataloging-in-Publication Data

Historical dictionary of the holiness movement / edited by William C. Kostlevy ;
   Gari-Anne Patzwald, associate editor.
     p. cm.—(Historical dictionaries of religions, philosophies, and movements ; no. 36)
   Includes bibliographical references.
   ISBN 0-8108-3955-5 (alk. paper)
   1. Holiness churches—History—Dictionaries. I. Kostlevy, William, 1952– II. Patzwald,
   Gari-Anne. III. Series.
   BX7990.H6 H55 2001
   270.8—dc21
                                00-048239

♾™ The paper used in this publication meets the minimum requirements of
American National Standard for Information Sciences—Permanence of
Paper for Printed Library Materials, ANSI/NISO Z39.48-1992.
Manufactured in the United States of America.

For my mother,
Dorothy Stuve Kostlevy,
and her friend from Olive Branch Mission
and Greenville College, Edith Tjepkema,
and their teachers, Helen I. Root and Mary Alice Tenney

Contents

Editor's Foreword

It is much harder to define a religious movement than a religion or denomination per se. That applies especially when that movement almost defies definition like the holiness movement. For one, its members come from rather different backgrounds, often Methodist, but other denominations as well, and that shapes a differing self-definition. More significant, however, is that despite any differences, one of the things they have in common is a dislike for rigid principles, rules and regulations, and church polities that could tie them down and get in the way of the search for a correct relationship with God. This underlying ethos left room for spiritual growth over the decades, meaning that the holiness movement is not the same today as it was yesterday. It has also enabled growth in numbers, growth far greater than initially expected, and also growth into other ethnic groups and abroad to other parts of Europe, Africa, Asia, and Latin America. That will bring even more change tomorrow.

Even if the holiness movement cannot be defined with any precision, it is essential to know more about a movement that already counts some ten million members around the world. It is necessary to take stock, and that is the purpose of this *Historical Dictionary of the Holiness Movement*. This is done largely through the dictionary entries, some of which describe the basic principles, rules, and policies, although loosely enough to accommodate variations. More important are the examples of leading persons, churches, and organizations, which show the activities of the people and structures that have shaped the movement. Further background is provided by a more general overview in the introduction, an indication of the path followed thus far in the chronology, a helpful list of acronyms and abbreviations, and an extensive bibliography. The many books and articles listed can fill the gaps and lead to a deeper understanding.

The broad range of individuals, groups, and concepts covered by this *Historical Dictionary of the Holiness Movement* required an exceptional degree of coordination. This was achieved by the compiler and editor, William Kostlevy, who wrote many of the entries and other parts of the book himself and liaised with an eminent panel of contributors. Dr. Kostlevy, who studies both history and theology, has already written and lectured extensively on many of the same topics. He is presently the archivist, special collections librarian, and associate director of the Wesleyan/Holiness Studies Center of Asbury Theological Seminary, the ideal place for a coordinator to be. He was ably assisted by associate editor Gari-Anne Patzwald. Together the editors and contributors have fashioned a unique introduction to a movement that is still inadequaly known and whose impact will be even greater in the future.

Jon Woronoff
Series Editor

Preface

The holiness movement traces its roots to John Wesley's insistence that Christians, in this life, might become perfect in love or intention. This teaching, and the experience known as "Christian perfection" or "entire sanctification" that grew out of it, found fertile ground in the perfectionistic climate of antebellum North America. By the late 1830s, three groups of closely related but distinct bodies of perfectionists could be found, especially in the northern United States and Canada. They included Methodists, often associated with New York lay evangelist Phoebe Palmer; Oberlin perfectionists, often associated with Asa Mahan and Charles G. Finney; and the so-called antinomian perfectionists, most notably associated with John Humphrey Noyes's Oneida community. The first two perfectionist denominations, the Wesleyan Methodist Church (1843) and the Free Methodist Church (1860), united features of Methodistic perfectionism and Oberlin perfectionism. In the years following the American Civil War, the holiness movement spread to England, the European continent, and around the world. In the 20th century, major holiness denominations, such as the Church of the Nazarene, the Evangelical Holiness Church of Korea, the Salvation Army, and the Church of God (Anderson), have experienced rapid growth. By the beginning of the 21st century, some estimates place holiness movement membership at nearly 10 million.

This *Historical Dictionary of the Holiness Movement* seeks to give basic information about important personalities and institutions. Its focus on the people draws its inspiration, in part, from the movement's own insistence that personal experience is a primary, although not the exclusive, source of theological authority. As a historical dictionary, its focus is on the founders and shapers and holiness thought and experience. Although I have sought to be inclusive and global, the limited availability of sources, especially relating to the recent rapid growth of the movement outside North America, is, unfortunately, reflected in the final product. As with all such projects, one of the real challenges is to define what should be included. I have purposely chosen a narrow definition. I have not included members of Pentecostal holiness churches, such as the Pentecostal Holiness Church and the Church of God (Cleveland), or individuals or groups primarily associated with the Keswick tradition. In fact, the holiness movement is historically prior to, and the ideological bridge between, these movements. In truth, a real understanding of the holiness movement is basic to an understanding of Evangelicalism and Pentecostalism. Words in bold type in the dictionary entries refer the reader to full dictionary entries on the persons or subjects bolded.

As with any work of this nature, its quality is dependent on the efforts of a number of contributors. I am especially grateful to the work of Stan Ingersol, Tim Erdel, Melvin E. Dieter, and Charles Edwin Jones and to the support I have received from the B. L. Fisher Library of Asbury Theological Seminary, D. William Faupel, director.

Contributors

Todd Bergman is a United Methodist pastor in Oklahoma.

Gary Bowell is a recorded minister in the Central Yearly Meeting of Friends.

Kenneth O. Brown is an independent scholar and authority on holiness camp meetings.

Barry L. Callen is University Professor at Anderson University, Anderson, Indiana, and editor of the *Wesleyan Theological Journal*.

Kenneth J. Collins is professor of church history at Asbury Theological Seminary, Wilmore, Kentucky.

Robert W. Cruver is president of Zarephath Bible Institute, Zarephath, New Jersey.

Melvin E. Dieter is professor emeritus at Asbury Theological Seminary, Wilmore, Kentucky.

Paul Arthur Erdel is a former missionary and minister in the Missionary Church.

Timothy Paul Erdel is on the faculty of Bethel College, Mishawaka, Indiana.

Wayne Jay Gerber is professor emeritus at Bethel College, Mishawaka, Indiana.

Barry W. Hamilton is a librarian at Northeastern Theological Seminary, North Chili, New York.

Thomas D. Hamm is archivist and professor of history at Earlham College, Richmond, Indiana.

R. Jeffrey Hiatt is a graduate student at Asbury Theological Seminary, Wilmore, Kentucky.

Christopher M. Howlett is pastor of the Vine Grove (Kentucky) United Methodist Church.

Wesley E. Humble is on the staff of Circleville Bible College, Circleville, Ohio.

Leon Orville Hynson is professor emeritus at Evangelical School of Theology, Myerstown, Pennsylvania.

R. Stanley Ingersol is archivist of the Church of the Nazarene.

David L. Johns is on the faculty of Wilmington College, Wilmington, Ohio.

Charles Edwin Jones is an independent scholar and the primary bibliographic authority on the holiness movement.

Richard M. Judy, Jr., is a minister in the Church of God (Anderson).

Paul L. Kaufman is dean at Allegheny Wesleyan College, Salem, Ohio.

William C. Kostlevy is archivist and special collections librarian at Asbury Theological Seminary and associate director of the Wesleyan/Holiness Studies Center.

Stephen J. Lennox is on the faculty of Indiana Wesleyan University, Marion, Indiana.

Kathryn T. Long is professor of history at Wheaton College, Wheaton, Illinois.

Herbert McGonigle is principal of Nazarene Theological College, Manchester, England.

David L. McKenna is president emeritus of Asbury Theological Seminary.

Edward H. McKinley is professor of American history at Asbury College, Wilmore, Kentucky, and an authority on the American Salvation Army.

Josef Moutz is a retired United Methodist minister.

J. Steven O'Malley is professor of history at Asbury Theological Seminary, Wilmore, Kentucky.

William Parkes is a retired English Methodist pastor and an authority on the holiness movement in English Methodism.

Gari-Anne Patzwald is an independent scholar and editor in Lexington, Kentucky.

Priscilla Pope-Levison is on the faculty of the Duke University, Durham, North Carolina.

Vic Reasoner is a minister in the Fellowship of Bible Churches.

R. David Rightmire is professor of historical theology at Asbury College, Wilmore, Kentucky.

William C. Ringenberg is professor of history at Taylor University, Upland, Indiana.

Delbert R. Rose is professor emeritus at Wesley Biblical Seminary, Jackson, Mississippi.

Neil Semple is an authority on Canadian Methodism and past president of the Canadian Methodist Historical Society.

E. Morris Sider is archivist for the Brethren in Christ Church, Messiah College, Grantham, Pennsylvania.

Dale H. Simmons is dean of Judson College, Elgin, Illinois.

Larry D. Smith is editor of *God's Revivalist*, Cincinnati, Ohio.

William Snider is on the faculty of Hobe Sound Bible College, Hobe Sound, Florida.

Howard A. Snyder is on the faculty of Asbury Theological Seminary, Wilmore, Kentucky.

Carole Spencer is on the faculty of George Fox College, Portland, Oregon.

Susie C. Stanley is professor of historical theology and women's studies at Messiah College, Grantham, Pennsylvania.

Merle D. Strege is on the faculty of Anderson University, Anderson, Indiana.

Douglas M. Strong is professor of church history at Wesley Theological Seminary, Washington, D.C.

Wallace Thornton, Jr. is on the faculty of God's Bible School and College, Cincinnati, Ohio.

John Paul Vincent is on the faculty of Asbury College, Wilmore, Kentucky.

Marilyn Färdig Whiteley is an independent scholar and authority on the Canadian holiness movement.

Jennifer Lynn Woodruff is a United Methodist minister and graduate student at the Duke University, Durham, North Carolina.

Acronyms and Abbreviations

ABI	Allentown Bible Institute
AEF	Association of Evangelical Friends
AIM	Association of Independent Methodists
AMEZ	African American Methodist Church, Zion
AME	African Methodist Episcopal
APCA	Association of Pentecostal Churches of America
ARBC	Alliance of Reformed Baptist Churches
ARW	American Rescue Workers
ATS	Asbury Theological Seminary
AWMC	Allegheny Wesleyan Methodist Connection
BHC	Bible Holiness Church
BMCC	Bible Methodist Connection of Churches
BIC	Brethren in Christ
BMiC	Bible Missionary Church
CBC	Church of the Bible Covenant
CCCU	Churches of Christ in Christian Union
CC(H)	Church of Christ (Holiness) U.S.A.
CEI	Chicago Evangelistic Institute
CG(A)	Church of God (Anderson)
CG(H)	Church of God (Holiness)
CGIHP	Churches of God/Independent Holiness People
CHA	Christian Holiness Association
CHC	Calvary Holiness Church
CHP	Christian Holiness Partnership
CMA	Christian and Missionary Alliance
CMC	Congregational Methodist Church
CN	Church of the Nazarene
CPC	Cumberland Presbyterian Church
EA	Evangelical Association
ECC	Evangelical Christian Church
ECNA	Evangelical Church of North America
EEI	Epworth Evangelistic Institute

EFA	Evangelical Friends Alliance
EFI	Evangelical Friends International
EmA	Emmanuel Association
EMC	Evangelical Methodists Church
EUB	Evangelical United Brethren
FEA	Florida Evangelistic Association
FJC	Friends of Jesus Christ
FMC	Free Methodist Church
FWBI	Fort Wayne Bible Institute
GBS	God's Bible School
GHA	Georgia Holiness Association
GMC	God's Missionary Church
GWC	Gospel Workers Church
HC	Holiness Church
HCC	Holiness Christian Church; Holiness Church of Christ
HFMA	Hephzibath Faith Missionary Association
HMC	Holiness Movement Church
HP	House of Prayer
IAHU	International Apostolic Holiness Union
IFBC	International Fellowship of Bible Churches
IGM	Immanuel General Mission
IHA	Illinois Holiness Association; Iowa Holiness Association
IHC	Inter-Church Holiness Convention
IHM	International Holiness Mission
InHC	International Holiness Church
JEB	Japanese Evangelistic Band
KCCBS	Kansas City College and Bible School
KEHC	Korea Evangelical Holiness Church
KMHA	Kentucky Mountain Holiness Association
MBIC	Mennonite Brethren in Christ
MC	Methodist Church
MCC	Mennonite Central Committe
MCA	Metropolitan Church Association
MEC	Methodist Episcopal Church
MECS	Methodist Episcopal Church, South
MiC	Missionary Church
MiCA	Missionary Church Association
MIT	Massachusetts Institute of Technology
MPC	Methodist Protestant Church
NAE	National Association of Evangelicals

NAHC	National Association of Holiness Churches
NCM	Nazarene Compassionate Ministries
NHA	National Holiness Association
NHMS	National Holiness Missionary Society
NIBS	Northwest Indian Bible School
NTCC	New Testament Church of Christ
NTS	Nazarene Theological Seminary
OMS	Oriental Missionary Society
PB	Pentecostal Bands
PCN	Pentecostal Church of the Nazarene
PHC	Pilgrim Holiness Church
PLP	Pentecostal League of Prayer
PMC	People's Methodist Church
POF	Pillar of Fire
PrMC	Primitive Methodist Church
SA	Salvation Army
SMEA	Scripture Meditation Evangelistic Association
UB	United Brethren in Christ
UHC	United Holy Church of America, Inc.
UMC	United Methodist Church
UMiC	United Missionary Church
USC	University of Southern California
WBS	Wesley Biblical Seminary
WC	Wesleyan Church
WCC	World Council of Churches
WCTU	Woman's Christian Temperance Union
WGM	World Gospel Mission
WHAC	Wesleyan Holiness Association of Churches
WHWC	Wesleyan/Holiness Women Clergy
WMC	Wesleyan Methodist Church
WMS	Women's Missionary Society
WTA	Wesleyan Tabernacle Association
WTS	Wesleyan Theological Society
WUHA	Western Union Holiness Association

Chronology

1824 Timothy Merritt edits *The Christian's Manual: A Treatise on Christian Perfection*.

1836 Sarah Worrall Lankford founds the Tuesday Meeting for the Promotion of Holiness in New York City. Charles Finney lectures on holiness in New York City. John Humphrey Noyes founds a perfectionist intentional community at Putney, Vermont.

1837 Phoebe Worrall Palmer experiences entire sanctification.

1838 Oberlin College begins to publish the *Oberlin Evangelist*.

1839 Asa Mahan publishes *Scriptural Doctrine of Christian Perfection*. Timothy Merritt founds the *Guide to Christian Perfection*, later *Guide to Holiness*. Thomas C. Upham experiences entire sanctification at the Tuesday Meeting for the Promotion of Holiness in New York City.

1841 James Caughey begins six-year itinerancy in England.

1843 Wesleyan Methodist Connection, later Church, is organized at Utica, New York. Phoebe Palmer publishes *The Way of Holiness*.

1848 John Humphrey Noyes founds the Oneida (New York) Community.

1850 Interest in reform and perfection declines at Oberlin College in the wake of Asa Mahan's resignation as president. The Five Points Mission is founded in New York City by Phoebe Palmer and other Methodist women.

1857 Extensive revivals break out in Ontario, Canada, as a result of Phoebe Palmer's ministry.

1858 W. E. Boardman publishes *The Higher Christian Life*.

1859 Phoebe Palmer publishes *The Promise of the Father*.

1860 The Free Methodist Church is organized by B. T. Roberts and John Wesley Redfield

1867   The first National Holiness Association (NHA) camp meeting is held at Vineland, New Jersey.

1868   The second NHA camp meeting attracts over 20,000 people to Manheim, Pennsylvania. Red Rock Camp Meeting is founded at Paynesville, Minnesota.

1869   The third NHA camp meeting is held at Round Lake, New York.

1871   Western Holiness Association is formed at Bloomington, Illinois.

1874   Broadlands and Oxford meetings in England for the promotion of holiness.

1875   Brighton (England) meeting for the promotion of holiness. First Keswick Convention meets.

1876   Rachel Bradley founds a ladies' sewing class that evolves into Chicago's first rescue mission, the Olive Branch Mission.

1877   General holiness conventions held in Cincinnati and New York City.

1878   William and Catherine Booth organize the Salvation Army.

1880   General holiness convention is held in Jacksonville, Illinois. Southern California and Arizona Holiness Association is organized. Prairie Camp Meeting is founded near Elkhart, Indiana.

1881   D. S. Warner founds the Church of God (Anderson).

1882   Heavenly Recruit Association is formed in Philadelphia, Pennsylvania. Mountain Lake Park (Maryland) Camp Meeting is founded.

1883   First Church of God (Holiness) Congregation is founded at Centralia, Missouri. Mennonite Brethren in Christ Church is founded.

1884   Cliff College is founded in England by Thomas Champness. The Salvation Army founds the first "Prison Gate Brigade" to minister to the imprisoned in Melbourne, Australia.

1885   General Holiness Assembly meets in Chicago, Illinois. Southport (England) Convention holds first meeting.

1886   Fiftieth anniversary of the Tuesday Meeting for the Promotion of Holiness. The Salvation Army establishes its first home for "fallen women" in New York City.

1888 Alliance of the Reformed Baptist Church is founded in Canada. The Salvation Army establishes a night shelter and food depot in East London.

1890 Asbury College founded. Indian Springs Camp Meeting is founded at Flovilla, Georgia.

1892 Hephzibah Faith Missionary Association is founded at Tabor, Iowa.

1894 First Convocation of the United Holy Church. A dispute over holiness in the Evangelical Association results in the formation of the United Evangelical Church.

1895 First Church of the Nazarene is founded in Los Angeles, California. Holiness Movement Church is founded in Canada. Association of Pentecostal Churches of America is organized in Brooklyn, New York.

1897 International Apostolic Holiness Union, later Pilgrim Holiness Church, is founded in Cincinnati, Ohio. Church of Christ (Holiness) is formed. A division occurs in the Church of God (Holiness).

1898 Missionary Church Association is founded.

1899 Metropolitan Church Association separates from the Methodist Episcopal Church.

1900 God's Bible School founded in Cincinnati.

1901 Martin Wells Knapp separates from the Methodist Episcopal Church. Charles and Lettie Cowman begin the Oriental Missionary Society (OMS) in Japan. General Holiness Assembly meets in Chicago. Alma White founds the Pentecostal Union, later Pillar of Fire.

1906 Azusa Street Revival in Los Angeles marks the beginning of Pentecostalism.

1907 Pentecostal Church of the Nazarene is organized in Chicago. OMS opens a Bible school in Korea, now Seoul Theological Seminary.

1908 Holiness Church of Christ joins the Pentecostal Church of the Nazarene at Point Pilot, Texas. This is the date that is formally celebrated as the founding date of the Church of the Nazarene.

1909 Churches of Christ in Christian Union founded at Washington Court House, Ohio. Holiness Methodist Church is founded as the Northwestern Holiness Association in Grand Forks, North Dakota

1910 National Holiness Association Missionary Society is founded as missionary arm of the NHA. Chicago Evangelistic Institute, later Vennard College, is founded. Brethren in Christ adopt a holiness statement on entire sanctification.

1915 Pentecostal Mission, Nashville, Tennesee, merges with the Church of the Nazarene.

1917 Laymen's Holiness Association is founded at Jamestown, North Dakota. Seth C. Rees is expelled from the Pentecostal Church of the Nazarene and forms the Pilgrim Church. African American members of the Church of God (Anderson) organize the West Middlesex (Pennsylvania) Camp Meeting.

1920 Bethel Mission of China is founded by Mary Stone and Jennie Hughes.

1921 First Cadle Tabernacle opens in Indianapolis, Indiana.

1922 Pilgrim Holiness Church formed by a merger of the International Apostolic Holiness Church and the Pilgrim Church. Laymen's Holiness Association joins the Church of the Nazarene. Church of God (Holiness) reunites. The Evangelical Association and United Evangelical Church merge to form the Evangelical Church.

1923 Asbury Theological Seminary is founded in Wilmore, Kentucky.

1925 Lela G. McConnell organizes the Kentucky Mountain Holiness Association.

1929 Merle E. Gaddis completes his University of Chicago Ph.D. dissertation, "Christian Perfection in America."

1930 National Holiness Association Missionary Society, later World Gospel Mission (WGM), establishes a mission in Kenya.

1933 E. Howard Cadle begins the *Nation's Family Prayer Period* on radio station WLW in Cincinnati.

1935 God's Missionary Church is organized in Pennsylvania.

1936 Roxbury (Pennsylvania) Camp Meeting is founded by the Brethren in Christ. Wesleyan Tabernacle Association is founded.

1937 The Emmanuel Association is organized by Paul Finch. Old Paths Tract Society is founded in Shoals, Indiana.

1938   Jim H. Green organizes the People's Christian Movement, later People's Methodist Church.

1939   The Methodist Church is formed by a merger of the Methodist Episcopal Church, the Methodist Episcopal Church, South, and the Methodist Protestant Church.

1940   Evangelical Holiness Church of Korea is organized.

1944   Canadian Holiness Federation is founded.

1945   Bethany Fellowship is founded by T. A. Hegre in Minneapolis. Nazarene Theological Seminary is founded in Kansas City, Missouri.

1946   Evangelical Methodist Church is organized. Florida Evangelistic Association is founded by H. Robb French. The Immanuel General Mission is organized in Japan. Asbury Theological Seminary founds the first scholarly holiness journal, the *Asbury Seminarian*. The Evangelical Church and the United Brethren Church merge to form the Evangelical United Brethren Church.

1947   Evangelical Friends Alliance is organized.

1951   First Inter-Church Holiness Convention meets in Salem, Ohio.

1953   Schmul Publishing Company is founded by H. E. Schmul.

1955   Bible Missionary Church is founded by Glen Griffith.

1956   Voice of the Nazarene Association of Churches is founded by W. L. King.

1957   Timothy L. Smith's *Revivalism and Social Reform* is published.

1959   Holiness Movement Church merges with the Free Methodist Church. Wesleyan Holiness Association of Churches separates from the Bible Missionary Church.

1961   Winona Lake Conference on the distinctives of Wesleyan-Arminian theology is held.

1962   People's Methodist Church merges with the Evangelical Methodist Church.

1963   Evangelical Wesleyan Church separates from the Free Methodist Church.

1966 Bible Methodist Church separates from the Wesleyan Methodist Church, and the Allegheny Conference of the Wesleyan Methodist Church separates from the parent body. First meeting of the Wesleyan Theological Society at Spring Arbor, Michigan.

1967 H. Robb French organizes the National Association of Holiness Churches.

1968 The Pilgrim Holiness Church and Wesleyan Methodist Church merge to form the Wesleyan Church. The Methodist Church and the Evangelical United Brethren Church merge to form the United Methodist Church. The Evangelical Church of North America is formed by former members of the Evangelical United Brethren in the Pacific Northwest.

1969 The Holiness Methodist Church merges with the Evangelical Church of North America.

1970 Asbury College revival occurs.

1971 National Holiness Association becomes the Christian Holiness Association.

1978 The Inter-Church Holiness Convention relocates its annual meeting to Dayton, Ohio.

1987 Donald W. Dayton's *Theological Roots of Pentecostalism* is published.

1991 Wesleyan/Holiness Studies Center is founded at Asbury Theological Seminary.

1994 First meeting is conducted by the Wesleyan/Holiness Women Clergy.

1998 Christian Holiness Association becomes the Christian Holiness Partnership.

1999 Northeastern Theological Seminary is founded in North Chili, New York.

Introduction

The holiness movement has deep roots in the perfectionist agitation that swept North American society in the 1830s. As historian Timothy L. Smith effectively argued in his award-winning book *Revivalism and Social Reform* (1957), the holiness movement was transcendentalism for the masses. Its founders were Methodist preacher and abolitionist Timothy Merritt, who published the *Guide to Christian Perfection*, later the *Guide to Holiness*, the first explicitly perfectionist periodical, in 1839; and a pair of Methodist sisters from New York City, Sarah Worrall Lankford and Phoebe Worrall Palmer, who instituted a weekly meeting for the promotion of holiness in 1836. These Methodists insisted that they were merely resurrecting the neglected Methodist teaching that all Christians might experience "Christian perfection" in this life. The common term for the experience became "entire sanctification," although it was known by numerous other titles such as "the second blessing," "the higher Christian life," "the rest of faith," "full salvation," and "perfect love."

In the optimistic climate of the 1830s, the nonliteral spiritual nature of Methodist perfectionism was challenged by a variety of more socially radical perfectionist options. Often rooted in the areas of Yankee migration, such as western New England, the so-called burned-over district of upstate New York, the Western Reserve of Ohio, and what has been termed the "third New England" of Michigan, these varieties of perfectionism vigorously attacked perceived social evils such as slavery and the oppression of women and occasionally, such as in the teachings of John Humphrey Noyes, founder of the Oneida Community, advocated the reconstruction of such intimate matters as the sexual relationship between men and women.

More closely related to Methodist perfectionism was the so-called Oberlin perfectionism that was formulated at Oberlin College in the late 1830s. Most commonly associated with Asa Mahan, president of the college (1835–1850), and with the nation's premier evangelist, Charles G. Finney, the teaching was deeply rooted in the traditional New England Congregationalism of Nathan Emmons (1745–1840) and Yale professor

William Nathaniel Taylor (1786–1858) and in the Methodist theology that Mahan and Finney eagerly devoured through the reading of the works of John Wesley, John Fletcher, and Adam Clarke. Frequently accused of Pelagianism, a theological heresy named for an early Christian author who had insisted that Christians could live without sin, Oberlin perfectionists taught that one could completely obey God. As a result, there was no excuse for sin, personal or public. Given this mindset, for example, once slavery was defined as sin, Christians became obligated to work for its demise. Methodists, such as Luther Lee and B. T. Roberts, who drank deeply at the Oberlin well, found the parlor perfectionism of fellow Methodists, such as Phoebe Palmer, sentimental and lacking in ethical vigor.

Other perfectionists, such as Bowdoin College professor Thomas E. Upham, were of a more mystical bent. Upham was a student of the work of the great Catholic mystic Madame Guyon, about whom he wrote a biography. Although Phoebe Palmer led Upham into the experience of full salvation, she remained suspicious of what she believed was his nonrational approach to the experience.

In spite of the fact that strands of all varieties of perfectionism continued to coexist in the holiness movement, it was the Methodistic perfectionism of the Worrall sisters, especially as articulated in Phoebe Palmer's *The Way to Holiness* (1843), that was most influential. Palmer's formulation of the experience of entire sanctification, which drew its inspiration from the thought and experience of such Methodist luminaries as John Fletcher and William Carvosso, taught that by a simple act of faith one could claim the experience of full salvation apart from any personal evidence. As Palmer insisted, if one had met the criteria of consecrating one's all to God, God would honor that commitment. By the late 1840s, testimonies to the experience of full salvation were commonplace. A decade later, prominent Presbyterians, Baptists, Episcopalians, Dutch Reformed, and Congregationalists had entered into the higher Christian life, even as North American–style perfectionism had spread to Great Britain through the ministries of James Caughey and Phoebe Palmer. In the decades following the Civil War, holiness agitation found a ready audience among smaller bodies, such as the Methodist related United Brethren and Evangelical Association, and among Friends and Mennonites.

Fueling the popular religious movement were the technological changes of the 1820s and 1830s that greatly reduced the cost of printing. As a result, the holiness movement was spread by a plethora of publications—magazines, books, tracts, and sermons—and a variety of people from laywomen, such as Phoebe Palmer, to the sons of holiness evangelists, such as A. B. Earle, became authors and publishers.

Another means by which the holiness movement was spread was through camp meetings. In 1867, Methodist perfectionists founded the National Camp Meeting Association for the Promotion of Holiness, later the National Holiness Association (NHA). The NHA sponsored several national camp meetings each year and eventually established a periodical, a publishing arm, and later a mission board, now World Gospel Mission. Dominated into the 20th century by the friends of Phoebe Palmer, such as John S. and Martha Inskip and George Hughes, the NHA vigorously opposed the growing sentiment to found distinctly holiness churches.

In spite of this, by the 1880s, independent holiness churches began to appear in New England, the Midwest, and California. Such developments led to an extended debate on the nature of the church that led to the formation of the Church of God reformation movement, now Church of God (Anderson), founded in 1881, and the Church of God (Holiness), founded in 1883.

Perhaps the most familiar public manifestation of the holiness movement has been urban holiness missions. Most often associated with the Salvation Army, these "rescue missions" have played a significant role in the life of the holiness movement, at least since 1850 when Phoebe Palmer played a pivotal role in the founding of the Five Points Mission in New York City. Often staffed by laywomen, or uniformed ordained workers, as in the case of the Salvation Army, these missions sought to meet human needs and to serve as advocates on behalf of the poor, while providing job training and, in recent years, drug addiction and alcoholism counseling. Today few people realize that the ministry of the Salvation Army or such splinter groups as the American Rescue Workers, the Volunteers of America, and the Bible Holiness Movement and lesser-known groups, such as the Peniel Missions, the Grace and Hope Missions, and the Olive Branch Mission, Chicago's oldest rescue mission, are living reminders of one of the most dynamic expressions of the holiness movement in American Christianity.

As early as the 1860s, missionaries, who were frequently associated with William Taylor, began spreading the holiness message in India, South America, and Asia, while holiness teaching in England resulted in the founding of the Salvation Army in 1878. Elsewhere in Europe, American perfectionist revivalists, such as William Boardman and Robert P. and Hannah Whitall Smith, organized higher life conferences that led to the establishment of the Keswick Conventions in 1875. Although Keswick eventually sought to distance itself from Methodistic views of Christian perfection, its insistence on a subsequent religious experience of empowerment remains difficult to distinguish from holiness formulations of the same experience.

By the 1890s, even as holiness teaching in Methodism became more controversial, Phoebe Palmer's "shorter way to holiness" was being challenged on the right by thoughtful Methodists and NHA leaders, such as Daniel Steele, and on the left by a growing body of radicals, such as Vivian Dake, who believed that entire sanctification was only gained after a long and difficult period of "dying to self." Frequently embracing such controversial new teachings as the premillennial return of Jesus, critics of the NHA, including Cincinnati publisher Martin Wells Knapp, founded the International Apostolic Holiness Union in 1897. By 1901, when Knapp left the Methodist Episcopal Church, the premillennial teaching had become the norm, even for NHA loyalists.

Beginning in the 1890s, the "come-outer" sentiment intensified, and additional independent churches and regional holiness denominations were founded. Increasingly radicalized by the depression of the 1890s, these churches, often convinced that the return of Jesus was around the corner, embraced such increasingly radical proposals as the redistribution of wealth and the communal ownership of property. In this climate, more moderate voices, such as California pastor Phineas Bresee, began laying the foundation for transcontinental holiness churches. In spite of the loss of many potential holiness adherents to Pentecostalism in the wake of the 1906 Azusa Street Revival, by the 1920s, the followers of Bresee and Knapp had organized two national holiness churches, the Church of the Nazarene and the Pilgrim Holiness Church.

Deeply committed to world missions, these bodies, along with such older holiness groups as the Salvation Army and the Church of God (Anderson), experienced explosive worldwide growth in the 20th century. In addition, the writings of Lettie Cowman, Hannah Whitall Smith, and Oswald Chambers have found a new audience among people who are frequently unaware that they are reading classic holiness literature. These writings, which include *Streams in the Desert*, *The Christian's Secret of a Happy Life*, and *My Utmost for His Highest*, continue to be among the most widely read Protestant devotional works.

The formation of new holiness denominations did not signal the demise of the holiness presence in such older bodies as the Evangelical Association and United Brethren or among Friends and Mennonites. In these bodies, holiness currents, often little noticed, continued to shape the contours of personal piety. Among Methodists, holiness camp meetings, distinctly holiness schools—such as Asbury College, Taylor University, and Chicago Evangelistic Institute—and periodicals—such as Henry Clay Morrison's *Pentecostal Herald*—continued to thrive. On the mission field, holiness-related Methodist missionaries, such as E. Stanley Jones, and missionary bishops, such as William Oldham and Arthur Wesley, continued to unapologetically urge Christians to seek deeper baptisms of the Holy Spirit.

In the years following World War II, the holiness movement has continued to experience steady growth. Reflecting the greater demand for an educated clergy, theological seminaries have emerged in North America, India, the Philippines, Africa, and Korea. In 1965, the Wesleyan Theological Society was founded, while a number of young Wesleyan scholars such as Timothy L. Smith, Donald W. Dayton, and Mildred Bangs Wynkoop emerged as international scholars of note.

As a movement deeply concerned with personal behavior, the holiness movement has struggled with changing cultural mores. In 1951, conservatives within the holiness denominations, especially the Church of the Nazarene and the Wesleyan Methodist Church, organized the Inter-denominational Holiness Convention, later Inter-Church Holiness Convention (IHC), which challenged the established NHA, now known as the Christian Holiness Partnership, for the position of primary ecumenical holiness body. Although a minority within the holiness movement, the IHC has grown into a significant international constituency consisting of a number of small denominations and independent congregations. In the 1990s, ironically amid discussions of the movement's presumed death, membership in holiness-related bodies, not including holiness Pentecostals or Keswick-related evangelicals, passed the 10 million mark. Although precise enumeration is difficult on the eve of the 21st century, some insiders believe that the holiness movement numbers more than 12 million adherents with roughly four million in North America, three million in Africa, four million in Asia, especially Korea and India, and significant numbers in the Caribbean and Australia. In fact, the discussion suggests that with most North American Christians, the holiness movement is in the midst of a serious identity crisis. It is perhaps a sign of the movement's continued vitality that holiness adherents from Africa, Asia, the Caribbean, and South America are increasingly setting the agenda for the movement.

William C. Kostlevy

The Dictionary

– A –

ADAMS, JOHN QUINCY (b. Philadelphia, 1825; d. New York City, July 1881). Baptist pastor and author. Adams was one of the first Baptist advocates of full salvation, or, as he preferred, "the higher Christian life." He began his ministry in Caldwell, New Jersey, in 1849. A rigorous champion of traditional Baptist ecclesiology, in his first book, *Baptists: The Only Thorough Reformers* (1853), Adams argued that the American principles of civil and religious liberty were, in fact, Baptist principles. In part, as a reward for his vindication of the Baptist tradition, Adams was named pastor of New York's North Baptist Church in 1856. Invited to attend the Tuesday Meeting for the Promotion of Holiness (see **Phoebe Worrall Palmer**), Adams, after a lengthy struggle, experienced **entire sanctification** on 25 March 1859. His new experience and perfectionist preaching created considerable controversy. Resigning his pastorate, he organized the Antioch Baptist Church on New York's Seventh Avenue in July 1859. Within a year, the church had 168 members. Deeply committed to the spread of full salvation among Baptists, Adams wrote tracts and booklets and established a periodical, *Experiences of the Higher Christian Life*. His most important work was *Experiences of the Higher Christian Life in the Baptist Denomination* (1870). At the time of his death, he was laying plans for a school to train Baptist clergy. Material documenting his work is located at the Baptist Historical Society, Rochester, New York. W.C.K.

ALLEGHENY WESLEYAN METHODIST CONNECTION (AWMC). In 1966, most of the congregations of the Allegheny Conference of the **Wesleyan Methodist Church** (WMC) withdrew from that body in opposition to the proposed merger of the WMC and the **Pilgrim Holiness Church** (PHC) and formed the AWMC. Located primarily in western Pennsylvania and eastern Ohio, these congregations accused the WMC of replacing its historic congregational polity

7

with a centralized bureaucracy. Deeply committed to localism and cultural conservatism, the AWMC even remained suspicious of the **Inter-Church Holiness Convention** (IHC). When two years of intense negotiations with the WMC failed to resolve differences, the AWMC was organized in 1968 with 96 churches, 13 mission appointments, and a total of 3,120 members. Although actual membership has remained stagnant, in North America the church has added 12 congregations and over 20 mission points since 1968. It has established missions among Native Americans in the United States and Canada, including the Northwest Indian Bible School (NIBS), Alberton, Montana. Founded in 1968 by Raymond Montour, the school has been directed by NIBS graduate Kenneth Hooper since 1984. Since 1973, the AWMC has operated Allegheny Wesleyan College in Salem, Ohio, and has 16 Christian day schools in Pennsylvania, Ohio, Montana, and New Mexico. It publishes a periodical, the *Allegheny Wesleyan Methodist*, and operates five **camp meetings**, including the historic Stoneboro (Pennsylvania) Camp Meeting. Since 1990, it has supported a radio program, *Wesleyan Gospel Echoes*. Among the most important AWMC leaders have been **H. C. Van Wormer**, conference president (1944–1968) and connection president (1969–1973), and Francis E. Mansell, director of World Missions (1969–1973) and president of the connection (1973–1982). W.C.K.

ALLIANCE OF REFORMED BAPTIST CHURCHES (ARBC). Organized at Woodstock, New Brunswick, in 1888 after five ministers in the Maritime provinces, who had angered denominational leaders for their continued holiness preaching, were expelled from the Free Christian Baptist Churches of Canada. During the following seven months, 22 churches with 540 members were organized in New Brunswick and Nova Scotia. In 1890, a periodical, the *King's Highway*, was established. In 1894, the Beulah Camp was established at Brown's Flat, New Brunswick, and a second camp, Riverside, was founded at Robinson, Maine, in 1902. In 1901, a medical doctor, H. C. Sanders, established the first ARBC foreign mission among the Zulus in Natal, South Africa. Under the direction of Sanders, I. F. Kierstand, and Kierstand's son Eugene, mission work was extended into the Transvaal and southern Rhodesia. By the late 1950s, the church's African membership stood at 358. In the first two decades of the 20th century, in part through the controversial ministry of famed anti-Catholic **L. J. King**, the movement experienced substantial growth in southwestern New

Brunswick, northern Nova Scotia, and northern Maine. In 1945, the church established Holiness Bible School in Woodstock, New Brunswick. Relocated to Yarmouth, Nova Scotia, in 1947, the school, now known as Bethany Bible College, remains an important Canadian holiness educational institution. In 1966, the ARBC merged with the **Wesleyan Methodist Church** (WMC). At the time of the merger, it had 60 congregations and 2,400 members in New Brunswick, Nova Scotia, and Maine. By 1990, membership in the **Wesleyan Church** (WC), successor to the WMC, in the Maritimes and Maine exceeded 4,000. W.C.K.

AMERICAN RESCUE WORKERS (ARW). In 1884, a dispute erupted between Thomas E. Moore, head of the **Salvation Army** (SA) in the United States, and General **William Booth** concerning Moore's decision to incorporate the SA in the United States as the Salvation Army of America (SAA). In 1889, Moore was replaced by Richard Holz, who arranged for the reunification of the SAA with the Booth-led international body. Twenty-five SAA corps rejected reunion and organized as the American Salvation Army with William V. Gratten as general. In 1896, James William Duffin was chosen general, a position he held until 1955. In 1913, as a result of a court challenge by the SA, the movement was forced to change its name to the American Rescue Workers. Similar to the SA, the ARW is a holiness denomination that seeks to combine evangelism and social service ministries. It is especially noted for its homeless shelters and food pantries. It also operates 19 thrift stores. In 1990, it had 18 corps and about 2,000 members in Maryland, Delaware, New Jersey, Pennsylvania, New York, and Ohio. It has published the *Rescue Herald* since 1884. Since 1896, its national headquarters has been in Philadelphia, Pennsylvania. W.C.K.

ANDERSON, T(ony) M(arshall) (b. Westport, Kentucky, 30 April 1888; d. Wilmore, Kentucky, 14 April 1979). **Church of the Nazarene** (CN) evangelist and teacher. One of the most notable holiness evangelists of the 20th century, Anderson spent 12 years in the pastoral ministry before becoming a full-time evangelist during the 1930s. He served as professor of Bible at **Asbury College** (1942–1950) and was a central figure in initiating the Asbury College revival of 1950. Granted a leave of absence by the college, Anderson was instrumental in spreading the revival across the country. He was one of the nation's most prolific **camp meeting** preachers, serving repeatedly as either Bible teacher or evangelist at such camp meetings as the Mount of Praise (Circleville, Ohio), Indian Springs (Georgia), Lakeland (Florida), and Hollow Rock (Ohio). One of the most distinctive characteristics of Anderson's ministry was his remarkable gift of discernment that allowed him insight into the spiritual struggles of many individuals. Deeply conservative, Anderson was an especially popular speaker among traditionalists in the holiness movement and especially the CN. He spoke at several of the early **Inter-Church Holiness Convention** (IHC) gatherings that were convened at **God's Bible School** in the early 1950s. Although remembered most as a camp meeting preacher, Anderson wrote for such periodicals as the *Herald of Holiness* and the *Pentecostal Herald*. He was the author of *After Holiness, What* (1929), reprinted as *After Sanctification: Growth in the Life of Holiness* (1978), and was the compiler of *Our Holy Faith: Studies in Wesleyan Theology* (1965). W.C.K.

ARMINIAN METHODIST CONNEXION (Derby Faith). The Arminian Methodist Connexion originated in 1832 in a division over holiness and revivalism in the Derby Wesleyan Circuit in England, and at its height, it extended into Manchester, Birmingham, Nottinghamshire, Leicestershire, Warwickshire, Staffordshire, and Cheshire. Highly charged in worship, it emphasized **entire sanctification**. Some leaders held semi-Pelagian views on human ability and did not believe that one should pray for faith. Consequently, the Arminian Methodist Connexion has frequently been described as a doctrinal deviation from Methodism. At its height, membership numbered 1,800. An article in the denominational discipline emphasized entire sanctification, and a testimony to such was required of all preachers. In 1837, most members became part of the Wesleyan Methodist Association, another small Methodist reform body. W.P.

ARTHUR, WILLIAM (b. Kells, County Antrim, Ireland, 3 February 1819; d. Cannes, France, 9 March 1901). British Wesleyan pastor, missionary, writer, and college president. Almost immediately following his conversion at age 16, Arthur began preaching. He attended college at the Wesleyan Theological Institute (Hoxton College). He served as a missionary to Gutti, Mysore, India (1839–1841), and in Boulogne and Paris, France (1846–1851). In 1851, he became secretary of the Wesleyan Missionary Society. In 1866, he was president of his conference. Arthur also was principal of Belfast Methodist College (1868–1871). He served for many years as a secretary of the Evangelical Alliance. He was honorary secretary of the Wesleyan Missionary Society (1871–1888). In

1888, he retired and lived out his days in southern France. His greatest impact on the holiness movement was through his widely read devotional classic, *The Tongue of Fire, or the Power of True Christianity* (1854), which went through 18 editions during Arthur's lifetime. As the most important Wesleyan work on the mission of the Holy Spirit, it has shaped subsequent holiness thought on the role of the Holy Spirit in Christian experience. Among his other books are *A Mission to Mysore* (1847), *The Successful Merchant* (1852), *The Pope, the Kings and the People* (1877), *Religion without God and God without Religion* (1883), and *Italy in Transition* (1860). T.B.

ASBURY COLLEGE was founded as Kentucky Holiness College in Wilmore, Kentucky, in 1890 by **John Wesley Hughes**. Renamed Asbury College in 1891, it was a coeducational college that promoted holiness piety in the context of a standard liberal arts education. Although not the oldest holiness college, Asbury College became the model for most of the holiness-related colleges established during the late 19th and early 20th centuries. Although Hughes served as president until 1905, it was **Henry Clay Morrison** (president, 1910–1925, 1933–1940) who established the institution's primary identity, which included a passionate commitment to world missions, old-fashioned Methodist revivalism, and the spiritual and theological renewal of North American Methodism. Missionaries such as **E. Stanley Jones**, Frederick B. Fisher, J. Waskom Pickett, J. T. Seamands, and Eugene Erny spread the holiness message around the world, even as Morrison and a number of Wilmore-based and Asbury College–related evangelists, such as **L. L. Pickett**, **Andrew Johnson**, **John Paul**, and **T. M. Anderson**, continued to fan the flames of Methodist revivalism. During Morrison's administration, Asbury College emerged as one of the principal centers of Methodist fundamentalism. Convinced that Methodist seminaries had largely abandoned orthodox Christian belief, Morrison established **Asbury Theological Seminary** on the campus of the college in 1923. The concerns of Morrison continued to shape Asbury College in the administrations of his successors as president, **Z. T. Johnson** (1940–1966) and **Dennis Kinlaw** (1968–1981, 1986–1991). Under Johnson's leadership, the institution achieved regional accreditation and financial stability. Among the most memorable events of the Johnson years were spontaneous revivals that occurred in 1950 and 1958. In 1970, a third revival swept the Asbury

College campus. Spreading to other evangelical colleges, the Asbury revival was an important catalyst in the national spiritual renewal of the early 1970s. Perhaps the most notable result of Kinlaw's leadership was an improved faculty and the strengthening of ties with non-Methodist holiness denominations such as the **Salvation Army** and the **Christian and Missionary Alliance**. W.C.K.

ASBURY THEOLOGICAL SEMINARY (ATS). A seminary founded on the campus of **Asbury College** in 1923. Taking its direction from its first president, **Henry Clay Morrison** (1923–1942), the school was established to fight the inroads of theological liberalism in the Methodist Episcopal Church (MEC) and MECS (Methodist Episcopal Church, South). Like Morrison, the early faculty members, including **George W. Ridout**, Fred H. Larabee, and Frank Paul Morris, were ministers and evangelists without terminal academic degrees. ATS was incorporated in 1931 and formally separated from Asbury College in 1941. Under its second president, **J. C. McPheeters** (1942–1962), the academic quality of the faculty was strengthened with the addition of several young scholars trained at Harvard University, including Harold Kuhn, Harold Greenlee, and **George Turner**, along with other accomplished scholars, including Curry Mavis, Claude Thompson, **Delbert R. Rose**, and **Robert Coleman**. Reflecting these changes, ATS established one of the nation's first evangelical scholarly periodicals, the *Asbury Seminarian*, in 1946 and received full academic accreditation. In spite of the temporary loss of its accreditation in the 1950s, the school emerged as one of the leading evangelical seminaries during the McPheeters presidency. Although noted for its evangelical theological commitments, the school's success rested perhaps even more on its strong affirmation of the subjective experiential piety of traditional Methodism. ATS maintained especially close ties to such Methodist champions of devotional piety as Harry Denman, for a time chairman of the board of trustees; Thomas Carruth, a prominent Methodist Church pastor and later ATS faculty member; and **E. Stanley Jones**. Following Jones, ATS has worked for racial justice for African Americans since the late 1940s.

Under the leadership of **Frank B. Stanger** (1962–1982) and **David McKenna** (1982–1994), who hired a new generation of faculty members that included Robert Traina, John Oswalt, Gilbert James, and Kenneth Kinghorn, student enrollment grew rapidly, a missions program was established, and ATS continued to strengthen its claim to be one of the nation's elite evangelical graduate schools of theology. In 1990, ATS received a substantial gift from the estate of Ralph Waldo Beeson, which has enabled it to expand its programs to include the establishment of several Ph.D. programs and a branch campus in Orlando, Florida. Under the leadership of Maxie Dunnam (1994–), in 1999 student enrollment stood at more than 1,200. ATS continues to be a center for evangelical concerns in the United Methodist Church and for experiential piety, as well as a significant graduate school for all North American Wesleyans. W.C.K.

ASHRAMS. Hindu spiritual retreats that have existed in India for centuries. As reformulated and given specifically Christian content by **E. Stanley Jones** in 1930, ashrams have proven to be valuable evangelistic tools in India, elsewhere in Asia, and throughout the world, especially in North America and Scandinavia. In 1940, the movement was organized as United Christian Ashrams. Shortly before his death in 1973, Jones established a system of government that included a self-perpetuating board of directors. Jones's son-in-law, United Methodist Church Bishop James Mathews, was named permanent chair. Since Jones's death, William Richardson, Paul Wagner, Lawrence Lykens, and William Pickard have served successively as general secretary. Papers of the United Christian Ashrams are located at the B. L. Fisher Library at **Asbury Theological Seminary**. W.C.K.

ASSOCIATION OF INDEPENDENT METHODISTS (AIM). Organized by former Methodist Church (MC) members in Jackson, Mississippi, in 1965 who argued that the MC was unresponsive to its members and supported social programs at variance with the beliefs of many Methodists. Critics of AIM charged that it was primarily organized by supporters of racial segregation, a charge denied by its founders. Today AIM has more than 50 churches in Alabama, Florida, Georgia, Mississippi, Tennessee, Texas, and Virginia with more than 4,000 members. It supports **Wesley Biblical Seminary** and sends missionaries through **World Gospel Mission**. Its radio broadcast, the *Methodist Bible Hour-International,* is heard throughout the southeastern United States and the Caribbean. It is a member of **Christian Holiness Partnership**. In 1999, its president was Roman J. Miller. W.C.K.

ASSURANCE. *See* WITNESS OF THE SPIRIT.

– B –

BAKER, SHERIDAN (b. near Cadiz, Ohio, 8 November 1824; d. Coshocton, Ohio, 30 March 1890). Methodist Episcopal Church (MEC) pastor, educator, evangelist, entrepreneur, and author. Baker was preparing for the ministry in the United Presbyterian Church at Richmond College, Jefferson County, Ohio, when he was converted on February 2, 1847, during revival services at a local Methodist church. He was admitted into membership in the Pittsburgh Conference of the MEC and served congregations in Pennsylvania and Ohio. In 1854, he became principal of Brownsville (Pennsylvania) Seminary and, in 1856, president of Beaver Seminary (Pennsylvania). In 1859, he accepted the pastorate of Hamline MEC, Steubenville, Ohio.

In 1864, Baker entered the mercantile business. Although meeting with immediate financial success, he longed for a deeper Christian experience, in part as a result of reading **J. A. Wood**'s book, *Perfect Love*. Convicted by Jesus' words in Matthew 19:21 that those who "would be perfect" must sell their possessions and give to the poor, Baker, in his own words, "became a steward and not a possessor." Experiencing **entire sanctification** in August 1870, Baker sold his business and returned to the active ministry in 1871. Although chronic rheumatism forced him to retire in 1875, Baker continued an active career as an evangelist and **camp meeting** preacher. Ironically, given his belief in faith healing, ill health continued to reduce his effectiveness. His mature reflections on divine healing were recorded in his book *The New Name* (1890). One of the most distinctive characteristics of Baker's teaching of holiness doctrine was his insistence on "progressive holiness." In his view, the experience of entire sanctification was not the end of one's spiritual quest but the beginning of a life of repeated "anointings" of the Holy Spirit. Biographical material is located in G. F. Oliver, "The Story of the Life and Evangelism of Rev. Sheridan Baker D.D.," which appears in Sheridan Baker, *A Peculiar People* (1890). W.C.K.

BALDWIN, HARMON ALLEN (b. Pierpont, Ohio, 3 June 1869; d. Wellsville, Ohio, 11 March 1936). **Free Methodist Church** (FMC) minister, district superintendent, evangelist, and author. Converted in 1890 while a student at Mount Union (Ohio) College, Baldwin entered **Vivian Dake**'s Pentecostal Bands (PBs). Emerging as a divisional leader of the PB, Baldwin was responsible for organizing a number of

FMC congregations from western Pennsylvania to Iowa. Separating from the PB following Dake's death, Baldwin was admitted into membership in the Pittsburgh Conference of the FMC and fully ordained in 1896. Also in 1896, he married former PB member and FMC minister Clara Etta Weatherly. A successful pastor, Baldwin served important FMC congregations in Pittsburgh, Pennsylvania, and Gerry, New York, and served as the West Virginia District elder on two occasions.

From 1917 to 1932, Baldwin was largely engaged in writing and evangelistic work. He was a thoughtful and unusually well-read champion of the Wesleyan doctrine of Christian perfection, and his work demonstrates a mastery of **John Wesley**, John Fletcher, and holiness movement writers, along with a sophisticated grasp of patristic, medieval, and early modern perfectionist literature. Deeply suspicious of the growing materialism of the early 20th-century holiness movement, Baldwin emphasized an interior mystical piety that rejected fundamentalist biblical literalism and premillennial **eschatology**. Among his most important books are *The Indwelling Christ* (1912), *Holiness and the Human Element* (1919), *The Carnal Mind* (1926), and *The Coming Judgement* (1927). His final work, a history of the doctrine of **entire sanctification**, was left uncompleted at the time of his death. His son, Leland Baldwin, was an important 20th-century American social and religious historian. W.C.K.

BANGS, NATHAN (b. Stratford, Connecticut, 2 May 1778; d. New York City, 4 May 1862). Methodist Episcopal Church (MEC) preacher, editor, missionary advocate, Methodist historian, and MEC book agent. Converted in 1799, Bangs began preaching in 1801 and served as a missionary to Canada (then part of the New York District) until 1808. In 1820, he became an agent of the Methodist Book Concern, solidifying its finances and extending its operation. During his 20 years as agent, he edited the *Christian Advocate,* the *Methodist Magazine,* and the *Quarterly Review*. In 1819, he was a chief founder of the MEC Missionary Society, writing its constitution and serving as its treasurer and corresponding secretary. In 1812, he was commissioned by the General Council to collect historical materials. His work culminated in the publication of the four-volume *History of the Methodist Episcopal Church* (1838–1841). An advocate of higher educational standards for Methodist ministers, Bangs served briefly as president of Wesleyan University, Middletown, Connecticut (1841–1842). Although a friend of **Phoebe Palmer** and regular attendee at her Tuesday Meetings,

Bangs publicly criticized her "altar theology" as "not sound," "unscriptural," and "anti-Wesleyan." D.H.S.

BAPTISM OF THE HOLY SPIRIT. A common term for **entire sanctification**. One of the most contested theological debates in the modern holiness movement has surrounded the meaning of the experience of the baptism of the Holy Spirit in the Christian life. Traditionally, the holiness movement taught that the first occurrence of the experience of entire sanctification was at Pentecost, as described in Acts 1:5. Although some 20th-century holiness proponents, most notably the so-called Pentecostal regenerationists, associated with **A. J. Smith**, did not subscribe to this view, it was not until the 1970s that a significant number of Wesleyan scholars began to question the legitimacy of seeing Pentecost as a paradigm of the experience of entire sanctification. Most significant was a 1973 address at the annual meeting of the **Wesleyan Theological Society** by **Donald W. Dayton** that argued that the Pentecostal model for entire sanctification had not been central to **John Wesley**'s articulation of Christian perfection. Going further, Dayton argued that the Pentecostal paradigm had been the creation of the 19th-century holiness movement, as evidenced in the writings of **Asa Mahan** and **Phoebe Palmer**. In spite of the fact that several Wesleyan scholars, most notably **Timothy L. Smith**, Charles W. Carter, and Larry Wood, have contested this view, Dayton's reconstruction has won wide scholarly acceptance. Part of its popularity clearly rests in its serviceability to a number of conflicting constituencies. Pentecostal holiness scholars see it as providing an explanation for the emergence of Pentecostalism out of the holiness movement. On the other hand, some Wesleyan fundamentalists have found that Dayton's efforts to disassociate Wesley from his heirs in the 19th-century holiness movement serve their own desire to create a wall separating themselves from Pentecostalism and the subjectivism of traditional holiness spirituality. Ironically, this last desire has found wide acceptance among many in holiness churches who have little regard for either fundamentalism or Pentecostalism. It seems clear that while the use of Pentecostal language to describe the experience of entire sanctification increased during the course of the 19th century, the Pentecostal paradigm was clearly itself used by such Wesley associates as John Fletcher, Hester Ann Rogers, and William Carvosso, and Wesley seems to have endorsed this use. W.C.K.

BASSETT, PAUL MERRITT (b. Lima, Ohio, 28 May 1935). **Church of the Nazarene** (CN) historian and theologian. A graduate of Olivet

Nazarene College with B.D. and Ph.D. degrees from Duke University, Bassett has taught at Trevecca Nazarene College (1965–1966), West Virginia University (1966–1969), and Nazarene Theological Seminary (1969–present). Although he is an authority on medieval and patristic Christianity, Bassett's most notable publications have been a series of carefully nuanced and influential essays on fundamentalism's impact on the holiness movement and the movement's theological development, which have appeared in *Methodist History* and the *Wesleyan Theological Journal*. As one of the most beloved professors at Nazarene Theological Seminary, he has had a profound impact on a generation of Nazarene pastors and scholars. Noted for his wit and the breadth of his learning, Bassett has frequently represented conservative Wesleyans in ecumenical conversations, including discussions of the Faith and Order Commission of the World Council of Churches. A past president of the **Wesleyan Theological Society**, he has also served as editor of the *Wesleyan Theological Journal*. W.C.K.

BAWA SALKA, JACOB (b. Salka, Niger State, Nigeria, 11 November 1938). **Missionary Church** (MiC) minister, educator, and diplomat. From the Kamberi tribe, Jacob Bawa Salka's status as an orphan led to providential opportunities for formal education. During his school days, Bawa Salka turned from tribal animism to Islam, then to Christianity. His early adult years were spent as a teacher, then as a pastor and the first Nigerian principal of Hausa Bible School in Salka. Theological studies in Nigeria (Ilorin) and North America (Bethel College [Indiana], Emmanuel Bible College [Ontario], and Trinity Evangelical Divinity School [Illinois]) prepared him for twin roles as president of the **United Missionary Church** (UMiC) Theological College in Ilorin, Nigeria, and senior pastor at the college chapel. Following studies at Michigan State University (M.A., Ph.D.), he served as president of the UMiC of Africa and in other major appointments, including superintendent of the Niger State public schools, chairman of the Niger State Board of Education, various university posts, director of the United Bank of Africa, and Nigerian ambassador to Spain, the Vatican, and the Republic of Chad. The Nigerian government and Pope John Paul II have awarded him special honors. Bawa Salka's life, ministry, and leadership are marked by humility, integrity, piety, and enthusiasm for Christian missions. In 1996, he quietly declined nomination to become secretary-general of the United Nations. Beginning in 1994, he served as visiting professor of Religion at Bethel College, Mishawaka, Indiana. T.P.E.

BELDEN, HENRY (b. Greenfield, Connecticut, 9 April 1813; d. New York City, 24 June 1884). Presbyterian and Congregational minister and evangelist. In 1838, following his education at Union College, Andover Theological Seminary, Princeton Theological Seminary, and Union Theological Seminary, Belden entered the Presbyterian ministry. In 1844, due in part to his abolitionist sensitivities, he entered the Congregational ministry, serving churches in Boonton and Washingtonville, New York (1844–1852). In 1852, he became pastor of the Free Church in New York City. Following his experience of **entire sanctification**, he served as a city missionary in Brooklyn (1856–1866) and as a Congregational pastor in New Providence and Parkville, New York (1866–1871). He was the recording secretary for the American Missionary Association (1854–1874). A leading advocate of holiness experience among Congregationalists, Belden was a frequent revival preacher and addressed some of the early National Holiness Association (see **Christian Holiness Partnership**) **camp meetings**. W.C.K.

BENNARD, GEORGE (b. Youngstown, Ohio, 4 February 1873; d. Reed City, Michigan, 10 October 1958). **Salvation Army** (SA), Methodist Episcopal Church (MEC), and Methodist Church evangelist and songwriter. The son of an Iowa coal miner, in 1889 Bennard began his own short career in the mines. In 1897, shortly after his conversion, he joined the SA, serving for a time as an officer. Joining the MEC, Bennard emerged as a prominent midwestern holiness evangelist, frequently serving with **D. Willia Caffray**. He was the author of the famous hymn "The Old Rugged Cross," which in a 1938 poll by a national radio network was determined to be the nation's most popular song. Written in 1913 and first performed at the Sawyer Friends Church, Sturgeon Bay, Wisconsin, the hymn was introduced to a national audience through the agency of Chicago Evangelistic Institute (see **Vennard College**). Bennard's career was closely associated with that of Methodist bishop Arthur F. Wesley (b. 1885). Together they founded the Old Rugged Cross Mission in Chicago and frequently ministered at its services. Bennard was the author of over 350 hymns, including "Have Thine Own Way, Lord," "Pentecostal Fire Is Falling," and "Love Never Faileth." W.C.K.

BETHANY FELLOWSHIP. An evangelical communal society founded in Minneapolis, Minnesota, in 1945 by Theodore A. Hegre (1908–1984). Hegre, the son of Norwegian Lutheran immigrants, was converted in 1935 and under the influence of Norman Grubb experienced **entire sanctification** in the 1940s. In 1943, Hegre established a church in Minneapolis. Two years later, based on their understanding of Acts 2, Hegre, his wife, and four other young couples adopted a communal living arrangement. In 1948, the community relocated to a 70-acre site in suburban Bloomington, Minnesota. Establishing a periodical edited by Hegre, the *Message of the Cross*; a missionary training school, Bethany Fellowship Training School, now Bethany College of Missions; a publishing arm, Bethany House Publishers; and, in 1963, its own mission, Bethany Fellowship Missions, this single congregation emerged as an important shaper of 20th-century evangelical culture.

By 1999, Bethany Fellowship had 130 missionaries on five continents. Its most notable mission work is in Brazil, where it has established 40 churches, three Bible institutes, and a thriving bookstore ministry. Equally successful has been Bethany House Publishers, which publishes the works of best-selling Christian writer **Janette Oke**, along with books by Hegre; Oberlin perfectionists, such as **Charles G. Finney**; **Keswick** authors, such as Andrew Murray; and holiness movement writers, including **Maynard James**, **Leonard Ravenhill**, **Delbert Rose**, **A. Skevington Wood**, and **Timothy L. Smith**. A member of the National Association of Evangelicals (NAE), Bethany Fellowship unites a Wesleyan emphasis on sanctification as a second work of grace with certain aspects of Pentecostalism, such as speaking in tongues, as a gift for the church. It rejects the notion that tongues is an evidence of the **baptism of the Holy Spirit**. The movement's distinctives are best expressed in such works by Hegre as *The Cross and Sanctification* (1960) and *The Will of God—Your Sanctification* (1961). W.C.K.

BETHEL MISSION OF CHINA. *See* STONE, MARY.

BHUJBAL, SAMUEL (b. Thana District, India, 1905; d. Bombay, India, 19 September 1978). **Church of the Nazarene** (CN) pastor, evangelist, and district superintendent. Bhujbal's parents began working for the CN mission in India when he was three. He was educated in mission and government schools and converted in 1921 through **H. F. Reynolds**'s preaching. As a young man, he proved an effective village evangelist, both as a preacher and as an organizer of evangelistic bands. Hundreds accepted the Christian faith through his ministry. He taught at the Nazarene Boy's School in Buldana (1926–1937). In 1937, he was ordained at the First India District Assembly, which also elected him district superintendent. He served in that office until 1945, as district evangelist (1945–1949), and again as district superintendent (1949–1959). He moved to Bombay in the early 1960s where he was a pastor-evangelist until his death. R.S.I.

BIBLE HOLINESS CHURCH (BHC). Founded by members of the Neosho Valley Holiness Association in 1890 as the South Eastern Kansas Fire Baptized Holiness Association. Under the leadership of B. H. Irwin, the association began to emphasize three works of grace: salvation, **entire sanctification**, and the **baptism of the Holy Spirit**. Spreading throughout the Midwest and Southeast, the movement experienced rapid growth that was only halted when its adherents divided after the advent of Pentecostalism in 1906. A significant body of members in southeast Kansas rejected Pentecostalism. In 1945, this group changed its name to the Fire Baptized Holiness Church (Wesleyan), which, in 1995, became the BHC. In 1988, the BHC had 1,200 members in 50 congregations. Its headquarters is at Independence, Kansas, where it operates a school. It supports missions in New Guinea and has published a periodical, the *Flaming Sword*, since 1935. A deeply conservative body, the church has prohibitions against television and encourages its members to be conscientious objectors in time of war. W.C.K.

BIBLE HOLINESS MOVEMENT (BHM). Originated as a single rescue mission established in Vancouver, British Columbia, in the 1940s by retired **Salvation Army** (SA) officer William James Elijah Wakefield. In 1949, Wakefield's son, Wesley H. Wakefield, became bishop-general of what was then known as the Bible Holiness Mission. The BHM unites the third-blessing theology of **Ralph C. Horner** and the social vision of the SA. It feeds the hungry, provides drug counseling, and holds open-air evangelistic meetings. It is committed to civil rights for racial minorities and protection of the environment, and its adherents are encouraged to become conscientious objectors to war. Typical of the movement's style was a 1992 debate between Wakefield and Sheik Ahmad Decdat at Toronto's famed Maple Leaf Gardens that was attended by 5,000 people. Outside Canada, the BHM has branches in the United States, India, Central Africa, the Philippines, Kenya, and South Korea. It is a member of the **Christian Holiness Partnership**. In 1988, the BHM reported 27,416 members, mostly outside North America. It publishes a periodical, *Truth on Fire*. W.C.K.

BIBLE METHODIST CONNECTION OF CHURCHES (BMCC). Organized in 1970 with 794 members in 44 churches. The BMCC was established by former **Wesleyan Methodist Church** (WMC) members in Ohio and Alabama who believed that the WMC–**Pilgrim Holiness Church** merger of 1968 had permanently altered the traditional congregational form of church government and represented further abandonment of the distinctive cultural mores of the WMC. In 1994, the United Holiness Church of North America, a group of former **Free Methodist Church** (FMC) members from Michigan who had left that body in 1955 in a reaction to cultural changes among members of the FMC, merged with the BMCC. As of 1997, the BMCC had 66 congregations with 1,033 members organized into three conferences: Alabama, Ohio, and the Great Lakes. Connectional missions were located in Mexico, the Philippines, South Africa, and France. Gary Brugger, missionary-secretary, was the only full-time officer. The BMCC publishes a monthly periodical, the *Bible Methodist*. W.S.

BIBLE MISSIONARY CHURCH (BMiC). Formed as the Bible Missionary Union in 1955 near Nampa, Idaho, in reaction to the increase of worldliness its leaders saw in the established holiness churches, particularly the **Church of the Nazarene** (CN). Led by **Glenn Griffith**, a former CN district superintendent in Idaho, the new denomination grew fairly rapidly. Elbert Dodd, a prominent former CN district superintendent, joined with the infant denomination at its first General Conference in Denver, Colorado.

Amid the monumental cultural changes taking place in the United States during the 1950s and 1960s, established holiness groups attempted to adjust to remain relevant to their contexts. These intra-church cultural changes were perceived by some to be unacceptable compromises with traditional holiness standards and practices. The BMiC was one of the first denominations in what has become known as the radical holiness movement. It continues to enforce strict standards of dress and Christian ethics, and it encourages traditional ecstatic worship experiences.

The church is organized into 14 districts in the United States and Canada and consists of 212 churches. It supports missions in 16 different countries with 35 missionaries. There are approximately 400 BMiC churches outside North America, primarily in Nigeria, New Guinea, Mexico, Nepal, and Myanmar. In 1958, the denomination founded the

Bible Missionary Institute, a four-year college in Rock Island, Illinois, with an enrollment in 1998 of more than 100 students. It has also supported Beulah Mountain Christian Academy, an orphanage in Beulah Heights, Kentucky, since 1959. C.M.H.

BOARDMAN, W(illiam) E(dward) (b. Smithfield, New York, 11 October 1810; d. London, 4 February 1886). Presbyterian minister, evangelist, and author. In the early 1840s, while attempting to establish a mercantile business in the mining community of Potosi, Wisconsin, Boardman experienced **entire sanctification**. He attended Lane Theological Seminary in Cincinnati, Ohio (1843–1846). After planting a Presbyterian church in Greenfield, Indiana, Boardman resumed his theological education at Yale University, New Haven, Connecticut. From 1852 to 1859, he worked with the American Sunday School Union in Detroit, Michigan, and Philadelphia, Pennsylvania. After a sojourn in California, Boardman, who was an ardent abolitionist, became secretary of the United States Christian Commission (1862–1866).

After several years in business, he resumed his ministerial career, becoming one of the key figures in the emerging transcontinental holiness and healing revivals. In 1873, while traveling in England with **Charles Cullis**, Boardman joined Cullis, **William Arthur**, and **R. P. Smith** in the promotion of a series of holiness meetings at the Broadlands, Oxford, and Brighton that evolved into the famous **Keswick** Conventions. The last years of his life were spent primarily in holiness evangelism in Europe and in the creation of a network of people committed to faith healing. Boardman's *The Higher Christian Life* (1858), although vigorously attacked by conservative Calvinists, including the editors of *Princeton Review*, played no small role in the spread of holiness teaching among Presbyterians and Congregationalists. Among his other significant books were *He That Overcometh* (1869) and *The Faith Work under Dr. Cullis* (1873). W.C.K.

BOOLE, ELLA ALEXANDER (b. Van Wert, Ohio, 26 July 1858; d. Brooklyn, New York, 13 March 1952). Temperance leader.

BOOLE, WILLIAM HILLIKER (b. Shelburne, Nova Scotia, 24 April 1827; d. Staten Island, New York, 24 February 1896). Methodist Episcopal Church (MEC) minister, U.S. Army chaplain, revivalist, author, temperance lecturer, founder of the Sea Cliff Grove Camp Meeting (Long Island, New York), and founder of the Home for Women (New York, New York).

William Boole's family moved to New York before he was six years old. He left legal studies to take up shipbuilding, which took him to Boston. He was converted while attending an MEC church in East Boston. Later he joined the New York East Annual Conference and served more than a dozen pastorates in a 30-year career. He also served as an army chaplain during the Civil War.

Boole was a gifted orator. He was well known as a temperance speaker, and some of his popular lectures were published. He became actively involved in politics and in 1868 traveled widely, promoting the interests of the Republican Party.

Evidence suggests that Boole joined the National Camp Meeting Association for the Promotion of Holiness (*see* **Christian Holiness Partnership**) in 1868. He preached at the 1868 and 1869 National Camp Meetings, held at Manheim, Pennsylvania, and Round Lake, New York. In 1869, he assisted William B. Osborn in the founding of the Ocean Grove (New Jersey) Camp Meeting as a permanent camp meeting resort. In 1871, he served on the West Coast with a team of revivalists from the National Camp Meeting Association. On the way home, the team pitched its tent in Salt Lake City, Utah, and held meetings during which Boole preached a powerful anti-Mormon sermon that created considerable excitement and nearly caused a riot.

Later in 1871, Boole purchased property on Hempstead Harbor, Long Island, New York, and founded Sea Cliff Grove as a holiness camp meeting resort where a National Camp Meeting was held in 1871. The same year, Boole founded the Home for Women in New York City.

In 1883, the twice-widowed Boole married Ella Alexander who, influenced by her husband's work, became active in the temperance movement, serving as president of the New York Woman's Christian Temperance Union (WCTU) from 1896 to 1925. She was president of the National WCTU (1925–1933) and of the World's WCTU (1933–1947). She also ran three strong but unsuccessful races for the United States Senate. K.O.B.

BOOTH, CATHERINE MUMFORD (b. Ashbourne, Derbyshire, England, 17 January 1829; d. Clacton-on-Sea, Essex, 4 October 1890). Preacher, social reformer, and cofounder of the **Salvation Army** (SA). Raised in a devoutly religious Methodist family, Mumford became an avid student of theology while she was a bedridden adolescent. About the time her family moved to London in 1844, she experienced **entire**

sanctification. She became active in a Wesleyan Methodist congregation in Brixton but was expelled from the church because of her involvement with a group seeking to reform the church. Among this group was preacher **William Booth**, whom Mumford married in 1855. She became actively involved in William Booth's evangelistic ministry. In 1859, Catherine Booth wrote a pamphlet entitled *Female Ministry* in which she presented the case for women taking an active role in the public ministry of the church. The following year, she began to preach. She was instrumental in William Booth's 1861 decision to abandon the Methodist Church in favor of a career as an itinerant evangelist that led to the founding of the SA. Catherine Booth was a tireless fund-raiser for the SA. She also championed many social causes, including temperance, aid to the poor, improvement of housing conditions, and humane treatment of animals. Among her eight children were Bramwell Booth (1856–1929), who followed William Booth as general of the SA; Ballington Booth (1857–1940), who, with his wife Maud, founded the Volunteers of America; Katherine Booth-Clibborn (1858–1953), for a time an associate of John Alexander Dowie and an early Pentecostal; Emma Booth-Tucker (1860–1903), who, with her husband, headed the American SA; Herbert Booth (1862–1926); and **Evangeline Booth**. G.A.P.

BOOTH, EVANGELINE CORY (b. London, 25 December 1865; d. Hartsdale, New York, 17 July 1950). Leader of the **Salvation Army** (SA) in the United States. Evangeline Booth was the fourth daughter and seventh of eight children of **William** and **Catherine Booth**, cofounders of the SA. Given high rank in the SA and placed in administrative positions at a relatively early age, Evangeline was strong-willed, notional, and melodramatic. As an administrator, however, she showed good judgment, foresight, and the ability to attract and hold dedicated and able subordinates. After eight years in charge of the SA in Canada, in 1904, she became leader of the SA in the United States, with the title of commander. Some of the most important developments in the history of the SA in the United States occurred during her long administration. She is the only national leader of the SA to become well known to the American public. In 1934, she was elected general of the international SA. She retired from active service in 1939 and returned to the United States. E.H.M.

BOOTH, WILLIAM (b. Nottingham, England, 10 April 1829; d. London, 20 October 1912). Cofounder of the **Salvation Army** (SA).

Raised in a Wesleyan home, Booth was converted in 1844 and almost immediately began preaching. He was licensed to the Methodist ministry in 1852 and served as a Methodist New Connection preacher (1854–1861). He married **Catherine Mumford (Booth)** in 1855. From 1861 to 1865, he was an itinerant evangelist, and in 1865, the Booths founded the Christian Mission in London's impoverished East End. It was reorganized as the SA in 1878. Although his critics found him autocratic and the SA was quite controversial in its early years, Booth emerged as one of the most beloved figures of late Victorian England. He was deeply concerned about poverty, and his widely read *In Darkest England and the Way Out* (1890) depicted the SA's vision of urban social redemption. Although he was to some degree committed to holiness teaching, it was Catherine Booth, not William, who systematically articulated the SA's early holiness teaching. Not surprisingly, the holiness emphasis of the SA became less pronounced in the years following Catherine's death in 1890. W.C.K.

BOWMAN, THOMAS (b. Lehigh Gap, Pennsylvania, 18 May 1836; d. Allentown, Pennsylvania, 19 March 1923). Prominent bishop and holiness leader in the Evangelical Association (EA). Converted at age 18, Thomas Bowman was licensed to preach in 1858 in the East Pennsylvania Conference. After serving effectively as a **camp meeting** preacher, holiness author, and presiding elder, he was elected bishop in 1875 and served in that capacity for 40 years. He was a prominent supporter of the majority party in the denominational schism of 1891–1921. He lived to see the parties in the schism reunite to form the Evangelical Church in 1922. J.S.O.

BRASH, JOHN (b. Garstang, Lancashire, England, 8 November 1830; d. Liverpool, 19 April 1912). British Wesleyan minister and cofounder of the *King's Highway* (1872). As an evangelist, Brash saw thousands of conversions during his ministry, which commenced in 1857. Revivals of deep intensity were part of his ministry in several northern towns. He led many into the experience of **entire sanctification** and was a popular speaker at the **Keswick** Convention and the **Southport Methodist Holiness Convention**. In 1872, he and three other young preachers, including **Isaac E. Page**, established the *King's Highway*, the first distinctly holiness publication in Europe. In retirement, he served the Liverpool Mission. His obituary declared, "In personal character an example of the beauty of holiness." W. E. Sangster considered him to be among the greatest saints. (Biography: Isaac E. Page, *John Brash* [London: n.d.]) W.P.

BRASHER, JOHN LAKIN (b. Attalla, Alabama, 20 July 1868; d. Attalla, Alabama, 25 January 1971). Methodist Episcopal Church (MEC) and Methodist Church (MC) minister, college president, and evangelist. Named for Arad S. Lakin, MEC abolitionist and defender of the recently liberated slaves in postbellum Alabama, Brasher was raised in the northern (or as some said, "Republican") Methodist stronghold in north Alabama. He was converted in 1886, ordained a deacon in 1893, and became an elder in 1896. Following graduation from U.S. Grant University School of Theology in 1899, he became pastor of the Simpson MEC in Birmingham. He served as conference secretary for the Alabama Conference (1903–1939) and was a delegate to five MEC general conferences. Although initially critical of the holiness movement, Brasher experienced **entire sanctification** in 1900 under the ministry of **Samuel Logan Brengle**. He served as president of John H. Sneed Seminary in Boaz, Alabama (1905–1911), and Iowa Holiness University, which he helped to rename John Fletcher College (1917–1926). He was president of the Iowa Holiness Association (1920–1922), pastor of the Detroit Holiness Tabernacle (1927), editor of the *Way of Faith* (1929–1931), founder and president of the Brasher **Camp Meeting** (1940–1969), and member of the faculty of **God's Bible School** (1943–1944, 1950).

A master of colloquial expression and the traditional use of metaphor, Brasher was one of the holiness movement's most articulate evangelists. During his active ministry, he preached at an estimated 200 camp meetings and participated in an estimated 700 revival meetings. He was the author of five books and many journal articles. Among his most notable works was *Glimpses* (1954), a thoughtful reminiscence of the many holiness evangelists he had known. A valuable collection of personal papers documenting Brasher's ministry and the holiness movement is housed at Duke University. His grandson, J. Lawrence Brasher, is author of a biography called *The Sanctified South: John Lakin Brasher and the Holiness Movement* (1994). W.C.K.

BREEDEN, HENRY (b. Southwell, Nottinghamshire, England, 11 August 1804; d. Leeds, Yorkshire, 24 November 1878). Wesleyan lay evangelist and holiness preacher who came to prominence as the prayer leader and associate of John Smith ("Smith of Cudworth") in his East Midlands Revivals. Breeden became the first Arminian Methodist itinerant in 1832 and acted as the general superintendent of the "Derby Faith" (**Arminian Methodist Connexion**) people until they ceased as a distinct body in 1837. His *A Call to Holiness and Usefulness* (1834) went into many expanded editions on both sides of the Atlantic. He deviated somewhat from the general Wesleyan understanding of grace by holding to a semi-Pelagian emphasis on people's ability to believe. He was also author of *Striking Incidents of Saving Grace* (1878; reprinted 1981). W.P.

BRENGLE, SAMUEL LOGAN (b. Fredericksburg, Indiana, 1 June 1860; d. Scarsdale, New York, 20 May 1936). Major exponent of holiness theology in the **Salvation Army** (SA). Growing up in the Methodist Episcopal Church (MEC), upon completion of his A.B. degree at Indiana Asbury University (now DePauw University) in 1883, Brengle began his ministry as a circuit preacher for the MEC in Indiana. The following year he began studies at Boston Theological Seminary, coming into the experience of **entire sanctification** under the influence of Professor **Daniel Steele** in 1885. Attracted by the SA's doctrine of social holiness, Brengle traveled to London to meet with **William Booth** in 1887. Becoming a cadet, he finished his training in London before assuming command of various SA corps in the United States.

After a near fatal encounter with a thrown brick in Boston in 1888, Brengle used his long recuperation period to write a series of articles for the *War Cry*, called "Helps to Holiness." His book, *The Soul-Winner's Secret*, was the outgrowth of another series of articles written for the *War Cry* in 1896. His other works include *Heart Talks on Holiness* (1897), *The Way of Holiness* (1902), and *When the Holy Ghost Is Come* (1906). These and other works were to prove very influential, not only in propagating holiness doctrine and practice throughout the holiness movement but also in further institutionalizing holiness doctrine within the SA. The immediacy of the experience of entire sanctification appropriated by simple faith was the predominant teaching of the early SA doctrine of the Holy Spirit, as mediated by William and **Catherine Booth** in the 1860s. Brengle's holiness theology, however, emphasized the tension between the immediacy of expectation and waiting on God for the assurance of sanctification. Thus, he served as a corrective to the emphases of **Phoebe Palmer** and the misuse of her "altar theology" within the movement. The ministry and message of Brengle helped to center SA theology in the tradition of Wesley, maintaining a tension between active faith and patient waiting in the experience of entire sanctification. R.D.R.

BRENNEMAN, DANIEL (b. Fairfield County, Ohio, 8 June 1834; d. 10 September 1919). Founder of the Mennonite Brethren in Christ (MBIC). Converted at the age of 22, in 1857, Brenneman was chosen by lot for ministry in the Mennonite Church. From the beginning of his ministry, he was known as an able preacher and evangelist.

In 1864, he moved to Elkhart County, Indiana, to serve as a minister of the Yellow Creek congregation. He soon came into conflict with a more conservative church than he had anticipated, and his progressive views were challenged by a bishop who was opposed to all new methods of extending the kingdom. He and an associate preached for the first revival meeting ever held in a Mennonite church in America in 1872. Brenneman was excommunicated from the church in 1874, and a number of members left the church with him. A warm relationship developed between Brenneman and some Mennonites he had visited in Ontario the previous year and who had also been excommunicated. Out of this relationship, the Reformed Mennonites were organized in 1874. Through a series of mergers, the MBIC was formed in 1883. Later, the name was changed to **United Missionary Church**, and a merger with the **Missionary Church Association** in 1969 formed the **Missionary Church** as it is presently known.

Brenneman and other church leaders were profoundly influenced by the Methodist **camp meetings** of their day. Holiness teaching was heralded in the masthead of the *Gospel Banner*, a publication founded by Brenneman in 1878. Preaching in English, singing in four-part harmony, Sunday schools, and many other progressive innovations were the result of the zeal of Brenneman and others of like mind. Brenneman served for many years as a pastor and as a presiding elder (district superintendent) in the MBIC. W.J.G.

BRESEE, PHINEAS F. (b. Franklin, New York, 31 December 1838; d. Los Angeles, California, 13 November 1915). Methodist Episcopal Church (MEC) minister, evangelist, and founder of the **Church of the Nazarene** (CN). Educated at the Delaware Literary Institute in Franklin, New York, Bresee was converted in 1856. In 1857, he moved with his family to Iowa where he was admitted into the Iowa Conference of the MEC and assigned to a grueling 40-mile circuit. In 1864, he was appointed a presiding elder in the West Des Moines Conference. Frustrated by his role as an administrator, Bresee was appointed to the Clariton circuit in 1866. Noted as a powerful evangelistic preacher, Bresee pastored important churches in Des Moines, Council Bluffs, Creston, and Red Oaks. As a conference leader, Bresee served on the board of Simpson College and was a delegate to the 1872 General Conference of the MEC.

Beginning in 1873, Bresee began selling stock in several silver mines in Mexico and, in 1881, was named president of Council Bluffs Gold and Silver Mining Company. In 1883, as a result of either fraud or a flood, the company failed. Since Iowa Methodists had heavily promoted and invested in the company, the failure was a source of embarrassment for both Bresee and the MEC. Relocating to Los Angeles, Bresee spent the next decade as pastor of a series of important MEC congregations in Los Angeles and Pasadena. He was a delegate to the 1892 General Conference of the MEC and served on the board of the University of Southern California (USC).

Deeply committed to evangelism, reaching the masses with the gospel, and demonstrative worship, Bresee, who had experienced **entire sanctification** in 1867, was increasingly drawn into leadership in the emerging holiness movement in Southern California. In 1894, he withdrew from the MEC and affiliated with the **Peniel Missions**. In 1895, Bresee, with his close friend, USC president J. P. Widney, organized the Church of the Nazarene. In 1898, Widney resigned, leaving Bresee as pastor of the Los Angeles church; editor of a growing holiness periodical, the *Nazarene Messenger*; and general superintendent of a small but growing holiness denomination. A skillful diplomat who worked well with both holiness radicals and conservative Methodist loyalists, Bresee orchestrated the creation of a transsectional holiness denomination, the Pentecostal Church of the Nazarene (PCN; see CN), through a series of mergers with several regional holiness bodies. Especially significant were a 1907 merger with the Association of Pentecostal Churches, a Northeastern holiness body; a 1908 merger with the Holiness Churches of Christ at Pilot Point, Texas; and a 1914 merger with Pentecostal Mission, a regional holiness body centered in Nashville, Tennessee. Reflecting Bresee's willingness to compromise on issues that he considered nonessential, the PCN combined elements of Congregational, Presbyterian, and Episcopal church government; infant and believer's baptism; and postmillennial and premillennial **eschatology**. W.C.K.

BRETHREN IN CHRIST CHURCH (BIC). Established in about 1780 in Lancaster County, Pennsylvania. The founders, led by Jacob

Engle, were largely Mennonites who had undergone crisis conversion experiences in meetings held by revivalist ministers such as Martin Boehm. Following their conversions, early BIC members met together in small groups, typical of Pietist conventicles, to discuss their experiences and to study Scripture. The founders called their new body "Brethren." Because they lived near the Susquehanna River, they were soon called "River Brethren" by outsiders to distinguish them from other Brethren groups who lived in the area.

In 1788, a small group of Brethren emigrated to the Niagara region of Canada. In the next century, other members moved to Michigan, Ohio, Indiana, Illinois, Iowa, Oklahoma, and California. These areas remain the chief centers of the denomination.

During the 19th century, the Brethren worked out a synthesis of their Anabaptist–Mennonite and Pietist beliefs. The former led them to emphasize separation from the world (nonconformity), which expressed itself, among other ways, in plain dress and prohibitions against worldly entertainment. Other marked signs of their Anabaptist background were their active stances on nonresistance, Christian community, church discipline, and obedience. The Pietist influence expressed itself in the more experiential areas of their lives. They emphasized the conversion experience, a strong devotional life, and testimony. Worship services, held in homes and barns, combined elements of Pietism and Anabaptism.

The Brethren formally adopted the name "Brethren in Christ" during the Civil War, when they registered with the federal government to obtain exemption from military service. In about 1880, the BIC began a program of aggressive evangelism, which included yearly revival meetings in many churches and institutional development. The BIC established a church periodical, *Evangelical Visitor*; foreign missions in Africa and India; educational institutions, such as Messiah College (Grantham, Pennsylvania); orphanages; and a retirement home, now Messiah Village. During this period, the holiness movement fundamentally altered the spirituality of the church. This change first occurred in the West where BIC youth from Iowa and Kansas were increasingly being educated at Hephzibah Faith Missionary Home and School in Tabor, Iowa (see **Hephzibah Faith Missionary Association**). After 1910, under the leadership of respected BIC evangelists **John** and Noah **Zook**, the holiness emphasis increasingly was felt in the eastern United States and Canada.

By 1910, the General Conference, the governing body of the BIC, officially accepted a statement that placed the BIC within the American holiness movement. In 1936, a holiness **camp meeting** was begun at Roxbury, Pennsylvania, and by 1950 similar camps had been established in Ohio, Kansas, California, and Ontario. More recently, a camp has been established in Florida.

By the 1950s, restrictions against worldly amusements were modified, even as the church adopted musical instruments for worship and programs for youth, while abandoning distinctive styles of dress. Accompanying these changes was a growing spirit of ecumenism. In 1941, the BIC became an integral part of the Mennonite Central Committee (MCC), and they joined the National Association of Evangelicals in 1949 and the National Holiness Association (NHA; see **Christian Holiness Partnership**) in 1950. Over the years they have provided key leadership in these three organizations, particularly in the MCC and the NHA. In 1957, the many small districts in North America were brought together into six regional conferences. Further structural reorganizations have combined a multiplicity of boards and committees into a few major boards. In 1984, the denomination instituted Cooperative Ministries, a concept of financing by which money given in congregational offerings goes in proportional amounts to congregational, regional, and denominational ministries. Since 1945, former mission areas have been indigenized. At the same time, the BIC has begun missions in other parts of the world, including Japan, Latin America, and Europe. In 1998, the BIC was in 17 countries outside Canada and the United States. Membership in Canada and the United States is nearly 21,000, while elsewhere membership is approximately 44,000. E.M.S.

BROCKETT, HENRY EDWARD (b. Bedford, England, 1893; d. Kent, England, 1976). Holiness author. Brought up in the Exclusive Brethren, Brockett came to personal faith in his youth, worked with the London Borough Council, and served in the British Army (1914–1917). Following his discharge on medical grounds, he returned to work with the London Council. Through contact with **David Thomas** and the International Holiness Mission, he moved away from dispensationalism and enthusiastically embraced Wesleyan holiness. A devout layman who spent much of his spare time in village evangelism, he promoted the doctrine of **entire sanctification** in three significant books. *The Riches of Holiness* (1936) was partly autobiographical and set out a simple outline of biblical teaching on the possibilities of a holy life. *Scriptural Freedom from Sin* (1939) was a carefully reasoned reply to Harry A.

Ironside's attack on Wesleyan teaching in his *Holiness: The False and the True*. His third work, *The Christian and Romans 7* (1972), argued that the experience delineated in Romans 7 is descriptive not of a Christian but of an awakened sinner. H.M.

BROOKS, D(elos) F(erdinand) (b. St. Albans Bay, Vermont, 10 October 1845; d. Round Lake, New York, 30 May 1935). Methodist Episcopal Church (MEC) minister, evangelist, and author. A Civil War veteran, Brooks entered the ministry of the Troy (New York) Conference, MEC, in 1873. Increasingly drawn to evangelistic work, he served as a conference evangelist (1899–1911). Although formally retiring in 1911, he continued to conduct revival services and preach at **camp meetings** into the 1930s. He was a vigorous apologist for the traditional holiness movement emphasis on two works of grace and spoke and wrote extensively against Christian Science, Pentecostalism, **Keswick** Movement formulations of holiness doctrine, and the distinctive teachings of Seventh-Day Adventism. Among his most widely read books were *Does St. John or Christian Science Tell the Truth?* (1902), *From Bethabara to Pentecost* (1905), and *What Is the Carnal Mind?* (1905). W.C.K.

BROOKS, JOHN P(etit) (b. Cincinnati, Ohio, 24 July 1826; d. Dallas, Texas, 16 June 1915). Methodist Episcopal Church (MEC) and **Church of God (Holiness)** (CG[H]) preacher and editor. Behind Brooks's role as a theologian and apologist for the Independent Holiness church movement lay half a lifetime devoted to the advancement of its supposed antithesis, the MEC. Throughout his career, Brooks displayed both the detachment and combativeness of the professional journalist, tendencies destined to placate as well as exacerbate conflict. In 1850, following service in the Mexican War and a brief stint as owner of the *Canton* (Illinois) *Register*, this son of pioneer Jacksonian Democratic newspaperman S. S. Brooks was licensed to preach in the Rock River Conference of the MEC. He was ordained a deacon in 1852 and an elder in 1856. Except for the years 1863 to 1865, during which he served as Illinois state superintendent of public instruction, he held conference appointments in the Rock River and Central Illinois conferences until 1880. He was for six years secretary of the Peoria, later Central Illinois, Conference, and Bishop Waugh is reputed to have said, "I consider Brother Brooks the ablest Conference Secretary in the Methodist Church." In 1869, Brooks, while under appointment to Peoria, professed **entire sanctification** under the ministry of **M. L. Haney**.

From 1872 to 1883, he served as editor of the Bloomington-based *Banner of Holiness*, organ of the Western Holiness Association and sounding board for the entire trans-Appalachian holiness movement, and was one of the conveners of transdenominational meetings in Cincinnati, Ohio (1877); Jacksonville, Florida (1880); and Chicago (1885).

Brooks's experience as spokesman for the holiness cause led him to question much that was occurring inside and on the periphery of official Methodism. His increasingly controversial views on the nature of the church resulted in his withdrawal from the MEC in 1880 and his being replaced as editor at the Western Holiness Association in 1883. In 1885, National Holiness Association (see **Christian Holiness Partnership**) leader **George Hughes** even refused to allow him to read a letter from independent holiness church advocates in California at the transdenominational holiness meeting in Chicago. Emerging as a leader in the CG(H), Brooks became the first editor of the *Good Way* to share fully in the emerging New Testament teaching that became the fundamental emphasis of the CG(H). The argument of his *Divine Church* (1891) must be viewed in the context both of connectional Methodism and the hyperspiritualism of the antiordinance agitation of A. L. Brewer (1848–1940). Initially a leader in the local church supremacy faction of the CG(H) (see **Churches of God**), Brooks eventually came to share the views of the elder supremacy faction. He served as editor of the *Church Advocate and Holiness Banner,* the *Church Witness,* and the *Church Herald* (1895–1904). During his last years, he continued to preach and to devote considerable time to an unpublished manuscript, "Observations on the Kingdom." C.E.J.

BROWN, CHARLES EWING (b. Elizabethtown, Illinois, 30 December 1883; d. Anderson, Indiana, 16 September 1971). **Church of God (Anderson)** (CG[A]) minister and writer. Brown's father, Willis, was converted in 1895, with Charles following shortly thereafter. In 1896, both Browns began traveling as holiness evangelists throughout southern Illinois, southeastern Missouri, and western Kentucky. In 1900, Charles attended **Asbury College** briefly and then left to resume evangelistic work with his father. After contact with CG(A) evangelists in 1901–1902, first Willis and then Charles affiliated with the CG(A).

Charles E. Brown served pastorates primarily in the Midwest but also as far east as Philadelphia, Pennsylvania. While at Detroit, Michigan, he helped to organize the Michigan State Assembly of the CG(A).

In 1925, he was elected chair of the General Ministerial Assembly. In 1930, Brown succeeded **F. G. Smith** as editor of the *Gospel Trumpet*, a post he held until 1951. A prolific writer, he approached topics historically and theologically and was the person primarily responsible for shifting the CG(A) away from a self-understanding grounded in biblical apocalyptic. M.D.S.

BURNS, NELSON (b. Niagara, Upper Canada, 22 March 1834; d. Toronto, 14 June 1904). Methodist minister, holiness preacher, author, and editor. As a boy of 14, Burns read **Phoebe Palmer**'s *Faith and Its Effects* and secured the "blessing of holiness." Following his ordination as a minister in the Wesleyan Methodist Church, Canada, in 1866, he became known as one who emphasized the doctrine of holiness. In 1878, poor health caused him to request supernumerary status. In 1879, he and others formed the Canada Holiness Association, and Burns became its president, a position he held until his death. While teaching in Milton (Upper Canada), he had become owner and editor of the *Herald* in nearby Georgetown and, consequently, in 1882, when the association began to publish a monthly paper, the *Expositor of Holiness*, Burns became editor. The association also held **camp meetings** and an annual convention.

Burns developed a strong theory of divine guidance, asserting that a Christian accepting God's absolute guidance could make no regrettable mistakes. After he elaborated on this in his book *Divine Guidance, or The Holy Guest* (1889), Methodist concern about his theories increased. At the 1894 meeting of the Guelph Conference, Burns was deposed from the ministry. Although he continued to lead the association and edit the *Expositor*, his previous cordial relations with holiness advocates in the United States deteriorated, and increasingly he opposed what he regarded as legalistic Christianity. In his later years, he pastored a Christian Association congregation in Toronto, although he resisted the idea that the holiness movement might become a denomination. (Autobiography: Albert Truax, ed., *Autobiography of the Late Nelson Burns* [Toronto: Christian Association, n.d.]) M.F.W.

BUTLER, CHARLES WILLIAM (b. Caro, Michigan, 13 May 1873; d. Detroit, Michigan, 17 April 1960). Methodist Episcopal Church (MEC) and Methodist Church minister, evangelist, editor, and president of the National Holiness Association (1928–1942; see **Christian Holiness Partnership**). Butler served as a pastor in the Detroit Conference of the MEC (1891–1906) and as an evangelist and **camp**

meeting preacher (1906–1921). During this period, he organized the Detroit Holiness Association and headed its mission in Detroit. Influenced by **Beverly Carradine**'s book *The Sanctified Life* (1897), Butler experienced **entire sanctification** in 1901. Although confessing that prior to his experience of "full salvation" he had been unable to locate verses that taught "a second work of grace," after his experience, he found ample scriptural justification. He served as president of Cleveland Bible Institute, now Malone College (1921–1936), and as president of John Fletcher College (1936–1946; see **Kletzing College**). He was also editor of the *Christian Witness* (1933–1947). In addition to numerous articles in holiness periodicals, such as the *Christian Witness* and the *Pentecostal Herald*, he wrote the *Holiness Manifesto*. His personal papers are located at **Asbury Theological Seminary**. W.C.K.

BYRUM, ENOCH E. (b. Randolph County, Indiana, 13 October 1861; d. Anderson, Indiana, 5 January 1942). **Church of God (Anderson)** (CG[A]) minister and editor. Byrum was raised in a devout United Brethren in Christ (UB) home, experiencing conversion at age 15. Through family influence, he was sanctified in a CG(A) revival in 1886. The following year, he purchased half-interest in the *Gospel Trumpet* and became its publisher. Byrum was especially interested in the practice of faith healing. In 1892, he published *Divine Healing of Soul and Body*. Claiming the gift of healing, he maintained this special ministry until his death.

Upon **D. S. Warner**'s death in 1895, Byrum succeeded him as editor of the *Gospel Trumpet* and thus became a de facto leader in the CG(A). A stolid manager and businessman, Byrum steered the church through its most serious theological crisis in 1898–1899. Byrum used the full weight of the editor's office to champion the holiness movement's view of sanctification. His heavy managerial hand eventually led to his being relieved of the editor's office in 1916. He produced an autobiography, *Life Experiences* (1928). M.D.S.

– C –

CADLE, E. HOWARD (b. Washington County, Indiana, 1884; d. Indianapolis, Indiana, 20 December 1942). United Brethren in Christ businessman, evangelist, and founder of the Cadle Tabernacle. Although raised in a pious home, as a young man Cadle became a gambler who owned a string of slot machines in Indiana, Illinois, and Kentucky. After Indiana banned slot machines, he operated a saloon in Indianapolis. Dramatically converted in 1914, Cadle taught Sunday school and began sharing his testimony throughout Indiana. A master at sales, Cadle worked as a traveling salesman and sold automobiles (1914–1916). In 1916, he founded the "While You Wait" chain of shoe repair shops. By 1918, he was operating 22 shops in the Midwest, including 4 in Chicago. In 1919, Cadle and a pastor from New Albany, Indiana, constructed a large tabernacle in Louisville, Kentucky. For a year, they held services that climaxed with a spectacular revival conducted by famed British evangelist "Gipsy" Smith (1860–1947). In 1921, Cadle built a second tabernacle in Indianapolis that led to the founding of the Cadle Tabernacle, a 10,000-seat religious complex in the center of Indianapolis. Suffering a series of business reversals, Cadle lost control of the tabernacle.

In 1927, Cadle became a full-time evangelist; by 1931, he had regained control of Cadle Tabernacle. In 1933, Cadle founded *The Nation's Family Prayer Period*, which was broadcast at seven A.M. on Cincinnati, Ohio, radio station WLW. Perhaps the nation's premier evangelist of the 1930s, Cadle, who once attracted a crowd of 28,000 at Cincinnati's Crosley Field, received an estimated 24,000 letters a month from his loyal listeners. Although he was heard throughout the Midwest, Cadle focused much of his evangelistic energy on the Appalachian region, where he remodeled more than 500 unused churches, providing each with a radio. In the process, he became the virtual pastor to the estimated 60,000 people who heard him weekly in these churches. Noted for his homespun humor and appeal to everyday aspects of life, Cadle was a nondogmatic holiness preacher who worked easily with Christians from a wide variety of backgrounds. He was the author of an autobiography, *How I Came Back* (1932). W.C.K.

CAFFRAY, D. WILLIA (b. Baton Rouge, Louisiana, 17 December 1880; d. Oskaloosa, Iowa, 16 January 1975). Methodist Episcopal Church (MEC) deaconess and evangelist. Although confirmed in the Episcopal Church, Caffray was converted in the MEC in 1897 and experienced **entire sanctification** in 1898. Feeling called to full-time Christian service, she attended the Chicago Training Institute. Following her graduation in 1902, Caffray served as a deaconess in the Wisconsin Conference of the MEC (1902–1904). Establishing a reputation as a forceful preacher, Caffray spent the next decade as a itinerant evangelist. After serving two years as associate pastor of the First MEC in Moscow, Idaho, Caffray spent a year as a postgraduate student at Chicago Evangelistic Institute (CEI; see **Vennard College**). While serving as an associate pastor of the First MEC in Wenatchee, Washington, Caffray became the first MEC woman to receive a local preacher's license. She was ordained a deacon in 1924 and an elder in 1929. Profiting from her association with CEI founder **Iva Durham Vennard**, Caffray emerged as a prominent holiness evangelist during the 1920s.

Although Caffray was a frequent speaker at such holiness schools as **Asbury College**, **Taylor University**, and CEI, it was her success as an international missionary evangelist that established her permanent reputation. Invited to tour South America in 1925 by MEC bishop and holiness sympathizer William Joyce, Caffray had remarkable success. During the next 30 years, she made 14 trips and visited over 50 countries in South America, Asia, and Africa. Following the culturally sensitive missional models of famous missionary bishop **William Taylor** and her friend **E. Stanley Jones**, she left a lasting legacy among nationals and missionaries. Deeply concerned with the waning influence of the holiness tradition among Methodists, Caffray was especially noted for distribution of holiness literature, especially the writings of **Samuel Logan Brengle** and **Harry Jessop**. In spite of her deep loyalties to the Methodist Church, Caffray served on the board of **World Gospel Mission** (1943–1967) and was a charter member of the National Association of Women Preachers. She received an honorary doctorate from **Kletzing College** in University Park, Iowa, in 1950. (Biography: Kenneth L. Robinson, *From Brass to Gold: The Life and Ministry of D. Willia Caffray* [1971]). W.C.K.

CAGLE, MARY LEE (b. Moulton, Alabama, 21 September 1864; d. Buffalo Gap, Texas, 27 September 1955). **Church of the Nazarene** (CN) evangelist and pastor. A schoolteacher, Mary Lee married revivalist Robert Lee Harris about 1891. In 1894, Harris established the first congregation of the New Testament Church of Christ (NTCC) in Milan, Tennessee, but he died soon afterward. With the help of other laity, mainly women, Mary Harris organized other churches in Tennessee, Arkansas, Alabama, and Texas. She was ordained by the NTCC in 1899. In 1900, she married Henry Cagle, a Texas cowhand who had been converted, sanctified, and called to preach under her ministry. In

1902, she organized the NTCC's Texas Council. She was deeply involved in mergers creating the Holiness Church of Christ (1904) and the Pentecostal Church of the Nazarene (1908). After 1900, her career was centered in the Southwest. She organized nearly 30 congregations and was elected district evangelist of the Abilene, New Mexico, and Arizona Districts at various times. Editor C. A. McConnell referred to her as the "Mother of Holiness in the West." R.S.I.

CALLEN, BARRY L. (b. New Brighton, Pennsylvania, 10 July 1941). **Church of God (Anderson)** (CG[A]) minister, educator, and theologian. A graduate of Geneva College (Pennsylvania), Anderson University School of Theology, **Asbury Theological Seminary**, Chicago Theological Seminary, and Indiana University, Callen served as a CG(A) minister (1966–1973) and has been on the faculty of Anderson University since 1973. At Anderson, he served as dean of the School of Theology (1974–1983) and dean of the Undergraduate College (1983–1988), and, since 1988, he has been University Professor. A preacher of note, Callen has addressed CG(A) gatherings in Australia and Germany. Also a prolific author, he has written a history of Anderson University and a history of higher education in the CG(A) as well as biographies of Lillie S. McCutcheon (1992), **D. S. Warner** (1995), and Clark Pinnock (2000). Callen was also the coeditor of a revised edition of **Russell Byrum**'s *Christian Theology* (1982). Other significant theological texts include *Contours of a Cause: The Theological Vision of the Church of God* (1995) and *God as Loving Grace: Systematic Theology* (1996). A truly "catholic" theologian, Callen unites traditional CG(A) ecclesiastical concerns and an Anabaptist emphasis on discipleship with a Wesleyan soteriology. Since 1993, Dr. Callen has been editor of the *Wesleyan Theological Journal*. W.C.K.

CAMP MEETING IN THE HOLINESS TRADITION. An institution for nurture and renewal in the holiness tradition. The first camp meeting ever held for the specific purpose of promoting the doctrine of Christian holiness convened at Vineland, New Jersey, in 1867. Methodist Bishop Matthew Simpson and his family attended, and the bishop preached to an estimated crowd of 10,000 on Sunday. So successful was this venture that its promoters formed the National Camp Meeting Association for the Promotion of Holiness (see **Christian Holiness Partnership**) and planned to conduct a second encampment the following summer. The 1868 National Camp Meeting at Manheim, Pennsylvania, attracted large crowds and made national celebrities of

John Inskip, **William McDonald**, **Alfred Cookman**, and other ministers. Moreover, it drew immediate national attention to the new grassroots holiness movement. In 1869, the association held its third annual encampment at beautiful new grounds at Round Lake, New York, and attracted a total aggregate attendance of 250,000. *Harper's Weekly* ran a two-page pictorial, and some called it "the Pentecost of 1869."

In the meantime, permanent holiness camp meetings were being established. Bentleyville (Pennsylvania) Holiness Camp Meeting was founded in 1867 and still ranks as one of the prominent holiness organizations in the state. **William B. Osborn** founded the Ocean Grove (New Jersey) Camp Meeting in 1869, and Ocean Grove, New Jersey, "God's Square Mile," continues to be one of the most popular Christian resorts on the East Coast. Osborn eventually helped to establish more than 30 camp meetings, including sites in Florida, Oregon, Niagara Falls, India, and Ocean Grove, Australia. **Barlow W. Gorham**, fresh from the fire of Vineland National Camp Meeting, held holiness meetings in Ohio that resulted in the founding of a camp meeting in 1870. The association acquired a permanent home near Mount Vernon, Ohio, and Camp Sychar remains one of the premier holiness camp meetings in the nation.

In 1874, **William H. Boole** and his wife **Ella Alexander Boole** helped to organize the National Temperance Camp Meeting Association on the grounds of the Old Orchard Beach (Maine) Camp Meeting. Patterned after the National Association, this organization used the holiness camp meeting idea to promote the temperance cause throughout New England. In 1875, Baptists **Edgar M. Levy** and George Morse founded the Douglas (Massachusetts) Holiness Camp Meeting, which became a mecca for holiness proponents in the East. William McDonald served as its president for many years. As of 1998, the association still conducted a camp meeting each summer.

As the national association marched across the country, numerous independent holiness associations and camp meetings were founded in an attempt to replicate its work. For example, the Landisville (Pennsylvania) Camp Meeting was established as a permanent encampment to continue the work of the 1868 Manheim National Camp Meeting. In 1871, John Inskip preached at special sessions of the Nebraska Annual Conference (Methodist Episcopal Chruch), and that summer a few of his converts held a holiness camp meeting. The next year they held another and founded the Nebraska State Holiness Association, which hosted National Camp Meetings 12 times. At the 1873 National

Camp Meeting in Cedar Rapids, Iowa, a Presbyterian minister named **Isaiah Reid** professed **entire sanctification**. Six years later he helped to form the Iowa Holiness Association (IHA), serving as its president for the next 29 years. This association organized separate holiness associations in almost every county of Iowa. Founded as an auxiliary to the state organization, each county association held its own camp meeting. The IHA invited the national association to conduct the camp meeting of 1892, but starting in 1902 the IHA hosted a National Camp Meeting for each of the following 23 years.

Hundreds of other independent holiness associations and camp meetings sprang up all over the country, and these formed the backbone of the holiness movement for the next 50 years. Besides those named previously, some of the most famous encampments were Red Rock Camp Meeting, Paynesville, Minnesota (founded 1868); Pitman Grove Camp Meeting, Pitman, New Jersey (1870); Beulah Park Camp Meeting, Oakland, California (1873); Hollow Rock Camp Meeting, Toronto, Ohio (1877); Mountain Lake Park (Maryland) Camp Meeting (1882); Central Illinois Camp Meeting, Normal, Illinois (1884); Eaton Rapids (Michigan) Camp Meeting (1885); Freeport (New York) Camp Meeting (1885); Waco (Texas) Camp Meeting (1886); Silver Heights Camp Meeting, New Albany, Indiana (1887); Beaulah Park Camp Meeting, Miltonvale, Kansas (1888); Wilmore (Kentucky) Camp Meeting (1889); Indian Springs Camp Meeting, Flovilla, Georgia (1890); Portsmouth (Rhode Island) Camp Meeting (1890); Ebenezer Camp Meeting, Montgomery, Louisiana (1895); Ferndale (Washington) Camp Meeting (1895); Main Spring (Arkansas) Camp Meeting (1896); Salem (Virginia) Camp Meeting (1896); Mount of Blessings Camp Meeting, Cincinnati, Ohio (1897); Ithiel Falls Camp Meeting, Johnson, Vermont (1898); and Morrison Park Camp Meeting, Glasgow, Kentucky (1900).

Many denominational holiness encampments were also established. The **Free Methodist Church** founded the Durley Camp Meeting at Greenville, Illinois, in 1870 and the Iowa Conference Meeting at Birmingham, Iowa, in 1874. Prairie Camp Meeting in Elkhart, Indiana, now operated by the **Missionary Church**, was founded in 1880. The Southwestern Holiness Association sprang from the 1879 National Camp Meeting at Bismarck Grove, Kansas, and in 1883, some members started one of the first "come-outer" denominations, the **Church of God (Holiness)**, which still holds annual camp meetings in at least five states. **Daniel S. Warner** and his followers conducted their first Michigan encampment also in 1883, and today the **Church of God (Anderson)** holds numerous camp meetings around the country, including Warner Memorial Camp Meeting at Grand Junction, Michigan. The **Wesleyan Methodist Church** founded several encampments during this time, including ones at Houghton, New York (1890), and Fairmount, Indiana (1894).

After 1900, the holiness camp meeting spread rapidly in newly founded denominations such as the **Church of the Nazarene**, **Churches of Christ in Christian Union**, and **Pilgrim Holiness Church**. These groups used the camp meeting as a central focus of church life. The campground not only served as the location for the annual district assembly but also sometimes housed district or general offices, the publishing house, and even the denominational Bible school. Some of these groups later merged to form national holiness denominations, and they eventually helped to bring new perspectives to the old campground. Wise church leaders saw the value of using camp meeting facilities more than just 10 days each summer. Since 1960, most holiness denominations, as well as the independent holiness camp meetings, have developed camping programs for all ages. Many campsites have been winterized for year-round use, such as for midwinter conferences and Christian retreats. Such innovations have pumped new life into the holiness camp meeting, and this institution is still vibrant with spiritual life and ministry. K.O.B.

CANADIAN HOLINESS FEDERATION (CHF). Founded in 1944 by representatives of Canadian holiness groups. In the early years of the organization, R. H. Hamilton served as president. Among the denominations active in the CHF were the **Free Methodist Church**, **Alliance of Reformed Baptist Churches**, **Holiness Movement Church**, **Church of the Nazarene**, **Pilgrim Holiness Church**, **Wesleyan Methodist Church**, **Salvation Army**, **United Missionary Church**, **Gospel Workers Church**, **Standard Church of America**, and the **Brethren in Christ**. It sponsored an annual meeting into the 1990s. W.C.K.

CARRADINE, BEVERLY (b. Yazoo County, Mississippi, 4 April 1848; d. Westmont, Illinois, 1931). Methodist Episcopal Church, South (MECS), minister and evangelist. Beverly Carradine was converted in July 1874. Licensed to the ministry of the MECS later the same year, he was assigned to an isolated rural circuit. His rise to prominence was meteoric. He become pastor of a prominent MECS congregation in

New Orleans in 1882 and established a reputation as a powerful preacher and social reformer. He was praised for his active participation in campaigns to prevent cruelty to children and animals, and his attacks on the highly profitable Louisiana lottery led to the lottery's demise and earned him a national reputation.

Carradine experienced **entire sanctification** on 1 June 1889. In 1890, he became pastor of a large MECS congregation in St. Louis, Missouri, where, dismissing his previous reform activities as the imperfect social engineering of an upwardly mobile aspirant to high ecclesiastical office, he angered wealthy parishioners and denominational leaders with his attacks on the dress, lifestyles, and social activities of upper-class urban Methodists.

In 1893, the charismatic Carradine entered full-time evangelistic ministry and became a popular and influential preacher, speaking at **camp meetings** and holding revival services throughout the United States and in England until he was injured in an accident in Seattle, Washington, and forced to retire from the active ministry in 1918. He edited the *Christian Witness*, the *Gospel Herald*, and *Way of Faith* and wrote numerous books, the most important of which were *Pastoral Sketches* (1895), *Sanctification* (1890), *The Sanctified Life* (1897), and *Living Illustrations* (1908). His autobiography, *Graphic Scenes*, was published in 1911. Among his descendants are several prominent American stage, television, and film actors. W.C.K. and G.A.P.

CARTER, R(ussell) KELSO (b. Baltimore, Maryland, 18 November 1849; d. Catonsville, Maryland, 23 August 1928). Presbyterian and Methodist Episcopal Church (MEC) faith healing advocate and professor of chemistry, mathematics, and civil engineering at the Pennsylvania Military Academy, Chester, Pennsylvania, and the Army War College, Carlisle, Pennsylvania (1869–1887). Led into the experience of **entire sanctification** and experiencing physical healing through the ministry of **Charles Cullis** in 1879, Carter left the Presbyterian Church for the MEC and emerged as a prominent advocate of divine healing. Because of his reputation as a scientist, Carter's book *The Atonement for Sin and Sickness; or a Full Salvation for the Soul and Body* (1884) greatly accelerated interest in divine healing. In 1887, Carter entered the ministry of the MEC and in the same year wrote an extensive defense of faith healing that was published in the *Century Magazine*. An early associate of **Christian and Missionary Alliance** founder **A. B. Simpson**, Carter was a coeditor of that movement's first hymnal. As a result of serious illness, Carter was forced to reevaluate his militant commitment to faith healing. In 1897, he published *Faith Healing Reviewed after 20 Years*. Although still acknowledging the reality of divine healing, Carter now insisted that "he could trust God as well with a physician or a little medicine as without either." Becoming a physician and novelist, Carter returned to the Presbyterian Church. Today he is primarily known as the author of the hymn, "Standing on the Promises." W.C.K.

CARY, C(lement) C. (b. Augusta, Georgia, 27 October 1847; d. Atlanta, Georgia, 25 November 1922). Methodist Episcopal Church, South (MECS), minister, evangelist, and author. Following his conversion in 1869, Cary was licensed to preach in the MECS. He was admitted into membership in the North Georgia Conference in 1872, where he served as an active minister until 1909. Cary served such influential churches as Second Church, Rome, Georgia (1885–1886); St. John's, Atlanta (1890–1893); and St. James, Atlanta (1898–1899). An impassioned partisan in theological debate, Cary was one of the few southern Methodist holiness adherents to remain staunchly committed to postmillennial **eschatology**. This view is reflected in his most important work, *The Second Coming of Christ: Showing Premillenarianism to Be Unscriptural and Unreasonable* (1902). A frequent contributor to **H. C. Morrison**'s *Pentecostal Herald*, Cary was an important actor in the creation of an enduring holiness presence in northern Georgia Methodism. W.C.K.

CATTELL, EVERETT LEWIS (b. Kensington, Ohio, 16 September 1905; d. Columbus, Ohio, 1 March 1981). Quaker minister, missionary, Yearly Meeting superintendent, and college president. Cattell was exposed early to missionary concerns through his mother's involvement with the Junior Band and his marriage (1927) to Catherine DeVol, daughter of medical missionaries to China. Cattell graduated from Marion (Indiana) College (A.B., 1927) and Ohio State University (M.A., philosophy, 1930). He spent nine years working as a Friends pastor in the Ohio Yearly Meeting before beginning a 21-year career in India missions (1936–1957). In India, he worked with Friends Missions, the Yeotmal Bible School, and the Evangelical Fellowship of India; he was the first chairman of the Board of Governors of India's Union Bible Seminary. Cattell served as the superintendent of the Ohio Yearly Meeting (now **Evangelical Friends Church**, Eastern Region) from 1957 to 1960. He was named president of Malone College in 1960, holding that position until his retirement in 1972. He was awarded honorary doctorates from Cleveland Bible College (1946; now Malone College), **Asbury College** (1963), and George Fox College (1972). After his retirement, he was visiting fellow at Princeton Theological Seminary (1972–1973) and held guest professorships at China Evangelical Seminary in Taipei (1973–1974) and George Fox College (1977). Among Cattell's many published works are *The Spirit of Holiness* (1963) and *Christian Mission: A Matter of Life* (1981). Cattell's vision of holiness was rooted in righteousness and the cross. He wrote, "There's far too much cheap and easy holiness these days based upon an emotional experience, whooping and hollering, but divorced from life and a stranger to the cross" (diary, 31 December 1941). He was highly regarded as a statesman among Friends and in the wider Christian community. His papers are located in the Malone College archives. D.L.J.

CAUGHEY, JAMES (b. the north of Ireland, 1811; d. Highland Park, New Jersey, 30 January 1891). Methodist Episcopal Church (MEC) minister and evangelist. Details of his early life are fragmentary, but it seems clear that in his youth, Caughey emigrated with his family to the United States, where he was converted under Methodist influence. He was ordained elder in the Troy Conference of the MEC in 1836. Appointed to circuit work in 1839, he preached with much success before making his first prolonged visit to Great Britain and Europe (1841–1847). His powerful revival preaching drew large crowds wherever he went, and his supporters calculated that in these six years, some 22,000 people confessed conversion and 9,000 professed **entire sanctification**. His revival methods were warmly welcomed by those in English Methodism who favored reform and longed for a return to the revival days of preachers like William Bramwell. The English Methodist Conference was unhappy with his long stay and because he ministered as an itinerant without supervision. Caughey's ministry drew strong disapproval from Jabez Bunting and other "High-Church" Methodists, and their influence persuaded the 1846 conference to petition the American Methodist bishops to recall him. Caughey made three more visits to Britain: 1857–1859, 1860–1862, and 1864–1866.

Caughey was a passionate advocate of entire sanctification. His preaching was characterized by bluntness, vivid portrayals of the reality of hell, and powerful emotional appeals, and it was punctuated by a ready supply of anecdotes and humor. He invited seekers to kneel at the communion rail, encouraging them to "call on the Lord" while he and his helpers moved among them giving spiritual counsel and exhortation. Although many Wesleyan superintendents and ministers were unhappy with Caughey's revivalism, requests for his impassioned oratory poured in from Primitive, New Connection, and United Methodist congregations. His ministry in the northeastern United States and Canada produced similar results. His soul-winning methods deeply influenced the young **William Booth**, whose subsequent revival ministry was patterned on Caughey's. Ill health forced Caughey into semi-retirement in the late 1860s, and he preached only occasionally in his last 20 years. H.M.

CENTRAL YEARLY MEETING OF FRIENDS. An Indiana denomination of conservative Friends was formed by a group of Friends in Westfield, Indiana, in 1924. The organizers were conservative Friends who were greatly concerned about elements of liberalism that they felt had entered some groups of Friends. By 1926, they had formally organized a new Yearly Meeting of Friends with **William M. Smith** as leader.

These Friends believe strongly in salvation and sanctification and have fellowship with other holiness groups. As of 1998, the membership in the United States was about 300. Organized meetings are held in Arkansas, Indiana, Ohio, and North Carolina. A yearly meeting and **camp meeting** are held each year near Muncie, Indiana. The Yearly Meeting has supported an extensive missionary work in Bolivia. It publishes a periodical, *Friends Evangel*. Within the United States, its ministers and song evangelists serve in camp meetings of various holiness groups. G.B.

CHADWICK, SAMUEL (b. Burnley, Lancashire, England, 16 September 1860; d. Cliff College, Derbyshire, 16 October 1932). British Wesleyan minister. Raised in very humble circumstances, Chadwick was converted at the age of 10. Greatly successful as a lay evangelist before entering the itinerancy, he spent his ministry in urban centers, where he focused on Christ and holiness. A pioneer of the central mission movement, he was appointed first as tutor in biblical subjects in 1907 and then principal of **Cliff College** in 1912. The influence of Cliff in mission and outreach as the "College of the Underprivileged" grew tremendously under his leadership, and "his passion for souls" kindled enthusiasm in thousands of students. A deep but popular expositor, he was considered to be one of Britain's great preachers. He edited *Joyful News* for 27 years, and, during a period when convinced Evangelicals were rarely in receipt of great recognition, he was elected president of the Wesleyan Conference in 1918, served for four years as president of the National Free Church Council, and was chairman of the Sheffield District (Wesleyan) for 15 years. He headed the **Southport Methodist Holiness Convention** for many years and invariably gave the keynote address. His writings include *Humanity and God* (1904) and *The Way to Pentecost* (1932). W.P.

CHAMBERS, OSWALD (b. Aberdeen, Scotland, 24 July 1874; d. Cairo, Egypt, 15 November 1917). Baptist and Pentecostal League of Prayer (PLP) educator and evangelist. The son of Baptist minister and temperance reformer Clarence Chambers, Oswald Chambers was educated at the National Art Training School, the University of Edinburgh, and the Gospel Training College in Dunoon, Scotland, where the school's founder, Duncan MacGregor, became his theological mentor. Chambers served on the faculty of the school (1897–1906). Following an intense religious crisis that resulted in an experience of **entire sanctification** in 1901, Chambers became actively involved in **Reader Harris**'s PLP. In 1907, Chambers, in the company of his friend **Jugi Nakada**, traveled to America and Japan. In America, he visited holiness **camp meetings** and taught at **God's Bible School**. While in Japan, he visited Nakada's Bible School and the God's Bible School–related mission of **Charles** and **Lettie Burd Cowman**. Returning to England, Chambers served as a PLP evangelist (1907–1911) and as principal of a PLP-sponsored school, the Bible Training College (1911–1915). He was serving as a YMCA chaplain in Egypt when he died unexpectedly.

Chambers was a mystic who created no small controversy among British evangelicals in 1902 when his public lectures on Emanuel Swedenborg were published by the Scottish Swedenborgians. Although suspicious of the literal tendencies of the turn-of-the-century holiness movement, Chambers was a demanding teacher who insisted that his students not substitute sentimental piety for serious study. Following his death, his widow, Gertrude (Biddy) Hobbs Chambers, edited a selection of Bible lectures that he had given between 1911 and 1917. Published in 1927 as *My Utmost for His Highest*, the book gradually became an international best-seller. It was, with the possible exception of his friend Lettie Burd Cowman's *Streams in the Desert*, the best-selling devotional book of the 20th century. Ironically, many people reading Chambers's work have no idea that they are digesting vintage holiness piety. W.C.K.

CHAMPNESS, THOMAS (b. Stratford, England, 19 July 1832; d. Lutterworth, Leicestershire, 30 October 1905). British Wesleyan minister. Possessed of an immense missionary and evangelistic zeal, Champness spent his first six years of ministry in West Africa. While district missionary in Bolton, he founded the weekly *Joyful News* (1883), which had a wide circulation through street and "pub" sales, and opened the Joyful News Home for Evangelists in Rochdale, a forerunner of **Cliff College**. He was devoted to rural work and established the training home largely to fortify country witness. He was a popular author of simple but gripping books that were particularly helpful to young men, and he was also a successful preacher in the United States, Canada, China, and Japan. His holiness preaching was always set within the wider context of a full gospel. W.P.

CHAPMAN, J(ames) B(laine) (b. Yale, Illinois, 30 August 1884; d. Vicksburg, Michigan, 30 July 1947). World's Faith Missionary Association, Independent Holiness Church, Holiness Church of Christ, and **Church of the Nazarene** (CN) minister, educator, editor, and administrator. Converted in 1899 and sanctified in 1900, Chapman served as an evangelist and minister (1900–1911), president of Peniel (Texas) College (1912–1918), editor of the *Herald of Holiness* (1920–1928), founding editor of the *Preacher's Magazine*, and general superintendent of the CN (1928–1946). Chapman is remembered as the "Nazarene Commoner," and his masterful use of illustrations from everyday experiences and the lives of ordinary people touched a responsive chord wherever he preached. Noted for his quick wit, effective articulation of the Wesleyan message, and skillful administration, Chapman was a living embodiment of the CN's movement from a populist religious denomination to a respected evangelical church. Fittingly, he was a champion of an educated ministry and one of the primary founders of Nazarene Theological Seminary. Among his most important books are *History of the Church of the Nazarene* (1926), *Holiness, the Heart of Christian Experience* (1941), and *The Terminology of Holiness* (1947). R.J.H.

CHRISTIAN AND MISSIONARY ALLIANCE (CMA). Founded in 1887 by **A. B. Simpson** as two nondenominational missionary agencies, the Christian Alliance and the Evangelical Missionary Alliance. The former was to be a body of Christians who retained membership in their own churches while holding regular meetings for fellowship, nurture, and support of world missions; the latter was to promote world missions, especially to areas that were deemed underevangelized. In 1897, the two bodies were united into the CMA. Although the CMA remained officially committed to its nondenominational status into the 1920s, in actual practice it began planting congregations in Ontario and Pennsylvania in the 1890s. Although never formally active in the institutional holiness movement, the CMA has been rightly viewed by many historians as a holiness body. Holiness movement leaders **W. E. Boardman**, **Charles Cullis**, **R. Kelso Carter**, John E. Cookman (brother of MEC holiness leader **Alfred Cookman**), and J. Gregory Mantle were Simpson's mentors and early coworkers. In truth, Simpson did reject the common late-19th-century Wesleyan/holiness teaching that the sinful nature is eradicated in **entire sanctification**, but he also insisted that the **Keswick** suppressionist view of sanctification failed to emphasize the decisive nature of the experience.

During the first three decades of the 20th century, CMA leaders remained active in national and regional holiness associations. This was especially true in western Pennsylvania and eastern Ohio, where, under the direction of holiness leader **E. D. Whiteside**, the CMA experienced its most rapid growth. From 1930 to 1960, much of the continued vitality of the holiness impulse in the CMA was the work of Whiteside's protégés, such as Paul Rader (1879–1938) and H. M. Shuman (1878–1967), who served as president of the CMA (1925–1954). Although always a diverse theological movement, since 1930, the CMA has abandoned its holiness heritage, in part as a result of the roles Bob Jones University and Wheaton College have played in training its leaders. Today the principal center of holiness agitation in the CMA is at Toccoa Falls (Georgia) College, which continues to maintain especially close ties to **Asbury College**. W.C.K.

CHRISTIAN HOLINESS PARTNERSHIP (CHP). An organization founded to facilitate cooperation among holiness denomination and institutions. The CHP has its roots in the holiness revival of the 19th century. Evidence suggests that **J. A. Wood**, a Methodist minister from Pennsylvania, first proposed the idea of conducting **camp meetings** to promote the doctrine and experience of Christian holiness. He mentioned the idea to a former parishioner, Harriet E. Drake, who enthusiastically supported the plan, offering to pay half the expenses if Wood would organize an encampment. Wood, **William B. Osborn**, **John S. Inskip**, and other holiness leaders held the first camp meeting at Vineland, New Jersey. The success of the meeting resulted in the creation of an organization to sponsor subsequent camp meetings, the National Camp Meeting Association for the Promotion of Holiness, with Inskip as president and **George Hughes** as secretary. The "National Association," as the organization came to be known, drew huge crowds to its 1868 and 1869 camp meetings in Manheim, Pennsylvania, and Round Lake, New York. As a result of this success, the members voted to hold three camp meetings in 1870, and this policy of multiple camp meetings stayed in effect almost continuously for 70 years. They also voted to purchase a large tent and in 1870 began to hold "tabernacle meetings" in strategic cities around the nation. In 1870, the organization began publication of a periodical, the *Advocate of Christian Holiness*, with **William McDonald** as editor. In 1874, it established a publishing company, the National Publishing Association for the Promotion of Holiness, headed by **Washington C. DePauw**, with headquarters in Philadelphia.

When Inskip died in 1884, the association elected McDonald president, a position he held for 10 years. He was succeeded by **Charles J. Fowler**, who served as president for the following 25 years. Since the ministry had expanded beyond camp meetings, the name was changed to the National Association for the Promotion of Holiness, and it was incorporated in 1899. State and local holiness associations were permitted to become auxiliary members and send delegates with full voting privileges to the annual meeting. In 1907, women were granted corporate membership, and by 1911 the membership rolls topped the 1,000 mark; by 1919, there were more than 1,600 members.

In 1910, **Iva Durham Vennard** helped to spearhead a drive to form the National Holiness Missionary Society (see **World Gospel Mission**) as the missionary arm of the association. The association's annual business meeting gradually evolved into a national holiness convention that wrestled with such issues as sectional divisions, theological tensions, new holiness denominations, and a global mission strategy. Study commissions held seminars for pastors and evangelists as well as camp meetings. As a result, the national camp meetings slowly disappeared. Evidence suggests that the last official encampment was held at University Park, Iowa, in 1942.

Fowler died in 1919 and was succeeded by **Will Huff** (1919–1921), George J. Kunz (1921–1925), **John Paul** (1925), **Joseph H. Smith** (1925–1928), and **Charles W. Butler** (1928–1942). Subsequent presidents were C. I. Armstrong, H. M. Couchenour, Paul F. Elliott, Myron R. Boyd, Morton W. Dorsey, Kenneth E. Geiger, and Paul L. Kindschi.

The National Holiness Association changed its name to the Christian Holiness Association in 1971 and adopted its current name, Christian Holiness Partnership, in 1998.

Due to the success of the camp meeting seminars, the CHP published the *Camp Meeting Manual* in 1963 and currently publishes the *Camp Meeting Challenge*, a periodical devoted to holiness camp meetings. Other publications of the CHP include *Proceedings of the Holiness Conferences* (1877), *Insights into Holiness* (1967), *Further Insights into Holiness* (1967), *The Word and the Doctrine* (1967), and *Projecting Our Heritage* (1967), and a periodical, *Holiness Digest*. Since 1970, the **Wesleyan Theological Society** has been a commission of the CHP. In 1970, the auxiliary Women's Aldersgate Fellowship was organized. K.O.B.

CHRISTIAN PERFECTION. *See* ENTIRE SANCTIFICATION.

CHURCH, JOHN R(obert) (b. Salem, North Carolina, 22 July 1899; d. North Carolina, 9 November 1984). United Methodist Church (UMC) minister, evangelist, and author. Church was converted in 1908 and sanctified in 1918. Admitted to the Western North Carolina Conference of the Methodist Episcopal Church, South (MECS), in 1922, he was ordained a deacon in 1924 and an elder in 1926. After serving as a pastor (1923–1934), Church became an evangelist in 1934. A founder of People's Bible College (now John Wesley College; see **People's Methodist Church**), Church was a trustee of John Wesley College and of **Asbury College**, from which he received an honorary doctorate in 1942. The same year, he founded the John Wesley Camp Meeting in High Point, North Carolina. The author of 21 books, Church was a vigorous champion of the traditional doctrines and experiences of the holiness movement and of evangelical concerns within the UMC. Among his most notable books are *After the H Bomb What?* and *A Bird's Eye View of God's Plan* (1936). Personal papers documenting Church's career are located at John Wesley College. W.C.K.

CHURCH OF CHRIST (HOLINESS) U.S.A. (CC[H]). A largely African American denomination that was organized in 1897 as the result of holiness conventions convened by **C. P. Jones** and C. H. Mason among black Baptists. Initially known as Church of God in Christ, the movement experienced rapid growth in Mississippi, Alabama, Tennessee, and Arkansas. In 1907, Mason took most of the body into Pentecostalism. In 1911, Jones reorganized the remnant that continued to hold the traditional Wesleyan view that salvation constituted two works of grace into the CC(H). Deeply rooted in the heritage of the fourfold gospel, the church emphasizes Jesus as savior, sanctifier, healer, and coming king. Although the church remains small, significant congregations have been established in Mississippi, Louisiana, Arkansas, and Georgia, and, beginning in the 1920s, California and such northern cities as Detroit, Chicago, and Gary, Indiana. The church has about 10,000 members in 170 congregations. Deeply committed to education, the church established Christ's Holiness School in 1897. Renamed Christ's Missionary and Industrial College in 1907, the school's most distinguished early graduate was A. B. Cobbins, a bishop and noted educator in Jackson, Mississippi, and Chicago who served as the school's president in the 1930s and 1940s. Although the church has conducted foreign missions in Liberia since the early 20th century, in recent years its mission focus has been in Mexico. The church has a denominational periodical, the *Truth Messenger*. Although discussions were held in the 1930s about a possible merger with the **Church of the Nazarene**, the CC(H) has remained independent. W.C.K.

CHURCH OF GOD (ANDERSON, INDIANA) (CG[A]). Among the oldest and largest of the holiness and Pentecostal bodies that refer to themselves with some variant of the phrase "Church of God," with general church offices in Anderson, Indiana. This group began in 1881 when small congregations at Beaver Dam, Indiana, and Carson City, Michigan, coalesced around the *Gospel Trumpet*, a holiness journal edited by **Daniel S. Warner**. The group had two strong theological commitments: a belief in **entire sanctification** as a second work of grace and a conviction that denominations were sinful divisions of the body of Christ, which, on the basis of the New Testament example, they felt should be unified as well as holy. Within an ethos of **camp meeting** revivalism, early Church of God people observed three ordinances: baptism, the Lord's supper, and foot washing.

In Warner's theology, the perfect love of sanctified believers created the only true and necessary bond of unity among Christians. Stated negatively, this conviction early yielded a strong and often harsh bias against any and all forms of ecclesial organization as examples of "sect Babylon" and a militant unwillingness to cooperate with other Christians. For most of the first 40 years of its existence, the Church of God movement (as its adherents preferred to name the group) lived and grew as a loose fellowship of congregations, evangelists, colporteurs, missionaries, and mission workers for whom the *Gospel Trumpet* and its parent Gospel Trumpet Company provided core ideas and examples.

Warner was succeeded as editor in 1895 by **Enoch E. Byrum**, who believed that he had received the gift of healing and made that a special feature of his work and the editorial policy of the paper. The doctrine and practices of the church historically have been the focus of the Church of God. During Byrum's tenure, the group customarily marked the true New Testament church as the place where sinners are saved, believers are sanctified, and the sick are divinely healed. Byrum served as editor until 1916 when he was replaced by his former secretary, **F. G. Smith** (1880–1947). Smith elaborated on apocalyptic themes initially found in Warner's later work in a way that intensified the group's militant separatism. During this era, the early theme of Christian unity through sanctification was recast to underscore even more strongly the group's "come-outer" preaching and tactics.

In the absence of governing boards or agencies, the Gospel Trumpet Company assumed many of the group's leadership functions. Thus, the editor's office took responsibility for ministerial certification as well as primary authority for teaching and practice. It was a situation bound to make some ministers restive in a movement that claimed to be governed only through the leadership of the Holy Spirit. During the 1920s, opposition to Smith arose among a small but vigorous group of ministers who successfully secured Smith's defeat when he stood for reelection as editor in 1930. Ironically, the years of Smith's tenure witnessed the wholesale development of a complete set of church boards and agencies, beginning with the General Ministerial Assembly in 1917. The degree of authority among these boards varied. In the case of the Board of Christian Education, the agency existed to assist congregations that might call on them. In other cases (e.g., the missionary board), agencies assumed direct supervisory roles.

Smith had championed the group's earlier view that the Holy Spirit endowed church leaders with the gifts required by their calling. He was succeeded as editor by **Charles E. Brown**, a self-taught historian who quickly set about the revision of several positions and policies. Advocating "spiritual democracy," Brown shifted responsibility for ministerial certification to state credentials committees. To those persons suspicious that the institutionalization of the 1920s was leading the Church of God down the road to denominationalism, Brown replied that boards and agencies organized the work of the church but not the church itself. Last and most significant, Brown's historical understanding of the church challenged Smith's apocalypticism and the "come-outerism" it so heavily underwrote. Hearkening back to Warner's early theology of "sanctified love works unity," Brown took the position that all who professed faith in Christ for salvation were already members of the Church of God, whether or not they left their denominations. Thus, Brown tacitly, if not intentionally, legitimated the denominational character of American Christianity and set the Church of God on the road from sectarian protest group to denomination.

The years of institutionalization coincided with the embourgeoisement of the Church of God movement. The first generation of leadership was located among the socially marginalized. As in the case of the other early holiness churches, women were free to preach and exercise authority. In 1924, one-third of the ordained ministers were women. Immigrants also occupied the margins of society, and the Church of God began outreach ministries to several immigrant groups including Hispanics, Germans, Scandinavians, Greeks, and Slovaks. Coupled with its message of Christian unity, the group's special location also positioned it to attract a significant number of African Americans. In 1886, the first congregation of African Americans was gathered through the work of Jane Williams in Charleston, South Carolina. The number of African American adherents grew significantly. In 1917, probably bowing to local sentiment, the white leadership of the church encouraged the separation and development of an African American camp meeting and general assembly at West Middlesex, Pennsylvania. This move created the National Association of the Church of God, which exists as an African American organization and fellowship within the Church of God. Approximately 20 percent of the Church of God constituency is African American.

In several instances, the Church of God created institutions to guide projects already begun through the initiative of individuals. Men and women began missionary works spontaneously in the 1890s. Soon mission fields could be found in Mexico, the Caribbean, England, Germany, Egypt, India, China, and Japan, all before the organization of the missionary board in 1909. The church has continued a strong commitment to foreign missions. Figures from 1997 indicate that the largest Church of God constituencies were in Kenya (106,200) and India (65,000). Total non–North American membership was 385,000 in 4,310 congregations. United States and Canadian membership was 221,000 in 2,327 congregations.

During its first two decades, the Church of God was hostile toward all formalized education from Sunday school through seminary. Ministerial education took the form of apprenticeships, often connected to one or more of 40 "missionary homes," centers for preaching and hostels for colporteurs and gospel workers. Between 1910 and 1917, the homes in Spokane, Kansas City, New York City, and Anderson, Indiana, developed Bible institutes independently of each other. Centrally located, the institute at Anderson was founded in 1917 as Anderson Bible Training School (later Anderson College). Now officially Anderson University, it is the oldest and largest of the colleges operated by the CG(A). The others are Warner Pacific College (Portland, Oregon), Mid-America Bible College (Oklahoma City), Warner Southern College (Lake Wales, Florida), Gardner College (Camrose, Alberta), and Bay Ridge Christian College (Kendleton, Texas). M.D.S.

CHURCH OF GOD (GUTHRIE, OKLAHOMA) (CG[Guthrie]). Founded in 1910 by conservative or radical **Church of God (Anderson)** (CG[A]) members, frustrated by the abandonment of such movement distinctives as racial integration and simple dress. As a result, they began uniting around CG(A) minister **Charles E. Orr**, publisher of the *Herald of Truth*. Similar to the teachings of the early CG(A), what became known as the CG(Guthrie) was committed to nonresistance, faith healing, and the idea of a literal millennium. In 1918, Fred Pruitt of Guthrie, Oklahoma, began publishing *Faith and Victory* and assumed leadership of the church. As with the early CG(A), the CG(Guthrie) is really an international fellowship united around a periodical, which, in 1961, had a reported circulation of 12,000. The Faith Publishing House, the publisher of *Faith and Victory*, maintains an active program of publication. The CG(Guthrie) does not keep membership records and is deeply suspicious of institutionalization. In 1938, a **camp meeting** was established at Guthrie, although other regional camp meetings are also held. Missions are supported in the Philippines, Nigeria, Mexico, and India. During the late 1980s, the CG(Guthrie) experienced a schism with a group of more radical members organizing the Church of God (Sumas, Washington) and establishing their own periodical, the *Gospel Trumpet*. W.C.K.

CHURCH OF GOD (HOLINESS) (CG[H]). Dates from the reunion in 1922 of the Unity Holiness People and the Independent Holiness People (see **Churches of God**). The CG(H), however, properly traces its roots to that portion of the Southwestern Holiness Association

(1879–1885), which regarded connectionalism as antithetical both to the one Church of God and to "true holiness." In 1883, attempting to actualize the New Testament ecclesia, a Church of God congregation was "set in order" at Centralia, Missouri. In succeeding decades, the churches formed according to this pattern in north-central and western Missouri, and eastern Kansas faced two challenges: the spiritual anarchism of the antiordinance teaching of A. L. Brewer (1848–1940) and a seemingly unsolvable dispute over clerical authority and local church autonomy that polarized the movement from 1897 to 1922. The first provides the background for **John P. Brooks's** magum opus *The Divine Church* (1891), which is a vindication of the order and ordinances of "the New Testament ecclesia." The second was resolved when most of the congregations of two factions reunited in 1922.

A. C. Watkins (1885–1945), R. L. Kimbrough (1889–1983), and other second-generation leaders, along with W. H. Graef (1891–1969) and F. B. Wisler (1880–1969) who came into the movement as a result of a merger with the Missionary Bands of the World, used the official organ, the *Church Herald and Holiness Banner;* delegated convention; "accredited" ministers roll; and general and regional **camp meetings** to bridge the chasm between competing points of view and to enhance collective vision. Wisler was the principal actor in the CG(H) expansion into Jamaica, the Caribbean, and Bolivia, where membership in the decades following World War II came to equal that of the parent body. Schools at College Mound and Clarence, Missouri, which had been closed before reunion, were replaced in 1927 and 1936 by regional schools at Gravette, Arkansas, and Ava, Missouri, and in 1938 by a general school and Bible college in Kansas City, Missouri. More than 12 local academies were to follow. Present as far east as West Virginia and as far west as California and Oregon, the 4,000-member constituency continues to be concentrated in Missouri and Kansas. Out-migration and the challenges of consensus account for the century-long flow of onetime adherents into the **Church of the Nazarene** and other like-minded bodies.

In 1945, the publishing plant and the editorial offices of the periodical moved from Fort Scott to Overland Park, Kansas, where the Bible college and national camp meeting had located four years earlier. From 1962 to 1994, the church refused to seat as general convention delegates anyone who owned a television set and worked in cooperation with the **Inter-Church Holiness Convention**. The works of CG(H) authors **C. E. Cowen** and **Dale Yocum** have a sizable readership in the wider holiness movement. C.E.J.

CHURCH OF THE BIBLE COVENANT (CBC). A conservative holiness denomination formed by a small group of **Church of Nazarene** (CN) ministers who believed that the CN had compromised its standards on several ethical and cultural issues. The most prominent minister was Remiss Rehfeldt, who was elected as one of two general superintendents of the fledgling CBC along with Marvin Powers, a CN pastor. Other major leaders of the CBC were Amos Hann, Jr., Donald Hicks, and Granville Rogers. Along with Powers, these three formed a steering committee in the fall of 1966 that eventually led to the formation of the CBC. In 1968, several **Pilgrim Holiness Church** ministers joined the CBC in protest of their denomination's merger with the **Wesleyan Methodist Church**.

The CBC founded Covenant Foundation College in Knightstown, Indiana, in 1968. The first two presidents were Rogers and Hicks. The school continued to operate until 1987. Missionary activity in the CBC included support of missionaries in the Philippines, Africa, Jamaica, and Mexico. Several independent CBC churches were founded in Mexico.

At its height, the denomination was composed of approximately 100 churches and more than 1,000 members. However, in 1986, the CBC began to lose ministers and churches due to disagreements on polity and on ethical and cultural issues. The church officially disbanded in August 1988. The **International Fellowship of Bible Churches** is a major heir to the CBC. Another group with significant numbers of former Covenanters is the International Conservative Holiness Association. Marvin Powers and others rejoined the CN. C.M.H.

CHURCH OF THE NAZARENE (CN). Developed out of Pentecostal Nazarene churches, the earliest of which were in New England. The People's Evangelical Church in Providence, Rhode Island, formed in 1887 after a schism over holiness teachings in St. Paul's Methodist Episcopal Church. Fred Hillery, former lay leader at St. Paul's, was ordained as first pastor. Similar congregations formed in Lynn, Massachusetts; Keene, New Hampshire; and elsewhere, and these united as the Central Evangelical Holiness Association in 1890. A similar group took shape in New York when **William Howard Hoople** organized three churches in Brooklyn in 1895 that united as the Association of Pentecostal Churches of America (APCA). Additional congregations formed in adjacent states. Hoople's group merged with the New England body in 1896. Hillery's the *Beulah Christian* became the official paper, while the APCA's name became that of the merged entity. **Hiram F. Reynolds** headed an ambitious missions program that placed missionaries in India in 1898 and in Cape Verde shortly thereafter. Some 50 churches, mainly on the eastern seaboard, stretched from Nova Scotia to Iowa by 1907.

A second body formed in the South. In 1894, the New Testament Church of Christ was organized as a restorationist body in Milan, Tennessee. Its early emphasis on "true church polity" waned after founder Robert Lee Harris died. A remarkable group of laity, largely women, organized churches in Tennessee, Arkansas, and Texas, and Harris's widow, **Mary Lee Cagle**, organized the Texas Conference in 1901. Leaders soon had contact with the Independent Holiness Church, which **Charles B. Jernigan** had founded in Texas in 1901 to gather up bands of holiness people alienated from established churches and restore them to a churchly way of life, including the sacraments. The Jernigan and Cagle branches merged in 1904 to form the Holiness Church of Christ (HCC). Some 80 congregations stretched from Georgia to West Texas by 1908, and the *Holiness Evangel* served as its official paper.

A third branch originated on the Pacific Coast. **Phineas F. Bresee** had an enviable record as a Methodist pastor and presiding elder but quit the itinerant ministry in 1894 after the bishop denied his request to pastor a city mission in Los Angeles. He and J. P. Widney, former University of Southern California president, worked at the **Peniel Mission** for one year and then organized an independent congregation, the CN, among the city's poor in 1895. Widney departed, leaving Bresee as sole pastor in Los Angeles and general superintendent of a small but vibrant denomination growing on the West Coast. By 1904, there were churches in the Midwest, including Chicago. Evangelist **C. W. Ruth** of Indianapolis, Indiana, joined in 1901 and was elected assistant general superintendent. The church was a democratized form of Methodism, or, as Ruth put it, "nothing in the world but old-fashioned Methodism with a Congregational form of government." Bresee edited the periodical, the *Nazarene Messenger*, and 52 churches existed by late 1907.

Leaders in the APCA, HCC, and CN sought a more comprehensive church, and Ruth, a visitor to every corner of America, introduced them to one another. Agreements between the APCA and CN led to the First General Assembly in Chicago in October 1907. The name Pentecostal Church of the Nazarene (PCN) was adopted. Bresee and Reynolds were elected general superintendents. The Second General

Assembly (1908), held at the HCC headquarters in Pilot Point, Texas, brought in the southern church amid great enthusiasm, and **E. P. Ellyson** joined the Board of General Superintendents. The 1923 General Assembly made 1908 the official anniversary date.

Critical elements united these churches. A common Wesleyan theology of the "way of salvation" stressed the doctrine of sin, justification by grace through faith, the sanctification of believers (including "initial sanctification" in the "new birth" and **entire sanctification** in a later experience), and the witness of the Spirit. A common "believers' church" perspective stressed a regenerate membership, church discipline applied to clergy and lay offenders, good works, care of the poor, and simple forms of worship. Each uniting church admitted women to all levels of participation and governance, including the ordained ministry, and women were ordained at the First and Second General Assemblies. Unlike more restrictive holiness churches, the PCN adopted no particular baptismal theology, allowing parents to baptize infants or not and leaving choice of mode to the individual; embraced no particular millennial theory; and affirmed divine healing without rejecting medical agencies and professionals.

These moderate positions later attracted other groups. The Pentecostal Mission, founded by Cumberland Presbyterian preacher **J. O. McClurkan** in Nashville, Tennessee, in 1898, merged in 1915, bringing a network of churches in the Southeast and missions in Cuba, Central and South America, and India. The Pentecostal Church of Scotland, founded by **George Sharpe** of Glasgow, united the same year, bringing another international dimension to the church. In the 1920s, many members of **J. G. Morrison**'s Dakotas-based Layman's Holiness Association united.

The word *Pentecostal* was dropped from the church name in 1919. The holiness movement had used it as a synonym for *holiness*, but the new 20th-century Pentecostalism was giving the term other meanings, and the General Assembly surrendered it.

Denominations formed through merger must find a common life. Nazarenes did this in various ways. Regional publishing ventures gave way to the 1911 decision to establish the Nazarene Publishing House in Kansas City, Missouri; and in 1912, *Herald of Holiness*, under editor **B. F. Haynes**, replaced regional papers. *Other Sheep* (later *World Mission*) appeared in 1913 to promote missions. Both were replaced in 1999 by *Holiness Today*, designed to serve the church's English-language readers worldwide. *El Heraldo de Santidad* serves Spanish-language readers. Lillenas Publishing Company, purchased from Nazarene songwriter **Haldor Lillenas** in 1930, is the music arm of the Nazarene Publishing House and a leading publisher of religious music.

Colleges inherited from parent bodies initially reinforced regionalism, but this was mitigated by consolidating some smaller schools and linking the surviving ones in a network guided by a sound philosophy of higher education. **H. Orton Wiley** and **J. B. Chapman** assisted in this process. In North America, there are nine liberal arts colleges and universities, a Bible college, and a graduate seminary. Other historic colleges are in Canada and England. The International Board of Education, created in 1989, assists these and a mosaic of 45 other institutions founded by the World Mission Division: Bible schools, liberal arts and nurses training colleges, and a graduate school of theology. The church's two graduate schools of theology are Nazarene Theological Seminary (Kansas City) and Asia Pacific Nazarene Theological Seminary (Manila, Philippines).

Auxiliaries also unified the church. The Woman's Missionary Society (now Nazarene World Missionary Society), authorized in 1915, was led by Rev. **Susan Fitkin** until 1948; men were later admitted. In 1998, there were 9,589 Nazarene World Missionary Society chapters worldwide with a combined membership of 712,355. Local youth societies held their first general convention in 1923, organizing the general Nazarene Young People's Society (now Nazarene Youth International). In 1998, there were 9,741 Nazarene Youth International societies and 312,674 members.

Commitment to missions was the primary goal to foster a common life among Nazarenes. This was a special cause of general superintendent Reynolds, who also headed the missions agency for many years and stamped his global vision on the church. Fields in Cape Verde, Japan, China, India, Mexico, and South Africa were augmented by the Pentecostal Mission's work in Latin America. Financial stress in the 1920s and 1930s led to retrenchment, including the closing of some fields, but a boom in the post–World War II era led the church into new areas such as the Philippines and the Pacific, and Europe. Small indigenous groups in Korea, Italy, Australia, and Canada united. Mergers with larger groups also occurred: The International Holiness Mission (IHM) (organized in London, 1907) merged in 1952, bringing work in southern Africa; the Calvary Holiness Church of England (organized in 1934) joined in 1955; and in 1988, a Nigerian group (organized in the 1940s) united, its name (Church of the Nazarene), doctrine, and polity shaped by a copy of the international church's *Manual* owned by its founder. Expansion led, in 1976, to a deliberate decision to embrace internationalism rather than create separate national churches. As a result, almost half of the nearly 1,000 voting delegates to the 1997 General Assembly were from outside North America. In 1998, the church reported 1,304,009 members, over half of whom lived outside North America. There were 12,165 churches in 389 districts. Of these, 5,101 churches and 79 districts were in the United States.

The church is organized at three primary levels: local, district, and general (international). The General Assembly is composed of lay and clergy delegates elected by the districts. It meets every four years and elects the general superintendents (currently six) and 60-member General Board, which meets annually, and boards of other general institutions of the church. It is the church's highest legislative body and court of final appeal. Its decisions are binding on all other levels of the church. The *Manual* is the church's book of order.

General superintendents fill the episcopal role and serve from one General Assembly to the next. They can be reelected. The general church agencies include the Office of General Secretary, the General Treasurer, Division of World Mission, Church Growth Division, Division of Sunday Schools, and Communications Division. Their executives are elected by the General Board, which shares in oversight of church agencies with the general superintendents.

Congregations are arranged in districts that hold annual assemblies, elect their district superintendents, and elect delegates to General Assembly. New ministers are elected to orders by district assembly action and ordained by the presiding general superintendent. The two permanent orders of ministry are elder (Ministry of Word and Table) and deacon (those called to full-time ministry but not primarily as preachers). Churches elect their pastors, subject to the approval of the district superintendent.

Prohibition politics, orphanages, and homes for unwed mothers were all part of the early Nazarenes' social vision. Later, social impulses were channeled primarily into medical ministries. Hospitals with teaching programs were built in Swaziland and China in the 1920s; others followed in India and Papua New Guinea. Surgeon David Hynd, a Scot, founded Swaziland's Red Cross while heading the church's hospital in that country. In the 1970s, a new engagement with urban problems led to the Community of Hope in the Washington, D.C. "riot corridor"; The

Lamb's in New York's Times Square; and social ministry–oriented churches in other cities. Nazarene Compassionate Ministries (NCM), emphasizing economic development, child sponsorship, and disaster relief, was established around 1981 and is now divided into NCM International and the NCM USA/Canada.

The CN is affiliated with the **Christian Holiness Partnership**, the NAE, and the Methodist World Council.

The systematic theologies of Methodists John Miley and Thomas Ralston dominated the Nazarene course of study for ministers until 1940. The first systematic theologies produced within the church were by **A. M. Hills** (*Fundamental Christian Theology*, 2 vols., 1931) and H. Orton Wiley (*Christian Theology*, 3 vols., 1940–1942), both from Pasadena College. **H. Ray Dunning** (*Grace, Faith, and Holiness*, 1988) and **J. Kenneth Grider** (*A Wesleyan-Holiness Theology*, 1994) have written later ones. Representative writings by other Nazarene theologians include those of biblical scholars **Olive Winchester**, Willard Taylor, and **William Greathouse**; systematic theologians **W. T. Purkiser**, Rob Staples, **Richard S. Taylor** and **Mildred Bangs Wynkoop**; and church historians **Timothy L. Smith** and **Paul M. Bassett**.

The holiness movement's revivalistic character shapes traditional Nazarene worship. Hymns, including Wesley compositions, remain popular but are usually supplemented with choruses or contemporary Christian music. The altar rail in the typical Nazarene church is often a place of prayer during public worship. Nazarene preaching is characterized by an intention to bring people to a point of decision in their spiritual lives, and most congregations conduct at least one special revival meeting a year. Some churches experiment with contemporary worship formats, while a smaller number do so with more liturgical formats. R.S.I.

CHURCHES OF CHRIST IN CHRISTIAN UNION (CCCU). Established in 1909, when five ministers and 60 laypeople withdrew from the Christian Union in Ohio. The primary leader, J. H. McKibban, had been publishing a holiness periodical, *Church of Christ Advocate*, since 1907. Among the issues contributing to the formation of the CCCU were opposition to the cultivation of tobacco and to secret societies and a restorationist belief that the New Testament name for the church was "churches of Christ" instead of "Christian union." Experiencing steady growth, the new church reported 1,400 members in 41 churches by 1915 and 2,100 members in 60 churches by 1925. In 1918, the church suffered a significant schism when Edward Runyan, Henry Leeth, and a number of church members left the parent body due to the teaching that Christians, following the biblical teaching in Acts 2, were to hold all property in common. The dissidents, under Leeth's leadership, established a **camp meeting** at Washington Court House, Ohio, and a periodical, *Herald of Perfect Christianity*, later, the *Repairer of the Breach*. Now known as the **House of Prayer**, this body continues as a small holiness denomination.

Although the CCCU was largely located in southern Ohio, Kentucky, and Tennessee before World War II, it has experienced both numerical and geographic growth since 1945; by 1998, it was found in 17 states. Especially significant was a 1952 merger with the Reformed Methodist Church, a body of nonepiscopal Methodists that had been established in 1814 in New York and New England. Among the CCCU's most important institutions is the Mount of Praise Camp Meeting in Circleville, Ohio, which was founded in 1918. The denomination operates eight camps, including Lily Lake Camp (New York), which was established by the Reformed Methodists in 1896. Although the church established a Committee on Foreign Missions in 1914, it initially supported the foreign mission program of the **Pilgrim Holiness Church** and by the 1930s was supporting missionaries through the National Holiness Missionary Society, now **World Gospel Mission**, a practice that has continued. One of the denomination's four districts is located in the Caribbean. Although the church operated a Bible school at Washington Court House from 1910 to at least 1917, it did not establish a permanent college until 1948 when Mount of Praise Bible School, later Circleville (Ohio) Bible College, was founded. In 1998, the church had 10,000 members in 225 congregations, with an average Sunday morning worship attendance of 14,000. W.E.H. and W.C.K.

CHURCHES OF GOD (commonly known as Independent Holiness People) (CGIHP). The CGIHP stands in the succession of the remnant of former Independent Holiness People (IHP; the Congregational Sovereignty faction) unwilling to reunite in 1922 with former Unity Holiness People (the Elder Supremacy faction) to form the **Church of God (Holiness)** (CG[H]). Gathered behind A. M. Kiergan, the group consisted of about 20 churches in Oklahoma, Illinois, Missouri, Kansas, and Mississippi that refused to compromise the congregational autonomy enshrined in the Declaration of Principles of 1897 that had split the CG(H). Although isolated, the splinter group was keenly aware of its roots, a fact made plain in the phrases composing the title of its official organ, the *Church Advocate and Good Way*. The paper, whose operations moved from Fort Scott, Kansas, to Delaware, Oklahoma, in 1992, reported a circulation of 670 in 1999. Expansionist but skeptical both of clericalism and connectionalism, the CGIHP has relied heavily on the initiative of freelancers, a strategy used in mission efforts in Mexico and Japan and among Native Americans in South Dakota and Wyoming. Particularly adept at operating in this way were Kiergan's successor, Otto Duecker (1882–1960), a convert from the German Reformed Evangelical Synod, and a pioneer missionary to Japan, Raymond Shelhorn (b. 1927), a World War II veteran who, under the aegis of the Church of God at Baden (IHP) of St. Louis, was to establish a thriving autonomous work in Japan. A convention, to which in 1997 only five churches sent representatives, meets in Fort Scott each October. Every year since 1948, this body has passed resolutions supporting conscientious objection to war. C.E.J.

CLARK, DOUGAN, JR. (b. Guilford County, North Carolina, 17 May 1828; d. Richmond, Indiana, 11 October 1896). Gurneyite Quaker physician, educator, and author. Trained as a physician and for much of his life a college professor, Clark attained considerable influence as a holiness preacher and writer. His parents were prominent Quaker ministers in North Carolina, and Clark was educated in Quaker schools before taking his degree at the University of Pennsylvania. In 1857, he moved his family to Indiana, where he lived most of his life. Clark was part of the Gurneyite group of American Quakers, the faction that, after 1850, moved consciously closer to the larger evangelical religious culture of the United States. In the 1860s, he was a leader among younger Gurneyite Friends who wanted to reform Quakerism, preserving distinctives such as unprogrammed worship, pacifism, and the ministry of women while purging it of what they considered anachronisms. In 1871, however, under the influence of **David B. Updegraff**, Clark experienced **entire sanctification**, and thereafter he was an aggressive proponent of second experience holiness. Clark became a leader in the holiness revival movement among Gurneyite Friends that was responsible, especially in the Midwest, for revolutionizing Quaker life; introducing music, pastoral ministry, and revivalism; and eschewing the Quaker plain life.

In 1884, Clark returned to Earlham College, where he had taught previously, to head its Biblical Institute, which focused on training Quaker ministers and pastors. Simultaneously, Clark came under increasing criticism for his advocacy of tolerating water baptism among Friends. In 1894, he caused a minor crisis among American Friends by undergoing the rite himself. Indiana Quakers sought to strip him of his standing as a Quaker minister, and Earlham's president maneuvered him out of his professorship. Clark, while active as a preacher and evangelist, also wrote on holiness subjects. In the 1870s, he published extensively in Quaker periodicals and in 1883–1884 published his own journal, *The Gospel Expositor*. His best-known books include *The Offices of the Holy Spirit* (1878), *Instructions to Christian Converts* (1889), *The Holy Ghost Dispensation* (1892), and *The Theology of Holiness* (1893). T.D.H.

CLARK, JOHN D(aughtrey) (b. Martin's Hill, Mandeville, Jamaica, West Indies, 18 July 1892; d. Clearwater, Florida, 1979). Missionary to Ecuador, affectionately known as its "Apostle of Love." Scion of devout British plantocracy families whose rural congregations gave rise to the **Christian and Missionary Alliance** (today the **Missionary Church Association**) in Jamaica, who brought **Keswick** conventions to the West Indies, and who include six generations of missionaries to five continents, Clark studied in Jamaica (Munro College), England (Weymouth College), and New York (Nyack Missionary Training Institute). He served as a missionary to Brazil (1922–1924) and Ecuador (1924–1948) with the CMA, then pastor of Surrey Chapel in Norwich, Norfolk, England (1948–1951). He returned to Ecuador to work with pioneer missionary radio station HCJB in Quito (1951–1978), which he and his brother, D(ouglas) Stuart Clark (1897–1995), had encouraged since its founding in 1931. Probably Ecuador's most beloved missionary, "Don Juanito" was a friend of presidents and bootblacks, generous to all in need, a constant evangelist, Bible institute director, hospital chaplain, pastor, and sterling radio preacher. P.A.E. and T.P.E.

CLARK, W(illiam) L(eslie) (b. Carroll County, Kentucky, 1 July 1875; d. Wilmore, Kentucky, 26 November 1960). Methodist Episcopal Church, South (MECS), minister, revivalist, presiding elder, and author. W. L. Clark entered the Kentucky MECS conference in 1895 as an on-trial member. In 1899, he was ordained into the conference. He graduated from **Asbury College** with A.B., M.A., and D.D. degrees. During his time as a member of the conference, Clark served as pastor of a number of churches, including three times as the pastor of the Wilmore (Kentucky) Methodist Church. He also served as a presiding elder for the Danville District. He is credited with holding more than 200 revivals and building five churches. He served as General Conference delegate in 1922, 1924, and 1926. While pastor of the Wilmore church, Clark also served a president of the Wilmore **Camp Meeting**. He was a trustee of Asbury College for 45 years and also served as the college's treasurer. He retired from the active ministry in 1947. Clark wrote *The Church Supper and the Lodge* and edited *Billy Sunday, U-N-M-A-S-K-E-D*, a critique of the famous revivalist. A chapel in the Wilmore United Methodist Church is named in his honor. T.B.

CLIFF COLLEGE. Founded as the Joyful News Mission in Rochdale, England, in 1884 by **Thomas Champness**. Following the example of the **Salvation Army**, Champness was convinced that the only way to evangelize common people was to train members of their own social class who, as a rule, were unqualified to be admitted to the normal ministerial training schools of British Methodism. Experiencing considerable growth, the school was forced to relocate in 1889 when the Methodist conference assumed responsibility for the school's funding. In 1903, **Thomas Cook**, head of the Home Mission Department of the Methodist Conference, assumed direction of the school. In 1904, the school was relocated to Derbyshire, where it occupied the grounds of Grattan Guinness's (1835–1910) missionary training school. Under the direction of a remarkable group of principals, including Cook (1903–1912), **Samuel Chadwick** (1912–1932), and J. A. Broadbelt (1932–1949), the school has remained the center of evangelical concerns and the holiness impulse in British Methodism. During the 1920s, Chadwick established a summer evangelism program known as "trekking" that would dispatch bands of Cliff students as evangelists throughout England. Attracting some notoriety and success, it remained a standard feature of the Cliff program into the 1960s. W.C.K.

COLE, MARY (b. near Decatur, Iowa, 23 August 1853; d. Anderson, Indiana, 27 August 1940). **Church of God (Anderson)** (CG[A]) minister and evangelist. Mary Cole spent much of her childhood in Missouri, where she was plagued with poor health and was an invalid by the age of 15. At 17, she joined the Methodist Episcopal Church. The same year, her oldest brother, Jeremiah, led her to the experience of **entire**

sanctification. Five years later, Cole received a call to preach and delivered her first sermon at a holiness meeting in Salisbury, Missouri.

Persecuted for her stand on sanctification and as a woman preacher, Cole remained a Methodist, preaching in Missouri holiness meetings with Jeremiah and their younger brother George until 1880, when she and her brothers came in contact with the CG(A) through the *Gospel Trumpet*. Initially put off by CG(A) radicalism, all three Coles eventually joined the new movement. Mary teamed with either of her brothers, but particularly with George, to conduct evangelistic meetings from Nebraska to Michigan. In 1899, she and George assumed management of a Chicago rescue mission that, in 1903, became the CG(A) missionary home. Mary remained in Chicago for 10 years before relocating to Anderson, Indiana, where she remained for the rest of her life. She wrote an autobiography, *Trials and Triumphs of Faith* (1914). M.D.S.

COLEMAN, GEORGE WHITEFIELD (b. Wyoming County, New York, 10 October 1830; d. Gainsville, New York, 3 July 1907). **Free Methodist Church** (FMC) minister and general superintendent (1886–1903). Raised on a farm in western New York, Coleman was a farmer and a lay preacher in the Methodist Episcopal Church. Joining the FMC in the early 1860s, Coleman was admitted to the Genesee Conference in 1863 and served charges in western New York, Pennsylvania, Ontario, and Washington. He served as chairman of the General Mission Board of the FMC (1891–1898) and on the Board of Trustees of Evansville (Wisconsin) Seminary (1892–1896). Conservative in temperament and often perceived by others to be autocratic in style, Coleman was the FMC's most articulate opponent of women's ordination. Ironically, his second wife, Laura Warren Coleman, was an outstanding evangelist who served as pastor of several congregations in Ontario. A son, J. Emory Coleman, was president of Evansville (Wisconsin) Seminary (1880–1894). W.C.K.

COLEMAN, ROBERT E. (b. Dallas, Texas, 4 April 1928). United Methodist Church (UMC) pastor, evangelist, and professor of evangelism. A graduate of Southwestern University (Georgetown, Texas), **Asbury Theological Seminary**, Princeton Theological Seminary, and the University of Iowa, Coleman has served as a Methodist pastor in Indiana, New Jersey, and Iowa (1949–1955) and as professor of evangelism at Asbury Theological Seminary (1955–1982) and Trinity International

University (1982–present). One of the most prominent authorities on evangelism, Coleman was the first professor of evangelism appointed in the Methodist Church. Beginning with his pioneer dissertation, "Factors in the Expansion of the Methodist Episcopal Church, 1784–1812," at the University of Iowa, Coleman became one of the foremost students of evangelism and church growth in the United States. He is a widely read author—his book *The Master Plan for Evangelism* (1964) has sold well over one million copies. A featured speaker at many conferences and seminars on evangelism, Coleman has been a delegate to the International Congress on Evangelism in Lausanne, Switzerland, and has served as a faculty member of the Billy Graham School for Evangelism, the Campus Crusade for Christ, and the Navigator National Conference on Disciple Making. A frequent speaker at revivals, **camp meetings**, retreats, seminars, **ashrams**, colleges, and theological seminaries, Coleman has also addressed national gatherings of the Southern Baptist Convention, **Church of God (Anderson)**, the **Evangelical Methodist Church**, and the Indiana Yearly Meeting of Friends, as well as international gatherings of Methodists, **Keswick** conventions in Hong Kong, and meetings in countries such as Singapore, South Korea, Holland, and the Czech Republic. Although deeply committed to holiness spirituality, he has been a member of the National Association of Evangelicals and Evangelical Theological Society. W.C.K.

COLT, W(ilder) B(runswick) M(ack) (b. Waterford, Pennsylvania, 9 February 1833; d. Litchfield, Illinois, 15 January 1899). Methodist Episcopal Church (MEC) minister and **Free Methodist Church** (FMC) minister and evangelist. Colt was educated in the public schools of Illinois and at Garrett Biblical Institute. Converted in 1843, he was licensed to preach by the Central Illinois Conference, MEC, in 1853. He served as a captain of Company B of the 73rd Illinois Volunteers during the early days of the Civil War. Honorably discharged in 1862, Colt experienced **entire sanctification** in 1863 and became a full-time evangelist. He had remarkable evangelistic success throughout the Midwest, Pennsylvania, and New York, and especially in Northern and Central Texas where thousands flocked to his meetings in 1877. In 1879, as a result of growing opposition to holiness doctrine in the Central Illinois Conference of the MEC, Colt united with the FMC. In 1886, he was elected General Conference evangelist of the FMC. Although he retired in 1890, he continued to preach until ill health forced him to stop in 1896. W.C.K.

COMPTON, LUCIUS BUNYAN (b. Haywood County, North Carolina, 21 April 1875; d. Asheville, North Carolina, 13 December 1948). International Apostolic Holiness Union (IAHU; see **Pilgrim Holiness Church**) and Methodist Episcopal Church, South (MECS), evangelist, rescue mission worker, and orphanage founder. The son of an impoverished Missionary Baptist minister from western North Carolina, Compton was converted in 1895 and sanctified at the Mount of Blessings **Camp Meeting** under the preaching of **Seth C. Rees** in 1899. Returning to North Carolina, Compton established a ministry to unwed mothers and prostitutes in 1903 and an orphanage, the Eliada Home, in Asheville in 1908. Deeply concerned about the quality of life in the mountains of western North Carolina, Compton added a dairy farm to his orphanage, in part to improve the quality of the mountain dairy industry. At the time of his death, it was estimated that 1,000 children and as many as 2,000 young women had benefited from the services of the home, while the home farm had established a reputation for producing award-winning cattle. An early leader in the holiness movement in North Carolina, Compton served as assistant general superintendent of the IAHU in 1905. Although a fervent supporter of the distinctive fourfold gospel of the IAHU, Compton's frustration with divisions within the IAHU resulted in his joining the MECS. In 1907, Compton established a periodical, the *New Testament Christian*. A leader of the interdenominational rescue mission movement, Compton served as president of the International Union of Gospel Missions and the Rescue Missions of America. Eliada Homes continues to meet the needs of children and families in Asheville. He wrote an autobiography, *Life of Lucius B. Compton, the Mountain Evangelist* (1903). W.C.K.

CONGREGATIONAL METHODIST CHURCH (CMC). The CMC was organized by laymen and local preachers who had withdrawn from the Georgia Conference of the MECS in 1852 over their belief that the Methodist system of itinerant ministers failed to meet the needs of local Methodists, while the local preachers who actually ministered to the daily needs of members were given no voice in the affairs of the annual conference. Although holiness experience played no role in the initial debate, the CMC affirmed the traditional Methodist teaching on **entire sanctification**. Primarily located in the southeastern United States, the CMC has about 17,000 members in the United States and supports mission work in Mexico. It has operated Wesley College in Florence, Mississippi, since 1953 and publishes a monthly periodical, the *Messenger*. In 1999, its president was David Frank Gilmore. It is a member of the **Christian Holiness Partnership**. W.C.K.

COOK, THOMAS (b. Middlesborough, Teeside, England, 20 August 1859; d. London, 21 October 1912). British Wesleyan minister. Thomas Cook was moved toward conversion at the age of seven. In his teens, he preached in the streets around his home, forming a youthful mission band and becoming associated with George Railton. As a layman, he witnessed crowds of several thousand at a mission he conducted in Newcastle. In 1878, he entered into the experience of **entire sanctification**, largely under the ministry of Joshua Dawson, a lay evangelist who was to become Cook's father-in-law. Becoming a lay district evangelist, he was accepted for the ministry in 1882 and immediately appointed as the first official Connexional evangelist. Direct simplicity was the key to his preaching, with great faith in immediate results. Frequently in Ireland, he also had successful tours in Australia, New Zealand, Ceylon, and Norway. According to **A. Skevington Wood**, "The dynamic of Thomas Cook's incredible ministry was devised from a personal experience of sanctification." Constantly proclaiming the highway of holiness, his message was scriptural, much in line with **John Wesley**, and centered on purity and growing maturity rather than power. As head of the gospel cars associated with the Joyful News Mission of **Thomas Champness**, he was appointed the first principal of **Cliff College** in 1903. His most notable work is *New Testament Holiness* (1902). W.P.

COOKE, BELLA BEETON (b. Hull, England, 13 July 1821; d. New York City, 15 November 1908). Methodist Episcopal Church laywoman and advocate for the poor. Raised in a devout Methodist home, Bella Beeton was converted in 1834. In 1840, she married a wealthy Methodist layman. Following business reversals, the Cookes relocated to New York in 1847. Befriended by **Sarah Worrall Lankford**, Cooke experienced **entire sanctification** in 1848. Following her husband's untimely death in 1849, she began an active ministry of soliciting funds on behalf of the poor. Although she dispensed thousands of dollars of financial aid, Cooke was equally noted for her wise spiritual counsel. Her accomplishments were especially noteworthy given the fact that she was bedridden after 1859. Although a lifelong Methodist and close friend of such distinguished Methodists as **Nathan Bangs** and the Palmers, she was universally respected among New York City evangelicals and maintained especially close ties to Quakers and Episcopalians.

Her widely circulated autobiography, *Rifted Clouds, or the Life Story of Bella Cooke* (1884), went through several editions during her life. W.C.K.

COOKE, SARAH ANN BASS (b. Olney, England, 10 November 1827; d. Chicago, Illinois, 9 July 1921). **Free Methodist Church** (FMC) lay evangelist who was instrumental in the spiritual life of noted evangelist D. L. Moody. Although an active Christian in England, it was only following her migration to the United States in 1864, with her husband (John Howes Cooke), that Sarah Cooke emerged as a leader in the holiness movement. Initially joining a Chicago Baptist church, Cooke became active in the noon prayer meetings held at the YMCA, where she first met Moody. In 1871, she experienced **entire sanctification** at the FMC-sponsored St. Charles (Illinois) **Camp Meeting**. Later the same year, according to an often recounted story, Cooke led Moody, at the time a young YMCA worker, into the experience of entire sanctification.

In the early 1870s, Cooke, in association with William Hamner, organized a band of interdenominational Christian workers who conducted services throughout the Midwest. Several of the band's early members became prominent Chicago religious leaders, including Methodist Episcopal Church minister R. S. Martin, FMC minister William Kelsey, and Chicago mission superintendent E. F. Dickinson. Perhaps the most notable convert was **S. B. Shaw**. One of Cooke's most significant ministries was her column "Wayside Sketches," which regularly appeared in the *Free Methodist*. Her autobiography, *Wayside Sketches, or the Handmaiden of the Lord*, was published in 1896. A widely read devotional classic, it is still in print. A passionate champion of demonstrative worship, holiness social ministries, evangelism, and the austere dress code of the early FMC, Cooke was a notable figure in the Chicago evangelical community for 50 years. Among those taking part in Cooke's funeral were James M. Gray of Moody Bible Institute, Baptist pastor C. S. Kerfoot, **Church of the Nazarene** minister H. W. Wallin, and prominent FMC leader W. B. Omstead. W.C.K.

COOKMAN, ALFRED (b. Columbia, Pennsylvania, 4 January 1828; d. Newark, New Jersey, 13 November 1871). Methodist Episcopal Church (MEC) minister, pastor, evangelist, author, delegate to the United States Christian Commission, and member of the National Holiness Association (NHA; see **Christian Holiness Partnership** [CHP]). Son of George and Mary (Barton) Cookman, Alfred grew up in a Methodist parsonage. His father, who gained immense popular recognition as an orator and served as chaplain of the United States Senate (1839–1841), died at sea when Alfred was just 13 years old.

Having been converted under his father's ministry at age 10, Cookman began preaching in 1846. He accepted his first pastoral appointment a year later and, at age 20, joined the Philadelphia Annual Conference of the MEC. He rose quickly in the ranks of the ministry. In 1855, Bishop Thomas Morris transferred him to Pittsburgh as pastor of the new Christ MEC. The year 1857 found him back in Philadelphia, Pennsylvania, riding the crest of the famous revival of 1857–1858 as pastor of the Green Street MEC. From this time forward, he became a flaming evangel for the doctrine and experience of **entire sanctification**. He carried his message to churches and **camp meetings** alike, and in 1863, founded the "Friday" meeting for the promotion of holiness in Philadelphia. Reports of this gathering appeared regularly in the *Christian Witness* for many years.

Following his father's example, Cookman took a strong stand against slavery before abolitionism became a popular movement. During the 1859 session of the Baltimore Annual Conference, he was one of only a handful of ministers who voted to exclude slaveholders from membership in the church. When the Civil War broke out in 1861, he took a strong stand for the Union. He gave patriotic speeches and personally wrote the resolutions passed by the 1863 session of the New York Annual Conference in support of Abraham Lincoln and the Union cause. In 1864, he joined the work of the United States Christian Commission, preaching on the front lines to the soldiers of the Army of the Potomac.

While these ministries endeared Cookman to the church, his preaching at various camp meetings, especially at the National Camp Meetings, brought him instant fame. Throughout the 1860s, he became a familiar figure at encampments in Sing Sing (New York), Shrewsbury (Pennsylvania), Penn's Grove (New Jersey), and other locations on the East Coast. When initial plans were made in 1867 to conduct a specifically holiness camp meeting, Cookman wrote the "call" for the friends of holiness to gather in Philadelphia and organize the event. He preached at all eight national encampments that preceded his death and ministered at other camp meetings as time allowed.

Strenuous labor eventually took its toll. On 22 October 1871, he preached his last sermon from the text "We all do fade as a leaf" and claimed it was prophetic. Less than a month later he died at his home. His death created a sensation because of his youth and his exceptional popularity. Although his dying testimony has been debated, it appeared in church papers all over the country as "I am sweeping through the gates, washed in the blood of the lamb." He was the subject of a widely read biography by H. B. Ridgaway, *The Life of Rev. Alfred Cookman* (1874). K.O.B.

COON, HARRIET ARVILLA DAMON (b. Geauga County, Ohio, 9 February 1829; d. Glen Ellyn, Illinois, 7 January 1922). **Free Methodist Church** (FMC) lay evangelist. "Auntie Coon," as she was popularly known, was the wife of Amos P. Coon, a lawyer and prominent Republican politician in Marengo, Illinois. In 1857, she was converted under the ministry of **John Wesley Redfield** and was actively involved in his ministry until his death. A charter member of the FMC, she was a frequent **camp meeting** and revival preacher whose ministry was promoted by FMC founder **B. T. Roberts**. Noted for the simplicity of her dress, spiritual insight, joyous and demonstrative worship, and advocacy of sexual abstinence within marriage (marital purity), Coon was the living embodiment of the puritanical radicalism that characterized the early FMC in northern Illinois. Appropriately, she was an early supporter of **Vivian Dake**'s Pentecostal Bands and frequently preached in Band-sponsored services. In 1887, she was responsible for the conversion of **E. E. Shelhamer**. After 1902, she was commonly associated with his ministry, which continued to advocate many of Coon's most controversial teachings, including the ministry of women, interracial services, simplicity of dress, and marital purity. Shelhamer edited her autobiography, *The Life and Labors of Auntie Coon* (1902). W.C.K.

COWEN, CLARENCE EUGENE (b. Fordland, Missouri, 24 September 1904; d. Denver, Colorado, 10 May 1975). **Church of God (Holiness)** (CG[H]) minister, educator, and author. Cowen was converted in 1922. From 1924 to 1928, he taught in rural grade schools in Missouri and preached in small rural churches on weekends. He held several pastorates in the CG(H), including more than 20 years of service in Columbia, Missouri. He graduated from John Fletcher College (see **Kletzing College**) and the University of Missouri at Columbia, where he earned a Ph.D., becoming one of the first leaders associated with the conservative holiness movement to earn a doctorate. Cowen was one of the founders of Kansas City College and Bible School, which serves the

COWLES, HENRY • 73

CG(H) and other conservative fellowships, and he served as president and professor there for 25 years. He later founded the Rocky Mountain Christian School in Denver, Colorado. Cowen was known as a passionate preacher, compassionate administrator, and erudite scholar. His doctoral dissertation, "A History of the Church of God (Holiness)," was the first scholarly history of a holiness denomination and won acclaim as an honest portrayal of the development of that fellowship. Cowen's truthful appraisal of the holiness movement in writing, preaching, and administration won him several opponents as well. However, his legacy remains a model of steadfast devotion to conservative holiness adherents who admire his saintliness as well as his sagacity. W.T.

COWLES, HENRY (b. Norfolk, Connecticut, 24 April 1803; d. Janesville, Wisconsin, 6 September 1881). Congregational minister, educator, and editor. Following graduation from Yale College (1826) and Yale's theological course (1828), Cowles was appointed by the Connecticut Home Missionary Society as a missionary to the Western Reserve of Ohio, where he served posts in Ashtabula and Sandusky (1828–1830) and Austinburg (1830–1835). Appointed as professor of languages at Oberlin College in 1835, Cowles served as professor of ecclesiastical history (1837–1840) and professor of Old Testament (1840–1848). In 1844, he assumed part-time responsibilities for editing the *Oberlin Evangelist* and was sole editor of the publication from 1848 to 1862. An important member of the Oberlin community, he served as a trustee of Oberlin College (1851–1881). From 1863 to 1881, he wrote an important 16-volume commentary on the Bible. His essays and sermons appeared in the *Oberlin Evangelist* and *Bibliotheca Sacra*.

As one of the founders of the Ohio Anti-slavery Society, Cowles was deeply committed to the Oberlin reform tradition and to **Oberlin perfectionism**. His most important holiness work, *Holiness of Christians in the Present Life* (1840), was both a critique of the antinomian perfectionism of **John Humphrey Noyes** and a vigorous defense of Oberlin perfectionism. Keenly aware of the charges that Oberlin, and especially **Charles G. Finney**, were thoroughly Pelagian and taught the possibility of individual perfection without divine assistance, Cowles emphasized the role of the Holy Spirit in both conversion and **entire sanctification**. Deeply respected during his life, Cowles was awarded an honorary D.D. by Hillsdale (Michigan) College in 1863. W.C.K.

COWMAN, CHARLES E(lmer) (b. near Toulon, Illinois, 13 March 1868; d. Los Angeles, California, 25 September 1924). Telegrapher and cofounder of the Oriental Missionary Society (OMS). Converted in 1881, Cowman began working as a telegrapher in 1883. Following his marriage to **Lettie Burd (Cowman)** in 1891, the Cowmans renewed their Christian commitments and experienced **entire sanctification** in the early 1890s. In part inspired by an 1894 address by **A. B. Simpson** at a missionary convention at Moody Bible Institute, Charles Cowman felt drawn to foreign missions. Although continuing with his lucrative position as a supervisor with the Western Union Telegraph Company, he also took courses at Garrett Biblical Institute and Moody Bible Institute.

In the fall of 1900, the Cowmans helped **Martin Wells Knapp** found **God's Bible School**. In December, they were ordained by **Seth C. Rees** in services at the Metropolitan Holiness Church (see **Metropolitan Church Association**) in Chicago. Leaving as missionaries for Japan in February 1901, the Cowmans, with the aid of **Jugi Nakada**, founded a Bible school in Tokyo. Drawing support from the readers of *God's Revivalist* and the early International Apostolic Holiness Union, the work in Japan proved quite successful. In 1907, a Bible school and mission were established in Seoul, Korea. In 1910, the Cowmans formally organized their work as the OMS with Charles Cowman as president. In 1918, Charles Cowman suffered a severe heart attack and was forced to retire from active leadership. Out of the pain of his suffering, Lettie Burd Cowman wrote her famous book *Streams in the Desert* (1925). The book, which has sold more than three million copies, became one of the best-selling devotional books of the 20th century. K.O.B.

COWMAN, LETTIE BURD (b. Thayer, Iowa, 3 March 1870; d. Los Angeles, California, 17 April 1960). Author and cofounder of the Oriental Missionary Society (OMS; see **OMS International**). Lettie Cowman served as president of the OMS (1928–1949). Becoming an evangelical celebrity, she spoke at numerous mission conventions and church meetings. Among her important books are *Streams in the Desert* (1925), *Charles E. Cowman: Missionary Warrior* (1939), and *Springs in the Valley* (1939). *See also* COWMAN, CHARLES E. K.O.B.

COX, LEO GEORGE (b. Windom, Kansas, 31 July 1912). **Wesleyan Church** (WC) minister and educator. Leo George Cox was converted, sanctified, and ordained in the **Wesleyan Methodist Church**. He attended Miltonvale (Kansas) and Marion (Indiana) Colleges, graduating in 1945. He earned M.A. (1957) and Ph.D. (1959) degrees from the University of Iowa. Cox started and presided over Melbourne Bible College in Australia (1948–1952). He was division chair at Marion College (1957–1969), president of Bartlesville (Oklahoma) Wesleyan College (1969–1975), and secretary of education and the ministry for the WC (1975–1980). He wrote *John Wesley's Concept of Perfection* (1964) and commentaries in the *Wesleyan Bible Commentary* (1956) and the *Beacon Bible Commentary* (1967). Cox was a cofounder of the **Wesleyan Theological Society** and its first president. S.J.L.

COX, WINFRED R. (b. 1880, North Carolina; d. Greensboro, North Carolina, 14 May 1955). International Apostolic Holiness Union (IAHU), **Pilgrim Holiness Church** (PHC), and **Church of the Nazarene** (CN) pastor, educator, and evangelist. One of the founders of the IAHU in North Carolina, in 1901, Cox was the founding pastor of the IAHU congregation in Greensboro, where he served as editor of the *Apostolic Messenger* (1901–1921). He was one of the founders of Greensboro Bible and Literary School in 1903 and served as its president (1905–1925). An able administrator, Cox served as chairman of PHC general assemblies (1924, 1926) and was general superintendent of the PHC (1922–1930). Deeply committed to higher education and church extension in the United States, Cox clashed with the foreign mission emphasis of **Ralph Finch**, who was general secretary for missions of the PHC during this period. Frustrated with the lack of consistent direction of the PHC, Cox withdrew from the church in 1930. He spent the last 25 years of his life as a general evangelist in the CN. Consistent with his love for young people and commitment to education, he was still on the faculty of People's Bible College at the time of his death. W.C.K.

CRAWFOOT, JAMES (b. Cheshire, England, 1758; d. Cheshire, England, 1839). "The Old Man of the Forest" or "The Forest Mystic." Crawfoot was hired at 10 shillings a week by Hugh Bourne as the first itinerant of what was to become the Primitive Methodists (Great Britain). A former Wesleyan local preacher, he formed small bands of highly charismatic followers largely in the Delamere Forest area of Cheshire. Most of these "Magic Methodists" linked with the Primitive Methodist movement. He placed great emphasis on the interpretation of dreams, prophecy, and trances in following the life of holiness. His gifts were best used in small groups, and he led many into a deeper life. He left the Primitive Methodists in 1813, possibly over personal problems with Bourne. W.P.

CRITTENTON, CHARLES NELSON (b. near Henderson, Jefferson County, New York, 20 February 1833; d. San Francisco, California, 16 November 1909). Episcopal merchant, evangelist, and founder of the Florence Crittenton Homes. In 1861, Crittenton founded a highly successful retail drug company in New York City. Following the tragic death of his daughter Florence in 1882, Crittenton had an intense conversion experience. Influenced by the Palmers' Tuesday Meeting for the Promotion of Holiness (see **Phoebe Worrall Palmer**), Crittenton rapidly emerged as an important figure in New York City's perfectionist community. In 1883, he established a mission for prostitutes, the Florence Crittenton Mission, on New York City's Bleecker Street. In 1890, a second mission was established in San Francisco. With the assistance of the widow of an Episcopal priest, Kate Waller Barrett, who had entered the experience of full salvation under Crittenton's preaching, the number of Florence Crittenton Missions grew rapidly to more than 70 at the time of Crittenton's death. Working closely with other perfectionist and semiperfectionist groups, such as the **Salvation Army** (SA), **Christian and Missionary Alliance** (CMA), the Woman's Christian Temperance Union, and the Door of Hope Missions, Crittenton was instrumental in the organization of the National Gospel Mission Union. He was an attendant at the General Holiness Assembly of 1901. A pioneer in the ministry to so-called fallen women, Crittenton inspired the significant ministries to unwed mothers and prostitutes of the SA, **Free Methodist Church**, CMA, **Pilgrim Holiness Church**, and **Church of the Nazarene**. W.C.K.

CROOKS, ADAM (b. Leesville, Ohio, 3 May 1824; d. Syracuse, New York, 15 December 1874). **Wesleyan Methodist Church** (WMC) minister, missionary to the South, abolitionist, and editor. Although not raised in a deeply religious home, Crooks was converted in 1838 and joined the Methodist Protestant Church (MPC). Influenced by the writings of William Carvosso, Crooks experienced **entire sanctification** in 1840. Convinced of the complicity of the MPC with slavery, Crooks joined the WMC in 1843. He was licensed to preach in 1844, admitted to membership in the Allegheny Conference in 1845, and ordained in 1847. Crooks served as a WMC missionary in North Carolina (1847–1852), an Allegheny Conference pastor (1852–1864), and editor of the *American Wesleyan* (1864–1874). While in North Carolina, Crooks was arrested and expelled from the state for violating the state's law against distributing abolitionist literature. A deeply committed reformer, Crooks was an outspoken temperance advocate and an organizer of the National Christian Association, a body of evangelical Protestants opposed to secret fraternal organizations such as the Masons and Odd Fellows. A fierce denominational loyalist, Crooks was a leading opponent of efforts to unite the WMC with the Methodist Episcopal Church and other efforts to create a united nonepiscopal Methodist body. Although not active in the early National Holiness Association (see **Christian Holiness Partnership**) **camp meetings**, Crooks was one of the early WMC advocates for the experience of Christian perfection. Following his death, his widow, Elizabeth Willits Crooks, wrote a biography of her husband, *The Life of Rev. A. Crooks*, based on his unpublished journal. W.C.K.

CROSSLEY, FRANCIS WILLIAM (b. Dunmurry, north of Ireland, 29 November 1839; d. Manchester, England, 25 March 1897). Founder of Star Hall. The eldest son of a military family, Crossley was set up in a rubber manufacturing business by his family in Manchester in 1867. A few years later, the firm began the manufacture of gas engines, and the business prospered until "Crossley engines" became a household word in Great Britain and elsewhere. Converted to Christ while he was an engineering apprentice, Crossley developed a reputation as a business entrepreneur and devoted Christian. Through his contacts with the **Salvation Army** (SA), he entered the experience of **entire sanctification**, became a personal friend of General **William** and **Catherine Booth**, and supported the SA enthusiastically. In 1889, he purchased a run-down music hall in Ancoats, Manchester's most notorious area, renovated it, and opened it as Star Hall. He and his wife, Emily, moved from the outskirts of Manchester to Star Hall. With a deep love for lost souls and the good of his fellow men, Crossley gave generously of his money, time, and strength, and the last seven years of his life were spent in making Star Hall a mission center, a home for unwed mothers, and the most significant holiness center in England. H.M.

CRUSADERS CHURCHES USA (CC). The CC was founded in 1972 in Urbana, Illinois, by former **Church of the Nazarene** (CN) pastor J. O. (Jack) Jones. Among the central issues in its founding was the growing acceptance of divorce and remarriage in the CN. A periodical, *Faith in the Future*, and Faith School of Theology were founded in Urbana at that time. By the mid-1990s, nine churches had been established in Illinois and Indiana and one in St. Louis. The Urbana congregation, under the leadership of Jones and his sons, Rick and Marsh, is the largest congregation and has gained considerable local attention for its public witness against pornography and abortion. In spite of its conservative theology, it is only loosely linked with the **Inter-Church Holiness Convention**. The CC has fewer than 1,000 members. W.C.K.

CULLIS, CHARLES (b. Boston, Massachusetts, 7 March 1833; d. Boston, 18 June 1892). Episcopal homeopathic physician, faith healer, author, and editor. After ill health ended Cullis's short career as a dry goods merchant, he entered medical school. In 1857, he received a medical degree from the University of Vermont and established a profitable medical practice in Boston. The tragic death of his young wife caused him to become far more introspective. Experiencing **entire sanctification** in 1862, Cullis, following the examples of Herman Francke and George Mueller, established a home for consumptives in Boston. Although supported entirely by volunteers and unsolicited contributions, Cullis's work experienced rapid growth. By 1870, his ministry included four consumptive homes, an orphanage, a deaconess home, and a dispensary. An ardent advocate of the message of full salvation, Cullis established a publishing arm, the Willard Tract Repository, in 1868 and a periodical, *Times of Refreshing*, in 1869. During the 1870s, Cullis's work expanded to include a cancer home, a spinal home, city missions, an orphanage and a normal school for ex-slaves in Virginia, a Chinese mission in California, and missions in India. In 1875, Cullis established the Faith Training College in Boston's famed Beacon Hill neighborhood. This coeducational and tuition-free theological seminary included faculty members such as **W. E. Boardman**, professor of Christian life; **A. B. Earle**, professor of revival work; and **Daniel Steele**, professor of systematic theology. By the 1870s, under the influence of European faith healers such as Johann Blumhardt, Otto Stockmayer, and Dorothea Trudel, Cullis began to conduct weekly meetings of prayer for the sick. In 1874, he began summer conventions dedicated to physical healing. Among those healed during Cullis's healing conventions was **A. B. Simpson**, founder of the **Christian and Missionary Alliance**. Increasingly concentrating on his ministry of healing, Cullis compiled several books of healing testimonies: *Faith Cures* (1879), *More Faith Cures* (1881), and *Other Faith Cures* (1885). A small collection of papers documenting Cullis's ministry is located at the American Antiquarian Society in Worcester, Massachusetts. W.C.K.

– D –

DAKE, VIVIAN ADELBERT (b. Oregon, Illinois, 9 February 1854; d. Sierra Leone, Africa, 5 January 1892). **Free Methodist Church** (FMC) evangelist and founder of the Pentecostal Bands (PB). Son of a Methodist Episcopal Church (MEC) pastor who became a Free Methodist in 1860, Dake was "wonderfully reclaimed" at Chili Seminary near Rochester, New York, after an earlier childhood conversion. He was influenced at Chili by **B. T. Roberts**, who later supported his radical holiness evangelism.

Dake studied at the University of Rochester (New York) but left to enter the FMC ministry. In 1885, he began organizing young men and women in Michigan into PB, which grew into a revival and church-planting movement of more than 300 workers, women outnumbering men two to one. Many FMC churches in the Midwest were started by these bands. The movement grew controversial because of aggressive methods, fund-raising for overseas mission ventures, and a "death-route" interpretation of holiness that, contrary to **Phoebe Palmer**'s shorter way, stated that the sanctification experience was only achieved after a slow and painful process. The FMC restricted PB activity, leading to the movement's becoming independent after Dake's death, taking the name Missionary Bands of the World. Always passionate for missions, Dake traveled to Africa, where he died of African fever. H.A.S.

DAMON, CHARLES MILTON (b. near Rushford, New York, 16 January 1846; d. Portland, Oregon, 21 August 1911). **Free Methodist Church** (FMC) minister, evangelist, educator, and reformer. Raised in a Methodist Episcopal Church (MEC) home, Damon was converted in 1857 and served as an MEC minister in Iowa (1867–1868). Following his experience of **entire sanctification** at the Round Lake (New York) **Camp Meeting** in 1869, Damon united with the FMC and married Frances E. Dunning, daughter of prominent FMC mission worker and preacher Jane Dunning. After two disappointing pastorates in New York, Damon joined the Iowa–Minnesota Conference of the FMC in 1871, serving as a minister until 1879, when he relocated to Kansas and established a homestead while serving as an FMC evangelist. In 1884, he was named the first president of Orleans Seminary in Orleans, Nebraska (now Central College). Relocating to Burlington, Iowa, in 1890, Damon served as an evangelist and held several brief pastorates in

Iowa, Minnesota, and Wisconsin. Fitting for an heir of Western New York's famed "burned-over district," Damon was a bitter foe of Masonry and an enthusiastic champion of civil rights for African Americans and Asian immigrants. Damon was a frequent correspondent for several holiness periodicals, especially the *Free Methodist*. His autobiography, *Sketches and Incidents* (1900), went through two editions. W.C.K.

DAYTON, DONALD W(ilbur) (b. Chicago, Illinois, 25 July 1942). **Wesleyan Church** (WC) librarian, ethicist, theologian, and historian. The son of prominent WC educator Wilbur T. Dayton, Donald Dayton is a graduate of Houghton College, Yale University, the University of Kentucky, and the University of Chicago. He has taught at **Asbury Theological Seminary** (1969–1972), North Park Theological Seminary (1972–1979), and Northern Baptist Theological Seminary (1979–1997) and is currently on the faculty of Drew University. Influenced by the cultural milieu of the 1960s, especially the civil rights movement, and the thought of Sören Kierkegaard and Karl Barth, Dayton emerged as a leader of the so-called New Evangelicals of the early 1970s. He was a contributing editor of *Post-American*, now *Sojourners*, a signer of the Chicago Declaration of Social Concern (1973), and a charter member of Evangelicals for Social Action.

Using history as a tool for evangelical renewal and transformation, Dayton, in a significant series of essays in the *Post-American*, later published as *Discovering an Evangelical Heritage* (1976), argued that evangelicals needed to embrace their 19th-century heritage and affirm such contemporary movements as civil rights, the women's movement, and the movement for economic justice. An avid spokesperson for the social significance of the holiness tradition, Dayton has tirelessly defended his spiritual heritage in the *Christian Century*; among gatherings of Evangelicals, Pentecostals, Methodists, and members of the Unification Church; and in discussions of the Faith and Order Commission of the World Council of Churches. As a mature scholar, Dayton has given special attention to the historiography of Evangelicalism and the origins of Pentecostalism in the 19th-century holiness movement. His book *The Theological Roots of Pentecostalism* (1987) has had an international impact and remains an essential text for understanding the holiness movement, Pentecostalism, and 20th-century Evangelicalism. Dayton has served on the boards of the Chicago Urban Life Center and Olive Branch Mission and has been president of both the **Wesleyan Theological Society** and the Society for Pentecostal Studies. W.C.K.

DE COSTA, LUCÍA CARMEN GARCÍA (b. Buenos Aires, Argentina, 12 November 1903; d. Buenos Aires, 22 May 1984). **Church of the Nazarene** (CN) evangelist, pastor, editor, and educator. Raised in a middle-class Catholic family, García was the first CN convert in Argentina (1919) and the first graduate of a Nazarene school for ministers in Argentina (1926). She and Soledad Quintana led Bible studies and started churches in the towns around Buenos Aires in the 1920s. Both women were in the Argentina District's first ordination class (1931). García married Italian immigrant Natalio de Costa in 1935. From 1927 to 1982, she was always pastor of one or more churches yet also taught at Nazarene Bible Institute in Buenos Aires (1935–1953), mastered nine languages, and earned a doctorate in linguistics (University of Buenos Aires, 1950). She translated into Spanish Adam Clarke's abridged commentary, **Hannah Whitall Smith**'s *The Christian's Secret of a Happy Life*, and other classic Wesleyan holiness texts; and edited the paper *La Via Mas Excelente*. She devoted her full energies to organizing and serving new congregations (1953–1969) and was credited in 1972 with the founding of more than one-third of her district's churches. R.S.I.

DEGEN, HENRY V(assel) (b. Leghorn, Italy, 14 December 1814; d. Boston, Massachusetts, 5 January 1897). Methodist Episcopal Church (MEC) minister, publisher, and editor of the *Guide to Holiness*. Son of a British consul to Italy, Henry Degen received an excellent education and was fluent in three languages. He became converted and joined the MEC. He worked for the Methodist Book Concern and served as a lay preacher in New Jersey. In 1840, he entered the ministry in the Maine Annual Conference of the MEC. At a **camp meeting** in 1842, he claimed the experience of **entire sanctification**.

In 1851, Degen became editor and publisher of the periodical, *Guide to Holiness*, which grew substantially under his management. In 1864, he sold *Guide to Holiness* to **Walter C.** and **Phoebe Palmer**. He joined the Episcopal Church and served Episcopal parishes on Long Island, New York, and in South Orange, New Jersey, until his retirement. K.O.B.

DEMARAY, C(alvin) DORR (b. Vermontville, Michigan, 21 October 1901; d. Seattle, Washington, 30 October 1992). **Free Methodist**

Church (FMC) educator, pastor, and college president. As a young man, C. Dorr Demaray began his association with the church as a youth evangelist. He studied at Greenville College and the University of Michigan, receiving a B.A. (1924) and M.A. (1927) from Michigan. For 23 years, he taught English and speech at Adrian (Michigan) College, Sterling (Kansas) College, and Los Angeles Pacific College. He also served as dean of students (1936–1941) and president (1941–1948) of Los Angeles Pacific College.

In 1941, Demaray was ordained in the FMC; he pastored the First Free Methodist Church in Seattle (1948–1959). He became a member of the Seattle Pacific College Board of Trustees and, in 1959, assumed the presidency of the college. During his tenure, 15 buildings were built or remodeled, enrollment increased by more than 60 percent, and faculty size doubled. His policy of openness to change enabled the college to survive the turbulence of the 1960s, and he attempted to increase its civic involvement. He was known for his gentility and high standards of scholarship.

After retirement from Seattle Pacific in 1968, Demaray traveled extensively as a Christian ambassador, leading nearly 20 tours to the Holy Land, pastoring a church in Japan, starting a Christian high school in Taiwan, and helping to raise money for a Taiwanese seminary. Among his children is **Donald Eugene Demaray**. J.L.W.

DEMARAY, DONALD EUGENE (b. Adrian, Michigan, 6 December 1926). **Free Methodist Church** (FMC) educator and author. The son of **C. Dorr Demaray**, Donald Demaray was educated at Los Angeles Pacific College (B.A.), **Asbury Theological Seminary** (B.D.), the Universities of California and Zurich, and the University of Edinburgh, where he received his Ph.D. in 1952.

Ordained in the FMC, Demaray pastored in the Seattle area before embarking on his academic career as a professor at Seattle Pacific College, where he taught from 1952 to 1959 and, in 1959, became dean of the School of Religion. In 1966, he joined the faculty of Asbury Theological Seminary, where he teaches in the areas of homiletics, healing, and Christian journalism. From 1967 to 1975, he served as dean of students at Asbury and, in 1991, was named Senior Beeson Professor of Biblical Preaching.

Demaray is well known as an evangelical author, having written more than 30 books on theology, preaching, and the Christian life, including *Basic Beliefs* (1958), *A Pulpit Manual* (1959), *Alive to God through Prayer* (1965, rev. as *How Are You Praying?* 1986), *Pulpit Giants* (1973), *Introduction to Homiletics* (1974), *Snapshots: The People Called Free Methodists* (1985), *Laughter, Joy, and Healing* (1986), and several devotional collections. He has also contributed many articles to religious magazines (most notably the FMC publication *Light and Life*) and journals, and he has been listed in *Who's Who in Religion* and *Leaders in Education*. J.L.W.

DEPAUW, WASHINGTON CHARLES (b. Salem, Indiana, 4 January 1822; d. New Albany, Indiana, 5 May 1887). Methodist Episcopal Church layman, National Holiness Association (NHA; see **Christian Holiness Partnership**) leader, banker, industrialist, and philanthropist. The son of a prominent Indiana lawyer, judge, and politician, DePauw served as Washington County (Indiana) clerk (1843–1853). Investing in saw and grist mills, DePauw was already a prominent businessman when he started a bank in Salem in 1853. Skillfully investing in government bonds during the Civil War, DePauw emerged from the war as perhaps the wealthiest individual in Indiana. Relocating to New Albany, Indiana, he became the chief stockholder in the Ohio Falls Iron Works and the New Albany Rolling Mill. In 1866, he was elected president of the Ohio Falls Nail Works and began operating a woolen mill. However, it was in the manufacturing of plate glass that DePauw made his real fortune. Acquiring the Star Glass Works, he skillfully invested vast sums of money and greatly increased both production and profits. Although at times controversial, DePauw was active in philanthropy and the promotion of education and missions in New Albany. In 1882, Indiana Asbury University (Greencastle, Indiana) was renamed DePauw University following his generous bequest to that college. A deeply committed Methodist layman, DePauw was a member of New Albany's Centenary Church and a delegate to the General Conferences of 1872 and 1876 and to the Ecumenical Methodist Council in London in 1881. Experiencing **entire sanctification** under the ministry of **John Inskip** in 1871, DePauw was a major financial supporter of the NHA, serving as head of its publishing arm during the 1870s. W.C.K.

DEPEW, MARY ELIZA KINNEY (b. near Warren, Ohio, 2 July 1836; d. Houghton, New York, 9 October 1892). **Wesleyan Methodist Church** (WMC) evangelist and dean of women, Houghton College (1885–1892). The daughter of a militant abolitionist who identified with the WMC in 1843, DePew was converted in 1849 and sanctified in 1866. Although never ordained, she felt called to spread the holiness message throughout the WMC. Leaving her husband to tend the family farm, DePew became one of the church's most notable evangelists. In fact, many Wesleyans were disappointed when she accepted the call to become dean of women at Houghton College. Establishing a daily prayer meeting in her home, DePew helped to make Houghton a center for the agitation for the experience of heartfelt holiness in the WMC. Along with her brother, D. S. Kinney, DePew was generally considered to have been the primary reason for the WMC's identification with the postbellum holiness movement. W.C.K.

DEWEERD, JAMES A. (b. Olivet, Illinois, 23 May 1916; d. Fairmount, Indiana, 29 March 1972). **Wesleyan Methodist Church** (WMC) and Evangelical United Brethren (EUB) minister and evangelist. The son of WMC missionaries Fred and Lelia DeWeerd, James DeWeerd was converted in 1930 and experienced **entire sanctification** in 1932. From 1933 to 1937, while a student at Marion (Indiana) College and **Taylor University**, he served as pastor of the Gaston (Indiana) WMC. Following graduation from Taylor in 1937, DeWeerd became an itinerant evangelist. During World War II, he served as a chaplain and was decorated with a Silver Star for bravery in combat. Resuming his career as a holiness evangelist after the war, DeWeerd served as editor of the *Christian Witness* (1948–1958); president of Kletzing College (Iowa); pastor of Cadle Tabernacle, Indianapolis (1952–1957); and a popular preacher on radio station WLW in Cincinnati, Ohio. Unlike the fundamentalistic literalism of many holiness figures of his time, DeWeerd's faith was decidedly pietistic and mystical. In an early thoughtful book, *The Realities of Christian Experience* (1940), DeWeerd, reminiscent of his hero **Samuel L. Brengle**, urged his readers to cultivate the interior life. Although one of the most popular holiness evangelists of the 1940s and 1950s, DeWeerd is ironically remembered today for his role in the life of Fairmount, Indiana's, most famous son, cultural icon James Dean. As a mentor of Dean and the officiant at Dean's funeral, DeWeerd has come to occupy a place in the James Dean legend. Although most scholars reject the widely circulated story of a Dean–DeWeerd sexual liaison, by the end of the 1950s DeWeerd was seldom asked to conduct evangelistic meetings. In 1963, DeWeerd joined the EUB Church and in 1968 received an M.A. degree from Ball State University (Indiana). W.C.K.

DIETER, MELVIN EASTERDAY (b. Cherryville, Pennsylvania, 12 October 1924). **Wesleyan Church** (WC) historian and minister. Melvin

Dieter was raised in Allentown, Pennsylvania, where his father, Harold Dieter, was president of Allentown Bible Institute (ABI). Educated in Lehigh Valley schools, he received an A.B. from Muhlenberg College, a Th.B. from ABI, and an M.A. from Lehigh University. In 1953, he received an S.T.M. from Temple University, where he also earned his Ph.D. in 1973. He served in the Naval Reserve and taught at ABI, where he became assistant to the president and then president (1961–1965). His doctoral dissertation was published in 1980 as *The Holiness Revival of the 19th Century*.

Dieter accepted the position of secretary of educational institutions in the WC in 1968. In 1974, he was named to the faculty of **Asbury Theological Seminary**, where he served as vice president and provost (1984–1987) and where he later developed the **Wesleyan/Holiness Study** Project.

Dieter was a master teacher, especially gifted at historical and theological summation. He edited or coedited *Five Views on Sanctification* (1987); *The Church in Wesleyan Theological Perspective* (1984); an anthology of **Hannah Whitall Smith**'s writings, *The Christian's Secret of a Happy Life* (1994), coedited with his wife Hallie; and *The 19th-Century Holiness Movement* (1998), Volume IV in *Holiness Classics*, completing the work of **Timothy Smith**. He has also written chapters and articles for books and journals. He contributed many entries to the *Beacon Dictionary of Theology* (1983) and major chapters to *Reformers and Revivalists: A History of the Wesleyan Church* (1992). A charter member of the **Wesleyan Theological Society**, he has served as its president and was honored by the society in 1996 with its award for Lifetime Service to the Holiness Tradition. He has been ever faithful in his presentation of the Wesleyan message of free salvation for all and full salvation from sin. L.O.H.

DODGE, WILLIAM A(sbury) (b. Columbia County, Georgia, 30 September 1844; d. Atlanta, 16 January 1904). Methodist Episcopal Church, South (MECS), minister, evangelist, editor, author, and one of the founders of the Georgia Holiness Association and Indian Springs Holiness **Camp Meeting**. William A. Dodge grew up in a Methodist home and became a Christian before his 14th birthday. Receiving his preacher's license on his 17th birthday, he entered the ministry of Georgia Annual Conference of the MECS in 1862. After serving as chaplain in the Confederate Army (1864–1865), he returned to the pastorate and was ordained an elder in 1869. He served as presiding elder (district superintendent) of the Dahlonega and Gainesville Districts and in 1875 to 1876 as pastor of a large MECS congregation in Atlanta. A friend introduced him to some popular holiness literature, including the writings of **Phoebe Palmer**, and a new southern periodical, the *Way of Holiness*. Dodge claimed **entire sanctification** in 1870 and again in 1873, but he lost the experience both times. Finally, in 1876, following a revival service in his church, he achieved a lasting conversion.

In 1880, **John S. Inskip** held successful holiness revival meetings in Augusta, Georgia. Shortly thereafter, Dodge and fellow Methodist pastor A. J. Jarrell laid plans to promote holiness in their district. In 1881, they organized the North Georgia Holiness Association with Dodge as secretary-treasurer. By 1882, they began to publish a paper, *Tongue of Fire*, with Dodge as editor. In 1883, 24 ministers and nearly 100 laypersons met in Gainesville and formally organized the Georgia Holiness Association (GHA). Within a few months, the name of the periodical was changed to *Way of Life*. In 1885, the association formed a separate organization for the southern part of the state, the South Georgia Holiness Association.

Dodge worked tirelessly for the cause of holiness in Georgia, sometimes traveling into other states to secure workers and supporting the National Camp Meeting held in Augusta in 1885. Dodge suffered professional reverses that resulted in his moving from a large important parish in the Gainesville District in 1885 to a rural circuit in Fulton County in 1887 and an appointment as a junior pastor in Atlanta in 1889. In 1894, he was appointed a city missionary in Atlanta, the same position he had held 20 years earlier.

Dodge became one of the most effective southern holiness leaders. He ministered at conventions of the GHA and preached at revivals and camp meetings in several states. In 1889, he and H. A. Hodges, J. H. Curry, and George W. Matthews selected a site near Flovilla, Georgia, for the Indian Springs Holiness Camp Meeting, the permanent camp meeting of the GHA. The first session of the camp meeting convened in 1890, and it quickly became one of the premier holiness camp meetings in the South. Dodge devoted the last 13 years of his life to the camp meeting. K.O.B.

DOTY, T(homas) K. (b. Barnardston, Massachusetts, 6 June 1835; d. Cleveland, Ohio, 13 October 1913). Methodist Episcopal Church (MEC) and **Wesleyan Methodist Church** (WMC) minister, editor, and reformer. As a child, Doty attended district schools in Waterbury Center, Vermont, where he worked with his uncle on the family farm and at the family-owned blacksmith shop. Learning the printing trade, he worked for newspapers in Montpelier and Northfield, Vermont, and Potsdam, New York. In 1855, he became the proprietor of the *Northern Freeman*, an abolitionist and Republican paper published in Potsdam. Converted in 1858, he was granted a local preacher's license in the MEC in 1859, received into membership in the Black River Conference in 1862, and ordained an elder in 1864. Forced to cease his ministerial labors as a result of ill health, Doty was a patient at the Jackson Sanatorium in Dansville, New York, from 1866 to 1868. In 1868, he relocated to Cleveland, Ohio. Beginning as a printer, Doty founded a holiness periodical, *Christian Harvester*, which he edited until June 1913. Joining the WMC, Doty served several terms as pastor of that denomination's Cleveland church. He was also instrumental in the founding of several WMC congregations in Ohio, in the organization of the denomination's Mission Board, and in the founding of Houghton College. Deeply committed to the reform tradition of the American WMC, Doty insisted that "holiness destroys the line of color-prejudice" and that it was sin "to padlock the lips" of anointed women preachers. Among his most significant books were *Lessons in Holiness* (1881) and *The Two-fold Gift of the Holy Spirit* (1890). W.C.K.

DOUGLAS, JOHN HENRY (b. Fairfield, Maine, 27 November 1832; d. Whittier, California, 24 November 1919). Gurneyite Quaker minister. Douglas moved to Clinton, Ohio, in 1852, where he resided until 1885. He then lived in Iowa and Oregon before settling in California in 1900. His family members were Gurneyite Friends, the Quaker faction that before 1860 had moved close to the dominant evangelical religious culture of the United States. Douglas was recorded a Quaker minister in 1858 and became prominent in Quaker affairs in the 1860s as part of a reforming group of young Friends who sought to proselytize among the freed people in the South. His views became more radical following his sanctification in 1871, after which he identified himself with the holiness movement. He traveled widely as a Quaker revivalist and evangelist, and he was an outspoken advocate of introducing the pastoral system among Quakers. He moved to Iowa in 1885. Douglas wrote occasionally for Quaker periodicals. T.D.H.

DRESS IN THE HOLINESS MOVEMENT. Dress has long been seen as a way that holiness people give evidence of Christian commitment. Convinced that expensive clothes led to pride and was a misuse of money better spent on the poor, **John Wesley** urged his followers to dress simply. Wesley's views on simple dress were continued by such early holiness champions as **Charles G. Finney** and **Phoebe Palmer**. It was a special emphasis of the **Free Methodist Church** (FMC), which required its preachers to read Wesley's sermon on dress to their congregations into the 1970s. Objects of special prohibitions concerning dress among men were neckties and later short-sleeve shirts, especially in the FMC and the **Church of God (Anderson)**. Concerning women's dress, the 19th-century holiness movement opposed fancy lace; in the 20th century, holiness churches opposed rising hemlines and the changing styles of women's clothing. Members of both sexes were prohibited from wearing wedding rings. Some holiness bodies, especially those engaged in mission work, adopted uniforms for both men and women. Among the most notable of these were the **Salvation Army**, **American Rescue Workers**, **Grace and Hope Mission**, the **Pillar of Fire**, and the **Metropolitan Church Association**. Beginning in the late 1940s, changing clothing styles in such holiness denominations as the **Church of the Nazarene** and the **Pilgrim Holiness Church**, especially among women, contributed to the formation of a series of new holiness denominations that united in the **Inter-Church Holiness Convention**. W.C.K.

DRYSDALE, J(ohn) D. (b. Edinburgh, 23 April 1880; d. Birkenhead, Cheshire, 15 January 1953). British pastor, evangelist, camp and convention teacher, author, church leader, and Bible college principal. Raised in "devout poverty" in a large family attached to the Free Church of Scotland, Drysdale received his call to the ministry prior to fully experiencing the new birth. This came about, together with the challenge of a clean heart, through **George Sharpe**, founder of what was to become the **Church of the Nazarene** in Great Britain. Not conforming to Scottish Presbyterianism, Drysdale stepped out in faith and established holiness work in Uddingston and Blantyre, both centers becoming Nazarene churches, although he never became a Nazarene minister. An entirely independent cause in Androssan grew considerably under his leadership, with an annual convention drawing speakers from Great Britain and the United States. Arriving in Birkenhead in 1915, he established Emmanuel Bible College with a clear holiness program, supported sacrificially by a few somewhat loosely knit Emmanuel Churches. Drysdale believed that Christians who had been made perfect in love could live in unity, and, practicing Bible "communism," no salaries were paid. A deeply committed pacifist, Drysdale insisted that mature Christians would refuse to take part in war. From this relatively small base, a considerable overseas work was established in Mauritius, Morocco, and Argentina, and outstanding members were trained for other holiness missionary societies. The work continued until 1997 when, faced with a very small enrollment, Emmanuel linked with the British Nazarene College. Drysdale's books include *The Price of Revival* (1938) and *Holiness in the Parables* (1952). W.P.

DUEWEL, WESLEY L(uelf) (b. St. Charles, Missouri, 3 June 1916). Fire Baptized Holiness Church (see **Bible Holiness Church**) and **Free Methodist Church** (FMC) missionary, educator, and author. A graduate of **God's Bible School** (1939) and the University of Cincinnati (1949, 1952), Duewel was one of the founders of the Oriental Missionary Society (see **OMS International**) work in India, where he served from 1940 to 1964. He was principal at Allahabad Bible Seminary (1946–1964) and director of the OMS work in India (1953–1964). He served as vice president of the OMS (1964–1969) and then president (1969–1982). He has continued his ministry with the OMS as a special assistant to the president for evangelism and prayer since 1982. In 1995, he was named president emeritus of the OMS. He has served as a board member of Union Bible Seminary in Pune, India (1953–1964), and **Asbury Theological Seminary** (1975–present). As a writer on prayer and revival, he is the author of *Touch the World through Prayer* (1986); *Revival Fire* (1995), an interpretative history of revival; and a general introduction to theology and experiential piety for working pastors and laypeople, *God's Great Salvation* (1991). He was a charter member of the **Wesleyan Theological Society**. W.C.K.

DUNN, L(ewis) R(omaine) (b. Brunswick, New Jersey, 1822; d. East Orange, New Jersey, 5 August 1898). Methodist Episcopal Church (MEC) pastor, National Holiness Association (NHA; see **Christian Holiness Partnership**) evangelist, and author. Converted at the age of 14, Dunn began supplying pulpits in 1838 and was admitted into membership in the New Jersey Conference of the MEC in 1841. An earnest student, he attended Dickinson College in Carlisle, Pennsylvania, and read widely in Methodist and Anglican theological literature. A successful pastor, Dunn was involved in the construction of new churches in Keyport, Madison, Springville, and Elizabeth, New Jersey. In 1876, he received an honorary degree from Wesleyan University in Middletown, Connecticut. In 1866, while serving as pastor of Newark's Central Methodist Church, he was led into the experience of **entire sanc-**

tification by **John Inskip**. An early leader of the NHA, Dunn spoke at virtually all of the early NHA **camp meetings**. With the possible exception of **Daniel Steele**, Dunn was the holiness movement's most articulate theological champion.

Dunn, whose writings were characterized by thorough research and clarity of style, was a frequent contributor to the *Methodist Quarterly Review*. His most notable book, *The Mission of the Spirit, or the Office and Work of the Comforter in Human Redemption* (1871), was one of the first books to argue that the church was on the eve of a new Pentecost. In his second book, *Holiness unto the Lord* (1874), Dunn argued that the experience of holiness would be the "grand universal characteristic of the millennial age." His final book, *A Manual of Holiness* (1896), was both a response to **James Mudge**'s critique of traditional Wesleyan theology and a profoundly personal defense of the experience of entire sanctification. Although less well known in the 20th century than his contemporary Daniel Steele, Dunn was certainly his equal as a defender of holiness experience and doctrine. W.C.K.

DUNN, SETHARD PIRLUM (b. Logtown, Louisiana, 18 April 1881; d. Chicago, Illinois, 13 November 1959). **Church of God (Anderson)** (CG[A]) minister. A graduate of Leland University in New Orleans, Dunn came into contact with the CG(A) in 1905 through the *Gospel Trumpet*. Although licensed to preach in the African Methodist Episcopal Church, Dunn left to affiliate with the CG(A), entering the ministry in 1907. Early in his career, he pastored in Texas, Arkansas, and Louisiana. Immediately after the Anderson **Camp Meeting** in 1920, Dunn succeeded J. D. Smoot as pastor of the five-year-old African American congregation in Chicago. Over 39 years, Dunn built Langley Avenue Church of God into a strong and influential church. Chicago also felt the influence of his voice as the "Radio Shepherd of Chicago" on radio station WCFL from 1955 to 1959. Dunn was frequently elected to several CG(A) agencies and boards. He was a charter trustee of Anderson College and a member of both the Board of Church Extension and the Missionary Board. M.D.S.

DUNNING H. R(ay) (b. Clarksville, Tennessee, 26 October 1926). **Church of the Nazarene** (CN) pastor, theologian, and ethicist. A graduate of Trevecca Nazarene College, Nazarene Theological Seminary, and Vanderbilt University, Dunning was a CN pastor in Tennessee and Arkansas for 14 years before becoming professor of theology at Trevecca Nazarene College (1964–1995), where he also chaired the Department of Philosophy and Religion. His concern to interpret Wesleyan holiness theology in relation to the broad Christian tradition is evident in his many writings, especially in *Reflecting the Divine Image: Christian Ethics in Wesleyan Perspective* (1998) and his primary work, *Grace, Faith, and Holiness: A Wesleyan Systematic Theology* (1988). In these books, a critical appropriation of **John Wesley**'s theology shaped Dunning's intellectual lens, and his conviction that Wesleyan theology brings together strands of Protestant, Roman Catholic, and Eastern Orthodox thought influenced his interactions with historical and contemporary Christian thought. R.S.I.

– E –

EARLE, A(bsalom) B(ackus) (b. Charlton, New York, 25 March 1812, d. Watertown, Massachusetts, 30 March 1895). Baptist minister, evangelist, and author. Converted in 1830, Earle was ordained in 1832 and became pastor of the Amsterdam (New York) Baptist Church, where he served until 1837. Although he served as pastor of several small Baptist churches in central New York, after 1837, Earle's ministry was largely devoted to evangelism. In the early 1840s, he relocated to Boston and entered full-time evangelistic work. Until the late 1860s, Earle's ministry was confined primarily to New England and New York. A firm advocate of union evangelistic efforts, Earle insisted that where possible all evangelical Christian churches should sponsor his meetings jointly. Perhaps Earle's most notable evangelistic effort was an 1866–1867 campaign on the West Coast. Invited by 14 different churches, Earle began his services in San Francisco in the early fall of 1866. The campaign included stops in Sacramento and San Jose, California; Portland and Salem, Oregon; and Virginia City and Carson City, Nevada. Upon his return to Boston, Earle published an account of his West Coast trip with some experiences from his earlier evangelistic ministry. The book, *Bring in the Sheaves* (1868), went through several editions, becoming something of a minor holiness classic. At the time of his death, it was estimated that 160,000 people had united with churches as a result of his meetings.

Earle's 2 November 1863 experience of **entire sanctification**—or, as he preferred to call it, "the rest of faith"—transformed his ministry. An ardent Baptist champion of the higher Christian life, he was the author of 18 books and tracts, mostly dealing with "the rest of faith," which is also the title of his most important holiness book (1873). A firm advocate of divine healing, Earle taught at **Charles Cullis**'s Faith Training School in Boston. At the time of his death, he had been a member of the famed Tremont Temple Baptist Church in Boston for more than 50 years. His son, James H. Earle, was a prominent holiness publisher. W.C.K.

EDWARDS, DAVID (b. North Wales, 5 May 1816; d. Baltimore, Maryland, 6 June 1876). United Brethren in Christ (UB) author and bishop. At an early age, Edwards emigrated to America with his family and settled in Ohio. While employed in a woolen mill, he was converted at a UB meeting in Lancaster, Ohio, and responded to the call to preach in 1836. Although plagued by ill health and forced to return to private employment on three occasions, he was elected editor of the *Religious Telescope* by the General Conference of the UB in 1845. Deeply influenced by the writings of **Thomas C. Upham**, Edwards experienced **entire sanctification** in 1845. After declining reelection to the office of editor in 1849, he was elected bishop and was reelected six times, serving until his death. He was an antislavery spokesman and holiness advocate, a well-published literary figure in his church, the editor of church publications, a pioneer leader in overseas mission work, and a founder of Otterbein College. J.S.O.

EHLERS, W. C. (b. Nicollet County, Minnesota, 27 March 1868; d. Minneapolis, Minnesota, 22 September 1916). Methodist Episcopal Church (MEC) and Northwestern Holiness Association minister and evangelist. Raised in a Lutheran family that occasionally worshipped with an Evangelical Association congregation, Ehlers was converted in a Baptist Sunday school in 1885. After experiencing a number of economic reversals as a worker and farmer in Minnesota and South Dakota, he renewed his Christian commitment in an MEC church at Bristol, South Dakota, in 1895. In 1897, he experienced **entire sanctification** during services conducted by **Henry Clay Morrison** in Mitchell, South Dakota. Granted a local preacher's license by the MEC in 1898, Ehlers served several congregations in North Dakota and South Dakota (1898–1907) and served as secretary of the North Dakota Holiness Association (1906–1907). In 1907, the North Dakota Conference rejected Ehlers's request to be appointed a conference evangelist. Following his refusal to accept an appointment by the conference, Ehlers was expelled by the North Dakota Holiness Association.

Teaming with fellow holiness evangelist C. A. Thompson, Ehlers embarked on an aggressive program of evangelism. In 1908, he organized his followers as the North Dakota County Holiness Association. In 1909, as the movement expanded beyond the boundaries of North Dakota, it was reorganized as the Northwestern Holiness Association and, after 1920, the **Holiness Methodist Church**. Ehlers and Thompson were named general superintendents. In 1913, Ehlers became sole general superintendent. Although Ehlers was opposed to the formation of another denomination, the Northwestern Holiness Association ordained ministers and established holiness chapels. At the time of his death, the association had 32 ministers and 30 deaconesses, primarily in the Dakotas and Minnesota. A pulpit orator and polemical writer, Ehlers was the author of a controversial and entertaining interpretation of world history, *Holiness and Its Opposition* (1915), the climax of which was the organization of the Northwestern Holiness Association and Ehlers's years of conflict with Upper Midwestern Methodism. Among his other works is an autobiography, *From Workshop to Pulpit* (1908). W.C.K.

ELLYSON, E(dgar) P(ainter) (b. Damascus, Ohio, 4 August 1869; d. Kansas City, Missouri, 24 August 1954). Quaker and **Church of the Nazarene** (CN) evangelist, educator, writer, and general superintendent. **ELLYSON, (MARY) EMILY** (b. Dunham, Quebec, 12 August 1869; d. Vicksburg, Michigan, 26 June 1943). Quaker and CN evangelist, educator, and writer. The Ellysons zealously promoted the holiness revival in the Ohio and Iowa Yearly Meetings of Friends and contributed frequent articles to the *American Friend*. In 1898, they founded the Christian Workers Training School in LaGrande, Iowa. They joined the CN two years after E. P. Ellyson became president of Peniel University (Greenville, Texas) in 1906. Emily was ordained at the church's Second General Assembly (1908), which elected E. P. Ellyson one of three general superintendents. E. P. Ellyson served one term, declining reconsideration in 1911. He was elected to the office again in 1915 and declined that election. He was subsequently president of Nazarene University (Pasadena, California) and Bresee College (Hutchinson, Kansas) and taught religion at other CN schools. Emily Ellyson taught in the religion departments of various schools. The Ellysons wrote Sunday school curricula for many years. In 1923, E. P. Ellyson became the first executive secretary of the CN Department of Church Schools, serving until 1948. R.S.I.

EMMANUEL ASSOCIATION (EmA). The EmA was organized in 1937 by **Ralph Finch** whose controversial teaching that **entire sanctification** was gained only after an extended period of "dying to self" had been deemed heretical by **Pilgrim Holiness Church** (PHC) leaders. Centered in Colorado Springs (where the EmA operated People's Bible College into the early 1990s), southern Indiana, and northwest Ohio, the EmA has experienced little growth. From the beginning, it suffered considerable internal dissent. In the early 1940s, the Immanuel Association, a group primarily located in southern Indiana, separated from the EmA. In the late 1980s, the Colorado Springs congregation, now known as Grace Tabernacle Church, separated from more moderate congregations in the Midwest. The EmA publishes the *Emmanuel Herald* from its headquarters in Logansport, Indiana, and has missions in Guatemala. It is opposed to owning and viewing television and encourages its members not to take part in warfare. By the 1990s, it had fewer than 400 members in the United States. W.C.K.

ENTIRE SANCTIFICATION. Distinctive expression used by the holiness movement to describe a religious experience that completes the process of salvation begun in conversion. Among the other expressions that are used for the same experience are "Christian perfection," "full salvation," "perfect love," "the second blessing," "the rest of faith," "the **baptism of the Holy Spirit**," and "the higher Christian life." In the thought of **John Wesley**, "perfect love," the term he preferred, implied the consistent intent to love God and neighbor. During the 19th century, it was primarily understood experientially and defended in periodicals and books that were primarily compilations of holiness testimonies and biographies. In addition to being understood as an experience, it was also understood as a way of life. This was especially evident in the portions of the holiness movement that were rooted in the areas of New England migration such as Upstate New York, the Western Reserve of Ohio, Michigan, and portions of Illinois, Wisconsin, and Iowa. It sees its clearest expression among members of the **Wesleyan Methodist Church**, **Free Methodist Church**, and **Salvation Army**, and among **Oberlin perfectionists**. A third 19th-century reading, closely associated with the first, interpreted the experience of full salvation as mystical union with Christ. This is found most clearly in the writings of **Thomas C. Upham**.

In the last century, as the holiness movement had evolved from a popular movement associated with noted evangelists and **camp meetings** into a network of churches, colleges, and even a scholarly society, the **Wesleyan Theological Society**, it increasingly understood entire sanctification as a doctrine to be defended. This natural tendency has been augmented by theological conflicts with Pentecostalism, which insisted that its adherents speak in unknown tongues, and with **Keswick** adherents, who saw the higher Christian life more as an experience of empowerment than heart purity. Although many holiness movement figures combined elements of these three understandings, one needs only compare the experiential and mystical vision of **G. D. Watson**, the ethical vision of **Mary Alice Tenney**, and the doctrinal vision, albeit sprinkled with an emphasis on experience, of **H. Orton Wiley** to appreciate the fact that the nature of full salvation remains contested. W.C.K.

ESCHATOLOGY. Term derived from the Greek word *eschatos* that refers to Christian teaching concerning the personal destiny of believers, the second coming of Christ, and the end of the world. In the holiness tradition, as in Christianity at large, it has often produced dubious speculation and considerable controversy. Concerning personal destiny, the holiness tradition has emphasized the reality of divine judgment, with the righteous inheriting eternal life and sinners eternal separation from God. A significant minority within the tradition, including such prominent figures as **Hannah Whitall Smith** and **Isaac Joyce**, has advocated the final salvation of all. In a similar manner, the holiness tradition's view of the second coming of Christ and the consummation of history has shown considerable diversity. In the 19th century, most advocates of the experience of full salvation believed that Christ would return after God's reign had been established on earth. Known as *postmillennialism,* this view was held by such diverse holiness figures as **Charles G. Finney**, most Methodist Episcopal Church advocates of Christian perfection, and such early denominational holiness leaders as **Phineas Bresee**, **A. M. Hills**, **Harmon Baldwin**, **John Paul**, and **J. Kenneth Grider**. In the early 20th century, *premillennialism,* the view that Christ would return and establish his kingdom on Earth, became the dominant eschatological view in the holiness movement. Among the most important early champions of this new vision were **G. D. Watson**, **W. B. Godbey**, **Seth C. Rees**, **L. L. Pickett**, and **Henry Clay Morrison**. Although such groups as the **Church of God (Anderson)** rejected elements of speculative eschatology, premillennialism remained the dominant vision of the last things into the 1970s. In recent years, the normative premillennial vision has been vigorously attacked by leading holiness theologians, including **H. Ray Dunning**, and it even seems to be losing ground among the holiness laity. W.C.K.

ESHER, JOHN JACOB (b. Alsatia, France, 11 December 1823; d. Naperville, Illinois, 16 April 1901). Prominent international leader of the Evangelical Association (EA). As a child, John Esher (also Escher) immigrated to America with his family and settled in Des Plaines, Illinois. Here he was converted at 11 and was licensed by the EA to preach in 1845. He served as a pioneer circuit preacher in the Midwest; presiding elder; editor of the *Christliche Botschafter*, a denominational journal that was a strong holiness organ; college founder; and bishop, elected in 1863 and reelected quadrennially until his death. He organized the first missionary conferences in Germany and Asia for the EA. A strong disciplinarian and tireless preacher and administrator, he was a fervent defender and advocate of the doctrine of **entire sanctification**, as found in the doctrines and discipline of his church. He was also the early leader of the majority party in the division of his denomination that occurred in 1891. Esher published a catechism for his church and an extensive three-volume work of systematic theology from a Wesleyan holiness perspective, *Die Christliche Theologie* (1899–1901), that was extensively used in North America and in Germany. J.S.O.

EVANGELICAL CHRISTIAN CHURCH (ECC). The ECC was founded as the Heavenly Recruits, later Heavenly Recruit Association, in 1882 in Philadelphia, Pennsylvania, by a recently converted hardware salesman, L. Frank Haas (1856–1953). By 1884, an estimated 1,400 people had been converted in Heavenly Recruit street meetings. In 1894, after Haas and his Philadelphia congregation separated from the movement, the church was reorganized as the Holiness Christian Association with **C. W. Ruth** as presiding elder. In 1897, it established a separate conference in the Midwest and a new name, the Holiness Christian Church (HCC). In 1908, C. W. Ruth and half of the congregations in Pennsylvania joined the Pentecostal Church of the Nazarene (see **Church of the Nazarene**). In 1919, about 50 congregations located in the Midwest joined the International Apostolic Holiness Union (see **Pilgrim Holiness Church**). Beginning in 1935, under the leadership of Ira W. Bechtel, the HCC began a period of extended growth. In 1937, it founded a periodical, the *Holiness Christian Messenger,* now the *Christian Messenger*. By 1970, the number of churches in the United States had more than doubled, while missions had been established in Jamaica and Nigeria. In 1976, the HCC was renamed the ECC. In Jamaica, the church has benefited from the outstanding leadership of A. B. Vassel (d. 1975) and his son Sam Vassel. Currently more than half of the ECC's 3,000 members are located in Jamaica. As of 1999, Kenneth W. Wooten, pastor of the ECC's Keymar, Maryland, church, was its general superintendent. The ECC is a member of the **Christian Holiness Partnership**. W.C.K.

EVANGELICAL CHURCH OF NORTH AMERICA (ECNA). The ECNA was organized in June 1968 by representatives of 51 congregations of the Pacific Northwest Conference of the Evangelical United Brethren (EUB) who opposed the merger of the EUB and the Methodist Church (MC). They were later joined by 23 congregations of the Montana Conference of the EUB and, in 1969, by the **Holiness Methodist Church**. With these additions, the ECNA had about 7,000 members in the United States. Although nationally the EUB and MC shared a common heritage and were quite similar, in the Northwest, EUB congregations were far more conservative than their MC neighbors. Deeply committed to personal conversion and **entire sanctification** as a second work of grace, the ECNA was from its beginning an active leader of the National Holiness Association (see **Christian Holiness Partnership** [CHP]) in the Pacific Northwest. The early leaders of the ECNA were former EUB district superintendents George K. Millen (b. 1918) and V. A. Ballantyne (b. 1916). In 1977, the Wesleyan Covenant Church (see **Metropolitan Church Association**), with several congregations and extensive mission work in Brownsville, Texas, and Mexico and among the Navajo Indians in New Mexico, joined the ECNA. Other missions are operated in Bolivia (see **Holiness Methodist Church**), where the ECNA has more than 200 congregations. The ECNA actively supports the work of the Oriental Missionary Society (see **OMS International**) and **World Gospel Mission**. In the United States, as of 1999, the ECNA had about 15,000 members. In 1993, the ECNA's Canadian General Conference and its 47 churches and approximately 4,000 members merged with the **Missionary Church** Canadian congregations to form the Evangelical Missionary Church. The ECNA publishes the *Challenge* from its Minneapolis, Minnesota, headquarters and is a member of the CHP. In 1999, its general superintendent was John F. Sills. W.C.K.

EVANGELICAL FRIENDS INTERNATIONAL (EFI). Organization originally established in 1965 by four independent Quaker Yearly

Meetings to cooperate in missions, publications, education, social concerns, youth work, and evangelism. At that time, it was called the Evangelical Friends Alliance (EFA). It grew out of an earlier renewal movement among individual Quaker leaders with fundamentalist and Wesleyan/holiness leanings within the Friends United Meeting (then known as the Five Years Meeting, established in 1902 to unite Orthodox Quakers). These Evangelical Quaker leaders were determined to challenge the modernist trends they perceived to be undermining the Orthodox faith within the Society of Friends. They organized a loosely knit movement known as the Association of Evangelical Friends (AEF), which met biennially from 1947 until 1970. The origins of this movement can be traced to 1927 when a group of 11 Quaker Evangelicals met in a YMCA in Cheyenne, Wyoming, to discuss ways to counter theological liberalism within the Society of Friends. The convener of the group was **Edward Mott** of Oregon, a leading Quaker fundamentalist voice. These Quaker leaders targeted organizations supported by mainline Quakers, such as the American Friends Service Committee, the Friends Committee on National Legislation, and the National Council of Churches, as symbols of liberalizing trends within Quakerdom.

The AEF was formally organized in 1956 in Denver, Colorado. Its two primary objectives were to promote revival throughout Quakerdom and to promote evangelization of the world. Its theological positions reflected those of the National Holiness Association (see **Christian Holiness Partnership** [CHP]). In its early years, members of the association exhibited a strong defensive and separatist stance against the prevailing liberalism within Quakerism. In later years, the movement adopted a restorationist stance, seeing itself as the true bearer of the evangelical and missionary vision of early Quakerism. The AEF published a journal, *Concern*, from 1959 to 1966, edited by Arthur Roberts, a professor of religion at George Fox College in Newberg, Oregon. The journal served to articulate a credible and thoughtful Quaker evangelical position. The AEF became a catalyst for the establishment of the EFA in 1964 (formally approved in 1965) to promote unity, efficiency, and cooperation among four independent Evangelical Yearly Meetings.

The original participating Yearly Meetings (YMs) were Ohio, the oldest of the four (established in 1913; now Eastern Region); Kansas (1872; now Mid-America); Oregon (1893; now Northwest); and Rocky Mountain (set off from Nebraska in 1957). All of these YMs were strongly influenced by the holiness revival and its **camp meetings**, the NHA, and the Bible School movement and were products of the westward migration of Quaker farming families in the 19th century. In 1996, Southwest YM (originally California YM) changed its affiliation from the theologically diverse Friends United Meeting to EFI.

The EFI holds membership in the National Association of Evagelicals and the CHP. The EFI has its own statement of faith, a primary tenet being the inspiration of the Bible as the rule of faith and the Holy Spirit as true interpreter. The EFI statement of faith includes in its position on salvation, a doctrine of sanctification with Wesleyan/holiness overtones blended with a traditional Quaker understanding. The EFI statement describes the experience of sanctification as "the work of God's grace by which affections of men are purified and exalted to the living Christ." This is accomplished by the **baptism with the Holy Spirit**, which cleanses the heart and begins a process of continuous discipline into paths of holiness. The article on sanctification of its predecessor, the AEF, included a more explicitly Wesleyan holiness position.

In 1989, the EFA changed its name to EFI and was divided into three regions: North America, Latin America, and Africa and Asia. EFI North America was joined by the Alaska YM. As of 1999, the EFI North America Region had an estimated membership of 36,382 in the United States and, largely as a result of missions in Latin America, Africa, and Asia, 68,910 members outside the United States. C.S.

EVANGELICAL METHODIST CHURCH (EMC). Founded in Memphis, Tennessee, in 1946 by former Methodist Church (MC) pastor J. H. Hamblen of Abilene, Texas. Theological conservatives, Hamblen and his followers were opposed to what they believed were the liberal trends of the MC. Although the church experienced rapid growth, it suffered a serious split in 1952 when W. W. Beckbill (d. 1974), who opposed Hamblen's holiness emphasis, organized his followers into the more fundamentalistic Evangelical Methodist Church of America. In 1960, about 400 members of a holiness splinter group in the California Yearly Meeting of Friends, the Evangel Church, joined the EMC; in 1962, the **People's Methodist Church** joined. In 1957, E. B. Vargas, head of the Mexican Evangelistic Mission that had been organized in 1926, brought that body into the EMC. The EMC supports the mission work of the Oriental Missionary Society (see **OMS International**) and **World Gospel Mission**. It currently has about 9,000 members in over 120 churches in the United States. It publishes the *Evangelical*

Methodist Viewpoint. Its headquarters is in Indianapolis, Indiana, and it is a member of the **Christian Holiness Partnership**. In 1999, Jack Wease was the general superintendent. W.C.K.

– F –

FAIRBAIRN, CHARLES V. (b. Ventnor, Ontario, Canada, 22 November 1890; d. Eskridge, Kansas, 20 February 1970). **Free Methodist Church** (FMC) bishop and evangelist. Fairbairn was educated in the public schools of Ontario and received college training at Queen's University. His career in Christian ministry began in the Methodist Church of Canada in 1913. In 1918, he joined the FMC and served both as an evangelist and as pastor in the East Ontario Conference. He was elected district elder in 1924 and entered General Conference evangelistic work in 1927.

In 1927, he moved with his family to McPherson, Kansas, where he served as pastor of the FMC church from 1932 to 1936. Later he served the Kansas Conference as district elder. In 1938, he was elected as bishop and served five four-year terms, retiring in 1961. During his episcopal tenure, he served as chairman of the Commission on Evangelism and as chairman of the Commission on Christian Education.

Bishop Fairbairn was known as a fiery and accomplished preacher. Besides many magazine articles, he wrote a number of books, including *Secret of True Revival* (1929); *Purity and Power* (1930), an important critique of the three-blessing theology as taught by the **Holiness Movement Church**; *Tarry Ye* (1943); *What We Believe* (1957); and an autobiography, *I Call to Remembrance* (1960). L.D.S.

FINCH, RALPH GOODRICH (b. Terrace Park, Ohio, 17 July 1881; d. Tolesboro, Kentucky, 23 July 1950). Methodist Episcopal Church (MEC), **Pilgrim Holiness Church** (PHC), and **Emmanuel Association** pastor, missionary, and evangelist. Raised in poverty, Finch was converted in 1904 and experienced **entire sanctification** while a student at **God's Bible School** in 1906. Although a brief pastorate in an MEC circuit in Aberdeen, Ohio, resulted in revival and considerable growth, Finch was not given a second appointment. Following several years as an itinerant evangelist, he was asked to accompany MEC evangelist James M. Taylor on a missionary trip to the West Indies and South America in the spring of 1912. Impressed by Finch's piety and compassion, Taylor asked him to assume direction of a string of missions that Taylor had established in the West Indies. Under Finch's leadership, these missions became the foundation for the successful PHC mission in the Caribbean.

Although ill heath forced Finch to return to the United States in 1920, his success in the mission field resulted in his appointment as general missionary superintendent of the PHC in 1922, a position he held until 1934. In 1933, Finch accepted a call to became pastor of a PHC congregation in Colorado Springs, Colorado. His conservative stand on dress and unguarded attacks on the wealthy, which seemed to have played well on the mission field, made him an increasingly controversial figure in the PHC. Convinced that much holiness teaching was sentimental and shallow, Finch insisted that holiness experience often consisted in a slow "dieing to self." It was this so-called death route teaching that led to his expulsion from the PHC in 1936. Organizing his followers into the Emmanuel Association, Finch served as general superintendent, pastor of the Colorado Springs congregation (1936–1945), and editor of the church's periodical, the *Emmanuel Herald*. He died while in prayer at the Hickory Grove **Camp Meeting**, Tolesboro, Kentucky. W.C.K.

FINNEY, CHARLES GRANDISON (b. Warren, Connecticut, 29 August 1792; d. Oberlin, Ohio, 16 August 1875). Presbyterian and Congregational evangelist, pastor, educator, and author. Following a dramatic conversion experience in 1821 in Adams, New York, where he was in preparation to become a lawyer, Finney began studying theology under the direction of Presbyterian pastor George W. Gale. Following his ordination in 1823, Finney was hired as a home missionary by the Female Missionary Society of the Western District. Igniting a series of highly publicized revivals in western New York, Finney's passionate preaching and use of controversial, although apparently effective, "new measures"—such as extended, or "protracted," meetings and allowing women to pray publicly, often for the conversions of their husbands and sons—angered not only such notorious enemies of revivals as Universalists and Unitarians but even Yale-educated clergy such as Lyman Beecher and Asahel Nettleton.

From 1827 to 1832, Finney took his controversial revivalism to such urban centers as Rochester, New York City, Philadelphia, and Boston. In part funded by Arthur and Lewis Tappan, Finney served as a Presbyterian and later Congregational pastor in New York City (1832–1837) and as pastor of the First Congregational Church in Oberlin, Ohio (1837–1872). He served as professor of theology (1835–1851) and president (1851–1866) of Oberlin College.

A product of the so-called burned-over district of western New York, Finney shared that region's twin commitments to revivalism and social reform. An important abolitionist, Finney was one of the founders of the Ohio Anti-slavery Society and an advocate of expanded roles for women. Passionately egalitarian, Finney's last crusade against oath-bound fraternal orders was rooted in their practice of denying membership to African Americans, women, and people with disabilities.

Although Finney is rightly honored as the father of American revivalism and his *Lectures on Revivals of Religion* (1835) has remained the standard revival textbook, at Oberlin he emerged as a gifted teacher and theologian. Skillfully integrating such popular emphases of the Edwardsian theological heritage as freedom of the will, disinterested benevolence, the moral government of God, and the simplicity of moral action with a modified Wesleyan understanding of Christian perfection, Finney's eclectic theology, although remaining controversial, was a potent shaper of American evangelical culture. In Finney's hands, **entire sanctification** consisted in the consecration of one's entire being to God. As Finney insisted, all acts must be performed in a spirit of entire devotion to God. As might be expected, such an emphasis on duty and law instead of grace, while stimulating moral idealism and social action, led to repeated charges of legalism and Pelagianism, even among Methodists. Although Finney was particularly critical of the sentimentalism, experiential emphasis, and a perceived lack of ethical vigor in American Methodist holiness teaching, his holiness teaching took deep root among antislavery Methodists, such as those in **Wesleyan Methodist Church** and **Free Methodist Church**. In spite of his criticisms of Methodist holiness teaching, Finney was a personal friend of **Walter** and **Phoebe Palmer**. Among Finney's most important works are *Lectures on Systematic Theology* (1878) and an autobiography, recently published as *The Memoirs of Charles G. Finney: The Completely Restored Text* (1989). W.C.K.

FIRE BAPTIZED HOLINESS CHURCH (WESLEYAN). *See* BIBLE HOLINESS CHURCH.

FITKIN, SUSAN NORRIS (b. Ely, Quebec, 31 March 1870; d. Oakland, California, 18 October 1951). Quaker and **Church of the Nazarene** (CN) evangelist and missionary society president. Fitkin was born to

Quaker parents active in the temperance reform movement. She entered evangelistic work and attended Friends Bible Institute in Cleveland, Ohio. After serving pastorates in New England, she returned to evangelism, marrying revivalist Abram Fitkin, later a Wall Street financier, in 1896. They joined the Association of Pentecostal Churches of America, and she helped organize its women to support missions. After the mergers that created the CN, Fitkin played a central role in organizing its Women's Missionary Society, serving as its executive secretary (1915–1948). The Fitkins financed four hospitals in memory of their son, Raleigh, including a children's wing at Yale University Hospital and the Raleigh Fitkin Memorial Hospital in Swaziland. Susan Fitkin's writings include *Holiness and Missions* (1940), a missiology; and an autobiography, *Grace Much More Abounding*. R.S.I.

FLEXON, RICHARD GANT (b. Williamstown, New Jersey, 18 June 1895; d. Salisbury, Maryland, 19 April 1982). **Pilgrim Holiness Church** (PHC) and **Wesleyan Church** (WC) minister, district superintendent, evangelist, educator, and administrator. Although raised in a Methodist home, Flexon was educated at Greensboro Bible and Literary School. He entered the ministry of the International Apostolic Holiness Union (IAHU; see PHC) in 1915. Following four years as a pastor in McKeesport, Pennsylvania, Flexon accepted a call to pastor an IAHU congregation at Shackleford, Virginia. While at Shackleford, he was named president of Beulah Holiness Academy and was appointed the first district superintendent of the Virginia District of the PHC. When the economic crisis of the 1930s forced the closing of Beulah Holiness Academy in 1931, Flexon was appointed district superintendent of the Pennsylvania District of the PHC. In 1938, he was appointed assistant secretary for foreign missions and subsequently served in several other positions with the PHC, including secretary for foreign missions (1946–1958), general superintendent (1958–1962), and member of the General Board (1930–1964). He was president of Central Pilgrim College in Bartlesville, Oklahoma (1962–1964), and an adviser and fund-raiser for **God's Bible School** (1964–1981). He was a regular contributor to the *Pilgrim Holiness Advocate* and was cofounder and, for a time, coeditor of the *American Holiness Journal*. An evangelist of note, Flexon had an estimated 120,000 seekers at the estimated 442 revivals and 154 **camp meetings** he conducted. He received an honorary doctorate from Eastern Pilgrim College in Allentown, Pennsylvania, in 1959. His autobiography, *In Christ, Seeking the Lost*, was published by God's Revivalist Press in 1981. W.C.K.

FLORIDA EVANGELISTIC ASSOCIATION. *See* FRENCH, H. ROBB.

FOOTE, JULIA A. J. (b. Schenectady, New York, 1823; d. 22 November 1900). African Methodist Episcopal (AME) and African Methodist Church, Zion (AMEZ), evangelist. The daughter of ex-slaves who had purchased their freedom, Foote was educated in rural schools near Schenectady. Following her conversion in 1838 and subsequent experience of **entire sanctification**, she joined the AME Church. In 1841, she married a sailor and relocated to Boston where she joined an AMEZ congregation. Foote's forceful holiness teaching angered her parents, husband, and pastor. Expelled from her home congregation in 1844, she began an itinerant evangelistic ministry. For several years, she conducted an active ministry in New England, the Middle Atlantic states, Michigan, and Ohio. In 1851, the loss of her voice and increased responsibilities for the care of her ailing mother forced her into temporary retirement in Cleveland. Experiencing divine healing in 1869, Foote resumed her evangelistic career. In part through contact with Cleveland holiness publisher **T. K. Doty**, Foote emerged as one of the most popular evangelists of the 1870s and 1880s. In 1878, an estimated 5,000 people heard her address a holiness encampment in Lodi, Ohio. Her 1879 autobiography, *A Brand Plucked from the Burning*, went through two editions. She attended the Western Union Holiness Convention in Jacksonville, Illinois, in 1880 and endorsed the call for the General Holiness Assembly shortly before her death. W.C.K.

FORD, JACK (b. Hull, England, 21 October 1908; d. Keighley, England, 25 September 1980). Calvary Holiness Church (CHC) and **Church of the Nazarene** minister and educator. Born into a Church of England home, Ford was converted in 1927 and joined the local International Holiness Mission (IHM). In 1929, he met **Maynard James** and the IHM trekking party, and his friendship with James remained unbroken until his death. Having studied at **Cliff College** under the principalship of **Samuel Chadwick**, he worked at the IHM headquarters in London and later pastored IHM churches. In 1934, he joined with Maynard James, **Leonard Ravenhill**, and Clifford Filer in leaving the IHM and founding the CHC. From 1950 to 1954, he was principal of the CHC's Beech Lawn Bible College in Lancashire and later tutor at the Nazarene Theological College in Manchester and principal (1966–1973). A graduate of London University, he was a very able scholar, especially in biblical languages, and published *What the Holiness People Believe* (1954) and *In the Steps of John Wesley: The Church of the Nazarene in Britain* (1968). Widely known for his gracious Christian spirit, Ford was an exegetical preacher of power and persuasion and did much to recommend and promote Wesleyan holiness teaching by his scholarship, writing, and influence. A collection of his papers is located at the Nazarene archives in Kansas City, Missouri. H.M.

FOSTER, RANDOLPH SINKS (b. Williamsburg, Ohio, 22 February 1820; d. Newton Center, Massachusetts, 1 May 1903). Methodist Episcopal Church (MEC) pastor, educator, and bishop. A gifted "boy preacher," Foster dropped out of Augusta (Kentucky) College in 1837 to join the Ohio Conference of the MEC. He was ordained a deacon in 1839 and an elder in 1841. He was noted as a skilled pulpit orator and an able defender of Methodist distinctives. His 1849 book, *Objections to Calvinism*, which was first delivered as a series of sermons while Foster was pastor of Cincinnati's influential Wesley Chapel, was hailed as the definitive American Wesleyan critique of Calvinism. In 1850, Foster was named pastor of New York City's Mulberry Street Methodist Church. With the exception of a three-year term as president of Northwestern University in Evanston, Illinois, Foster served the next 18 years in New York as pastor of some of Methodism's most important churches, such as Greene Street, Trinity, and Sing Sing. In 1868, he was named professor of theology at Drew University where he became president in 1870. He was elected bishop of the MEC in 1872.

In 1851, Foster published *The Nature and Blessedness of Christian Purity*, the first of his books dedicated to the subject of Christian perfection. In 1869, Foster thoroughly revised the text and reissued it under a new name, *Christian Purity, or the Heritage of Faith*. Although continuing to affirm the Wesleyan doctrine of Christian perfection and maintaining close relationships with holiness adherents such as **Alfred Cookman**, Foster expressed reservations about certain features of the recently organized National Holiness Association (see **Christian Holiness Partnership**), such as the practice of creating special meetings outside the normal life of the church for the propagation of holiness teaching. In 1890, in his Merrick Lectures at Ohio Wesleyan University, "The Philosophy of Christian Experience" (which later appeared in book form), Foster continued to affirm that holiness, or "the perfecting of the soul in love," remained a distinct possibility for all God's children. Although still a popular speaker, in later life, Foster was troubled by charges that his views on the resurrection and afterlife were too dependent on Emanuel Swedenborg. In his last years, Foster devoted most of his time to his six-volume *Studies in Theology* (1892–1896). W.C.K.

FOWLER, CHARLES JOSEPH (b. Bristol, New Hampshire, 6 February 1845; d. West Newton, Massachusetts, 30 September 1919). Methodist Episcopal Church (MEC) minister, pastor, revivalist, editor, author, and president of the National Holiness Association (NHA; see **Christian Holiness Partnership**). Charles Fowler was converted during an 1869 revival in Bristol and began to preach shortly thereafter. For 11 years, he served as a lay evangelist in communities throughout New Hampshire and Massachusetts.

In 1883, Fowler joined the New Hampshire Conference of the MEC and served pastorates in several cities. In 1885, he claimed the experience of **entire sanctification** under the ministry of Deacon George Morse, a well-known New England Baptist holiness advocate. Fowler quickly became a leading proponent of the doctrine of holiness in his conference and by 1890 had become active in the National **Camp Meetings**. Three years later, **William McDonald** recommended him to succeed McDonald as president of the NHA, which he did in 1894. In 1895, **Taylor University** awarded him an honorary doctor of divinity degree.

Fowler was the ideal man to head the NHA. He was a Methodist revivalist who reminded people of both McDonald and **John Inskip**. He took a conservative stance on issues such as "come-outism," yet he strongly supported independent holiness ministries. In 1897, the NHA passed several resolutions that forbade the preaching of the doctrines of healing and premillennialism at National Camp Meetings, and they called the holiness movement back to its original mission to spread scriptural holiness. These resolutions led opponents to form the International Apostolic Holiness Union, later the **Pilgrim Holiness Church**.

Fowler traveled extensively promoting the work of the NHA in churches and camp meetings around the nation. The organization grew rapidly under his leadership, and, by 1911, membership topped 1,000. In 1910, the association organized the National Holiness Missionary Society, which grew to become an independent organization known today as **World Gospel Mission**.

Fowler wrote extensively. He served as contributing editor of the *Christian Witness*, and his articles, sermons, and reports appeared regularly. He also wrote several tracts and books, including *Judas* (1896), *Back to Pentecost* (1900), *Christian Unity* (1907), *Thoughts on Prayer* (1912), and *Chair Talks on Perfection* (1918). In 1919, Fowler had charge of the National Camp Meetings at University Park, Iowa, and Mooers, New York. After his death, the NHA erected a monument at his grave to honor his many years of service, and the Missionary Society erected a new church in Tung Changfu, China, naming it the C. J. Fowler Memorial Chapel in honor of his worldwide vision. K.O.B.

FREE METHODIST CHURCH OF NORTH AMERICA (FMC). Church founded in 1860 by a union of laity from northern Illinois under the leadership of **John Wesley Redfield**, who had been expelled from the Methodist Epsicopal Church (MEC), and ministers under the leadership of **B. T. Roberts**, who had been expelled from the Genesee Conference of the MEC. Roberts emerged as the dominant personality in the movement, serving as general superintendent (1860–1893); editor of the movement's unofficial publication, the *Earnest Christian;* principal evangelist, and apologist. In Roberts's words, the goals of the FMC were "to maintain the Biblical standard of Christianity, and preach the Gospel to the poor." A distinct product of the so-called burned-over district of western New York, the FMC was committed to abolitionism, anti-Masonry, and the plethora of other reform movements characteristic of upstate New York.

During Roberts's lifetime, the church experienced steady growth, primarily in the areas of New England migration such as western New York, the Western Reserve of Ohio, Michigan, parts of northern Illinois, southwestern Wisconsin, and Kansas. In 1890, membership in the United States stood at 22,000; by 1916, it had become a transcontinental denomination with 35,000 members. As the literal heirs of the New England Puritans, Free Methodists were noted for their asceticism, even by Victorian standards; deep commitment to education; demonstrative, although instrument-free, worship; and passion for evangelism and missions. In North America, the FMC has operated 17 colleges, including Roberts Wesleyan College, North Chili, New York (founded as Chili Seminary in 1866); Spring Arbor (Michigan) College (1873); Central Christian College, McPherson, Kansas (founded as Orleans Seminary, Orleans, Nebraska, 1884); Seattle (Washington) Pacific University (1891); Greenville (Illinois) College (1892); Los Angeles

(California) Pacific College (1903; now part of Azusa Pacific University); Lorne Park College, Port Credit, Ontario (1924–1966); and Wessington Springs (South Dakota) College (1887–1968).

Although traditionally a largely rural denomination, the FMC has been sponsoring **Salvation Army**–style missions among the urban poor since the ministry of Jane Dunning among African Americans in New York City during the 1860s, including the Olive Branch Mission in Chicago (1873). Although the FMC did not formally send its first foreign missionary until 1885, FMC member Ernest F. Ward began serving in India in 1880. The church established missions in India (1885), Portuguese East Africa (1885), South Africa (1891), Transvaal (1895), Japan (1895), China (1905), the Dominican Republic (1908), Brazil (1928), Rwanda (1935), Paraguay (1946), and the Philippines (1949). In North America, the FMC established missions among Appalachians in Kentucky; Japanese in Oregon, Washington, and California; Hispanics; African Americans; and Native Americans. The FMC currently has about 322,000 members outside North America, with the largest memberships being in the Congo, Rwanda, Egypt (founded by the **Holiness Movement Church**), South Africa, and Malawi.

As a denomination, the FMC has combined a tradition of outstanding educated and socially concerned leaders such as Roberts, **W. T. Hogue**, Gilbert James, **Leslie R. Marston**, **David McKenna**, **Mary Alice Tenney**, and **Howard A. Snyder** with equally socially concerned but emotional evangelists such as Redfield, **Vivian A. Dake**, and **E. E. Shelhamer**. Under the leadership of Leslie R. Marston, who was the church's dominant leader from the 1930s to 1970s, the FMC increasingly emerged as an important leader in the neo-Evangelicalism of the post–World War II era. The FMC has also been active in the **Christian Holiness Partnership** and the World Methodist Council. The FMC has published a periodical, the *Free Methodist,* now *Light and Life,* since 1868. Among its most notable editors have been B. T. Roberts (1886–1890), W. T. Hogue (1894–1903), J. T. Logan (1907–1923), and C. L. Howland (1931–1955). Its publishing house and denominational headquarters have been located in Chicago (1886–1935); Winona Lake, Indiana (1933–1992); and Indianapolis, Indiana (1992–present). Beginning in 1944, the FMC sponsored a weekly radio program, *The Light and Life Hour,* which by 1960 was heard on 135 radio stations in North America.

Even though evangelism has remained a stated objective for the church in this generation, total membership growth in North America has floundered, while overseas churches have grown at a rate to triple the U.S. membership in 1997. Along with other denominations, the FMC went through the throes of membership decline, financial crisis, organizational restructuring, decentralization of ministries, and diversification of churches, all at the same time. The FMC has shown significant gains along the eastern and western seaboards of the United States as well as in pockets across the country, especially in urban and ethnic ministries. At the end of 1996, its membership in the United States was approximately 74,000. As the FMC anticipates its ministry in the 21st century, it is guided by the expanded mission statement "to make known to all people everywhere God's call to wholeness through forgiveness and holiness in Jesus Christ and to invite into membership and equip for ministry all who respond in faith." In this mission, the FMC has such strengths as an unswerving commitment to the doctrine of holiness; worldwide support for a global church through the Free Methodist World Conference; a working history of shared governance between clergy and laity at all levels of church organization; a strong, growing, and loyal system of Christian higher education; a long-standing record of tithing; a story of growing churches in selective pockets, especially in new church plants appealing to young adults and to ethnic and racial minorities in urban settings; and pastoral leadership dedicated to evangelistic outreach. D.L.M.

FRENCH, H(amilton) ROBB (b. Denver, Colorado, 26 December 1891; d. Jupiter, Florida, 24 January 1985). **Wesleyan Methodist Church** (WMC) and **Bible Methodist Connection** minister, evangelist, and administrator. The son of R. A. French, a pioneer WMC minister in Kansas and Alabama, French was educated at Miltonvale (Kansas) College and the Missionary Training Institute, now Trevecca Nazarene College, in Nashville, Tennessee. Following graduation in 1915, he was the founding pastor of the Tuscaloosa (Alabama) WMC. In 1919, he married Geraldine Trusher, a teacher at Kingswood (Kentucky) Holiness College. Together they founded a WMC congregation in Birmingham, Alabama, serving as pastors until 1929. Serving as a full-time evangelist (1929–1976), French emerged as a sought-after interdenominational speaker. In 1946, sensing the need for a spiritual retreat center in Florida, the Frenches established the Florida Evangelistic Association (FEA) at Hobe Sound, Florida. During the next two decades, the FEA evolved into a series of ministries including the Sea

Breeze **Camp Meeting**, established in 1947; Hobe Sound Bible College, established in 1960; a local church; and a mission, which operated in Latin America, Africa, Asia, and Eastern Europe. In 1951, French was the inspiration behind the organization of the first **Inter-Church Holiness Convention** at which he was one of the principal speakers. In 1967, French was one of the organizers of the **National Association of Holiness Churches**, an organization that primarily provided ministerial credentials for evangelists and pastors of nondenominational churches. He was the author of *The Revival Secret* (1934). Noted in his later years for his militant anticommunism, French was the author of *The Rape of America* (1950s). W.C.K.

FRIENDS OF JESUS CHRIST (FJC). The FJC is the ministry of James and Paula McCusker of Farmington Falls, Maine. Following their conversion in the early 1970s while involved in the counterculture movements of the time, they established an intentional community in Maine. They sought to duplicate the experiences of the early Quakers through simplicity of dress, confrontational public witnessing, and the republication of early Quaker writings. Led into the experience of **entire sanctification** through reading the Garland Press Higher Life Series edited by **Donald W. Dayton**, the McCuskers began reprinting holiness literature while continuing to publicly confront the Farmington area with their understanding of the Christian way of life. In the process, like the early Quakers, they have achieved some local notoriety. W.C.K.

FUHRMAN, ELDON RALPH (b. Mound City, Missouri, 24 April 1918). Evangelical United Brethren and **Evangelical Church of North America** evangelist and educator. Converted in his teens and shortly thereafter entirely sanctified, Fuhrman earned his B.A. in 1942 from John Fletcher College (see **Vennard College**). After receiving a divinity degree from **Asbury Theological Seminary** in 1946, for the next five years he traveled widely in the United States and Canada in full-time evangelism. In 1951, Western Evangelical Seminary called Fuhrman to its faculty. On leave of absence from the seminary, he earned an S.T.M. at Biblical Seminary in New York, where he explored John Fletcher's writings. He secured his Ph.D. from the University of Iowa in 1963. His dissertation was a study of **John Wesley**'s theology of grace.

In September 1974, Fuhrman joined the founding faculty of **Wesley Biblical Seminary** in Jackson, Mississippi, becoming president in

1978. Retiring as president in 1985, he continued to teach until 1989. Fuhrman served as a board member of **World Gospel Mission** and Vennard College. The Christian Holiness Association (see **Christian Holiness Partnership**) chose him as "Holiness Exponent of the Year, 1993." D.R.R.

FUNDAMENTAL WESLEYAN SOCIETY. Organized in 1979. The founding resolution stated that within the holiness movement there had been a serious deviation from the scriptural teaching developed by **John Wesley** and early Methodist writers that had led to a shallow preaching of the new birth. As a result, confusion had developed concerning Christian experience that led many to profess salvation without victory over the power of sin or a direct witness of the Holy Spirit and others to profess **entire sanctification** without being made perfect in love. The founders, many of whom had been influenced by **A. J. Smith**, saw a need for a fellowship that would teach and promote scriptural holiness as taught by Wesley. Their statement of faith declares the inerrancy of Scripture; total depravity; the necessity of the new birth through the **baptism of the Holy Spirit** whereby the believer is delivered from the guilt and power of sin; that faith is a gift of God to all who truly repent and is always accompanied by the witness of the Spirit; that there is yet in the believer the "remains of sin," even after he or she has been born of the Spirit; and that the believer may be cleansed by the perfecting work of the Spirit. Membership in the society is open to anyone who agrees with the statement of faith. The society has published the *Arminian Magazine* since its inception and has concentrated on extending its influence through printing, including the publication of *The Hole in the Holiness Movement* by Victor Reasoner (1991). In 1995, the society established the Fundamental Wesleyan Bible Institute. V.R.

– G –

GADDIS, MERLE E(lmer) (b. near College Springs, Iowa, 21 December 1891; d. Fayette, Missouri, 16 January 1958). Methodist Episcopal Church (MEC) and Methodist Church (MC) historian. A graduate of Iliff School of Theology and the University of Denver, Gaddis served as an MEC minister in Colorado and, after graduation, taught rural sociology at Iliff (1926–1928). He entered the University of Chicago in the late 1920s where he studied with William Warren Sweet (1881–1959). In his Ph.D. dissertation, "Christian Perfectionism in America," Gaddis, following Sweet, argued that the holiness currents in U.S. history were largely the product of the American frontier and had been in decline since the 1840s. Gaddis did acknowledge that perfectionist currents continued to find large numbers of adherents among impoverished people in isolated rural communities and in the nation's urban ghettos. He believed that some of the fastest-growing holiness groups, such as the **Church of the Nazarene**, were rapidly losing their distinctly perfectionist heritage. At the time of his death, it was reported that Gaddis's dissertation had been the most requested Ph.D. dissertation at University of Chicago. From 1929 to 1956, he served on the faculty of Central Methodist College in Fayette, Missouri. W.C.K.

GAITHER, WILLIAM "BILL" (b. Alexandria, Indiana, 28 March 1936), and **GAITHER, GLORIA (SICKAL)** (b. Battle Creek, Michigan, 4 March 1942). Lyricists and authors. William "Bill" Gaither grew up in a **Church of the Nazarene** family and later attended Anderson College, where he graduated with a degree in English in 1959. Gloria Sickal was born into the family of a **Church of God (Anderson)** (CG[A]) minister. She also attended Anderson, earning a degree in English in 1962. The two met while teaching in Alexandria and were married in 1962. White gospel quartet music fascinated Bill Gaither, and as a teenager, he formed his own quartet and later sang locally with a brother and sister. He began writing songs in 1960. After their marriage, the Gaithers formed the Bill Gaither Trio with Bill's brother Danny. They became full-time gospel entertainers in 1968 and subsequently became among the most recognized gospel music artists in the United States, their work having won numerous Dove Awards and several Grammy Awards.

The Gaithers have written lyrics for some of the most popular gospel songs of the 1960s and 1970s, and Gloria has authored several best-selling devotional books, including *Let's Hide the Word* (1994) and *Let's Make a Memory* (1983), both coauthored with Shirley Dobson; and *What My Parents Did Right* (1991). Bill earned a reputation for developing new talent, often trained in the Gaither Vocal Band. He also founded and produces annual multiple-day festivals of conferences and worship services in Indianapolis, Indiana; Gatlinburg, Tennessee; and Charlotte, North Carolina. More recently, Gaither has produced a series of videotaped recordings featuring performers of the 1940s and 1950s. M.D.S.

GERIG, ZENAS (b. near Auburn, Indiana, 27 February 1927). **Missionary Church** (MiC) missionary, statesman, and leading catalyst for theological education and evangelical cooperation in the Caribbean. Gerig made a personal commitment to Christ at the age of eight. A graduate of Fort Wayne Bible College (1951), the Biblical Seminary in New York City (1954), and Indiana University (M.S., 1965; Ph.D., 1967), he became a **Missionary Church Association** missionary to Jamaica in 1954, pastoring the Emmanuel Missionary Church in Mandeville. In 1959, he was appointed founding principal of Jamaica Theological Seminary to which he gave firm leadership until 1983, when he turned his attention to founding the Caribbean Graduate School of Theology. Before retiring from active missionary service with World Partners of the MiC in 1997, he also helped to found, organize, or give leadership to some 32 other organizations, including the Jamaica Association of Evangelicals, the Evangelical Association of the Caribbean, the Caribbean Evangelical Theological Association, the International Council of Accrediting Agencies of the World Evangelical Fellowship, and the Congress on the Evangelization of the Caribbean. Among his many honors are a theological library named for him in Kingston, Jamaica, and an honorary D.D. degree from **Taylor University** (1998). T.P.E.

GILL, JOSHUA (b. Burnet, Vermont, 16 August 1834; d. Boston, Massachusetts, 25 September 1907). Methodist Epsicopal Church (MEC) and Evangelical Association (EA) pastor and publisher. Converted in the MEC at Hopkinton, Massachusetts, Gill was educated at the Newbury (Vermont) Academy and at Boston University Divinity School. In 1856, he was received into the Vermont Conference of the MEC and was admitted into the New England Conference in 1866. Although accounts differ concerning the time of his experience of **entire sanctification**, he was increasingly drawn into the holiness movement. In 1881, he became publisher of the *Advocate of Bible Holiness*, later the *Christian Witness*. He was for many years the treasurer of the Douglas (Massachusetts) **Camp Meeting** Association. He was a partner with National Holiness Association (see **Christian Holiness Partnership**) president **William McDonald** in the Boston publishing firm of McDonald and Gill. In 1887, he received a distinct religious experience that he believed was a final testimony that he had a "clean heart." Separating from the MEC in 1893, Gill joined the EA. He served as pastor of an EA congregation in Boston (1893–1900) and was presiding elder of the New England Conference of the EA (1894–1902). A poet and songwriter, Gill edited several songbooks. One of Gill's most notable edited works, *The Book of Hearts*, became the basis for one of the most influential religious tracts of the 20th century, *The Heart of Pak*, which played a decisive role in the evangelization of Korea and was widely used later in the United States. W.C.K.

GODBEY, W(illiam) B(axter) (b. Pulaski County, Kentucky, 3 June 1833; d. Cincinnati, Ohio, 12 September 1920). Methodist Episcopal Church, South (MECS) pastor and evangelist. W. B. Godbey was converted in a revival in 1849 and licensed to preach in 1853 by the Kentucky Conference of the MECS. He taught in rural schools and received a baccalaureate degree from Georgetown (Kentucky) College in 1859. He served as president of Harmonia College in Perryville, Kentucky (1859–1869), temporarily moving the college to Indiana during the Civil War. He was admitted to the pastorate on trial in 1866 and into full connection in 1868. He experienced **entire sanctification** in December 1868 and became a strong holiness advocate. From 1868 to 1869 he preached on the Perryville circuit. He served several pastoral appointments (1870–1872, 1877–1888) and was as presiding elder (1873–1876). He served as tract and book agent for the Maysville District of the MECS in 1882 and served as pastorate in Vanceburg, Kentucky, in 1883. In 1884, Godbey was listed in the minutes of the Kentucky Conference as being without an appointment. In 1883 and 1884, Godbey conducted revivals and promoted holiness in Kentucky and Missouri. In 1884, he carried his holiness revival campaigns to Texas where he exercised a wide-ranging ministry. In Godbey's revival at Alvarado in 1886, **Reuben A. ("Bud") Robinson** learned of the experience of entire sanctification for the first time. Godbey made four international tours (1895, 1899, 1905, 1912), spending much of his time in Palestine.

Godbey published more than 200 books and pamphlets on a wide range of topics, including doctrine, new religious movements, the Second Coming, and divine healing. He wrote several books and pamphlets on the Holy Land and gained an extensive reputation in the holiness movement as a Bible teacher and scholar. He recounted his travels in *Around the World, Garden of Eden, Latter-Day Prophecies and Missions* (1907). After 1895, he was a prominent exponent of premillennialism, and many of his publications were attempts to discern the "signs of the times" preceding the return of Christ. He produced a seven-volume *Commentary on the New Testament* (1887) and a translation of the New Testament, and was regarded in many circles as the

Greek scholar of the holiness movement. He wrote numerous columns for holiness periodicals, including *God's Revivalist*, achieving distinction for his Sunday school lessons.

He was influential in keeping Pentecostalism out of most of the holiness movement. He was also an articulate exponent of the "holiness or hell" position in the movement's eradicationist wing. His numerous friends included **Martin Wells Knapp**, founder of **God's Bible School**, and **Alma White**, who experienced conversion in a Kentucky schoolhouse revival in 1878 under Godbey's preaching. In later years, Godbey taught at God's Bible School. He has an enduring reputation as one of the most prominent evangelists of the early holiness movement but is also known for eccentricities in dress and lifestyle. Godbey is buried in Perryville, Kentucky. B.W.H.

GOD'S BIBLE SCHOOL (GBS). Now known as God's Bible School and College. GBS was founded in Cincinnati, Ohio, in the fall of 1900 by **Martin Wells Knapp**. Following Knapp's death in December 1901, the school was administered by three trustees: Minnie Ferle Knapp, Mary Story, and **Bessie Queen [Standley]**. After Story's death in 1906, Standley, who served as editor of *God's Revivalist*, a magazine published by the school, and her husband, **M. G. Standley** (president 1910–1950), emerged as the principal leaders of the school. The Standleys were the recipients of the support of holiness evangelist **W. B. Godbey**, whose regular columns in *God's Revivalist* and personal support of Bessie Queen proved decisive in the Standleys' consolidation of power following the founder's death. Surviving a court challenge from Knapp's son, John Franklin Knapp, which resulted in the school's becoming a ward of the Ohio courts, and controversies over the use of funds, GBS, especially through its early, although informal, associations with the **Pilgrim Holiness Church** and the Oriental Missionary Society (see **OMS International**), sent its graduates throughout the United States and around the world.

As a faith school that did not charge tuition or, for that matter, pay regular salaries, GBS provided rudimentary training for ministers and missionaries who often had few alternatives. As one of the GBS's early supporters and sometime faculty member **Oswald Chambers** noted, it was, in fact, an expression of "Christian communism." Given the lax administration of funds, it was perhaps inevitable that the Standley administration would end in scandal. In 1950, unable to account for how the school's funds had been spent, M. G. and Bessie Queen Standley were forced to resign. In the early 1950s, GBS, in part through the work of dean **Leslie D. Wilcox**, emerged as a center for the growing **Inter-Church Holiness Convention** (IHC)–related conservative holiness movement. It spite of its continued close association with the IHC, the school continues to serve members of the **Church of the Nazarene** and **Wesleyan Church** and has a significant international constituency, while *God's Revivalist*, under the editorship of Larry Smith, remains an important holiness periodical. W.C.K.

GOD'S MISSIONARY CHURCH (GMC). The product of a revival that originated in Pennsylvania's sparsely populated Lykens Valley in 1931. Two converts of the revival, George I. Straub and Truman C. Wise, emerged as leaders of the new denomination that was formed by those converted at the revival in 1935. By 1990, GMC had more than 500 members in more than 40 congregations located primarily in Pennsylvania and Florida. It operates Penn View Bible Institute in Penns Creek, Pennsylvania, and missions in Haiti and among Cuban immigrants in Miami, Florida. One of the most conservative holiness bodies, it ordains women and urges its members not to take part in war. It has published *God's Missionary Standard* since 1949. W.C.K.

GOFF, FRANK DELORMEY (b. near Gananoque, Ontario, June 1873; d. Clarksburg, Ontario, 7 July 1944). Evangelist and founder of the **Gospel Workers Church**. Converted in a **Holiness Movement Church** congregation in 1895 and sanctified in 1896, Goff began his ministry in Eastern Ontario and Southern Quebec. In February 1898, he began services in the Beaver Valley community of Meaford. Meeting with immediate success, Goff held tent meetings and revivals in the nearby communities of Clarksburg and Heathcote. In 1902, he organized the Holiness Workers Church and established a periodical, the *Holiness Worker*. In 1918, the church was renamed the Gospel Workers Church, and the periodical was retitled the *Gospel Worker*. In 1906, Goff established the Clarksburg (Ontario) **Camp Meeting** and served as pastor of his denomination's Clarksburg church until his death. Although an advocate of the controversial theory that the **baptism of the Holy Spirit** was a third work of grace subsequent to conversion and sanctification, Goff was active in the **Canadian Holiness Federation**. Goff's distinctive theological views are expressed in his book, *The Promised Enduement, or the Baptism with the Holy Ghost* (1921). A son, Reginald Goff, became a successful Methodist pastor, evangelist, and organizer of Prayer Unlimited, a mission dedicated to deepening Christians' prayer life. W.C.K.

GOODWIN, JOHN WESLEY (b. North Berwick, Maine, 13 March 1869; d. Pasadena, California, 26 January 1945). Free Will Baptist, Advent Christian, and **Church of the Nazarene** (CN) minister and administrator. A factory worker who was converted in a Free Will Baptist church in 1887, Goodwin eventually joined the Advent Christian Church, entering the ministry in 1892 and serving appointments in Haverhill and Springfield, Massachusetts, until 1905. Although he had experienced **entire sanctification** in 1892 and had been associated with such holiness evangelists as **C. J. Fowler**, **H. C. Morrison**, and **Phineas Bresee**, he only gradually adopted a more specifically Wesleyan theological perspective. Especially decisive in this regard was his introduction to the classics of Methodist theology through the correspondence program of **Taylor University**. Relocating to southern California in 1905, Goodwin joined the CN and was responsible for establishing CN congregations in Pasadena, San Diego, and Whittier. He was one of the founders of Pasadena College, now Point Loma Nazarene University, where he served for a time as campus pastor. He served as general superintendent of the CN (1916–1940). Following his retirement, he was professor of homiletics at Pasadena College. Although honored as a skillful administrator, Goodwin was also a thoughtful exponent of holiness teaching. His most important book, *The Gospel for Our Age* (n.d.), went through several editions. W.C.K.

GORHAM, B(arlow) W(eed) (b. Danbury, Connecticut, 25 June 1814; d. Sea-Cliff, New Jersey, 11 April 1889). Methodist Episcopal Church (MEC) pastor, evangelist, author, and editor. Converted at a **camp meeting** near Philadelphia in 1832, Gorham was admitted to the Oneida (New York) Conference of the MEC in 1836. He was ordained a deacon in 1839 and an elder in 1841. He was a pastor in the Oneida Conference (1836–1852) and the Wyoming (New York) Conference (1852–1864), where he served as conference secretary (1853–1857). He later held appointments in the New England and Northwest Iowa Conferences. Gorham was a successful evangelist and a noted singer and songwriter. Following his experience of **entire sanctification** in 1844, he became one of the first Methodist evangelists to emphasize **Phoebe Palmer's** teaching that entire sanctification was obtainable instantly by faith. He was coeditor of the *Guide to Holiness* (1854–1863). Gorham's first book, *Camp Meeting Manual* (1854), was both a defense of the camp meeting as a religious institution and an instructional guide for the creation and management of camp meetings. A second book, *God's Method with Man* (1879), was a phenomenological description of progressive Christian experience including salvation, entire sanctification, continual baptisms of the Spirit, and growth beyond entire sanctification. W.C.K.

GOSPEL WORKERS CHURCH (GWC). **Frank Delormey Goff** began annual tent meeting revivals in Grey County, Ontario, in 1898. Over the winter of 1902–1903, he and several young lay evangelists organized the Holiness Workers Church. The church began building small churches, principally in Grey County, and established a permanent **camp meeting** site south of Clarksburg in 1906. Upon incorporation in 1918, the name of the church was officially changed to the Gospel Workers Church. The church published a monthly periodical, initially the *Holiness Worker*, then the *Gospel Worker*, from 1904 until 1955. Like other holiness churches, the GWC was socially conservative and emphasized moral conduct, simple dress, and a modest lifestyle. It also promoted temperance and social purity. It believed in universal conversion and instantaneous sanctification and looked for the empowerment of the **baptism of the Holy Spirit**. However, Goff never permitted speaking in tongues or the teaching of premillennialism in his denomination. The church was organized along Methodist lines, with an ordained clergy and lay leadership, and Goff served as the annually elected president until his death in 1944.

After five years of church building and substantial expansion and another five years of more modest growth in its narrow geographic region, the church experienced retrenchment, declining numbers of members, and a diminished revival spirit. Goff's arbitrary leadership—especially his investment policies, personal lifestyle, and expulsion of members who disagreed with his evangelical priorities—prevented significant growth. Rural depopulation, the inability of the church to retain adherents who moved out of the county, and the difficulties in sustaining emotional enthusiasm, particularly among second-generation members, also contributed to the church's demise. After unsuccessful attempts to unite with the **Holiness Movement Church** during the 1940s, the majority of the few hundred remaining members joined the **Church of the Nazarene** in 1957, while a minority allied with the **Free Methodist Church** or the United Church of Canada. The Gospel Workers' influence is nevertheless still felt in the spiritual ethos of the region and as an evangelical leaven in various Protestant denominations. N.S.

GOVAN, JOHN GEORGE (b. Glasgow, Scotland, 19 January 1861; d. Perth, Scotland, September 1927). Converted in 1873 and claiming cleansing from all sin in 1883, Govan became a hardworking evangelist with a deep passion for the lost. He was strongly influenced by D. L. Moody's evangelistic preaching in Glasgow in 1882 and also by the example of the holiness evangelism of **William** and **Catherine Booth**. In 1886, he founded the Faith Mission, an interdenominational mission for evangelizing the rural areas of Scotland. The workers, both men and women, were called "pilgrims," and although interdenominational, the Faith Mission was strongly full salvation in its emphasis. In 1887, "Prayer Unions" were organized as a means of uniting converts in a prayer fellowship for spiritual growth and revival. By 1900, the work had spread to England and Ireland. In 1924, the African Evangelistic Band was organized in South Africa along similar lines; in 1927, the Faith Mission was established in Canada. A bimonthly magazine, *Bright Words*, was launched in 1889 and renamed *Life Indeed* in 1966. In 1922, a Training Home and Bible College was opened in Edinburgh, which still prepares men and women for evangelistic ministry. A man of prayer, dedication, and discipline, John George Govan inspired his followers with a passion for holiness evangelism. H.M.

GRACE AND HOPE MISSION. Founded in Baltimore, Maryland, in 1914 by Mamie E. Caske (1880–1959) and Jennie E. Goranflo (1880–1941), urban mission workers with the interdenominational Gospel Workers Society. By 1927, the group was operating five missions in Baltimore; York, Philadelphia, and Reading, Pennsylvania; and Norfolk, Virginia. By 1939, it had expanded into New York City; Newark, New Jersey; Boston; Providence; and Scranton, Pennsylvania. It currently operates 10 missions. It is exclusively led and staffed by uniformed women workers. Its statement of faith is distinctly Wesleyan. From 1927 to 1941, it published the *Grace and Hope Evangel*. Typical of most rescue missions, it provides food, clothing, Christian instruction for children, religious services, and drug and alcohol counseling. In 1988, it was providing regular services to about 800 people. W.C.K.

GREATHOUSE, WILLIAM M. (b. Van Buren, Arkansas, 29 April 1919). **Church of the Nazarene** (CN) theologian and general superintendent. Raised in Jackson, Tennessee, Greathouse graduated from Lambuth College, Trevecca Nazarene College, and Vanderbilt University. He exemplifies a rare combination of traits: competence in both theology and educational administration. Long associated with Nashville, Tennessee, he was instructor (later professor) of Bible at Trevecca (1945–1958), pastor of historic Nashville First CN (1958–1963), and president of Trevecca (1963–1968). He became president of Nazarene Theological Seminary (Kansas City, Missouri) in 1968, leading it in a period when enrollment surged from 260 to nearly 500. He was elected a general superintendent of the CN in 1976, retiring in 1989. Greathouse assembled a talented religion faculty at Trevecca that shared his vision for recovering a more catholic Wesleyanism, including **Paul Bassett**, John Knight, **H. Ray Dunning**, and **Mildred Wynkoop**. Biblical theology was his specialty, but his intense interest in the doctrine of Christian holiness was reflected in published studies touching on homiletics, historical theology, and systematic theology. A later work, *Wholeness in Christ* (1999), reflects on the theme of sanctifying grace. R.S.I.

GREAVES, J. CLAPHAM (b. Birstall, Yorkshire, 11 December 1842; d. 28 March 1908). British Wesleyan minister. Desiring to see a resurgence of holiness teaching and experience at the heart of the major British Methodist Church, in 1872, J. Clapham Greaves joined with three other young preachers, **John Brash**, W. G. Pascos, and **Isaac E. Page**, in establishing the first distinctly holiness publication in Europe, the *King's Highway*. Perhaps more than any other source, this magazine acted as the stimulus for a renewal of holiness interest in Methodism and as an interpreter of the higher life movement worldwide. It was said of Greaves that his whole life and message were holiness. W.P.

GREEN, JIM H. (b. Ashe County, North Carolina, ca. 1880; d. Greensboro, North Carolina, 23 May 1955). Methodist Episcopal Church, South (MECS), and **People's Methodist Church** pastor, evangelist, and educator. Educated at the Ashe Academy and Business College in the 1890s, Green taught school in Ashe County during the late 19th and early 20th centuries. Following a profound religious experience, he was admitted into the North Carolina Annual Conference of the MECS in 1905. Rapidly emerging as one of the most effective evangelists and holiness advocates in Western North Carolina, Green served circuits in Transylvania, Haywood, and Buncombe Counties from 1905 to 1918. Following five years as an evangelist and several short pastorates, he separated from Methodism in 1926. Although denouncing the inroads theological liberalism was making within the MECS, Green suggested that other issues, especially the wealth and quest for worldly recognition by Methodists, were equally important factors in his decision to leave the MECS.

After briefly serving as an itinerant evangelist, Green pastored the
Light House Mission in St. Louis from 1929 to 1931. Always deeply
concerned with education of the poor, in January 1932, Green established People's Bible School on the property that had formerly housed
Greensboro Bible and Literary Institute. Beginning with four faculty
and 18 students, the school, known as John Wesley College since 1959,
has continued to train church workers faithful to the vision of its
founder. In May 1938, Green, in part to find preaching opportunities
for the Bible school's growing student body, founded the People's
Christian Movement, renamed the People's Methodist Church in
1948. He was chosen general superintendent, a position he held until
1951. He also served as founding editor of the movement's periodical,
the *People's Herald*. Deeply committed to the **camp meeting** tradition, Green founded three camp meetings, Camp Free in Connelly
Springs, North Carolina, in 1921; the White City Camp in Avon Park,
Florida, in 1940; and the Sunny South Camp in Greensboro in 1946.
Although some of Green's followers were troubled by the name "People's," especially during the Red Scare of the early 1950s, Green never
abandoned his suspicion of wealth and the religious institutions that
serve mammon. W.C.K.

GRIDER, J(oseph) KENNETH (b. Madison, Illinois, 22 October
1921). **Church of the Nazarene** (CN) pastor and theologian. Con-
verted in 1939 and sanctified in 1940, Grider was educated at Olivet
Nazarene College, Nazarene Theological Seminary (NTS), and Drew
University and was awarded a Ph.D. by Glasgow University (1952).
Grider has served as a CN pastor in Illinois and Missouri (1944–1947)
and Glasgow, Scotland (1951–1952). He was a professor of theology at
Pasadena College (1952–1953) and NTS (1953–1992). Following retirement from NTS, he served as visiting professor of theology at Olivet
Nazarene University. As a biblical scholar, Grider has written commentaries on Ezekiel (1966) and Zechariah (1969) and several articles
in the *Wycliffe Encyclopedia of the Bible* (1975) and the *International
Standard Bible Encyclopedia* (1979). He was one of the two associate
editors of the *Beacon Dictionary of Theology* (1983). As a theologian,
he has published work in the *Wesleyan Theological Journal* and in *Contemporary Wesleyan Theology* (1983). He is the author of an important
defense of traditional holiness soteriology, *Entire Sanctification: The
Distinctive Doctrine of Wesleyanism* (1980), and his magnum opus, *A
Wesleyan–Holiness Theology* (1994). Although Grider is committed to

traditional holiness theology and spirituality, his work as a theologian is marked by originality. For example, he has proposed that predestination is temporal and unrelated to individual eternal destiny. As such views suggest, Grider is an unabashed lover of theological speculation and debate whose legacy has deeply touched two generations of CN pastors. W.C.K.

GRIFFITH, GLENN (b. Augusta, Kansas, 17 August 1894; d. San Antonio, Texas, 12 January 1976). **Church of the Nazarene** (CN) minister, conservative holiness leader, and denominational founder. Griffith was converted and called to preach in 1912 but rejected this call and served as a U.S. Army sergeant during World War I. In 1925, he joined the CN and pastored several churches prior to becoming a full-time itinerant evangelist. Griffith quickly became known as one of the most effective holiness evangelists, a reputation that helped to earn him positions as district superintendent in Idaho-Oregon (1937–1945) and Colorado (1946–1951).

After serving as superintendent, Griffith returned to evangelism. He became increasingly discontented with what he perceived to be a worldly trend in the CN. This precipitated his separation from that body in September 1955. He then held an eight-week tent meeting near Nampa, Idaho, which resulted in the formation of the Bible Missionary Union (later **Bible Missionary Church** [BMiC]). Griffith was unanimously elected as general moderator of this group, which was dedicated to maintaining traditional behavioral standards. He served in this capacity until a rift developed with another BMiC leader, Elbert Dodd, over the issues of divorce and remarriage. As a result of his more rigid view, Griffith left the BMiC in 1959 and formed the **Wesleyan Holiness Association of Churches**, of which he became the general superintendent. While he served in several administrative positions, Griffith always retained his greatest reputation as a fiery revivalistic preacher. W.T.

– H –

HAMLINE, L(eonidas) L(ent) (b. Burlington, Connecticut, 10 May 1797; d. Mount Pleasant, Iowa, 22 February 1865). Methodist Episcopal Church (MEC) minister, editor, and bishop. **HAMLINE, MELINDA JOHNSON TRUESDALE** (b. Hillsdale, Columbia County, New York,

29 September 1801; d. Evanston, Illinois, 1881). MEC educator, author, and convener of a Tuesday Meeting for the Promotion of Holiness. Raised in a pious Congregational family deeply committed to the teachings of Samuel Hopkins, L. L. Hamline was educated at an academy in Andover, Massachusetts. Following a brief career as a teacher, he settled in Zanesville, Ohio, where he married Eliza Price, a young woman of considerable wealth. In 1827, he became a lawyer. Following the tragic death of his young daughter and his introduction to the writings of John Fletcher, Hamline was converted. He was licensed to the ministry in 1829 and was named a presiding elder in the Pittsburgh Conference, MEC, in 1830. In 1834, he was named pastor of Wesley Chapel in Cincinnati, Ohio. Following the death of his first wife in 1835, he married a young widow, Melinda Truesdale, in 1836. He was named associate editor of the *Western Christian Advocate* in 1836 and was founding editor of the *Ladies' Repository* in 1841. In 1844, following an important speech in which he defended the right of the General Conference to suspend Bishop James Osgood Andrew for owning slaves, Hamline was elected a bishop. In 1852, he was forced to resign from the episcopacy due to ill health. An ardent champion of holiness currents in Methodism, Hamline had experienced **entire sanctification** on 22 March 1842.

Like many married couples in the holiness movement, the Hamlines were a formidable team. Highly educated, Melinda Hamline took an active role in the editorship of the *Ladies' Repository*. She was a regular contributor to the magazine and, following her experience of entire sanctification, to the *Guide to Holiness*. Closely associated with **Sarah Lankford** and **Phoebe** and **Walter Palmer**, the Hamlines played no small role in the growth of the holiness movement from the 1840s to the 1870s. In fact, Walter Palmer was L. L. Hamline's first biographer. Following the death of Bishop Hamline, Melinda Hamline retired in Evanston, Illinois, where she convened a regular Tuesday Meeting for the Promotion of Holiness. Hamline University (St. Paul, Minnesota) was named for the bishop who was noted for his generosity and who gave the school a gift of $25,000. W.C.K.

HANEY, MILTON LORENZO (b. Richland County, Ohio, 23 January 1825; d. Pasadena, California, 20 January 1922). Methodist Episcopal Church minister, pastor, U.S. Army chaplain during the Civil War, evangelist, editor, author, and member of the National Holiness Association (NHA; see **Christian Holiness Partnership**). Son of James Haney, a local preacher for more than 50 years, Milton became a Christian at the age of 16 and received his first appointment at Dixon, Illinois, five years later. In 1847, he experienced **entire sanctification** at a Methodist **camp meeting**. Evangelistic in his parish ministry, Haney soon became a holiness revivalist and early joined the holiness movement in Illinois.

In 1861, shortly after beginning his pastorate in Bushnell, Illinois, Haney enlisted in the Army. He served with distinction and was awarded the Congressional Medal of Honor in 1896.

By 1872, Haney had become a full-time holiness revivalist. He joined the NHA in 1878 and served for many years as a vice president. When the association considered starting a missionary endeavor in 1910, he supported the project and sat on the committee that organized the National Holiness Missionary Society (now **World Gospel Mission**). He participated in the Western Union Holiness Convention in Jacksonville, Illinois, in 1880, and the General Holiness Convention, held in Chicago in 1901. He served for several years in the Iowa Holiness Association. He helped to organize the Wesleyan Holiness Association in Illinois and founded one of the earliest western holiness periodicals, *Repository of Holiness*. It soon ceased for financial reasons. In 1881, he published his first book, *Inheritance Restored*, followed by *Story of My Life* in 1904, reprinted as *Pentecostal Possibilities* in 1906. In 1910, he published *Tares Mixed with the Wheat* and in 1911 issued *Impatience and Its Remedy*. He served as a contributing editor of the *Christian Witness* for several years, and he wrote several tracts. K.O.B.

HARDING, U(lle) E(arl) (b. Shoals, Indiana, 16 May 1883; d. Pasadena, California, 8 May 1958). **Free Methodist Church** (FMC) and **Church of the Nazarene** (CN) minister, district superintendent, and evangelist. One of the most influential folk evangelists of the early-20th-century holiness movement, Harding was raised in poverty and educated in the country schools of southern Indiana, the Indiana School for the Blind, and, following his conversion in 1902, **God's Bible School**. Although his eyesight was so poor that he was unable to read, Harding served as an FMC minister. In 1911, he joined the Pentecostal Church of the Nazarene (see CN), founding churches in Evansville and Indianapolis, and serving as a district superintendent of the Indianapolis District of the CN. During his career, he organized 55 CN congregations in Indiana. He also served as executive secretary for the Home Mission Board of the CN and as pastor of congregations in Walla Walla, Washington, and Berkeley and Pasadena, California. In 1938, he gained national prominence when he received the first successful cornea transplant, which enabled him to have limited vision for the rest of his life. Harding was typical of the brilliant, if eccentric, popular holiness preachers who were capable of turning a disability like blindness into an asset. He was noted for his optimism, skillful employment of metaphors drawn from the experiences of common people, celebration of demonstrative worship, and commitment to an austere holiness lifestyle. Among his most widely read books were *A New Grip on God* (1938), *Pen Pictures from Life* (1938), *Movie Mad America* (1942), and *Roads to Reno: How to Avoid Divorce* (1940s). W.C.K.

HARRIS, MERNE A. (b. Aberdeen, South Dakota, 5 June 1923). **Wesleyan Methodist Church** (WMC) and **Wesleyan Church** minister, evangelist, and educator. Harris was educated at Chicago Evangelistic Institute (CEI; see **Vennard College**), William Penn College (Iowa), Drake University, and Iowa State University, where he received a Ph.D. in 1966. Following a two-year WMC pastorate in Michigan, Harris joined the faculty of CEI where he served as field representative (1948–1950), dean of men (1950–1952), registrar (1952–1956), dean of the college (1956–1968), and president (1968–1988). As a noted evangelist, Harris has conducted revival meetings throughout the United States. He was one of the founders of the **Wesleyan Theological Society**, serving as its secretary (1965–1968) and president (1968–1969). His published work has appeared in the *Wesleyan Advocate*, *Wesleyan Theological Journal*, and the *Beacon Dictionary of Theology*. He is the author of *The Torch Goeth Forth* (1985), an interpretive history of Vennard College. W.C.K.

HARRIS, R(ichard) READER (b. Worcester, England, 5 July 1847; d. London, 30 March 1909). Episcopal railway engineer, lawyer, and founder of the Pentecostal League of Prayer. Harris was called to the bar in 1883 and later had the distinction of being appointed a queen's counsel. Converted to Christ from agnosticism, in 1889, he attended services in London conducted by the prominent American holiness preacher **G. D. Watson** and claimed the blessing of **entire sanctification**. For the rest of his life, he was an indefatigable promoter of scriptural holiness. In 1891, he organized the Pentecostal League of Prayer, an interdenominational mission and prayer fellowship for the purpose of mutual prayer support, which promoted evangelistic outreach and the experience of the infilling of the Spirit in every Christian. The league's holiness emphasis was further strengthened when Harris launched its periodical, *Tongues of Fire*, in 1891. By the time of Harris's death, the league had 150 missions in Great Britain and 12 overseas. One of his converts, **David Thomas**, became a prominent supporter who founded the Holiness Mission in 1906. Harris disapproved, believing that the truth of full salvation should be spread through the existing denominations. For some 20 years, Harris was one of the most prominent and forthright holiness leaders in Britain. H.M.

HATFIELD, JOHN T. (b. near Cleveland, Indiana, 8 August 1851; d. Los Angeles, California, 14 December 1934). Methodist Episcopal Church (MEC) and **Church of the Nazarene** evangelist. Popularly known as the "Hoosier evangelist," Hatfield was a farmer and dry goods merchant who experienced salvation in 1872 and sanctification in 1880. Following his experience of full salvation, Hatfield, although not yet licensed to the ministry, began a career as an itinerant evangelist. An immensely popular, if eccentric, holiness preacher, Hatfield held services that were punctuated with shouting, jumping, and numerous other physical manifestations. Acknowledging that he had experienced all the divine gifts, including speaking in tongues, Hatfield affirmed the traditional holiness experience, insisting that "there is one Holy Ghost and many anointings." He was a contributor to holiness periodicals, such as the *Nazarene Messenger, God's Revivalist,* and the *Herald of Holiness,* and the author of an autobiography, *Thirty-three Years a Live Wire: Life of John T. Hatfield* (1913). In 1901, he was one of the founders of a **camp meeting** near Cleveland, Indiana, now known as the John T. Hatfield Camp Meeting. W.C.K.

HAWKINS, RICHARD WATSON (b. Youngstown, Pennsylvania, 16 March 1835; d. Olean, New York, 18 January 1892). Methodist Episcopal Church (MEC), **Free Methodist Church** (FMC), and **Wesleyan Methodist Church** (WMC) minister and author. Converted in 1851, Hawkins experienced **entire sanctification** under the ministry of **Phoebe Palmer** in the late 1860s. Although he had served as a presiding elder in the Erie Conference of the MEC, Hawkins joined the FMC in 1870 and organized an FMC society near Oil City, Pennsylvania. In 1883, he was one of the primary organizers of the Pittsburgh Conference of the FMC, where he served as a presiding elder. In 1891, Hawkins joined the WMC and was chosen general mission superintendent. Hawkins was one of the most controversial figures of the late-19th-century holiness movement. His 1888 book, *Redemption or the Living Way: A Treatise on the Redemption of the Body*, which insisted on the possibility of the direct spiritual translation of individual Christians to paradise apart from death, struck a responsive chord in the optimistic atmosphere of the late 19th century. However, Hawkins was censured for its controversial teaching by the General Conference of the FMC in 1890. Especially troubling to FMC leaders were the all-too-common divorces and remarriages among Hawkins's followers. Although Hawkins rejected the frequent changing of marital partners—the so-called practice of "spiritual affinity"—his view that such a "heresy" was a special danger to the spiritually advanced angered many in the FMC. In spite of Hawkins's censure, his insistence that Christians need not die continued to be taught well into the 20th century. W.C.K.

HAYNES, BENJAMIN FRANKLIN (b. Franklin, Tennessee, 1851; d. Nashville, Tennessee, 2 October 1923). Methodist Episcopal Church, South (MECS), and **Church of the Nazarene** (CN) minister, educator, and editor. Trained as a printer and editor, Haynes was editing the *Williamson Journal*, Franklin, Tennessee, when he felt called to the ministry in the early 1870s. Establishing a reputation as a forceful preacher and militant social reformer, Haynes was named pastor of Nashville's prominent McKendree Church in 1888. In 1890, following what he believed to be his premature replacement as pastor of McKendree Church, he became editor of a reform periodical in the Tennessee Conference, the *Tennessee Methodist*. Although he was primarily known for his active leadership of the Prohibition Movement in Tennessee Methodism, Haynes's experience of **entire sanctification** in 1894 made him a natural leader of the holiness movement in the Volunteer State. Although continuing to edit the *Tennessee Methodist*, Haynes was increasingly assigned to isolated circuits. In 1898, he further angered MECS loyalists by publicly dissenting from a claim that the U.S. government owed money to the church for damages done to the MECS Publishing House during the Civil War.

In 1900, he sold his interest in the *Tennessee Methodist* to holiness leader **J. O. McClurkan**. As Haynes noted in his 1921 autobiography, *Tempest-Tossed on a Methodist Sea*, the pastoral appointments he received from 1898 to 1905 were the most poorly paying and undesirable in the Tennessee Conference. From 1905 to 1908, Haynes served as president of **Asbury College** and, in 1911, joined the faculty of Texas Holiness University. Following his decision to join the Pentecostal Church of the Nazarene (see CN) in 1912, Haynes was named editor of the church's new periodical, the *Herald of Holiness*, a position he held until his retirement in 1922. Although increasingly drawn to premillennial **eschatology**, Haynes, like his good friends **H. C. Morrison** and **L. L. Pickett**, remained a champion of poor and working people. W.C.K.

HEPHZIBAH FAITH MISSIONARY ASSOCIATION (HFMA). Founded in 1893 in Tabor, Iowa, by George Weavers (1840–1914), president until his death, and L. B. Worcester (d. 1926), vice president (1893–1912) and president (1914–1926). The HFMA operated a missionary training school, an orphanage, and a **camp meeting** and published a periodical, *Sent of God*. Following Worcester's death, J. M. Zook served as president (1926–1944). Following Zook's death, most of the HFMA's 20 congregations and 700 members united with the **Wesleyan Methodist Church** (WMC). In 1950, the school, camp meeting, and church at Tabor, Iowa, joined the **Church of the Nazarene** (CN). At the time of the mergers, the HFMA mission in China had become part of the mission work of the Oriental Missionary Society (see **OMS International**). Its missions in India were merged with the **United Missionary Church** work in that country, while its work in Haiti became part of the WMC and its work in South Africa became part of the CN work in that country. In 1966, Paul W. Worcester, son of L. B. Worcester, wrote an uncritical account of the history of the HFMA, *The Master Key: The Story of the Hephzibah Faith Missionary Association*. W.C.K.

HILLS, A(aron) M(erritt) (b. Dowagiac, Michigan, 4 February 1848; d. Pasadena, California, 11 September 1935). Congregational and **Church of the Nazarene** minister, evangelist, and educator. Converted in a Baptist church in 1859, Hills was educated at Oberlin College and Yale University. He served as a Congregational pastor in Ravenna, Ohio (1874–1884); Allegheny, Pennsylvania (1884–1890); and Olivet, Michigan (1890–1892). Noted as a successful evangelical preacher, Hills served as state evangelist for the Home Missionary Society of the Congregational Church in Michigan until he accepted a call to teach at **Asbury College** in 1898. He was the founding president of Texas Holiness University (1899–1906) and Iowa Holiness University (1906–1908). On three separate occasions between 1908 and 1915, Hills taught at the Star Hall School and Mission in Manchester, England. Returning to the United States, he taught religion at Pasadena (California) College (1916–1932).

Hills was an author of note whose most important and widely read book was *Holiness and Power* (1897). In this work, which has gone through four English editions, Hills argued that the social, religious, and moral crisis of the late 19th century was fundamentally a spiritual crisis that could only be resolved by full salvation. Among his other works were criticisms of secret societies, the use of tobacco, fanaticism in the holiness movement, and the **Keswick** movement and Pentecostalism. In 1932, Hills published his two-volume *Fundamental Christian Theology*. Written in his usual polemical style, the work ridiculed the theory of verbal inerrancy of the Bible, higher criticism of the Bible, and Charles Darwin's theory of evolution, and it rejected premillennial **eschatology**. Not surprisingly, the book was privately printed and never received wide use or circulation. Written largely between 1910 and 1915 and reflecting his training at Oberlin and Yale and his wide reading in Methodist theology, Hills's theology follows the logic of Charles Finney and the soteriological concerns of the American holiness movement. Although Hills left an unpublished autobiography, serious students will turn to L. Paul Gresham's biography, *Waves against Gibraltar: A Memoir of Dr. A. M. Hills* (1992). W.C.K.

HOGUE, W(ilson) T(homas) (b. Lyndon, New York, 6 March 1852; d. Michigan City, Indiana, 13 February 1920). **Free Methodist Church** (FMC) minister, educator, editor, and bishop. Educated at Ten Broeck Academy in Franklinville, New York, W. T. Hogg, who changed the spelling of his last name to *Hogue,* was converted in 1861 and entirely sanctified in 1873. Appointed to the Dunkirk and Jamestown Circuit of the FMC in 1873, Hogue served congregations in Buffalo, Albion, and Rochester, New York (1873–1892). Although he did not attend college in his youth, he received his higher education through the nonresidence course at Illinois Wesleyan University (A.B., 1897; A.M., 1899; Ph.D., 1902). Hogue was deeply committed to education in the FMC and served as president of Greenville (Illinois) College (1892–1904). He was editor of the *Free Methodist* (1894–1903) and the *Earnest Christian* (1908–1909). Following the death of **B. T. Roberts** in 1893, Hogue was named to complete Roberts's term as general superintendent (1893–1894). He served as an FMC bishop in his own right from 1903 to 1920.

In spite of suffering from partial paralysis in 1908, Hogue faithfully executed his duties as bishop while writing a two-volume definitive history of the FMC. He was a noted author. His work *A Handbook of Homiletics and Pastoral Theology* (1886), although originally given as a series of lectures to the ministerial association in Albion, New York, remained the standard pastoral theology in the FMC until the 1960s.

Although deeply suspicious of the then incipient fundamentalism and materialism of the early-20th-century holiness movement, Hogue was an early FMC champion of premillennial **eschatology**. His vision of a nonliteral Wesleyan spirituality received classic expression in a 1916 work on the Holy Spirit. Among his other works was an important book on the class meeting. A collection of important papers documenting Hogue's life is located at the Free Methodist Historical Library in Indianapolis. W.C.K.

HOKE, JACOB (b. McConnellsburg, Pennsylvania, 17 March 1825; d. Chambersburg, Pennsylvania, 29 December 1893). United Brethren in Christ (UB) merchant, philanthropist, and author. Although raised in a Presbyterian home, Hoke was converted in a UB revival in 1841 and united with a UB congregation in Chambersburg in 1843. A prominent dry goods merchant in Chambersburg, Hoke served the UB church as a Sunday school teacher, a member of the denomination's mission board, missionary secretary, and treasurer of the Pennsylvania Conference (UB) Missionary Society, and he was a trustee of both Union Bible Seminary and Otterbein College. One of the primary advocates of the experience of full salvation among the UB, Hoke served as editor of a UB holiness periodical, *Highway of Holiness* (1875–1887). He was the author of four books including the widely circulated holiness classic, *Holiness, or the Higher Life* (1870). W.C.K.

HOLINESS CHRISTIAN CHURCH. *See* EVANGELICAL CHRISTIAN CHURCH.

HOLINESS CHURCH (HC). Product of the itinerant ministry in 1880 of **Free Methodist Church** (FMC) evangelists Harden Wallace and Henry Ashcraft. Converts of their meetings organized the California and Arizona Holiness Association and established a **camp meeting** at Downey, California. Under the leadership of James W. Swing and James F. and Josephine Washburn, distinctly holiness congregations were formed and organized into the HC, with Swing serving as president. In 1885, a periodical, the *Pentecost*, later the *Standard Bearer of Bible Holiness*, was founded. Besides California, churches were planted in Oregon, Tennessee, and Kentucky. From its beginning, the HC was interracial. In the Midwest and South, the work was directed by African American evangelist George A. Goings. In 1906, in the wake of the Azusa Street Revival, a significant number of members became Pentecostal, while increasing numbers of other members joined the

Church of the Nazarene. In spite of these setbacks, the church founded missions in Peru and Palestine. In 1931, the HC acquired property at El Monte, California, where a camp meeting and a Bible college were established. In 1946, the final 19 congregations, 17 of which were located in California, with approximately 400 members, joined the **Pilgrim Holiness Church**. In 1912, Josephine Washburn compiled an important early history of the HC, *History and Reminiscences of the Holiness Church Work in Southern California and Arizona*. W.C.K.

HOLINESS METHODIST CHURCH. Established as the Northwestern Holiness Association in Grand Forks, North Dakota, on 24 March 1909, it was the creation of former Methodist ministers **W. C. Ehlers** and C. A. Thompson, who were named joint general superintendents. Although it was initially committed only to the creation of countywide interdenominational holiness associations, by 1912, the Northwestern Holiness Association had dedicated its first chapel. The association founded a periodical, the *Northwest Holiness Advocate*, in 1910 and a school of theology in 1914. In 1913, following an internal dispute between Ehlers and Thompson, Ehlers was elected sole general superintendent. Under his aggressive leadership, the association experienced steady growth and, by the time of his death in 1916, had more than 30 ordained ministers and preaching points throughout the Dakotas and Minnesota.

Following Ehlers's death, J. Hamilton Irwin was named general superintendent. In 1920, he was reelected general superintendent, and the association was renamed the Holiness Methodist Church. Although several new churches were planted during the 1920s, the church experienced little overall growth. In 1948, it assumed responsibility for a mission in Bolivia. During the 1950s and 1960s, merger discussions were held with both the **Free Methodist Church** and the **Wesleyan Methodist Church**. In 1969, 20 of the church's 22 congregations voted to merge with the **Evangelical Church of North America**. At the time of the merger, the church had approximately 900 members in the Dakotas, Minnesota, and Illinois. The Holiness Methodist School of Theology (Minneapolis) continued to operate until 1973. W.C.K.

THE HOLINESS MOVEMENT CHURCH IN CANADA (HMC). The rise of controversial American-style holiness enthusiasm in Canada in the 1880s culminated in the expulsion of **Ralph Horner** from the Methodist ministry in 1895 and his formation of the HMC the same year. Centered in the Ottawa Valley and eastern Ontario, the church opened a publishing house and Holiness Movement College in Ottawa in late 1895. By 1900, when the church organized a General Conference and received a federal charter, it had expanded its work throughout western Canada and into New York state and opened successful missions in Egypt (Asyut, 1899), the Sudan, and Belfast in Ireland. Later, missions were started in China and Australia. In 1911, the church claimed 3,600 adherents in Canada but laid its greatest emphasis on missionary operations.

From its formation until 1916, the HMC was led by Bishop Ralph Horner and Bishop A. T. Warren. In that year, Horner and a large number of members left the HMC to establish the **Standard Church of America**. Warren continued as bishop until 1925. The following year, the church replaced its episcopacy with a general superintendent elected by the General Conference. The Annual, Missionary, and General Conferences had approximately equal lay and ministerial representation. By organization and doctrine, the church followed the teachings of **John Wesley**, but it added a third baptism of Pentecostal spiritual empowerment to conversion and **entire sanctification**. This permitted prophecy and speaking in tongues, which would later divide the denomination and cause difficulties with other holiness churches. Over time, the overseas operations expanded, except in China, and grew more independent, while the church in Canada faltered under the stress of past schism, lack of financial and numerical strength, and, particularly, the difficulty in sustaining emotional enthusiasm among second-generation members. By 1958, the church had only about 800 members in Canada, and it sought an alliance with stronger holiness bodies. Most of its members united with the **Free Methodist Church** in 1959. N.S.

HOOPLE, WILLIAM HOWARD (b. Herkimer, New York, 6 August 1868; d. New York City, 29 September 1922). Leather merchant, pastor, YMCA worker, and holiness movement leader. Raised in a Baptist home, Hoople was converted at the age of 18 during a YMCA meeting conducted by D. L. Moody and experienced **entire sanctification** in 1893.

Hoople attracted many followers as he attempted to fulfill a vision from the Lord to plant churches in Brooklyn, New York. This vision took shape in 1894 with the founding of the Utica Avenue Pentecostal Tabernacle. Hoople and the church stood firmly in the Wesleyan "second blessing" camp of independent holiness groups that emerged nationwide during the 1890s.

Two more Brooklyn churches were founded. In 1895, they joined with the first, and at their annual meeting in 1896, they took the name Association of Pentecostal Churches of America (APCA). The APCA continued to expand under Hoople's leadership, and by 1907, there were 47 member churches. During 1906–1907, the APCA and the **Church of the Nazarene** (CN) seriously discussed joining forces. Hoople advocated submerging "secondary issues" in favor of a combined attack on evil and persuaded both groups to vote for union. The resulting merger formed the Pentecostal Church of the Nazarene (see CN). Hoople continued to serve the united group as the district superintendent of the New York District and as a local pastor until his death. R.J.H.

HORNER, RALPH CECIL (b. near Shawville, Quebec, 22 December 1854; d. Ivanhoe Camp Meeting, near Ottawa, Ontario, 12 September 1921). Holiness evangelist and church founder. Raised in an Anglican farm family, Horner was converted and **entirely sanctified** in 1872. After two years of probationary study at Victoria University and further oratory training, he was ordained in the Methodist Church in 1887. Horner believed this was a special ordination as an evangelist. While serving successfully as Montreal Conference evangelist, he was accused of unsound doctrinal teaching and promoting excessive enthusiasm in his holiness preaching. After refusing circuit work and condemning the conduct and spirituality of his colleagues, he was expelled from the conference in 1895. He then organized the **Holiness Movement Church** (HMC) in Canada, serving as its first bishop. After several years, Horner claimed that the church was abandoning its principles, and, in 1915, he and many supporters formed **Standard Church of America**, which he led until his death. Horner was a forceful leader and dynamic preacher whose authoritarianism did much to undermine his overall success. He was noted for his distinctive teaching on the third blessing (see HMC). N.S.

HOUSE OF PRAYER (HP). The HP traces its roots to the ministry of Edward Wayne Runyan (1864–1945), who followed the example of the **Metropolitan Church Association**, which taught that Christians should live communally, holding "all things in common." By 1917, Runyan had won several converts among ministers in the **Churches of Christ in Christian Union** (CCCU), including one of its founders,

Henry C. Leeth. In 1918, the CCCU expelled 14 ministers for supporting Runyan's teaching. These ministers formed the HP with Leeth serving as bishop from 1919 until his death in 1967. In 1919, the HP began publishing a periodical, the *Herald of Perfect Christianity*, and established its headquarters at Washington Court House, Ohio. Although a communal farm and store established near Urbana, Ohio, failed, the HP did found a church in Washington Court House, known as God's Non-Sectarian Tabernacle, and an annual **camp meeting**, held at the church. Although many churches were established during Leeth's lifetime, the movement has been in decline since his death. In 1999, the HP had two congregations and about 200 members. It continues to hold its annual camp meeting. K.O.B.

HUFF, WILL H. (b. Glasgow, Ohio, 25 October 1874; d. Cincinnati, 28 September 1928). Methodist Episcopal Church (MEC) evangelist and missionary. Trained as a potter in East Liverpool, Ohio, Huff was converted during the 1890s and educated at **Asbury College** and Texas Holiness University. Deeply influenced by **A. M. Hills** and **Bud Robinson**, Huff lived for a time in the Robinson home in Greenville, Texas. In fact, Huff established his reputation as a polished and skilled pulpiteer in joint evangelistic meetings that he held with Robinson during the first decade of the 20th century. He was a serious student of Scripture and of the culture of the people among whom he ministered. As a friend of Methodist missionary bishop **William Oldham**, Huff made five missionary trips to Latin America and even transferred his membership to the South America Conference of the MEC. Deeply concerned about the plight of African Americans, Huff spent a substantial portion of each year ministering in the South under the direction of MEC bishop Robert Elijah Jones. An especially gifted storyteller, Huff collected many of his stories from African Americans. He served as president of the National Holiness Association (1919–1921; see **Christian Holiness Partnership**). Fittingly, at the time of his death, he was conducting evangelistic meetings at the Hyde Park Community Methodist Church in Cincinnati. W.C.K.

HUFFMAN, JASPER ABRAHAM (b. Elkhart County, Indiana, 28 February 1880; d. Berne, Indiana, 7 December 1970). Mennonite Brethren in Christ (MBIC; later **United Missionary Church** [UMiC]; now **Missionary Church**) author, editor, publisher, and educator. With only a grammar school education, Huffman began as a pastor in the MBIC and was soon in demand as a Bible teacher and conference speaker. Later he graduated from seminary and college and began a 50-year career as a teacher and administrator at Bluffton (Ohio) College, Marion (Indiana) College, **Taylor University**, and Winona Lake (Indiana) School of Theology. In 1947, he was one of the founders of Bethel College (Indiana). Huffman served as editor of the *Gospel Banner*. He also served for many years as editor of the Higley Sunday School Lesson Commentary and was founder and editor of the Bethel Series of Sunday school literature. Huffman published 32 books and booklets, founding a publishing and retail book business in his home. Huffman Book and Bible House developed into Bethel Publishing Company, which became the publishing arm of the UMiC. In his later years, Huffman established Standard Press to continue publication of his works. W.J.G.

HUGHES, GEORGE (b. Manchester, England, 22 February 1823; d. East Orange, New Jersey, 8 October 1904). Methodist Episcopal Church (MEC) minister, editor, and author. The son of a British Wesleyan Methodist local preacher, Hughes migrated to Philadelphia in 1837 and was converted under the ministry of Charles Pitman. Entering the New Jersey Conference of the MEC in 1844, Hughes was a successful pastor and presiding elder. While on leave in England during the American Civil War, he experienced **entire sanctification** through the ministry of **Phoebe Palmer**. He was one of the founders of the National Holiness Association (NHA; see **Christian Holiness Partnership**) in 1867 and served as its first secretary. During the 1870s, he served as editor of the *Methodist Home Journal* and the *New Jersey Methodist*. From 1880 to 1902, he served as editor of the *Guide to Holiness*. At the time of his death, he was one of the editors of *Consecrated Life*. A Methodist loyalist, Hughes used his position as chairman of both the 1885 and 1901 General Holiness Assemblies to keep the holiness movement loyal to Methodism. The unofficial historian of the 19th-century holiness revival, Hughes was the author of *Days of Power in the Forest Temple* (1873), an account of the first 14 NHA **camp meetings**, and *Fragrant Memories* (1889), an account of the first 50 years of the Palmers' famous Tuesday Meeting for the Promotion of Holiness in New York City. In spite of his years of loyal service to Methodism, two of his daughters, Jennie and Anna, were leaders in the Volunteers of America at the time of his death. W.C.K.

HUGHES, HUGH PRICE (b. Carmarthen, Wales, 7 February 1847; d. London, 17 November 1902). British Wesleyan minister and president of the British Wesleyan Conference, 1889. Hughes was a man of prophetic insight who, more than any other, planned the use of the Methodist 20th Century Fund for a significant extension of the church in greater London. A radical Wesleyan, through his influence on government leaders, he helped to formulate a stronger social policy with regard to the poor and neglected. Suspect in many circles because of his involvement with the government, he was nevertheless equally at home on holiness platforms and in the inner circle of national affairs. He was the outstanding figure of his day in seeking to bring together genuine expressions of Wesleyan Christianity with the emerging social gospel. W.P.

HUGHES, JOHN WESLEY (b. Owen County, Kentucky, 16 May 1852; d. Wilmore, Kentucky, 22 February 1932). Methodist Episcopal Church, South (MECS), minister, evangelist, and educator. Raised in poverty on a Kentucky farm, Hughes was converted in 1869. Educated at Kentucky Wesleyan College and Vanderbilt University, he was admitted into the Kentucky Conference, MECS, in 1876. Experiencing **entire sanctification** under the ministry of **W. B. Godbey** in 1882, Hughes quickly established a reputation as a successful evangelist. In 1890, he established Kentucky Holiness College, later **Asbury College**, where he served as president and professor of theology (1890–1905). Following a trip to the Holy Land, in 1906, he established Kingswood (Kentucky) College, where he served as president until 1917. Retiring to Wilmore, Kentucky, in 1917, Hughes served as an evangelist and wrote *The Autobiography of John Wesley Hughes, D.D.* (1923). W.C.K.

HUNTER, NORA SIENS (b. near Chanute, Kansas, 16 August 1873; d. Altadena, California, 27 January 1951). **Church of God (Anderson)** (CG[A]) minister and women's leader. Although raised in a religious milieu, Nora Siens remained spiritually dissatisfied until she experienced **entire sanctification** in 1892. The following year, she joined the Gospel Trumpet Company. From 1893 to 1896, she evangelized throughout the Midwest and Mid-Atlantic states, most successfully in a team with Lena Shoffner. In 1896, she married Clarence Hunter, a minister, and they formed a new evangelistic and pastoral team, with Nora taking the lead. A 1929 tour abroad introduced Hunter firsthand to problems confronting foreign missionaries. Three years later, she won approval for the National Women's Home and Foreign Missionary Society of the CG(A) and served as its president until 1948. The society quickly became a major source of financial and material support for CG(A) missions. M.D.S.

– I –

IMMANUEL GENERAL MISSION (IGM). Founded by former Oriental Missionary Society (see **OMS International**) pastor **David T. Tsutada** in 1945, the IGM sought to duplicate the early Methodism of **John Wesley** in a Japanese context. Augmented by the additions of congregations founded by **Wesleyan Methodist Church** missionary Maurice Gibbs and the work of **World Gospel Mission** in Japan, the new body experienced steady growth during Tsutada's lifetime. Establishing a Bible School, now located at Yokohama; missions in India, Jamaica, Taiwan, and Laos; and a significant publishing ministry, the IGM had become a respected denomination of more than 7,000 members at the time of the founder's death. Under the leadership of Yohane Fukuda (1971–1978), Hiroshi Asahira, and the founder's sons, John M. and Joshua T. Tsutada, the church has grown to more than 10,000 members. The majority of the church's pastors are women. Following the puritanical example of its founder, the IGM remains one of Japan's most conservative holiness bodies. W.C.K.

INSKIP, JOHN S(wanel) (b. Huntingdon, England, 10 August 1816; d. Ocean Grove, New Jersey, 7 March 1884). Methodist Episcopal Church (MEC) minister, pastor, revivalist, editor, author, and first president of the National Holiness Association (NHA; see **Christian Holiness Partnership**). **INSKIP, MARTHA JANE FOSTER** (b. Cecil County, Maryland, 11 August 1819; d. Eggleston Heights, Florida, 26 December 1890). Holiness evangelist. John Inskip converted at age 16 under the preaching of Levi Scott. He joined the MEC and received his license to preach in 1835. In 1836, the Philadelphia Annual Conference received him on trial and appointed him to the Cecil Circuit (Maryland). Here John met Martha Jane Foster, whom he married in 1836.

John and Martha Inskip accepted the pastoral ministry as their calling and vocation. They served parishes in Pennsylvania and then transferred to Ohio. John was censured by the Ohio Conference over his belief in "promiscuous sittings," the practice of allowing men and women to sit together in church. John Inskip defended the practice in a book, *Methodism Explained and Defended* (1851), which also promoted the building of elaborate churches to appeal to increasingly wealthy Methodists. Even though he was vindicated by the General Conference of the MEC in his dispute with the Ohio Conference, John Inskip transferred to the New York East Annual Conference.

In 1861, Inskip joined the Union Army and served as a chaplain until 1862 when he resigned his commission and returned to the pastorate. Martha Inskip attended the Palmers' Tuesday Meeting (see **Phoebe Palmer**), and in the summer of 1864, she and John attended the Sing Sing **Camp Meeting**, near Ossining, New York, where Martha professed her experience of **entire sanctification** under the guidance of **Sarah Lankford**. Two weeks later, while preaching in the morning worship service at his church, John made his own public confession of entire sanctification.

John and Martha Inskip quickly gained prominence among the "friends of holiness." They conducted holiness meetings in their home and were among the first to support the idea of holding a camp meeting for the specific purpose of promoting the doctrine of entire sanctification. John was a leader in the 1867 National Camp Meeting at Vineland, New Jersey. At the close of the encampment, a committee organized the National Camp Meeting Association for the Promotion of Holiness (NHA) and elected John Inskip as president, a position he held until his death.

To meet the growing needs of the NHA's ministries, John Inskip and **William McDonald** entered into full-time evangelism and preached at camp meetings and church revivals around the country. Martha Inskip often sang and gave her testimony. She also helped pioneer youth and children's ministries in the camp meetings. Through 1883, John Inskip presided at 49 National Camp Meetings and 11 "Tabernacle Meetings," which employed a large tent, including campaigns in California, Utah, Ohio, and Indiana. For a short while he edited both the NHA periodical *Advocate of Christian Holiness* and the *Christian Standard and Home Journal*, and he served as an agent for the National Holiness Publishing Association. In 1880, he led a team from the NHA on a global evangelism tour to England, Rome, India, and Australia.

After John Inskip's death, Martha Inskip began to hold revival meetings and ministered in several National Camp Meetings. In 1887, she held revivals at the Cookman Institute in Jacksonville, Florida, and founded the Inskip Memorial Methodist Episcopal Church in Eggleston Heights, Florida. K.O.B.

INTER-CHURCH HOLINESS CONVENTION (IHC). The idea for the Inter-Denominational (later Church) Holiness Convention was first proposed in a discussion between two Wesleyan Methodist evangelists, **H. Robb French** and **H. E. Schmul**, on 8 June 1951, during the General Conference of their denomination in Fairmount, Indiana. The first convention was held at the Emmanuel Wesleyan Church (now Salem Pilgrim Church) in Salem, Ohio, from 31 December 1951 through 1 January 1952, with about 200 in attendance. The success of the first convention led to a subsequent meeting at the Vine Street Wesleyan Methodist Church in Cincinnati, Ohio. However, overflow crowds soon precipitated a move of evening services (and later all services) to the campus of **God's Bible School**, which was the home of the IHC until 1966. From 1967 to 1978, annual meetings were held at Huntington, West Virginia. Since 1978, annual spring conventions have been conducted at the Convention Center in Dayton, Ohio. Evening crowds in the 1990s have tended to number around 6,000.

From the beginning, the leading figure in the convention was H. E. Schmul, who often referred to himself as the convention "chore boy," handling organizational details and platform management as the general secretary for more than 40 years. Schmul was joined by a multitude of other conservative holiness leaders such as V. O. Agan, D. P. Denton, S. I. Emery, **Glenn Griffith**, S. D. Herron, and **Dale Yocum** in guiding the convention to become the primary institutional embodiment of unity among holiness conservatives. In 1997, Rev. Leonard Sankey, who had served as Schmul's assistant for several years, became the general secretary. Under his leadership, the IHC continues to stand for the early commitments that brought it into existence.

The concerns that led to the formation of the IHC are expressed succinctly in the original invitation sent to various church leaders in 1951:

> Because of the moral corruption nationally and internationally; because of the lethargy of the Church world; because the Holiness Movement is losing her identity and distinguishing doctrine of Holiness; because much of the ministry is neglecting the unpopular Bible themes on Holiness, adornment and separation from the world, we call this convention for fasting, prayer, humiliation and heart searching, that the Holy Spirit may visit us again with old-time power.

Positive and negative emphases thus characterized the convention. Positively, the IHC was a revival endeavor, promoting such activities as prayer and fasting in an effort to elicit God's blessing. It also served as a forum in which conservatives could derive mutual encouragement. Negatively, the convention served as a "resistance movement" in which manifestations of worldliness (e.g., television, immodesty, and jewelry) among "old-line" holiness groups were staunchly condemned.

An early common perception of the IHC, among friends and foes alike, was that the convention involved an attempt to form a new conservative holiness denomination that would draw constituents from several old-line denominations. However, Schmul and other convention leaders protested this charge, and such a denomination never developed. While it is true that many leaders associated with the convention did lead efforts to form various conservative denominations, the IHC remained true to its original purpose of providing interchurch fellowship for all holiness conservatives. Eventually, the IHC came to be seen by some as the conservative counterpart to the **Christian Holiness Partnership** (CHP), and to some extent this comparison is accurate. However, while the CHP primarily functions as a fellowship of church leaders (denominational executives, college officials, and so on.) from the old-line holiness churches, the IHC involves a much larger number of laypersons, almost functioning like a large "homecoming" for holiness conservatives.

Since its early days, many conservatives have applauded the function of the IHC as a forum for fellowship. The IHC has also functioned as a platform for promoting various conservative holiness agencies, particularly Bible colleges, missions organizations, and publishing companies. At the convention, a display area is popular, and much of the music is provided by Bible college choirs. The IHC conducts many regional conventions throughout the year and has provided various services for specific groups, including Women of Worth, School of the Prophets (ministerial seminars), and Singles Soar. Other auxiliary activities have included Overcomers (a youth organization) and Aldersgate School of Religion (graduate school).

The IHC is undoubtedly the greatest single unifying institution among holiness conservatives. Its leaders have attempted to preserve traditional holiness lifestyle commitments while providing an inclusive area in which all holiness people might receive fellowship and seek God's blessing. Such a commitment to a tenuous balance has been challenging and prompted criticism from those who see the IHC as too rigid and others who see it as too open. However, the IHC has unarguably been a defining force in the development of the conservative holiness movement and will likely continue to be so. W.T.

INTERNATIONAL APOSTOLIC HOLINESS UNION (IAHU). *See* PILGRIM HOLINESS CHURCH.

INTERNATIONAL FELLOWSHIP OF BIBLE CHURCHES (IFBC). Organized in August 1988 in Siloam Springs, Arkansas, as a voluntary fellowship of ministers and churches within the conservative holiness movement. From 1988 to 1998, it was led by Donald Hicks, a former **Church of the Nazarence** pastor and general superintendent of the **Church of the Bible Covenant** (CBC). Hicks incorporated a large number of former CBC churches and ministers into the formation of the IFBC. Largely because of negative experiences with controversy and hierarchical polity in the past, especially among members of the CBC, the polity of the IFBC is extremely decentralized and congregational. It basically operates for the purpose of ordaining clergy and sending missionaries. It consists of more than 130 ministers and supports missionary activities in the Philippines, Honduras, Guatemala, Mexico, and Lesotho. The IFBC publishes a quarterly newsletter titled *The Fellowship*. In the summer of 1998, William Sillings, a former CBC minister, was elected as the IFBC's second chief executive officer. C.M.H.

INWOOD, CHARLES (b. Woburn Sands, Bedfordshire, 25 March 1851; d. Hove, Sussex, 12 October 1928). Irish Wesleyan Conference minister, world evangelist, and spiritual life leader of the **Keswick** Convention Council. An Englishman serving an Irish church, Inwood was the strongest bridge between classical Wesleyan teaching and the more Reformed emphasis of the Keswick Convention. Equally at home on both platforms, he believed that the distinctives could be reconciled. He was the last Wesleyan for a long period to hold leadership in Keswick circles. His greatest interest was in the establishment of faith missions, and several came into being under his leadership, including the Egypt General Mission and some in Europe. He visited 35 countries, introducing Pastor's Conferences and Conventions, and played an important part in the great African revivals of the early 20th century. W.P.

– J –

JAMES, MARY DAGWORTHY YARD (b. Trenton, New Jersey, 7 August 1810; d. New York City, 4 October 1883). Methodist Episcopal Church (MEC) writer, hymn lyricist, reformer, and evangelist. The daughter of a Hicksite Quaker father and a Baptist mother, James was converted at the age of 10 at a meeting in a Methodist church. Two years later, she experienced **entire sanctification**. In 1840, on a visit to New York, she came into contact with **Phoebe** and **Walter Palmer**, and she soon became a contributor to the *Guide to Holiness*. She wrote many poems and hymns, including "Stand Up for Jesus," "All for Jesus," and "All Bright Above," as well as an account of her own religious experience written for children. An active reformer, in 1859, James was one of the founders of the Trenton (New Jersey) Children's Home, supported early legislative efforts to limit the sale of liquor in New Jersey, and was later active in the Woman's Christian Temperance Union. In later years, she took an active role in **camp meetings** conducted at Ocean Grove, New Jersey, often conducting meetings when the Palmers were absent and leading meetings for children. M.F.W.

JAMES, MAYNARD GEORGE (b. Bargoed, Wales, 17 April 1902; d. Birkenhead, England, 21 May 1988). International Holiness Mission (IHM), Calvary Holiness Church (CHC), and **Church of the Nazarene** (CN) minister, evangelist, and editor. Brought up in a godly home, Maynard James came to faith as a boy and, in 1927, began theological training at **Cliff College**. In 1928, he pioneered the Holiness Trekkers, groups of young men who walked across England in the summers of 1928 through 1934 preaching, mainly for the IHM, and raising up new IHM churches. In 1934, James found himself at odds with the IHM leadership due to his emphasis on divine healing in his revival services and his refusal to condemn the Pentecostal practice of *glossolalia*, speaking in unrecognizable languages. With others, he founded the CHC in 1934, which, like the IHM, was enthusiastically committed to promoting full salvation. In 1935, he launched *The Flame*, a holiness periodical that he edited for the next 48 years. In 1955, the CHC united with the **CN**. In 1945, James published his first book, *Evanglise*, and three other titles followed: *Facing the Issue* (1945), *When Thou Prayest* (1963), and *I Believe in the Holy Ghost* (1964). Gifted with outstanding oratorical power and a man of deep prayer practice with a passion for holiness evangelism, Maynard James had an international preaching ministry and for 50 years was the best-known holiness preacher in Great Britain. H.M.

JENNINGS, A(rthur) T. (b. Yates County, New York, 21 July 1858; d. Houghton, New York, 20 March 1914). **Wesleyan Methodist Church** (WMC) pastor, evangelist, and editor. The son of a pioneer WMC minister, Jennings was converted in 1873, and following a brief career as a schoolteacher, he entered the ministry of the WMC in 1878. Following pastorates in Ontario and New York and Seneca Falls, New York, he was elected editor of the *Wesleyan Methodist* in 1891, a position he held until failing health forced him to retire in 1913. A frequent speaker at holiness **camp meetings**, Jennings was influential in the WMC's close identification with the holiness movement while remaining faithful to the WMC's reform heritage. Deeply committed to holiness ecumenism, Jennings was one of the leaders of the unsuccessful negotiations for a merger between the WMC and the **Free Methodist Church** (1908–1909). He served as WMC representative on the committee that compiled the hymnal that was jointly published by the two groups in 1910. He also authored a WMC history (1902). W.C.K.

JERNIGAN, C(harles) B(rougher) (b. Casilla, Mississippi, 4 September 1863; d. Nashville, Tennessee, 21 June 1930). **Church of the Nazarene** (CN) district superintendent and evangelist. **JERNIGAN, JOHNNY HILL** (d. Nashville, Tennessee, 17 February 1940). CN evangelist and social worker. The Jernigans were ordained by **Seth Rees** in 1902. C. B. Jernigan cofounded the Holiness Association of Texas, an interchurch body, and founded the Independent Holiness Church, a sectarian one, believing that the scattered holiness bands needed the sacraments and a more churchly life. He guided the International Holiness Church into union with the New Testament Church of Christ, creating the Holiness Church of Christ (1904). As founding editor of the *Holiness Evangel*, he advocated the Holiness Church of Christ's union with the Nazarenes in 1908. His leadership of the Oklahoma District paved the way for the state to become one of the two fastest-growing sectors of the Pentecostal Church of the Nazarene. This included the founding of Bethany, Oklahoma, and Oklahoma Holiness College, now Southern Nazarene University. Later, he was superintendent of districts in New York, Florida, and Tennessee. *Pioneer Days of the Holiness Movement in the Southwest* (1915) was his most significant book. Much of Johnny Jernigan's ministry was directed to assisting prostitutes and unwed mothers, first at Rest Cottage, a home for unwed mothers, and later at the Nazarene Home, which she founded in Bethany, Oklahoma. R.S.I.

JESSOP, HARRY E. (b. Yorkshire, England, 7 March 1884; d. Largo, Florida, 13 January 1974). International Holiness Mission (IHM) and **Church of the Nazarene** (CN) minister and educator. Raised in a Baptist home, Jessop was converted in 1901. Following his experience of **entire sanctification** in 1916, he joined the Pentecostal Church of the Nazarene in England. In 1919, Jessop was appointed to an IHM congregation in South Wales; in 1920, he was named superintendent of the IHM work in northern England. During the 1920s, he served as visiting lecturer at **Cliff College**. In 1929, he was appointed guest pastor at the Northwest Tabernacle in Chicago. In 1930, he was named pastor of Austin CN in Chicago and joined the faculty of Chicago Evangelistic Institute (see **Vennard College**), where he served as dean (1934–1945), editor of the school's periodical, *Heart and Life* (1938–1954), and president (1945–1951). Perhaps the 20th century's most articulate holiness exponent, Jessop wrote the notable work *Foundations of Doctrine in Scripture and Experience* (1938), which reflects a classic Wesleyan emphasis on looking to Scripture, reason, tradition, and experience when defending holiness doctrine. Consistent with the heritage of the holiness movement, Jessop was a forceful champion of experiential religion, especially conscious divine guidance. This emphasis found expression in his important 1942 work, *The Lord Shall Guide Thee Continually,* and his widely read autobiography, *I Met a Man with a Shining Face* (1941). W.C.K.

JOHNSON, ANDREW NATHAN (b. Jackson County, Kentucky, 1876; d. Lexington, Kentucky, 22 August 1959). Methodist Episcopal Church, South, and Methodist Church (MC) evangelist and lecturer. Educated at **Asbury College**, Northern University (Ohio), and Milton University (Pennsylvania), Johnson was a gifted evangelist, temperance advocate, and critic of theological modernism, the theory of evolution, and postmillennialism. In an evangelistic career that lasted for 65 years, he conducted an estimated 1,000 revival meetings. An unusually gifted street preacher, Johnson often held street meetings during the annual meetings of the Kentucky Conference of the MC. As an ardent premillennialist and prohibitionist, Johnson rejected the notion that premillennialism was socially pessimistic, and he was the 1928 Prohibition Party vice presidential candidate. A frequent contributor to holiness periodicals, such as the *Pentecostal Herald* and *God's Revivalist*, Johnson was the author of *Twelve Striking Sermons* (1918) and *The Trial of John Barleycorn* (n.d.) and coauthor, with **L. L. Pickett**, of *Post-Millennialism and the Higher Critics* (1923). He was a board member of Asbury College (1919–1959). W.C.K.

JOHNSON, Z(achary) T(aylor) (b. Athens, Georgia, 18 June 1897; d. Lexington, Kentucky, 30 May 1981). Methodist Episcopal Church, South (MECS), Methodist Church, and United Methodist Church pastor, evangelist, and educator. Converted in 1913, Johnson served MECS pastorates in Georgia and Kentucky. He received an A.B. from **Asbury College** (1925), an M.A. from the University of Kentucky

(1926), and a Ph.D. from George Peabody College for Teachers (1929). He taught history at Mississippi State Teachers College (1927–1932). In 1934, he was named pastor of the Wilmore (Kentucky) Methodist Church and, in 1935, was appointed executive vice president of Asbury College, where he served as president (1940–1966). Although remembered most for his frugal fiscal policies that erased the college's indebtedness, Johnson also provided the leadership that resulted in accreditation for the college. As a student of southern culture and a product of his time and place, Johnson opposed the civil rights movement and the admission of African American students. Always primarily a southern holiness preacher, Johnson vigorously championed Asbury's **camp meeting** and holiness heritage. Among his most important publications were articles on southern history and culture in the *Georgia Historical Quarterly* and *School and Society* and several important defenses of holiness doctrine: *What Is Holiness?* (1936), *We Believe* (1950s), *Essential Holiness* (1960s), and *The Story of the Indian Springs Holiness Camp Meeting, 1890–1965* (1965). W.C.K.

JONES, CHARLES EDWIN (b. Kansas City, 1 June 1932). **Church of God (Holiness)**, **Church of the Nazarene**, and Reformed Episcopal bibliographer and historian. Educated at Bethany-Peniel College (Oklahoma), the University of Oklahoma, the University of Michigan, and the University of Wisconsin, Jones has served as a librarian at Nazarene Theological Seminary, Park College (Missouri), and Brown University and manuscript curator of the Michigan Historical Collections; and he has taught history at Tuskegee Institute and Houghton College. He is noted for his pioneer social history of the holiness movement, *Perfectionist Persuasion* (1974), and his published work includes significant essays in the *Missouri Historical Review*, *North Dakota Quarterly*, *Chronicles of Oklahoma*, *Methodist History*, and the *Wesleyan Theological Journal*. Equally important have been his trilogy of bibliographies: *A Guide to the Study of the Holiness Movement* (1974), *A Guide to the Study of the Pentecostal Movement* (1983), and *The Charismatic Movement: A Guide to the Study of Neo-Pentecostalism* (1995). W.C.K.

JONES, C(harles) P(rice) (b. near Rome, Georgia, 9 December 1865; d. Los Angeles, California, 19 January 1949). Baptist and **Church of Christ (Holiness)** minister, songwriter, and bishop. Following his conversion in 1884, Jones served as a Baptist minister in Arkansas (1888–1892) and Alabama (1892–1895). He experienced **entire**

sanctification. After his vigorous advocacy of full salvation among African American Baptists angered traditionalists, Jones, with his close friend, C. H. Mason, organized a series of holiness conventions among African Americans that resulted in the formation of the Church of God in Christ in 1897. Under the leadership of Jones and Mason, holiness or "sanctified" churches spread rapidly throughout the South and Southwest. In 1907, the movement was permanently fractured when Mason embraced Pentecostalism. In 1911, Jones, who continued to affirm a traditional holiness movement understanding of the **baptism of the Holy Spirit**, reorganized his followers into the Church of Christ (Holiness). Although respected as a preacher and church leader, Jones is primarily remembered as a songwriter. Among his most notable gospel songs are "I'm Happy with Jesus Alone," "Jesus Only," and "Perfect, Perfect." W.C.K.

JONES, E(li) STANLEY (b. Clarksville, Maryland, 3 January 1884; d. Bareilly, India, 25 January 1973). Methodist Episcopal Church (MEC), Methodist Church, and United Methodist Church missionary and author. Honored in a 1938 *Time* magazine article as the greatest missionary of our time, Jones was converted in 1899 and experienced **entire sanctification** in 1902 after reading **Hannah Whitall Smith**'s *Christian's Secret of a Happy Life*. Desiring to preach like the famed holiness evangelist **H. C. Morrison**, Jones enrolled at **Asbury College**, graduating in 1906. Appointed as an MEC missionary to India, Jones served as pastor of an English-language church in Lucknow (1907–1911) and then was appointed conference evangelist. Following a physical and emotional breakdown in 1915, Jones gradually experienced healing. No longer content with defending the certainties of his western evangelical faith, Jones became convinced that the living Christ transcended national and cultural boundaries. In his best-seller, *The Christ of the Indian Road* (1925), which made him an international celebrity, he articulated his vision of a Christ-centered non-Western Christian faith. Continuing his intentional effort to root Christianity in indigenous social institutions, Jones created the first Christian **ashram**, modeled after Hindu spiritual retreats, in 1930.

Equally important for Jones's mature articulation of the Christian faith was a 1934 visit to Moscow. Keenly aware of the attractiveness of Marxism to intellectuals in the Depression-ridden decade of the 1930s, Jones was deeply moved by Russian social and economic experiments aimed at improving the lives of peasants. Convinced that the West had much to learn from these experiments, Jones nevertheless believed that Christ's teaching in the Sermon on the Mount and the biblical image of the Kingdom of God offered a superior model of social regeneration. In *Christ's Alternative to Communism* (1935), *The Choice before Us* (1937), and *Is the Kingdom of God Realism?* (1940), Jones outlined his vision of a noncapitalist egalitarian social order.

On furlough in the United States during the early 1940s, Jones directly confronted America's history of racial discrimination. In his 1944 book, *The Christ of the American Road*, he urged African Americans to employ Gandhian style civil disobedience to achieve a racially integrated society. A friend of Gandhi, Jones wrote *Mahatma Gandhi: An Interpretation* (1948) following the Indian leader's assassination.

Although he was immensely popular, Jones's commitment to pacifism, socialism, and racial integration did not go unchallenged. Dismissed as a naive liberal by writers as diverse as Walter Horton, Reinhold Niebuhr, **Keswick** writer Robert C. McQuilkin, and holiness evangelist **John Paul**, Jones remained an unreconstructed holiness evangelist who united Wesleyan personal piety and social gospel activism. Although convinced that much of his training at Asbury College, such as premillennialism and dogmatic style apologetics, was anachronistic, Jones remained deeply rooted in the experiential piety of historic Methodism. In his widely read devotional books and especially in his important later work, *Victory through Surrender* (1966), Jones taught that in self-surrender to Christ an individual realized his or her true potential. W.C.K.

JONES, WILLIAM (b. Cadiz, Ohio, 22 October 1832; d. Kansas City, Missouri, 1 January 1898). Physician, Methodist Episcopal Church (MEC) minister, pastor, evangelist, author, and member of the National Holiness Association (see **Christian Holiness Partnership**). Raised a Methodist, William Jones was converted at the age of 10 and trained as a medical doctor. He accepted a call to preach in 1855, joining the North Ohio Conference of the MEC in 1863. He served pastorates in Ohio, Kansas, and Missouri; spent five years as presiding elder in Missouri; and served as a member of the General Conference of 1892. He twice turned down nominations to serve in the U.S. Congress. Jones joined the holiness revival after the second National **Camp Meeting** held at Urbana, Ohio, in 1872. He quickly gained prominence through his writing and preaching, and his testimony appeared in *Forty Witnesses* by Olin Garrison. Jones published at least seven books and pamphlets. Two of these, *The Doctrine of Entire Sanctification* (1890) and *From Elim to Carmel* (1895), became classics in holiness literature. K.O.B.

JOYCE, ISAAC W. (b. near Cincinnati, Ohio, 11 October 1836; d. Minneapolis, Minnesota, 28 July 1905). Methodist Episcopal Church (MEC) minister, National Holiness Association (see **Christian Holiness Partnership**) member and bishop. Converted in a United Brethren in Christ revival, Joyce was educated at Hartsville (Indiana) College and Indiana Asbury University, now De Pauw University. After a short career as a schoolteacher, Joyce joined the Northern Indiana Conference of the MEC in 1859. Rapidly emerging as an influential pastor, he served the Ninth Street MEC in Lafayette, Indiana (1866–1876). In 1880, he transferred to the Ohio Conference and was appointed pastor of St. Paul's Church in Cincinnati. Experiencing **entire sanctification** in 1883 under the ministry of **William Jones**, Joyce emerged as the most prominent MEC advocate of holiness doctrine during the last two decades of the 19th century. Joyce served as bishop of the Chattanooga Conference (1888–1896) and the Minnesota Conference (1896–1905). During his first five years in Tennessee, he also served as president of U. S. Grant University. Deeply interested in missions, Joyce presided over conferences and made episcopal tours to Europe, Mexico, China, Japan, India, and South America. One of the great evangelistic MEC bishops, Joyce could keep an audience spellbound for two hours. Convinced that spiritual growth took precedence over the routine business of the church, Joyce turned the conferences over which he presided as bishop into **camp meetings**. Frequently accompanied by holiness evangelists **S. A. Keen** and Edward S. Dunham, Joyce initiated so-called Pentecostal meetings that urged conference attendees to seek a deeper religious experience. Fittingly, his last message was delivered at the famous Red Rock Camp Meeting in Minnesota. W.C.K.

– **K** –

KEEN, S(amuel) A(shton) (b. Harrison, Ohio, 12 May 1842; d. Delaware, Ohio, 11 November 1895). Methodist Episcopal Church (MEC) minister, evangelist, and author. Following three years of service with the Union Army in the Civil War, Keen enrolled at Ohio Wesleyan University.

Following his graduation in 1868, he entered the Ohio Conference of the MEC. Experiencing **entire sanctification** in 1869 during his first pastorate in Chillicothe, Keen established a reputation as an effective pastor and skilled evangelist. Following pastorates in Ohio and Indiana, Keen entered full-time evangelistic work in 1891. Perhaps the most notable feature of his evangelistic career were the so-called Pentecostal meetings he conducted during regular sessions of many annual conferences. Instituted by Bishop **I. W. Joyce**, these meetings were the primary source of holiness agitation in the MEC during the last decade of the 19th century. Keen was a frequent contributor to a variety of religious periodicals and wrote several books, including *Praise Papers: A Spiritual Autobiography* (1895). Following his death, his widow, Mary Keen, prepared a biography, *Memorial Papers, or Records of a Spirit-Filled Life* (1899), based on his letters and journals. W.C.K.

KENT, L(yman) B(lakemarr) (b. Wyoming County, New York, 2 July 1830; d. Jacksonville, Illinois, 24 May 1911). Methodist Episcopal Church (MEC) and Pentecostal Church of the Nazarene (PCN; see **Church of the Nazarene**) minister, evangelist, and editor. Converted in 1847, Kent entered the ministry of the MEC in 1849 in the Northern Indiana Conference. After serving circuits in such Indiana communities as Valparaiso, Laporte, Rochester, and New Carlisle, Kent transferred to the Central Illinois Conference in 1859. Following pastorates in Galesburg and Rock Island, he was appointed presiding elder of the Peoria District in 1866. He later served as pastor of congregations in Macomb and Lacon. In 1871, he was one of the founders of the Western Union Holiness Association (WUHA), known after 1898 as the Illinois Holiness Association (IHA). In 1878, as holiness agitation in the conference became increasingly controversial, he was denied an appointment. Beginning a full-time ministry in evangelism, Kent became one of the Midwest's most notable holiness evangelists. He served as president of the WUHA/IHA (1872–1906) and as editor of its periodical, the *Banner of Holiness* (1883–1890). Although highly critical of the MEC, Kent opposed the formation of distinctly holiness churches. He remained convinced that the experience of full salvation was not the unique property of any sect or denomination. In spite of these convictions, by the time of his death, he had affiliated with the PCN. Following his death, Bertha Corson and **Iva Durham Vennard** edited his journals, correspondence, and writings into a biography, *A Stalwart of the Old Guard: The Life and Labors of Lyman Blackmarr Kent* (1911). W.C.K.

KENTUCKY MOUNTAIN HOLINESS ASSOCIATION. *See* Mc-CONNELL, LELA GRACE.

KESWICK. A specific teaching on **entire sanctification**, or, as its proponents prefer, "the higher Christian life"; an annual convention held at Keswick, England; and related conventions held around the world. The term's origins lie in a series of "higher life meetings" held by **Robert P.** and **Hannah W. Smith** and **W. E. Boardman** in 1873 and 1874. In 1874, the Smiths and Boardman were invited to hold a higher life meeting at the Broadlands, the estate of W. Cowper-Temple, later Lord Mount Temple. This led to similar 1875 meetings at Oxford and Brighton, which resulted in an invitation by the Anglican curate at Keswick, T. D. Herford-Battersby, for the Smiths to hold a similar meeting at Keswick. Just before the meetings, rumors of sexual indiscretion on the part of Robert P. Smith resulted in others assuming the Smiths' roles as leaders of the meetings.

After Smith's so-called fall, the meetings came under the control of Anglican and Reformed evangelicals who sought to articulate a doctrine of full salvation that was free of American and Methodistic perfectionism. In its classic form, Keswick teaching holds that the sinful nature is not extinguished or eradicated but "counteracted" by a second distinct religious experience following salvation, the **baptism of the Holy Spirit**. Introduced into North America by D. L. Moody, Keswick teaching was quickly wedded to premillennial **eschatology** and often to faith healing as well, creating the so-called fourfold gospel of Jesus as savior, sanctifier, healer, and coming king. This popular articulation received its classic expression in the writings of **A. B. Simpson** and continues as the unifying element in the theology of Billy Graham's revivalism. Although often considered an advocate of Keswick theology, Simpson, in fact, insisted that his own formulation lay between eradication and suppression or counteraction. The relation between Keswick and holiness teaching on full salvation remains complex. Although some holiness movement figures, such as **W. B. Godbey** and **A. M. Hills**, attacked Keswick views, others, such as **H. C. Morrison**, insisted that both groups of teachers were merely using different terminology to describe the mystery of the "baptism of the Holy Spirit." In the mid–20th century, although both holiness and Keswick proponents of full salvation continued to cooperate in ecumenical evangelical ventures, such as the ministry of Billy Graham or the support of *Christianity Today*, it was a rare holiness figure, such as **Paul S. Rees**, who would become a regular speaker at Keswick Conventions around the world.

Less definite than holiness teaching on full salvation, Keswick teaching has come under increasing attack for its lack of social vision and its tendency to encourage (at least its critics believe) spiritual complacency. At the beginning of the 21st century, although the institutions created by Keswick spirituality, such as *Christianity Today*, Moody Bible Institute, Wheaton College, and Dallas Theological Seminary, are flourishing, it is hard to find specific supporters of Keswick teaching on full salvation. Nevertheless, it should be noted that the classic Keswick texts continue to be read around the world.

In the final analysis, it is probably not the distinctive contours of Keswick theology but the social location and aspirations of its promoters that proved most troubling to holiness critics of this inventive reconstruction of holiness experience. For evangelists such as W. B. Godbey, holiness was an experience that led to a life lived in radical nonconformity to the world, while for Keswick adherents, the higher Christian life was an experience that liberated one from the uncomfortable implications of Jesus' teachings on possessions, allowing one to gain relief from the nagging feeling that Christians were not to be too comfortable this side of paradise. W.C.K.

KHAN, JOHN A. D. (b. Mymensing, East Bengal, India, 22 November 1877; d. Cuttack, Orissa, India, 8 October 1922). **Church of God (Anderson)** (CG[A]) minister and church leader. Alla-ud-Din Khan was born a Muslim and converted through the work of Australian Baptist missionaries in 1893. While studying in Calcutta, Khan, now "John," was called to the ministry. He affiliated with the CG(A) because it shared his view of the New Testament church.

Under Gospel Trumpet Company sponsorship, Khan founded a paper, the *Firebrand* (later *Victory*), and the Shelter, a girls orphanage, at Cuttack in the 1890s. In 1903–1904, Khan toured the United States and wrote *India's Millions* (1903), all the while recruiting missionaries and galvanizing interest in missions. Khan was the key figure in a circle of converts and missionaries whose efforts produced the then largest missionary field of the CG(A). Khan's gifted and determined leadership did not sit well with the church's colonial-minded missionary board. He and close friend George Tasker were determined to have their way, but Khan died of pneumonia in 1922, and Tasker resigned in 1925. M.D.S.

KILBOURNE, E(rnest) A(lbert) (b. Niagara Falls, Ontario, 13 March 1865; d. Los Angeles, California, 13 April 1928). Methodist Episcopal Church (MEC) and **Pilgrim Holiness Church** (PHC) missionary. A Western Union telegraph operator, in the early 1890s, Kilbourne was converted at the Grace MEC through the influence of his supervisor, **Charles E. Cowman**. With Cowman, Kilbourne was one of the organizers of the Telegrapher's Mission Band in 1894. Joining the International Apostolic Holiness Union (IAHU) (see PHC) in 1900, Kilbourne assumed direction of the Telegrapher's Mission Band in 1901 when Charles and his wife, **Lettie Burd Cowman**, established the IAHU mission work in Japan. In 1902, he joined the Cowmans in Japan. It was through the work of Kilbourne that several young Japanese telegraph operators, including Akiji Kurumada, Teiji Yamazaki, and Goro Mori, were converted. In 1902, Kilbourne became one of the founding editors of the mission's first publication, *Electric Messages*. Returning to the United States in 1917, Kilbourne assumed administrative leadership of the Oriental Missionary Society (see **OMS International**) in 1918 and, following the death of Charles Cowman in 1924, was named president, a position he held until his death. His son, E. L. (Bud) Kilbourne, was an important second-generation OMS leader. W.C.K.

KING, L(ouis) J. (b. Fredericton, New Brunswick, 1866; d. Toledo, Ohio, 18 November 1948). **Alliance of Reformed Baptist Churches** (ARBC) and **Church of God (Holiness)** (CG[H]) evangelist, author, and editor. Raised in a staunchly Catholic home, King was converted in a Canadian Methodist church in 1891 and experienced **entire sanctification** later the same year. Attracted to the ARBC cause in part because of its commitments to entire sanctification and believer's baptism, King emerged as a successful ARBC evangelist and anti-Catholic lecturer who greatly increased ARBC membership in the southern maritime provinces and northern Maine. In 1906, King began an evangelistic and anti-Catholic campaign in St. Louis, Missouri. He became associated with the CG(H) during a highly publicized anti-Catholic lecture series at Clarence, Missouri. Although he was admittedly the most successful CG(H) revivalist of the era, King's confrontational tactics and vicious attacks on Catholicism led to conflicts with CG(H) leaders that resulted in his disassociation with the CG(H) by 1911. King's attacks on the Catholic Church and sexually explicit depictions of life in convents led to repeated arrests for slander and distributing obscene literature. Settling in Toledo, Ohio, in 1908, King published his autobiography, *The Scarlet Mother on the Tiber: or The Trials and Travels of Evangelist L. J. King* (1908), operated a book room, and published a periodical, the *Converted Catholic*. Although still selling **W. B. Godbey's** *Commentary on Revelation* in the 1930s, he had largely dropped out of the holiness movement. W.C.K.

KING, W(alter) L(ee) (b. Dunbar, West Virginia, 12 October 1923). **Church of the Nazarene** (CN) minister and radical holiness leader and editor. King was converted in 1950 and began pastoring in the CN the same year. He followed **Glenn Griffith** out of the CN into the Bible Missionary Union in 1955. However, in 1956, he left this group to form the Voice of the Nazarene Association of Independent Churches, which now has approximately 42 ministers. He has also served as superintendent of God's Acres **Camp Meeting**, first located in Eighty-Four, Pennsylvania and later in Sun City Center, Florida. King's most significant contribution to the radical conservative holiness cause has been as an editor. In 1950, he began publishing the *Voice of the Nazarene*, which had a circulation of about 8,000 in 1998. This periodical gained and has retained a reputation for being among the most radical instruments of conservative holiness propaganda. King, who has been editor since the paper's inception, has persisted in aggressive assaults against liberalism both within and outside the holiness movement.

King's urgent warnings against apostasy, often couched in vitriolic language, have been frequently oriented against the Roman Catholic Church, the National Council of Churches, the charismatic movement, and such ecumenical endeavors as Promise Keepers. These disputations have sometimes led to the courtroom. For example, many holiness people applauded King's 1962 victory in a libel suit brought by the Roman Catholic Knights of Columbus.

Some of King's most intense criticism has been reserved for those within the holiness movement whom he has viewed as guilty of compromise with the world, especially those who have violated traditional holiness taboos. King has thus unreservedly declared himself a "**Sweet Radical Holiness**" adherent, condemning culture-accommodating holiness people. W.T.

KINLAW, DENNIS FRANKLIN (b. Lumberton, North Carolina, 26 June 1922). Methodist Church and United Methodist Church minister and educator. Educated at **Asbury College**, **Asbury Theological Seminary**, Princeton Theological Seminary, the University of Edinburgh, and Brandeis University, which awarded him a Ph.D. in 1967, Kinlaw served as a pastor in North Carolina, Indiana, New York, and Massachusetts. He has taught at Seoul (Korea) Theological Seminary (1959), and Asbury Theological Seminary (1963–1968, 1982–1983, 1993–1994) and served as president of Asbury College (1968–1981, 1986–1992). He is the author of commentaries on Ecclesiastes (1968) and Song of Songs (1968) in the *Wesleyan Bible Commentary* and Leviticus in the *Beacon Bible Commentary* (1969). His published articles have appeared in the *Asbury Seminarian, Wesleyan Theological Journal,* and *Christianity Today.* Deeply respected as a diplomat and educator, Kinlaw brought unity to a greatly divided campus when he assumed the presidency of Asbury College. Although he was rooted in experiential piety, Kinlaw made appointments that greatly strengthened the college's academic program. Reminiscent of the scholar-pastor-presidents of antebellum America, such as **Asa Mahan** of Oberlin, whom he admired, Kinlaw was the undisputed intellectual, spiritual, and moral leader of Asbury College. Fittingly, his administration included the 1970 Asbury revival, which spread to numerous college campuses and had a nationwide impact. Although he is respected as a teacher and scholar, Kinlaw's greatest impact has been as a preacher. He has served on the boards of the Oriental Missionary Society (see **OMS International**), Christian Holiness Association (see **Christian Holiness Partnership**), *Christianity Today*, Toccoa Falls (Georgia) College, and Catherine Booth College (Canada). W.C.K.

KINNE, CLARENCE J. (b. Knoxville, Iowa, 12 December 1869; d. Los Angeles, California, 19 October 1932). Methodist preacher, **Church of the Nazarene** (CN) publisher and missionary. Kinne entered the Methodist ministry about 1890, joined the Nazarenes in 1905, and became manager of the Nazarene Publishing Company in Los Angeles. He was founding manager of the Nazarene Publishing House of Kansas City, Missouri (1911–1915), a leading publisher of holiness literature and Christian music. He returned to California and became a full-time promoter of Nazarene missions. He founded the Nazarene Medical Missionary Union to build support for medical missions and to build a hospital in China. On three extended trips to China in the 1920s, he selected a site and supervised construction of Bresee Memorial Hospital in Tamingfu, which began receiving patients in 1925 and was completed in 1930. Kinne returned to California and, in 1931, published **A. M. Hills**'s *Fundamental Christian Theology.* R.S.I.

KITAGAWA, HIROSHI (b. Kumamoto, Japan, 11 January 1888; d. Yokohama, Japan, 1975). **Church of the Nazarene** (CN) preacher, district superintendent, educator, and editor. Raised in a predominantly Buddhist area of Japan, Kitagawa, who rejected Christianity in his youth, was embarrassed by his father's conversion to Russian Orthodoxy. He emigrated to San Francisco in 1906 and was converted to Christ two years later near Upland, California. He graduated from Nazarene University (Pasadena, California) in 1914 and was ordained by **Phineas Bresee**. Returning to Japan that year, he helped to organize the first CN church in his homeland at Kumamoto and became its pastor. He opened a school to train pastors in 1915 and soon began publishing the paper *Heavenly Way*. In 1922, he became pastor of a church in Kyoto and moved the school and paper there. Without dropping these responsibilities, he also served for 13 years (1922–1935) as a district superintendent. Kitagawa helped to rebuild the CN in Japan after World War II. His final pastorate was at Yokohama. R.S.I.

KLETZING, H(enry) F(rick) (b. Fairview, Montgomery County, Pennsylvania, 24 November 1850; d. Naperville, Illinois, 15 August 1910). Evangelical Association minister, educator, and publisher. Overcoming a childhood illness that left him partially disabled, Kletzing was educated at North Central College, Naperville, Illinois. Following graduation in 1879, he joined the faculty of North Central College, where he taught until 1896. Entering the publishing field with his brother, E. L. Kletzing, H. F. Kletzing was the author of *Progress of the Race* (1897), a celebration of the accomplishments of African Americans. Also, he was the coauthor, with his brother, of *Traits of Character* (1899). This biographical analysis of the character of a diverse body of 19th-century Victorian heroes was notable for its inclusion of people of color and, perhaps even more remarkably, Roman Catholics. He served as part owner of the Christian Witness Company and as publisher of the *Christian Witness* (1901–1910). Deeply committed to holiness higher education, he was one of the founders of Chicago Evangelistic Institute (see **Vennard College**) in 1910. Following his death, his brother, E. L. Kletzing, assumed direction of the *Christian Witness* and the Christian Witness Company. W.C.K.

KLETZING COLLEGE. Founded in 1906 as Iowa Holiness University, later John Fletcher College, Kletzing College (named after **H. F. Kletzing**) had a distinguished heritage as an interdenominational holiness college with close ties to the National Holiness Association (see **Christian**

Holiness Partnership) and the holiness element in the Methodist Episcopal Church. Its presidents included some of the most distinguished holiness evangelists of the 20th century, including **A. M. Hills** (1906–1908), **G. A. McLaughlin** (1910–1917), **J. L. Brasher** (1917–1926), **John Paul** (1933–1936), and **C. W. Butler** (1936–1946). In its early years, the school showed great promise. It opened with 224 students in 1906 and had an enrollment of 345 in 1909. Unfortunately, a theological controversy concerning a popular faculty member and the general economic decline of southeastern Iowa greatly reduced the school's viability. Attempts were made to merge the school with **Taylor University** in the 1920s and with **Asbury College** in the 1930s. At the time it closed, the school had 181 students. Nevertheless, through its graduates, including Sue Schultz, **Delbert Rose**, and Ivan Howard, it has continued to play an important role in the holiness movement. W.C.K.

KNAPP, MARTIN WELLS (b. Calhoun County, Michigan, 27 March 1853; d. Cincinnati, Ohio, 7 December 1901). Methodist Episcopal Church (MEC) and International Apostolic Holiness Union (IAHU; see **Pilgrim Holiness Church** [PHC]) minister, evangelist, author, and editor. Raised in a pious and poor MEC home, Knapp was converted while a student at Albion (Michigan) College in 1872. He entered the ministry in the Michigan Conference of the MEC in 1876. Although he was successful as a minister and evangelist, his experience of **entire sanctification** in 1882 seemed to invigorate his preaching. In 1887, Knapp entered full-time evangelistic work. In 1888, he founded the *Revivalist*, a monthly periodical dedicated to evangelism. In 1892, following the tragic death of his young wife, fellow evangelist Lucy Glenn Knapp, he relocated his ministry to Cincinnati.

During the next decade, Knapp's ministry flourished. Even as the *Revivalist* became a nationally circulated holiness periodical, he founded a publishing company, a school in southeastern Kentucky, and several rescue missions in the Cincinnati area. In 1893, Knapp established the International Revival League, an informal organization of individuals who covenanted to pray daily for revival, which was renamed the International Revival Prayer League in 1895. In effect, Knapp's practice of publishing lists of accredited ministers made the body a quasi-denomination. In the fall of 1897, after the National Holiness Association (NHA; see **Christian Holiness Partnership**) moved to limit premillennial preaching and faith healing at NHA camp meetings, Knapp's International Revival Prayer League became the IAHU, with

Seth C. Rees as president and Knapp as vice president. Although still a member of the MEC, Knapp had created an institution that would evolve into a separate church, the PHC.

As Knapp's ministry began to transcend denominational boundaries, worship became more demonstrative, and he began to emphasize such radical social and economic theories as God's ownership of all. Attacking elaborate churches and their wealthy parishioners, Knapp began teaching that, following Acts 2, Christians were to sell their possessions and distribute their resources to those in need. Sensing the imminent return of Jesus, Knapp deeded his property to God. *The Revivalist* became *God's Revivalist,* and the school that he established was named **God's Bible School**. In 1901, Knapp left the MEC. Ironically, Knapp's decision to deed his property in Cincinnati to God had unintended consequences. In a property dispute following Knapp's tragic death in 1901, a Hamilton County court ruled that God could not hold property in Hamilton County. It would not be until the 1970s that God's Bible School would be released from a court-appointed trusteeship. Among Knapp's most notable books were *Christ Crowned Within* (1885), *Impressions* (1892), and *Lightning Bolts from Pentecostal Skies* (1898). W.C.K.

KOREA EVANGELICAL HOLINESS CHURCH (KEHC). The roots of the KEHC are in the mission of the Oriental Missionary Society (OMS; see **OMS International**) to Korea, which was begun in 1907 by Bin Chung and SangJun Kim, two Korean students trained at the OMS-sponsored Tokyo Bible School. Under the direction of E. L. (Bud) Kilbourne, a Bible school, now Seoul Theological Seminary, was established. By the early 1920s, the Bible school had trained more than 300 Korean pastors. Beginning in 1927, the holiness movement in Korea, which had already shown signs of significant growth, was greatly energized by the success of evangelists Robert Nam Soo Chung, a graduate of **God's Bible School** and **Asbury College**, and Sung Bong Li, later known as the "Billy Graham of Korea." In 1940, the KEHC had 230 congregations and 40,000 members. In 1935, MyungJik Lee (also Chik Li) assumed direction of the Bible School. Lee (b. 1890), who had experienced **entire sanctification** under the ministry of **E. E. Shelhamer**, served as teacher, principal, and president of the school (1916–1968). He served as editor of the denominational periodical, *HwalChun* (*Living Water*); its principal holiness theologian; and an advocate of "oriental Christianity."

Although not a charismatic preacher, Lee was especially adept at keeping the Koreans and Western missionaries working together.

Under his leadership, Seoul Theological Seminary became one of the largest graduate schools of theology in the world. The 1930s and 1940s were particularly difficult times for the KEHC. In 1935, most of the congregations in northern Korea withdrew to organize the Church of God in Korea. During World War II, the pro-Japanese policies of Lee resulted in the sale of all of the church properties. It was not until 1953 and the end of the Korean War that the church started experiencing rapid growth. By 1995, it had nearly 1 million members, while other holiness bodies such as the Korea Jesus Holiness Church, a 1961 split from the KEHA, had 400,000 members; the Korea Holiness Church had 1.5 million members; Korea Holiness Church of the Nazarene had 100,000 members; and the Church of God in Korea had about 70,000 members. W.C.K.

KRING, J(ames) A(rthur) (b. Douglas, Illinois, 5 October 1873; d. North Long Beach, California, 1955). Methodist Episcopal Church (MEC), **Church of God (Holiness)** (CG[H]), and **Church of the Nazarene** (CN) minister, editor, and evangelist. Converted in 1884, Kring served as pastor and evangelist in the Southwest Kansas Conference of the MEC (1895–1901). In 1902, he became associated with the so-called elder supremacy faction of the CG(H) and received his education at that movement's McGee College in College Mound, Missouri. A forceful and demonstrative evangelist, Kring was the most successful evangelist in the supremacy faction during the first two decades of the 20th century. He served as editor of the movement's periodical, *Church Herald* (1906–1922). Like many members of the CG(H), Kring joined the larger CN in 1922. Continuing his career as an itinerant evangelist, he was an important holiness evangelist in the Midwest and Pacific Northwest during the next two decades. As a preacher and author, Kring was a master of the use of metaphor and the nonliteral interpretation of biblical texts. An especially notable exposition of his hermeneutical principles is found in his classic commentary on the book of Joshua, *The Conquest of Canaan* (1930). Shortly before his death, he published a volume of his evangelistic messages, *Vital Gospel Truths* (1955). W.C.K.

KULP, GEORGE B(rubaker) (b. Philadelphia, Pennsylvania, 23 July 1845; d. Battle Creek, Michigan, 21 July 1939). Methodist Episcopal Church (MEC) and **Pilgrim Holiness Church** (PHC) minister, evangelist, and author. Educated in the public schools of Philadelphia, Kulp, a Civil War veteran, was converted in 1871 and was licensed to preach in

1872. Following a 10-year ministry in Philadelphia, he transferred to the West Michigan Conference of the MEC. In Michigan, Kulp served churches in Martin, South Haven, Otsego, Battle Creek, and Grand Rapids (1882–1898). After a short but fruitful ministry at Holbrook, Nebraska, Kulp returned to Michigan in 1900. In Holbrook, Kulp had an intense experience of spiritual revitalization that resulted in his decision to leave the MEC and cast his lot with **Seth C. Rees** and **Martin Wells Knapp** in the International Apostolic Holiness Union (IAHU; see PHC). Renewing his ministerial vows at the Metropolitan Holiness Church in Chicago in March 1901, Kulp served as pastor of an important IAHU congregation in Battle Creek, Michigan (1900–1931). He was general superintendent of the IAHU (1905–1921). A cultured, if colorful, holiness preacher, Kulp was a frequent contributor to *God's Revivalist* and the author of such books as *Nuggets of Gold* (1908) and *Truths That Transfigure* (1927). W.C.K.

– L –

LANKFORD (PALMER), SARAH WORRALL (b. New York City, 23 April 1806; d. New York City, 24 April 1896). Founder of the Tuesday Meeting for the Promotion of Holiness. Following her experience of **entire sanctification** in 1835, in part through the ministry of **Timothy Merritt**, Sarah Worrall Lankford established the Tuesday Meeting for the Promotion of Holiness in her home in 1836, bringing together leaders of various denominations and about 200 laypeople for Bible study, prayer, and personal testimony. These meetings became the prototype for similar meetings held throughout the world. Lankford, who had been inspired by *The Life of Hester Ann Rogers*, had gained her breakthrough experience by abandoning the Wesleyan belief that one must have a palpable witness of the spirit. Henceforth, the ground for her assurance was belief in the naked scriptural promise. This controversial discovery became the foundation on which her sister, **Phoebe Palmer**, built her distinctive "altar theology." Two years after Phoebe's death, Sarah married **Walter Palmer** and assumed her sister's editorship of the *Guide to Holiness*. D.H.S.

LEE, LUTHER (b. Schoharie, New York, 30 November 1800; d. Flint, Michigan, 13 December 1889). A founder of the **Wesleyan Methodist Church** (WMC), reformer, and Methodist Episcopal Church (MEC) minister. Born on the eastern periphery of the "burned-over district" of New York, Lee underwent a religious conversion at the age of 21 and subsequently served several rather obscure pastorates in the Genesee and Black River Conferences of the MEC. In 1837, he became an abolitionist and served as a counselor to ministers standing trial for promulgating abolitionism within MEC conferences. By 1839, Lee had accepted the position of general agent for the Massachusetts Antislavery Society. He lectured throughout New England for the next two years, during which time he edited the *New England Christian Advocate* from his home in Lowell, Massachusetts. He, along with **Orange Scott**, La Roy Sunderland, Jotham Horton, and **Lucius C. Matlack**, withdrew from the MEC in 1842, calling for an antislavery convention in February 1843 at Andover, Massachusetts. That led to an organizing convention to form the WMC in May 1843 at Utica, New York. In 1844, in Cleveland, Ohio, Lee was elected the first president of the new denomination.

While president, Lee resided in Syracuse, New York, where he participated in the formation of the Liberty Party. He later served pastorates at Felicity, Claremont County, Ohio, and Chagrin Falls, Ohio. For 12 years he edited the *True Wesleyan*, the official organ of the WMC. In 1853, he preached the ordination sermon of Antoinette Brown (Blackwell), the first female ordained in America. In 1856, he published *Lee's Theology*, which earned him a professorship at Leoni (Michigan) College. The college soon closed; subsequently, he became professor of theology at the new WMC college in Adrian, Michigan. In 1857, he received an honorary D.D. from Middlebury College. On 4 July 1860, he delivered a speech at the grave of John Brown in North Elba, New York. In 1866, he returned to the MEC, pastoring churches in Flint, Northville, and Ypsilanti, Michigan. His writings include *Universalism Examined and Refuted* (1836); *Ecclesiastical Manual, or Scriptural Church Government Stated and Defended* (1850); *The Revival Manual* (1850); *The Evangelical Pulpit* (1854, 1864); *Slavery Examined in the Light of the Bible* (1855); *Elements of Theology* (1856); *Wesleyan Manual: A Defence of the Organization of the Wesleyan Methodist Connection* (1862); and *Autobiography of Reverend Luther Lee, D.D.* (1862). P.L.K.

LEVY, E(dgar) M(ortimer) (b. St. Mary's, Georgia, 23 November 1822; d. Philadelphia, Pennsylvania, 29 October 1906). Baptist minister and evangelist. Although raised in a Presbyterian home, as a youth Levy frequently attended Methodist church services. Converted in 1835, he began his ministerial career as pastor of the First Baptist Church in West Philadelphia in 1844. Noted as a successful evangelist, Levy served as a Baptist pastor in Newark, New Jersey (1858–1868), and as pastor of Philadelphia's Berean Baptist Church (1868–1894). He was one of leaders of the Newark Baptist City Mission, which resulted in the establishment of Sunday schools for poor children and seven Baptist churches during the 1850s and 1860s. Following his experience of **entire sanctification** in 1871, Levy emerged as the most prominent Baptist champion of full salvation. He was still a forceful champion of holiness experience and doctrine at the time of his death. Today he is primarily remembered for giving the invocation at the first Republican National Convention in 1856. W.C.K.

LILLENAS, HALDOR (b. Island of Stord, Norway, 18 November 1885; d. Aspen, Colorado, 18 August 1959). **Peniel Mission** and **Church of the Nazarene** (CN) minister, evangelist, and songwriter. Converted through the ministry of the Peniel Mission in Astoria, Oregon, in 1906, Lillenas united with the Pentecostal Church of the Nazarene (PCN; see CN) in 1908 and briefly attended Pasadena (California) College. He married PCN minister Bertha Mae Wilson in 1909, and the couple served as pastors in California, Illinois, Texas, and Indiana. As a ministerial team, the Lillenases preached and wrote and performed numerous gospel songs. In 1924, while serving as pastor of the First Church of the Nazarene in Indianapolis, Haldor Lillenas founded the Lillenas Publishing Company. In 1930, he sold the company to the Nazarene Publishing House, where he served as music editor until his retirement in 1950. He was author of more than 4,000 gospel songs, which celebrated Jesus as savior, sanctifier, healer, and coming king. Among Lillenas's most notable songs were "Wonderful Cross of Jesus," "A Closer Walk with Thee," "Jesus Can Heal," "My Wonderful Lord," and "Holiness Forevermore." He was the compiler of the first CN hymnal, *Glorious Gospel Hymns* (1931). He also wrote an autobiography, *Down Melody Lane* (1953). W.C.K.

LINCICOME, F(orman) (b. Noble County, Ohio, 2 February 1879; d. Gary, Indiana, 18 May 1960). **Free Methodist Church** (FMC) pastor, evangelist, and writer. Lincicome, though an effective pastor, is remembered chiefly as a gifted evangelist and wordsmith. Though a loyal member of the FMC, he is representative of the sizable cadre of preachers who, with passionate devotion to the cause of holiness, itinerated, sans portfolio, throughout the movement in the decades between the world wars. Readers of *A Lot in Sodom* (1932) and other much-reprinted sermons of Lincicome—who even one-time hearers long remembered for his skill with words—far outnumbered those who ever heard the evangelist in person. Characteristic of his style was his description, drawn from Bernie Smith's *Flames of Living Fire* (1950), of pride as an issue facing him and other seekers after **entire sanctification**: "Pride was my besetting sin. Some are proud of one thing, some of another. Some are proud of their face, others of their lace, others of their race, others of their place, and still others of their grace; and of all the most abominable forms of pride in the sight of God, it is a man who is proud of his grace." C.E.J.

LINN, OTTO F. (b. Falun, Kansas, 1887; d. Portland, Oregon, 17 June 1965). **Church of God (Anderson)** (CG[A]) minister and college professor. Converted in 1905, Linn joined the Gospel Trumpet Company after experiencing **entire sanctification** in 1907. From 1910 to 1930, he served churches in Kansas, Oklahoma, New York, and Denmark. During his Oklahoma pastorates, he earned B.A. and M.A. degrees at Phillips University. In 1930, he joined the faculty of Anderson College; while there, he earned a Ph.D. from the University of Chicago. In 1942, Linn was named dean and professor of New Testament at Pacific Bible College (later Warner Pacific College) in Portland, Oregon. Linn was the first minister of the CG(A) to earn an academic doctorate and the church's first scholarly writer. He introduced elements of the historical-critical study of the Bible to the CG(A) and to his college students. He participated in the translation of the RSV New Testament, and, in 1941 and 1942, he published *Studies in the New Testament*. M.D.S.

LOWREY, ASBURY (b. Goodwin's Point, New York, 20 March 1816; d. Germantown, Pennsylvania, 5 August 1898). Methodist Episcopal Church minister, presiding elder, editor, and author. Educated at Genesee Wesleyan Seminary in Lima, New York, Lowrey was admitted into membership in the Ohio Conference in 1840. He rapidly emerged as one of Ohio's most prominent Methodist leaders, serving eventually as pastor of Cincinnati's Morris Chapel. In 1860, he was named a presiding elder of the Springfield (Ohio) District. An articulate defender of the Wesleyan experience of Christian perfection (see **entire sanctification**), Lowrey was the founding editor of the *Methodist Home Journal*, later the *Christian Standard*, and was a founder and editor of *Divine Life* (1878–1896). A thoughtful defender of Methodism and holiness distinctives, Lowrey was the author of *Positive Theology* (1853) and *Possibilities of Grace* (1884). Although he was the author of a detailed response to **James Mudge**'s controversial critique of Wesleyan perfectionism that appeared in the *Methodist Quarterly Review* in 1895, he repeatedly urged holiness advocates to concentrate on the positive and on points of agreement among all Christians who desired to follow Christ faithfully. W.C.K.

LUCE, ALBERT L(aurence), Sr. (b. La Grange, Illinois, 26 June 1888; d. San Francisco, California, 16 November 1962). Methodist Church layman and philanthropist. During the 1920s, Albert L. Luce owned a Ford agency in Fort Valley, Georgia. In 1927, he manufactured a bus body that was used to carry children to school. A committed Christian, Luce believed that God led him to sell his car dealership and start a business building bus bodies. The Blue Bird Bus Company grew steadily and in 1935 opened a new manufacturing plant, which included a chapel. The company continued to prosper and after World War II became one of the largest school bus–manufacturing firms in the world.

Albert Luce and his wife, Helen, daughter of one of the founders of the Indian Springs Holiness **Camp Meeting**, committed their lives and resources to God. They gave millions of dollars to missions and other Christian causes. Albert served on the boards of numerous Christian organizations and institutions, including Indians Springs Holiness Camp Meeting, Chicago Evangelistic Institute (see **Vennard College**), and **Asbury College**. K.O.B.

LUDWIG, S(ylvester) T. (b. Moweaqua, Illinois, 2 April 1903; d. Kansas City, Missouri, 3 March 1964). **Church of the Nazarene** (CN) minister, educator, and denominational official. The son of pioneer CN evangelists Minnie and Theodore Ludwig, S. T. Ludwig was educated at Olivet Nazarene College in Kankakee, Illinois; Northwestern University; and the University of Kansas. He served on the faculties of Northwest Nazarene College in Nampa, Idaho, and Bresee College in Hutchinson, Kansas (1925–1936). A skilled administrator, Ludwig served as executive secretary of the Young People's Society of the CN (1936–1942); president of Bethany-Peniel College in Bethany, Oklahoma (1942–1944); and general secretary of the CN (1944–1964). He was the denomination's first full-time secretary. While fulfilling his duties as general secretary, he served at various times as executive secretary of the Department of Education, executive secretary of the Department of Home Missions and Evangelism, general stewardship secretary, and director of the Nazarene Information Service. He is remembered today, in part, as the father-in-law of former U.S. senator and presidential hopeful Gary Hart. W.C.K.

– M –

MAHAN, ASA (b. Vernon, New York, 9 November 1799; d. Eastbourne, England, 4 April 1889). Presbyterian and Congregational minister, educator, and author. Educated at Hamilton College and Andover Theological Seminary, Mahan served as pastor of Presbyterian churches in Pittsford, New York (1829–1831), and Cincinnati, Ohio (1831–1835). He was elected to the board of Lane Theological Seminary in Cincinnati, where his support for a group of dissident abolitionist students resulted in his being called to assume the presidency of Oberlin College, where many students who had been expelled from Lane had resumed their studies. Under Mahan's leadership, the college became noted for its commitment to abolitionism, women's rights, and other popular reform causes of the period. Following an experience of **entire sanctification** in 1836, Mahan emerged as one of the primary defenders of **Oberlin perfectionism**. He was the author of the first book-length defense of Oberlin teaching, *The Scriptural Doctrine of Christian Perfection* (1839). Insisting that the final goal of the Christian life was renewal in the image of Christ, Mahan vigorously defended the unity of the old and new covenants in the work of redemption.

Radical in temperament, Mahan loved spirited debate and angered many of the Oberlin community's more conservative members. Forced to resign as president in 1850, he served as president of the short-lived University of Cleveland (1850–1852) and as pastor of Congregational churches in Jackson, Michigan (1855–1858), and Adrian, Michigan (1858–1860). Returning to education, he was president of Adrian College (1859–1871). As was the common practice of 19th-century college presidents, he taught moral philosophy. Deeply wedded to Scottish commonsense realism, Mahan was the author of several important texts, including *A System of Intellectual Philosophy* (1845), *The Science of Moral Philosophy* (1848), and *A System of Moral Philosophy* (1882). Among his other works are a critique of spiritualism, *Modern Mysteries Explained and Exposed* (1855), and a history of the American Civil War (1877). Retiring to England in 1872, Mahan emerged as a leader of the British holiness movement and, in 1876, was the founder of a periodical, *Divine Life*. While in England he wrote two autobiographies, *Out of Darkness and Into Light* (1875) and *Autobiography* (1882). His mature reflections on the doctrine of Christian perfection, *The Baptism of the Holy Ghost* (1870), suggest a growing reliance on Wesleyan presuppositions. W.C.K.

MAINS, LURA ANN (b. Brownhelm, Lorain County, Ohio, 9 May 1847; d. Coldwater, Michigan, 27 February 1896). Free Will Baptist minister and evangelist. Educated at Olivet (Michigan) College and Hillsdale (Michigan) College, Mains taught school before being ordained as a Free Will Baptist minister in 1876. She capitalized on her skill as an evangelist and notoriety as a woman preacher, and her early ministry was marked with considerable success. Deeply impressed by the simplicity and spirituality of Free Methodists she encountered in Coldwater, Michigan, Mains sought and eventually received the experience of **entire sanctification** at the Old Orchard Beach (Maine) **Camp Meeting** in the early 1880s. Although much of her ministry centered in Michigan, Mains made several evangelistic forays into Kentucky, especially focusing her ministry in Berea. In 1883, she assumed direction of a church and school at Camp Creek, Kentucky. Deeply concerned about the lack of educational opportunities for poor children, especially girls, Mains established a coeducational boarding school, Mizpah Academy, in Coldwater in 1884. In 1886, the school was relocated to Dutton, Michigan. As an important leader in the interdenominational holiness movement in Michigan, Mains championed demonstrative worship and divine healing. Influenced by the Pentecostal Bands, she embraced a controversial teaching that encouraged sexual abstinence in marriage, commonly known as marital purity. Although the author of several tracts and periodical articles, she is best remembered for her autobiography, *Mizpah: Autobiographical Sketches* (1892). W.C.K.

MALLALIEU, W(illard) F(rancis) (b. Sutton, Massachusetts, 11 December 1828; d. Auburndale, Massachusetts, 1 August 1911). Methodist Episcopal Church (MEC) minister and bishop. Raised in poverty, Mallalieu was converted in 1839 and in his youth worked in the woolen mills of Massachusetts and Connecticut. He was educated at Wesley Academy in Wilbraham, Massachusetts, and Wesleyan University in Middletown, Connecticut, and he was admitted into membership in the New England Conference in 1858. Following a series of successful pastoral appointments in and near Boston, Massachusetts, Mallalieu was named presiding elder of the Boston District in 1882. In 1884, he was elected a bishop. Noted for his success as an evangelist and polished orator, he gained national prominence for his stirring tribute to controversial New England Methodist abolitionist and bishop Gilbert Haven at the MEC general conference of 1880. Although he shared Haven's commitment to civil rights for African Americans, Mallalieu was noted most as a champion of personal evangelical conversion. He was a supporter of evangelist D. L. Moody and the experiential piety of the holiness movement. He was chairman of the MEC General Commission on Aggressive Evangelism. Nevertheless, Mallalieu served as president of the Massachusetts Anti-Saloon League and vice president of the New England campaign to prevent cruelty to animals. His concerns for evangelism and experiential Wesleyanism are expressed in his two most notable books, *The Why, When, Where and How of Revivals* (1901) and *The Fullness of the Blessing of the Gospel of Christ* (1903). Following his retirement as a bishop in 1904, he wrote the introduction to G. W. Wilson's controversial critique of turn-of-the-century Methodist theologians, *Methodist Theologians vs. Methodist Theology* (1905). W.C.K.

MALONE, J(ohn) WALTER (b. Clermont County, Ohio, 11 August 1857; d. Cleveland, Ohio, 30 December 1935). Society of Friends minister, reformer, and educator. **MALONE, EMMA BROWN** (b. Pickering, Ontario, 30 January 1859; d. Cleveland, Ohio, 10 May 1924). Society of Friends minister and educator. Raised in a Quaker center of revivalism in New Vienna, Ohio, J. Walter Malone migrated to Cleveland in 1880 to join his brother in his stone-quarrying business. After experiencing **entire sanctification** under the ministry of **Dougan Clark**, Walter and Emma Malone founded Cleveland Bible Institute, now Malone College, in 1892. Deeply committed Quaker reformers and pacifists, the Malones established the Whosoever Will Mission in a Cleveland red light district and opposed the growing militarism in American society. Malone vigorously opposed the growing practice of adult believer's baptism among Evangelical Friends in the late 19th century. Emma Brown Malone, a convert of evangelist D. L. Moody, shared in every phase of her husband's ministry, including assisting her husband in his 25 years as pastor of First Friends Church in Cleveland. In 1922, the onset of Parkinson's disease forced Walter Malone to relinquish the presidency of Cleveland Bible Institute. W.C.K.

MARSTON, LESLIE R. (b. Maple Ridge, Michigan, 24 September 1894; d. Warsaw, Indiana, 14 July 1979). **Free Methodist Church** (FMC) bishop, educator, and author. Marston was reared by parents who served alternately in the FMC and **Wesleyan Methodist Church** (WMC) ministry. At the age of 17, he enrolled at Greenville (Illinois) College, from which he received a B.A. degree in 1916. An apt student, he completed an M.A. at the University of Illinois (1917) and a Ph.D. at the University of Iowa (1925), the latter in the field of child psychology. He served as executive secretary of the National Research Council's Committee on Child Development (1926–1928) and, in 1930, was appointed to the White House Conference on Child Health and Protection.

After serving six years as professor and dean at Greenville College, he became president of that institution in 1927. His professional academic experience also included service on the summer staffs at the state universities of Illinois, Iowa, and Michigan, as well as the Winona Lake (Indiana) School of Theology. He was a member of the Central Illinois Conference of the FMC in which he completed the requirements for ordination. In 1935, he was elected bishop and served in that capacity until his retirement as bishop emeritus in 1964.

From 1947 until 1964, he was senior bishop and president of the church's board of administration. He traveled twice around the world, visiting FMC churches. He also assisted in the organization of the World Fellowship of Free Methodist Churches, serving as its first president (1962–1964). Known for his administrative skills, personal integrity, and force of personality, he also led his denomination to adopt a commission form of government. He was one of the founders of the National Association of Evangelicals, serving as its president (1944–1946).

During his retirement, Bishop Marston, in conjunction with his daughter (Evelyn Mottweiler), organized the archives and historical center at FMC denominational headquarters. His published works include *The Emotions of Young Children* (1925); *From Chaos to Character* (1935); *Youth Speaks* (1939); and a monumental FMC history, *From Age to Age a Living Witness* (1960).

In a memorial tribute, Bishop W. Dale Cryderman wrote that "the long shadow of his influence covers the full length and breadth of the evangelical church world. Through his pen, pulpit, classroom, boardroom, and personal leadership, he molded the Church and many of its institutions." L.D.S.

MASSEY, JAMES EARL (b. Ferndale, Michigan, 4 January 1930). **Church of God (Anderson)** minister, preacher, and educator. James Earl Massey earned degrees from Detroit Bible College (later William

Tyndale College), Oberlin Graduate School of Theology, and **Asbury Theological Seminary**. He pastored the Metropolitan Church of God in Detroit (1954–1976) and was associated with Anderson College for many years between 1969 and his retirement in 1996, serving as campus pastor, professor of New Testament and preaching, and dean of the School of Theology. From 1977 to 1982, he was preacher for the *Christian Brotherhood Hour*, a national radio ministry of the CG(A), and from 1984 to 1989 served as dean of the chapel and university professor of religion at Tuskegee University, a position to which he returned following his retirement from Anderson. He has written and edited numerous books and has delivered many distinguished lectures. Massey has served on the Board of Trustees of Asbury Theological Seminary and was named a Life Trustee of the Seminary. He is the recipient of several honorary degrees and, in 1995, was honored by the **Wesleyan Theological Society** with its award for Lifetime Service to the Holiness Tradition. In 1996, Abingdon Press published *Sharing Heaven's Music,* a series of essays on homiletics written in his honor. B.L.C.

MATLACK, LUCIUS C(olumbus) (b. Baltimore, Maryland, 28 April 1816; d. Cambridge, Massachusetts, 24 June 1883). Methodist Episcopal Church (MEC) and **Wesleyan Methodist Church** (WMC) minister and reformer. Matlack was converted and admitted to the MEC at Philadelphia in 1827. Although licensed to preach in 1837, he was denied ordination. In 1839, he served as a junior pastor under **Orange Scott**. The New England Conference of the MEC stationed him as pastor in Holliston and later in Boston, Massachusetts. Frustrated by opposition to abolitionism, Matlack and others seceded from the MEC in 1842, and he became a founder of the WMC in 1843. He served as a WMC pastor; book agent; editor of the *Juvenile Wesleyan*, the *Wesleyan Magazine*, and *Family Mirror*; treasurer of the Wesleyan Missionary Society; and president of the Illinois Institute (now Wheaton College; 1856–1860). He entered the Union Army in 1861 as chaplain of the Eighth Illinois Cavalry, but was soon transferred to the fighting ranks as a major, and for heroic services was breveted colonel of the 17th Illinois Cavalry. He also served as Provost Marshal at St. Louis.

After the WMC refused to merge with the Methodist Protestant Church, Matlack returned to the MEC in 1866. He received an honorary M.A. from Adrian (Michigan) College and a D.D. from Indiana Asbury University (now DePauw University). He wrote *The Life of*

Rev. Orange Scott (1848); *The History of American Slavery and Methodism, 1780–1849* (1849), *History of the Wesleyan Methodist Connection of America* (1849), *Proceedings and Debates at the Convention of Laymen of the Methodist E. Church* (1852), and *The Antislavery Struggle and Triumph in the Methodist Episcopal Church* (1881). P.L.K.

McCLURKAN, J(ames) O(ctavius) (b. Houston County, Tennessee, 13 November 1861; d. Nashville, Tennessee, 16 September 1914). Cumberland Presbyterian Church (CPC) and **Christian and Missionary Alliance** (CMA) minister, evangelist, editor, author, and founder of the Pentecostal Literary and Bible Training School, now Trevecca Nazarene University (Nashville). The son of a CPC clergyman, McClurkan was converted in 1875. He was licensed to preach by the Charlotte Presbytery of the CPC in 1879. McClurkan served as a CPC pastor in Texas (1886–1888) and California (1888–1897). Although McClurkan never formally left the CPC, his experience of **entire sanctification**, under the ministry of **Beverly Carradine** in San Jose, California, in 1895, transformed his ministry. Returning to Tennessee in 1897, McClurkan, working closely with the CMA, established the Pentecostal Alliance, an independent ministry that eventually included a church, Bible School, orphanage, homeless shelter, periodical (the *Living Word*), and a missions program that would eventually send 33 missionaries to eight countries. In 1901, McClurkan severed his ties with the CMA, renaming his organization the Pentecostal Mission. McClurkan's theology united a Calvinist understanding of unmerited grace with an Arminian-Wesleyan emphasis on human responsibility. Although not unique, McClurkan's belief that entire sanctification was not the ultimate spiritual experience and was often followed by "a deeper death to self" was not the common understanding of Wesleyan perfectionists. Following **A. B. Simpson**, McClurkan was more interested in the ongoing relationship to Christ in the life of the believer than in the initial experience of full salvation. Among his most important books are *Wholly Sanctified* (1895), *Chosen Vessels* (1901), and *How to Keep Sanctified* (1914). R.J.H.

McCONNELL, LELA GRACE (b. Honey Brook, Pennsylvania, 1 June 1884; d. Vancleve, Kentucky, 7 April 1970). Methodist Episcopal Church (MEC) and Methodist Church minister and founder of the Kentucky Mountain Holiness Association (KMHA). McConnell was converted in 1898 and **entirely sanctified** under the ministry of **George Ridout** at the Delanco (New Jersey) Holiness **Camp Meet-**

ing. Her early adulthood was spent as a public school teacher in Pennsylvania and New Jersey. She was educated at Kutztown (Pennsylvania) State Normal School (1909), Chicago Evangelistic Institute (now **Vennard College**; 1915), and **Asbury College** (1924). Following two years as a teacher in a Bible school in Edmonton, Alberta (1915–1917), she served as a pastor's assistant in MEC churches in Philadelphia and Bristol, Pennsylvania (1918–1919). Becoming one of the first women licensed into the ministry of the MEC, McConnell served as an itinerant evangelist (1919–1922).

While a student at Asbury College, McConnell felt called to begin a ministry in eastern Kentucky. After organizing the KMHA in Jackson, Kentucky, in 1924, she established a permanent base of operation on a 12-acre site in Breathitt County, near Vancleve, in 1925. With the support of students from Asbury College and publicity generated by **Henry Clay Morrison**, especially through the *Pentecostal Herald*, McConnell established a string of missions and preaching points throughout eastern Kentucky. In 1925, she established Mount Carmel High School and, in 1930, Kentucky Mountain Bible Institute. In 1948, she founded the first radio station in Breathitt County (WMTC).

Following the faith model advocated by pioneer Methodist bishop **William Taylor**, McConnell and her workers received no salaries and lived in an intentional community supported by free will gifts and the produce of the community's farm. A leader in the Woman's Christian Temperance Union, McConnell was instrumental in ending legal liquor sales in Breathitt County in 1948. A frequent contributor to the *Pentecostal Herald* and *Heart and Life*, she was also the author of five autobiographical works. Especially notable was her first book, *The Pauline Ministry in the Kentucky Mountains* (1942). Shortly before her death, she named Karl Paulo to be her successor as president of the KMHA. In 1990, the KMHA had about 16 churches located in eastern Kentucky and continues to operate Kentucky Mountain Bible College. W.C.K.

McDONALD, WILLIAM (b. Belmont, Maine, 1 March 1820; d. West Somerville, Massachusetts, 11 September 1901). Methodist Episcopal Church minister, evangelist, editor, publisher, and author. Entering the ministry in 1840, McDonald rapidly emerged as one of the most prominent Methodist ministers in Maine, serving as pastor of several Portland congregations. His chronic health problems resulted in his transfer to the Wisconsin Conference in 1855. While serving as pastor of an

Appleton, Wisconsin, congregation, he experienced **entire sanctification** in 1857. Returning to New England, he served pastorates in Providence, Boston, and Brooklyn, New York (1859–1871). One of
the founders of the National Holiness Association (NHA; see **Christian Holiness Partnership**), McDonald served as vice president
(1868–1884) and president (1884–1893). One of the most prominent
NHA **camp meeting** evangelists, McDonald, who was often accompanied by **J. A. Wood**, spread the holiness message throughout North
America, and he traveled twice to Europe and once to India.

McDonald served as editor of the *Advocate of Bible Holiness*, later
the *Christian Witness* (1870–1894) and, with his partner **Joshua Gill**,
operated one of the most successful holiness publishing companies
during the 1880s and 1890s. He was a founder and president of the
Douglas (Massachusetts) Camp Meeting. Also a noted songwriter,
McDonald edited several songbooks, beginning with *The Wesleyan
Minstrel* (1850). Decidedly a Methodist loyalist who urged holiness adherents to remain faithful to Methodism or other evangelical denominations, McDonald vigorously opposed the growing movement to organize independent holiness churches. A critic of premillennial
eschatology and faith healing, he wrote *Modern Faith Healing Scrip-
turally Considered* (1892). Among his other books were *The New Testament Standard of Piety* (1860), *Scriptural Views of Holiness* (1877),
biographies of **Alfred Cookman** and **John Inskip**, and a study of
Wesley's teaching, *John Wesley and His Doctrine* (1892). Although his
sudden resignation as president of the NHA and of the Douglas Camp
Meeting and the dissolution of his partnership with Joshua Gill occurred amid an air of scandal, old associates, such as J. A. Wood, and
nonholiness Methodists staunchly defended his character. W.C.K.

McKENNA, DAVID L(oren) (b. Detroit, Michigan, 5 May 1929). **Free
Methodist Church** (FMC) educator. Following his education at
Spring Arbor (Michigan) Junior College, Western Michigan University,
Asbury Theological Seminary, and the University of Michigan
(Ph.D., 1958), McKenna joined the faculty of Spring Arbor Junior College. In 1960, he was named to the faculty of Ohio State University. In
1961, he assumed the presidency of Spring Arbor Junior College,
where he established a reputation as an educational innovator while directing the college's evolution from a struggling junior college into a
fully accredited four-year liberal arts college. He served as president of
Seattle Pacific University (1968–1982) and Asbury Theological Semi-

nary (1982–1994). A gifted communicator of the evangelical and Wesleyan messages, he is a much sought-after conference speaker. Among his most notable books are *The Jesus Model* (1977), *Megatruth* (1986), and *The Coming Great Awakening* (1990). W.C.K.

McLAUGHLIN, G(eorge) A(sbury) (b. Nashua, New Hampshire, 13 October 1851; d. Walnut Park, California, 10 March 1933). Methodist Episcopal Church (MEC) minister, evangelist, editor, and author. The son of an MEC minister, McLaughlin was educated at Phillips Exeter Academy and Wesleyan University in Middletown, Connecticut. Entering the ministry in 1875, he served congregations in New Hampshire and Massachusetts until 1892. Relocating to Evanston, Illinois, in 1892 to assume direction of the Christian Witness Company's Chicago office, McLaughlin centered his ministry around evangelism and editing. He served as an editor of the *Christian Witness* from 1891 to 1933. He was president of Iowa Holiness University, later **Kletzing College** (1911–1917). In 1918, he moved to southern California, where he taught at California Bible College (1918–1922) and the Training School for Christian Workers (1919–1933). As an author, he was most noted for his Bible commentaries, which included works on Matthew (1909), Mark (1910), Luke (1911), John (1913), and Romans (1925). Shortly before his death in the Los Angeles earthquake of 1933, he completed his final book, *The Autobiography of George Asbury McLaughlin* (1933). McLaughlin's career as a holiness evangelist was augmented by that of his wife, Mary Ella Henshaw McLaughlin, who convened a weekly holiness meeting in their Evanston home from 1892 until her death in 1910. She also served as Chicago office manager of the Christian Witness Company (1892–1907). Following her death, her husband wrote a biography, *The Beauty of Holiness, As Exemplified in the Life of Mrs. Mary McLaughlin* (n.d.). W.C.K.

McLEISTER, IRA FORD (b. Taylorsville, Pennsylvania, 22 April 1879; d. Alliance, Ohio, 7 May 1963). **Wesleyan Methodist Church** (WMC) minister, editor, and author. **McLEISTER, CLARA ORRELL** (b. Newport, Kentucky, 8 August 1882; d. Syracuse, New York, 2 January 1958). WMC minister and author. A third-generation WMC leader, Ira McLeister was educated at Houghton College and served as a pastor in the Allegheny Conference (1903–1919). Following their marriage in 1906, the McLeisters served as joint pastors of a WMC congregation in Akron, Ohio. In 1919, Ira McLeister was named denominational Sunday school editor. In 1927, he was named editor of the *Wesleyan Methodist*, a position he held until 1943. Deeply concerned with the denomination's history, Ira McLeister was author of a 1934 history of American Wesleyan Methodism and a leader in the celebration of the church's 1943 centennial. During Ira McLeister's tenure as a denominational leader, Clara Orrell McLeister served as pastor of the Canandaigua (New York) WMC (1921–1930) and president of the Woman's Missionary Society of the WMC (1923–1943). Her most noted literary work, *Men and Women of Deep Piety* (1920), remains in print. In retirement, the McLeisters founded the Lyncourt WMC. Following his wife's death, Ira McLeister wrote a brief biography, *The Life and Work of Rev. Clara McLeister* (n.d.). W.C.K.

McPHEETERS, JULIAN C. (b. Oxley, Missouri, 6 July 1889; d. Lexington, Kentucky, 31 October 1983). Methodist Episcopal Church, South (MECS), Methodist Church (MC), and United Methodist Church (UMC) minister, evangelist, and educator. Educated at Marvin College in Frederickton, Missouri, and Meridian (Mississippi) College where he taught (1910–1911), McPheeters served pastorates in the St. Louis, Arizona, and California–Nevada Conferences of the MC (1911–1948). He was pastor of the influential Glide Memorial Church in San Francisco (1931–1948). A frequent **camp meeting** preacher, McPheeters developed close ties with **Henry Clay Morrison**. In 1935, he began a weekly column in Morrison's *Pentecostal Herald*. He was named president of **Asbury Theological Seminary** and editor of the *Pentecostal Herald* upon Morrison's death in 1942. He remained president of Asbury until 1962 and editor of the *Herald* until 1975. Following his retirement as president of the seminary, he served the institution as representative for development. A weekly column McPheeters wrote for the *San Francisco Examiner*, and later published in booklet form, is considered to have been the model for the widely circulated Methodist devotional, *The Upper Room*. Deeply committed to holistic evangelism, McPheeters was instrumental in the integration of nutrition, exercise, physical healing, and social justice, especially racial justice, into the Asbury Theological Seminary curriculum. Shortly after his death, his son, Chilton McPheeters, wrote a popular biography, *Pardon Me, Your Halo's Showing: The Story of J. C. McPheeters* (1984). W.C.K.

MENNONITE BRETHREN IN CHRIST. *See* UNITED MISSIONARY CHURCH.

MERRILL, STEPHEN MASON (b. Mount Pleasant, Ohio, 16 September 1825; d. Keyport, New Jersey, 12 November 1905). Methodist

Episcopal Church (MEC) minister, editor, bishop, and author. Although trained as a shoemaker, Merrill became a teacher after his conversion in 1842. He entered the ministry in Georgetown, Ohio, in 1848. He served MEC circuits in Ohio and Kentucky (1848–1868). In recognition of his wide range of reading and dedicated scholarship, he was awarded an A.M. degree by Indiana Asbury (now DePauw) University in 1864. After serving as editor of the *Western Christian Advocate* (1868–1872), Merrill served as an MEC bishop (1872–1904). Never noted as an evangelist, Merrill was a skilled parliamentarian and an authority on Methodist constitutional law. Known for his wit and skill in the art of peacemaking, Merrill was a vigorous defender of the peculiar doctrines of Methodism. Among his most important works were defenses of Methodist baptismal practices, the doctrine of eternal punishment, and a critique of premillennial **eschatology**. His writings on Christian perfection, *Aspects of Christian Experience* (1882) and *Sanctification* (1901), were conciliatory in tone, even as they vigorously defended classic Wesleyan understandings of Christian experience. W.C.K.

MERRITT, STEPHEN (b. New York City, 6 March 1833; d. New York City, 29 January 1917). Methodist Episcopal Church (MEC) minister and philanthropist. A prominent New York undertaker, Merritt gained considerable notoriety for his handling of the funeral of President Ulysses S. Grant. Although he served for more than 40 years as a Methodist minister and as pastor of 15 New York City MEC parishes, Merritt was primarily noted for his generosity to New York City's rescue missions and soup kitchens. An early supporter of the **Christian and Missionary Alliance**, Merritt served as vice president of its board of managers. As the person who funded holiness icon **Sammy Morris's** education at **Taylor University**, Merritt became part of the Morris legend. He was coauthor, with **T. C. Reade**, of an 1897 biography of Morris. W.C.K.

MERRITT, TIMOTHY (b. Barkhamstead, Connecticut, October 1775; d. Lynn, Massachusetts, 2 May 1845). Methodist preacher and writer. Merritt was converted in 1792, and four years later he entered the Methodist ministry. He was stationed first on the London (Connecticut) circuit, and then in 1797, he began work in the Penobscot area of Maine. In 1803, Merritt located, but he continued to preach over the next 14 years. He returned to active work in 1817 and subsequently served in such centers as Lynn and Boston, Massachusetts. In 1824, Merritt published *The Christian's Manual: A Treatise on Christian Per-*

fection. Although the manual was primarily a compendium of statements by **John Wesley** and John Fletcher, Merritt stressed the distinction between justification and sanctification and the need for **entire sanctification**. To this he added the idea of a covenant with God, which he saw as a step toward attaining sanctification, an experience that he considered to be instantaneously available.

In 1831, Merritt began to serve part-time as an editor of *Zion's Herald* and, in 1832, became an assistant editor of the *Christian Advocate* (New York). He was committed to the abolitionist movement; in 1838, he was elected as one of the officers of the third general convention of the Methodist antislavery movement.

In the years following the writing of the *Manual*, Merritt joined the small but growing network of people committed to the spread of holiness. He counted both **Phoebe Palmer** and her sister **Sarah Lankford** among his friends. A zealous promoter of holiness in the church, Merritt envisioned a monthly publication to encourage those who were becoming interested in holiness. With the support of Palmer and Lankford, in 1839, he published the first issue of the *Guide to Christian Perfection*, which featured testimonies of entire sanctification and exhorted ministers to give extra effort to its promotion through special meetings. It also carried reports of **camp meetings** and revival services. Under Merritt's leadership, the *Guide* was a significant force in the spread of the Wesleyan holiness revival. It continued under other editors; in 1864, it was renamed the *Guide to Holiness*. M.F.W.

MESSENGER, F(rank) M(ortimer) (b. Stoddard, New Hampshire, 3 April 1852; d. Chicago, Illinois, 5 February 1931). Methodist Episcopal Church (MEC), **Metropolitan Church Association** (MCA), and **Church of the Nazarene** (CN) mill superintendent and publisher. Raised on a farm in rural New Hampshire, Messenger began working in the textile industry in Winchester, Massachusetts, in 1871. In 1884, he was hired as a superintendent of the Grosvenor-Dale Company in North Grosvenor, Connecticut, becoming sole manager in 1887. A nominal church member, Messenger was converted in the company-sponsored MEC church in 1893 and shortly thereafter experienced **entire sanctification** at the Douglas (Massachusetts) **Camp Meeting**. Separating from Methodism in 1898, Messenger emerged as a leader of those who advocated the organization of independent holiness churches. Following the tragic death of his son, Frank, Messenger invited MCA evangelists to conduct services in New England. In the ensuing controversy inspired by the evangelists, Messenger was terminated as manager of the Grosvenor-Dale Company.

Messenger joined the MCA and assumed direction of the movement's growing intentional community in Chicago. In 1906, he directed the MCA's relocation to Waukesha, Wisconsin. As a member of the MCA, Messenger began production of the Scripture Text Calendar, which included daily Bible verses and a monthly picture of a biblical story. In 1913, Messenger separated from the MCA, established the Messenger Publishing Company in Chicago, and began the mass marketing and distribution of the Scripture Text Calendar, or Messenger calendar.

Joining the CN, Messenger served as chairman of the CN Pension Board. In 1919, he was named chairman of the church's unified board. A frequent contributor to holiness periodicals such as *God's Revivalist,* the *Burning Bush,* and the *Herald of Holiness*, Messenger authored several books, including an early semiautobiographical work, *Catacombs of Worldly Success, or History of Coarsellor Dell* (1910); *The Time of the End, or the Book of Revelation* (1925); and *The Coming Superman* (1928). W.C.K.

METROPOLITAN CHURCH ASSOCIATION (MCA). Also known as the Burning Bush. The MCA was founded in 1894 by hotel owner Edwin L. Harvey (1865–1926) and banker Marmaduke (Duke) M. Farson (1863–1929). Initially a mission congregation of the Rock River Conference of the Methodist Episcopal Church (MEC), the MCA emerged as an important center for the holiness movement in Chicago, Illinois, which attracted nearly 1,000 Sunday School pupils and 200 adults by the time it separated from the MEC in 1899. The MCA's insistence that physical manifestations, especially jumping, were regular features of authentic worship resulted in the common practice of referring to MCA members as "jumpers." In the fall of 1900, Farson hired **Seth C. Rees** to assume direction of the Chicago ministry. In early March, a scheduled two-week evangelistic campaign initiated a revival that attracted front-page coverage in Chicago newspapers. Within three months, an estimated 2,200 people had experienced salvation.

In May 1902, the MCA established a periodical, the *Burning Bush.* Adopting the features commonly associated with mass circulation periodicals, the *Burning Bush* became a religious expression of the muckraking journalism of the early 20th century. Employing a professional cartoonist, it used caricature and publication of private correspondence in a never-ending war against the wealthy, prominent evangelists, established denominations, and alleged holiness compromisers. The MCA attracted the adherence of several colorful religious figures, such as **Alma White**, colorful African American preacher Susan Fogg, and **Reuben A. (Bud) Robinson**.

Especially significant was the MCA's role in the origins of Pentecostalism. In April 1906, A. G. Garr, an MCA evangelist, led part of the MCA's Los Angeles mission to Seymour's Azusa Street Mission. Following his experience of Pentecostal baptism, Garr returned to Chicago and to Danville, Virginia, and even attempted to spread the Pentecostal message to MCA missions in India. In retaliation, the MCA used the full force of its muckraking journalism in a series of graphic exposés of Pentecostalism.

The most controversial feature of the MCA was its rejection of private property. Organizing intentional communities in Waukesha, Wisconsin, and Bullard, Texas, the MCA, with more than 1,000 residents, was one of the largest communal societies in American history. Experiencing a steady decline following World War I, the Burning Bush movement gradually evolved into a conventional evangelical religious body. Having abandoned the remaining features of communalism, the MCA sold its Waukesha property in 1956. As of 1999, the MCA continued to publish the *Burning Bush* and operate a church in Milwaukee, Wisconsin. Its continued vitality is as an indigenous international movement with more than 50,000 members in India and churches in South Africa, Swaziland, and Mexico. W.C.K.

MISSIONARY CHURCH ASSOCIATION (MiCA). Founded in 1898 in Berne, Indiana, after a **Christian and Missionary Alliance** (CMA) Bible convention. Many early MiCA members came from the nearby "Egly Amish" and from the mostly Mennonite German branch of the CMA. All accepted **A. B. Simpson**'s emphasis on the fourfold gospel. From the beginning, the MiCA had close ties to the CMA. Its first president, A. E. Funk, was a close associate of Simpson. Other early leaders were **J. E. Ramseyer** and **J. A. Sprunger**. Although early missionaries usually served under other bodies, especially the CMA, the MiCA did eventually establish missions in Sierra Leone, Ecuador, Haiti, the Dominican Republic, Jamaica, and Hawaii. An ecumenical evangelical body from the beginning, the MiCA founded institutions, such as Fort Wayne Bible College and Jamaica Theological Seminary, and served a broad evangelical constituency, while a number of MiCA leaders were active in the creation of such agencies as the National Association of Evangelicals, the Evangelical Missions Association Information Service, the American Association of Bible Colleges, and the Caribbean Evangelical Theological Association. In 1969, when it merged with the **United Missionary Church**, the MiCA had about 110 churches and 9,000 members. T.P.E.

MISSIONARY CHURCH (MiC). Headquartered at Fort Wayne, Indiana. The MiC grew out of the 1968–1969 merger of the **Missionary Church Association** (MiCA) and the **United Missionary Church** (UMiC). Both churches shared an Anabaptist history influenced by Pietism and by the Wesleyan–holiness and **Keswick**–holiness movements, including the fourfold gospel of **A. B. Simpson**. By the time of the merger, both were active in the National Association of Evangelicals; earlier trademarks such as a peace witness and commitment to women in ministry had faded, while elements of fundamentalism had emerged. The MiC practices believer's baptism and has a congregational polity. As the name suggests, overseas missions and evangelism were a fundamental source of self identity. At the time of merger, the MiC had 273 congregations with 17,700 members and an average Sunday worship attendance of 25,500. In the United States, membership was concentrated in Indiana, Michigan, Ohio, and California. In 1987, the Canadian congregations formed the Missionary Church of Canada and, in 1993, merged with the Evangelical Church of Canada to form the Evangelical Missionary Church of Canada.

By the late 1990s, in the United States, the MiC had 340 congregations with 31,640 members, an average Sunday worship attendance of 45,500, and a constituency of 72,000. One-third of the denomination's congregations were less than nine years old, and one-third of the new churches were non-European. New districts included Puerto Rico and Texas. At the time of the merger, outreaches were maintained in Nigeria, India, Sierra Leone, Ecuador, the Dominican Republic, Jamaica, Haiti, Brazil, Mexico, and Cyprus. National churches are autonomous members of the International Fellowship of Missionary Churches. Since the merger, new missions have been established in France (1979), Spain (1985), and, in the 1990s, Indonesia, Thailand, Portugal, Russia, Arab nations, Vietnam, China, Cuba, Chad, Venezuela, South Africa, and Germany and among Kurds. In Nigeria, membership exceeds that of the U.S. church. The MiC is the primary supporter of Jamaica Theological Seminary. Not all features of the merger have worked. Bethel Publishing Company attempted to expand too rapidly and was forced out of business in 1998. Meanwhile, Bethel College (Mishawaka, Indiana; UMiC) and Fort Wayne (Indiana) Bible College (MiCA) struggled to serve the same constituency, with the latter eventually merging with **Taylor University**. T.P.E.

MORGAN, JOHN (b. near Cork, Ireland, November 1802; d. Oberlin, Ohio, 27 September 1884). Congregational minister and educator. The son of an impoverished Irish local Methodist preacher, Morgan was educated at Stockbridge, Massachusetts, and Williams College, where he was valedictorian in 1826. Morgan served as a teacher in New York City (1826–1832) and as professor of general studies at Lane Seminary in Cincinnati, Ohio (1832–1835). As a result of his abolitionist convictions, Morgan was relieved of his duties at Lane in early 1835. He served on the faculty of Oberlin College (1835–1881), where he was professor of New Testament and Hebrew. He was acting president of Oberlin College (1850–1851) and assistant pastor of First Congregational Church, Oberlin (1851–1872). Although remembered as a conservative and a champion of conventional educational theory, Morgan was an ardent abolitionist and an important exponent of **Oberlin perfectionism**. He was the author of significant articles in such periodicals as the *Oberlin Evangelist* and *Bibliotheca Sacra* and a short book, *The Gift of the Holy Spirit* (1875). W.C.K.

MORRIS, SAMUEL (b. West Africa, 1873; d. Fort Wayne, Indiana, 12 May 1893). Spiritual icon. Sammy, or Kaboo, his native name, was the son of a Kru nation chief, probably from near the Po River in southern Liberia. Enslaved as a youth, Morris escaped and found employment on a plantation in Liberia. Following conversion to Christianity, he was encouraged to seek further training in America. Through the intervention of **Stephen Merritt**, Morris was accepted as a special student at **Taylor University** in 1892. Although his tragic death a year later was little noticed outside the Taylor community, Taylor University president **T. C. Reade**'s inspirational biographical pamphlet of 1896 turned Morris into an evangelical legend. Selling more than 200,000 copies by the 1920s, Reade's tract and its numerous imitations were skillfully used in the promotion of Taylor University, especially through a special fund for international students and in the construction of the Sammy Morris dormitory. Many believe that funds raised by Reade's tract literally kept the school open at a crucial period in its history. In effect, the image of Morris, as presented by Reade, and perfect surrender to the love and will of God would remain a standard of evangelical devotion throughout the 20th century. W.C.K.

MORRISON, H(enry) C(lay) (b. Bedford, Kentucky, 10 March 1857; d. Elizabethton, Tennessee, 27 March 1942). Methodist Episcopal Church, South (MECS), and Methodist Church (MC) minister, evangelist, editor, and author. Morrison was raised on his grandfather's farm and educated at Ewing Institute in Perryville, Kentucky, and Vanderbilt University. Entering the ministry of the MECS in 1878, Morrison experienced success as a pastor and evangelist, serving appointments in Kentucky at Stanford, Covington, Danville, and Frankfort. During the late 1880s, he experienced **entire sanctification** and rapidly emerged as one of the most notable holiness evangelists in the South.

Leaving the pastoral ministry in 1890, Morrison became an evangelist, editor, and publisher. In 1888, he founded the *Kentucky Methodist*, a paper dedicated to revivalism, holiness, and the traditional conservative lifestyle of primitive Methodism. In 1897, the paper, now with a national circulation, was renamed the *Pentecostal Herald*. Although Morrison remained editor until his death, much of the paper's success was due to the contributions of his wife, Elizabeth Whitehead Morrison (1867–1945). A former teacher at **Asbury College** and **Taylor University**, she served as office editor (1906–1916) and associate editor (1916–1945). H. C. Morrison also served as president of the Pentecostal Publishing Company, which was one of the primary holiness publishers of the era. As one of the great showmen and religious orators of his day, Morrison conducted a reported 1,200 revival meetings and preached at an estimated 250 **camp meetings**. He served as president of Asbury College (1910–1925, 1933–1940) and as founder and first president of **Asbury Theological Seminary** (1923–1942).

As a Bryan Democrat, Morrison was deeply concerned about the economic plight of farmers and workers and was critical of the emerging capitalist class. Although an economic liberal, he remained a social conservative who supported Prohibition, Sunday blue laws, and anti-Catholicism, and he opposed the teaching of evolution in the public schools. Despite being committed to traditional holiness teaching, Morrison easily formed coalitions with non-Wesleyans, such as **Keswick** holiness advocates, nonholiness Methodist fundamentalists, and national fundamentalist leaders, such as William Jennings Bryan. He was the author of more than 20 books dealing with evangelism, holiness, and premillennialism and two autobiographical works, *Life Sketches and Sermons* (1903) and *Some Chapters from My Life* (1941). W.C.K.

MORRISON, JOHN A. (b. Phelps County, Missouri, 6 February 1893; d. Anderson, Indiana, 23 December 1965). **Church of God (Anderson)** (CG[A]) minister and educator. Born into a family with a history of interest in holiness, John A. Morrison left a career as a teacher when he was called into the ministry in 1917. While serving as a pastor in Colorado, he was invited to become principal of Anderson Bible Training School in 1919. He accepted the position and subsequently presided over the development of the school until his retirement in 1958. Morrison's folksy storytelling endeared him to generations of students, and, with longtime friend and partner **Russell Olt**, Morrison guided Anderson College through the Depression years to reach its goals of accreditation and academic respectability. M.D.S.

MORRISON, J(oseph) G(rant) (b. Oskaloosa, Iowa, 27 March 1871; d. Kansas City, Missouri, 23 November 1939). Methodist Episcopal Church (MEC), Laymen's Holiness Association, and **Church of the Nazarene** (CN) pastor, editor, evangelist, and denominational leader. Converted in a Methodist revival in 1887, Morrison entered the MEC ministry in 1893. Following his experience of **entire sanctification** under the ministry of bishop **Isaac Joyce** in 1895, Morrison emerged as a prominent leader at the Jamestown (North Dakota) **Camp Meeting** and in the Holiness Movement in the Upper Midwest. Following service in the Spanish-American War, he served MEC congregations in Minneapolis and Fergus Falls, Minnesota (1899–1907); Jamestown (1907–1912) and Dickinson (1912–1915), North Dakota; and Fort Lauderdale, Florida (1916–1917). Morrison, who had served as coeditor and then editor of the *Little Methodist*, later the *Holiness Layman* (1908–1925), was especially critical of Methodist Sunday school materials and the course of study for Methodist ministers. When he was ousted from the MEC ministry in 1917, his followers organized the Laymen's Holiness Association with Morrison as president. In 1922, Morrison led his followers into the CN. As a member of the CN, Morrison served as general superintendent of the Minneapolis District (1922–1927), president of Northwest Nazarene College (1927), and general missionary secretary of the CN (1927–1939). Although Morrison's bitter attacks on theological liberalism in Methodism have led some to dismiss him as a Wesleyan fundamentalist, he is best understood for his commitment to the traditional optimistic spirituality of the holiness movement, which received classic expression in his most important book, *Achieving Faith* (1926). W.C.K.

MOTT, EDWARD (b. Saratoga County, New York, 9 December 1866; d. Portland, Oregon, 31 May 1955). Society of Friends minister, evangelist, and educator. Following his experience of **entire sanctification** in 1886, Mott entered the Friends ministry. In 1887, he was recorded as a minister in the New York Yearly Meeting. He served as minister of Friends meetings in Macedon Center, New York (1889–1891); Adrian, Michigan (1891–1900); and Tecumseh, Michigan (1900–1904). Although self-educated, he taught the Bible and theology at Cleveland Bible Institute (1904–1920), where he served for a time as editor of the *Evangelical Friend*. After serving as a Friends minister in Long Beach, California (1920–1922), Mott was president of Northern Pacific Evangelistic Institute, later Portland Bible Institute and Cascade College (1922–1933), and served on the faculty (1933–1938). He was presiding clerk of the Oregon Yearly Meeting of Friends (1924–1944). A bitter critic of theological liberalism, Mott was a vigorous defender of the evangelical and holiness legacy of such Quaker figures as George Fox and Joseph John Gurney (1788–1847). Among his most important books were *The Christ of the Eternities* (1936), *God's Plan for the Restoration of Man* (1941), *Christ Preeminent* (1943), and an autobiography, *60 Years of Gospel Ministry* (1947). W.C.K.

MUDGE, JAMES (b. West Springfield, Massachusetts, 5 April 1844; d. Malden, Massachusetts, 7 May 1918). Methodist Episcopal Church (MEC) minister, missionary, and author. A fourth-generation New England Methodist, Mudge was converted in 1856 and experienced **entire sanctification** in 1860. Following education at Wesleyan University in Middletown, Connecticut, and the Boston University School of Theology, he was admitted into membership in the New England Conference in 1868. He served as an MEC pastor in New England (1868–1873, 1883–1908) and as a missionary in India (1873–1883), where he was editor of the *Lucknow Witness* and wrote an introduction to Methodist history and doctrine, *Handbook of Methodism* (1877). Later, he served as a lecturer in missions at the Boston University School of Theology (1888–1913) and secretary of the New England Conference (1889–1918).

An active participant in the holiness movement, whose testimony was included as a standard example of Christian experience in S. Olin

Garrison's *Forty Witnesses* (1887), Mudge came to the conclusion that **John Wesley's** teaching on Christian perfection (see **entire sanctification**) and the views of the holiness movement were sadly deficient. His controversial *Growth in Holiness toward Perfection, or Progressive Sanctification* (1896) was judged to be the most serious challenge to holiness teaching in the late 19th century and drew book-length responses from **Daniel Steele** and **L. R. Dunn**. Mudge insisted that sanctification was entire up to the light given at conversion and continued to be entire during later fillings of the Spirit. As a result, he emphasized the progressive nature of the Christian life. Mudge's mature view of full salvation appears in *The Life of Love* (1902). A lifelong student of Christian experience, Mudge was the author of *Faber* (1885), *Fenelon* (1906), and several volumes of spiritual biographies, including *The Saintly Calling* (1905) and *The Perfect Life* (1911). W.C.K.

MUNRO, BERTHA (b. Saugus, Massachusetts, 19 February 1887; d. Wollaston, Massachusetts, 19 January 1983). Association of Pentecostal Churches of America and **Church of the Nazarene** (CN) educator. Nurtured in a pioneer holiness congregation in Cliftondale, Massachusetts, Munro was converted at the Douglas (Massachusetts) **Camp Meeting** in 1902. Following graduation from Boston University in 1907, she taught foreign languages in area public schools (1907–1910) and was on the faculty of Pentecostal Collegiate Institute in North Scituate, Rhode Island (1910–1915). After receiving a master's degree in English from Radcliffe College in 1916, Munro taught at **Taylor University** (1916–1919). She served as professor of English and dean at Eastern Nazarene College (1919–1957). During the 1920s, she continued her education at Harvard University, studying with Irving Babbitt and Kenneth Murdock. Following her formal retirement from Eastern Nazarene College, she continued to teach part-time until 1968. She wrote numerous articles that appeared in the *Herald of Holiness*; several devotional books, including *Truth for Today* (1947) and *Strength for Tomorrow* (1954); and an autobiography, *The Years Teach* (1970). Although deeply rooted in holiness spirituality, Munro's thought bore the decided imprint of the personalist philosophy in which she had been nurtured at Boston University under William M. Warren and especially Borden Parker Bowne. This is reflected in point 3 of her famous Munro Doctrine: "persons are more important than things." The dominant personality at Eastern Nazarene College during its first five decades, Munro was committed to consecrated scholarship, which inspired several generations of CN youth to seek advanced academic training. W.C.K.

MUSSELMAN, W(illiam) B(runner) (b. Zionsville, Pennsylvania, 3 October 1860; d. Cleveland, Ohio, 21 February 1938). Mennonite Brethren in Christ (MBIC; now Bible Fellowship Church) colporteur and missionary administrator. The son of Jonas Musselman, an Evangelical Mennonite preacher, W. B. was converted at 16, began preaching at 23, and built four churches in the first seven years of his ministry. Elected presiding elder in 1892, he found that his heart was more in colportage work. In 1898, he declined reelection so that he could devote himself to missions at home and abroad, whereupon the conference named him missionary presiding elder. An energetic and progressive leader, he started tent meetings, hall meetings, and mission **camp meetings**. In 1895, he organized the Gospel Workers Society, which provided a means for unmarried women to do city mission work. Several missions in Pennsylvania and New Jersey were placed in charge of young women who developed them into permanent congregations. Musselman founded and managed Union Gospel Press in Cleveland to provide books, tracts, and Sunday school literature for distribution. He also founded the *Gospel Herald*, a leading religious periodical of the time. In addition to his home mission activities, W. B. managed the foreign missionary outreach of the Pennsylvania district of the MBIC Church for 40 years. W.J.G.

– N –

NAKADA, JUGI (b. Hirosaki, Japan, 27 October 1870; d. Tokyo, 24 September 1939). Methodist Episcopal Church (MEC), Pentecostal League of Prayer, and Japan Holiness Church minister, evangelist, editor, and bishop. The son of a samurai and an expert in judo, Nakada was converted in 1887 and admitted into the MEC ministry in 1891. Following his marriage to fellow Methodist minister Katsuko Odate in 1894, Nakada was invited by D. L. Moody to study at Moody Bible Institute. Influenced by R. A. Torrey and **A. M. Hills**, Nakada experienced **entire sanctification** in 1897. Returning to Japan in 1899, Nakada established a holiness periodical, *Tongue of Fire*, which he edited until his death. With **Charles Cowman**, Nakada established a mission and Bible school in Tokyo in 1901. When the Oriental Missionary Society (see **OMS International**) was established in 1901, Nakada became one of its directors. In 1917, Nakada resigned as a director of the OMS when he was named bishop of the recently organized Japan Holiness Church, a movement with 46 churches and about 1,500 members that, by 1923, had 2,783 members and in 1933, 19,523 members. A noted evangelist, Nakada established the first regular Christian radio program in Japan. By the early 1930s, he was an increasingly controversial figure. Influenced in part by the commentaries of **W. B. Godbey**, Nakada became convinced that Japan had been chosen to play an important role in preparing the world for the return of Jesus. His book *Japan in the Bible* (1933) resulted in internal conflict, and Nakada and his supporters withdrew to organize the Kiyome Kyokai, a Japanese holiness church, in 1933. W.C.K.

NAST, WILHELM (William) (b. Stuttgart, Germany, 15 June 1807; d. Cincinnati, Ohio, 16 May 1899). Methodist Episcopal Church (MEC) minister and editor. Deeply influenced in his youth by mystical and pietistic writers, such as Thomas à Kempis and Johann Arndt, Nast began preparation for the Lutheran ministry at Blaubeuren and Tübingen, where he studied under F. C. Bauer and was the roommate of David F. Strauss. In 1828, with his evangelical faith shattered, Nast migrated to the United States. Continuing his spiritual quest, he taught at the U.S. Military Academy (West Point, New York), Gettysburg (Pennsylvania) College, and Kenyon (Ohio) College (1829–1835). Following an intense conversion experience on 11 January 1835, he entered the ministry of the MEC. He served as a missionary to German immigrants in the Cincinnati area from 1835 to 1839. In 1839, he was appointed editor of the *Christliche Apologete*, a position he held until 1892. Using Cincinnati as his primary base of operations, Nast, who was a popular revival and **camp meeting** preacher, emerged as the primary leader of the rapidly growing German Conference of the MEC. He made several extended missionary trips to Germany, where his ministry resulted in a substantial MEC presence. At its height, before World War I, the German Conference had more than 60,000 members, while the mission in Germany had more than 65,000 members. Deeply committed to the experience of Christian perfection (see **entire sanctification**), Nast was active in the National Holiness Association (NHA; see **Christian Holiness Partnership**) and was a frequent speaker at holiness camp meetings. He was the first president of German-Wallace (now Baldwin-Wallace) College in Ohio, where he served from 1864 to 1893.

Nast was an author of note, and his published works appeared in the *Methodist Quarterly Review*, his own *Christliche Apologete*, and a number of books. His most important English-language work was *The Gospel Record* (1866), which defended the historicity of the New Testament against the skepticism of his old Tübingen associates Bauer and Strauss. His son, Alfred Nast, was active in the NHA and served as editor of the *Christliche Apologete* (1892–1918); a daughter, Fanny, married William A. Gamble, cofounder of the Procter and Gamble Company; while a grandson, Condé Nast, became publisher of *Vogue*, *Vanity Fair*, and several other magazines. W.C.K.

NATIONAL ASSOCIATION OF HOLINESS CHURCHES (NAHC). Founded in 1967 by **H. Robb French**. The NAHC exists to provide credentials for evangelists and pastors of **Inter-Church Holiness Convention**–related nondenominational churches. Following French's resignation in 1973, Steven D. Herron headed the body. In 1990, it provided credentials for more than 200 ministers, evangelists, song evangelists, and missionaries. Membership includes more than 30 congregations, missions, and **camp meetings**. W.C.K.

NATIONAL HOLINESS ASSOCIATION. *See* CHRISTIAN HOLINESS PARTNERSHIP.

NAYLOR, CHARLES WESLEY (b. Athens County, Ohio, 8 January 1874; d. Anderson, Indiana, 21 February 1950). **Church of God (Anderson)** (CG[A]) minister, poet, and writer. In 1895, following affiliation with a CG(A) congregation, Charles Wesley Naylor joined the Gospel Trumpet Company as a worker. His talent for poetry and writing was quickly recognized, and he became an editorial assistant for the *Gospel Trumpet*. An accident in 1908 left him with severe internal injuries and bedridden for the remainder of his life, a situation that was theologically problematic for a religious community strongly committed to faith healing. Nevertheless, Naylor continued to write devotional books and poetry that, when set to music, created some of the most popular gospel songs in the CG(A). M.D.S.

NDZIMANDZE, JULIET KAYISE (b. Hhelehhele, Swaziland, 1929; d. Manzini, Swaziland, 4 May 1996). **Church of the Nazarene** (CN) pastor and evangelist. Juliet Ndzimandze was the daughter of Solomon Ndzimandze, a pioneer Swazi CN preacher. She was educated in mission schools, converted in 1947, and professed a call to preach the following year. She was the first woman to be elected president of the

Swaziland District's young people's society. She was pastor at Magugu for five years and a teacher at the Nazarene Bible School in Siteki, her alma mater, from 1950 to 1971. In 1965, she became the first Swazi woman ordained by her denomination. She became a full-time evangelist in 1971. Admirers dubbed her "the Billy Graham of Swaziland," and her well-received revivals in other African nations, including Zambia, Malawi, and Kenya, helped her church to reach beyond its longtime base at the southern tip of the continent. She also conducted revivals in Europe and North America. Declining health forced her to retire in 1991. R.S.I.

NEASE, ORVAL J(ohn) (b. Nashville, Michigan, 25 December 1891; d. Pasadena, California, 7 November 1950). International Apostolic Holiness Union (IAHU; see **Pilgrim Holiness Church**) and **Church of the Nazarene** (CN) minister, evangelist, educator, and denominational leader. The son of prominent United Brethren in Christ (UB) and IAHU evangelist William O. Nease, Orval Nease was educated at Bible Holiness Seminary in Owosso, Michigan; Pasadena (California) College; Boston University; and Ohio State University. Entering the CN ministry in 1917, Nease served as pastor of such important congregations as Malden, Massachusetts (1920–1925); Columbus, Ohio (1926–1928); and Detroit, Michigan (1933–1938). He served as president of Pasadena College (1928–1933) and head of the CN Sunday school program (1938–1940). He served as one of the four CN general superintendents (1940–1944, 1948–1950). One of a generation of young CN leaders nurtured by **Seth C. Rees** during Rees's tenure as pastor of the Pentecostal Church of the Nazarene congregation in Pasadena, Nease was a masterful evangelistic preacher and skilled administrator. After his death, his widow and sons edited a volume of his sermons, *A Vessel unto Honor: Seven Sermons and a Life Sketch* (1952). His brother, Floyd Nease (1893–1930), served as a CN minister and president of Eastern Nazarene College. W.C.K.

NICHOLSON, ROY S(tephen) (b. Walhalla, North Carolina, 12 July 1903; d. Central, South Carolina, 2 March 1993). **Wesleyan Methodist Church** (WMC) and **Wesleyan Church** (WC) minister and denominational leader. Nicholson was converted in his youth and experienced **entire sanctification** in 1925 while a student at Central Wesleyan College. He was also educated through the extension program of Moody Bible Institute. Ordained an elder in the WMC in 1923, he served as a minister in Virginia and North Carolina (1923–1934). Nicholson was superintendent of the WMC Young People's Society (1934–1935), Sunday school editor (1935–1939), home missionary secretary (1939–1943), editor of the *Wesleyan Methodist* (1943–1947), and president of the General Conference of the WMC (1947–1959). He served on the faculty of Central Wesleyan College (1959–1968). Following his retirement in 1968, Nicholson continued his active ministry of speaking and writing and was for a time supply pastor of the Brooksville (Florida) WC. A frequent contributor to the *Wesleyan Methodist, Wesleyan Advocate,* and the *Christian Minister,* he was the author of *Wesleyan Methodism in the South* (1934) and an editor of the revision of **Ira McLeister's** history of the WMC in 1951. He wrote several doctrinal works, including *Studies in Christian Doctrine* (1947) and *The Arminian Emphasis* (1963). With **Stephen Paine** and Wilbur T. Dayton, Nicholson was one of the chief architects of the WMC's movement in a neo-evangelical direction during the 1950s. A founding member of the **Wesleyan Theological Society**, Nicholson was named Holiness Exponent of the Year by the Christian Holiness Association (see **Christian Holiness Partnership**) in 1972. W.C.K.

NOYES, JOHN HUMPHREY (b. Brattleboro, Vermont, 3 September 1811; d. near Niagara Falls, Ontario, 13 April 1886). Minister, editor, and founder of the Oneida Community. Educated at Dartmouth College, Andover Theological Seminary, and Yale College Divinity School, Noyes was converted in 1831 and claimed freedom from sin in 1834. Although he was influenced by the logic of his Yale theological professor Nathaniel William Taylor, Noyes's confession of personal perfection resulted in the revocation of his ministerial license. In 1834, he began publication of the *Perfectionist,* which was the first of several periodicals that he would edit. Noyes united the revivalism of Taylor and a radical Pauline understanding of justification by faith with a realized **eschatology** that was rooted in his belief that Christ had returned in 70 A.D., making it possible for Christians to live without sin.

In the perfectionistic climate of New England and New York's so-called burned-over district, Noyes's ideas attracted a significant following. In 1836, he established a Bible school at Putney, Vermont. By 1844, he had established an intentional community at Putney in which believers, following Acts 2, held "all things in common." In 1847, after initiating a practice known as "complex marriage," Noyes was indicted for adultery and fled Vermont. As Noyes taught, it was a sin for married couples to establish exclusive sexual relationships.

In 1848, Noyes organized a second community in Oneida, New York. At Oneida, more than 300 people lived communally, shared mates, disciplined themselves through mutual correction, practiced divine healing, engaged in experiments in eugenics, and prospered economically. Among Noyes's most significant publications were *Bible Communism* (1848), *Salvation from Sin, the End of Christian Faith* (1869), and *The History of American Socialism* (1870). Widely read in the perfectionist literature of his era, Noyes distinguished Bible communism from the emotional perfectionism of Methodism and the legal perfectionism of Oberlin. Although the holiness movement has long sought to disassociate its understanding of Christian perfection from that of Oneida, their common history, shared theology, and the movement's repeated social, economic, and sexual experimentation suggest otherwise. W.C.K.

– O –

OBERLIN PERFECTIONISM. A form of Christian perfectionism propagated at Oberlin (Ohio) College beginning in the late 1830s. First tentatively stated by **Charles G. Finney** in the spring of 1836 in New York City and expanded in a series of articles by Finney, **John Morgan**, **Henry Cowles**, and **Asa Mahan** published in the *Oberlin Evangelist* from 1838–1840, Oberlin perfectionism maintained that fully sanctified Christians would perfectly obey God and act in what they believed to be the best interests of the universe. Oberlin perfectionists were careful to distinguish their brand of full salvation from that promoted by **John Humphrey Noyes** and the Oneida community, which taught that perfected Christians were no longer subject to moral law. Although dependent on Methodism for much of their vocabulary, Oberlin perfectionists were critical of what they believed to be the excessive emotionalism of Methodism and its lack of ethical vigor. Among the most notable assertions of Oberlin perfectionism were Mahan's *The Scriptural Doctrine of Christian Perfection* (1839) and Finney's *Views on Sanctification* (1840). Although intensely controversial and bitterly attacked by Congregational and Presbyterian critics, Oberlin perfectionism has long been seen by scholars as lying behind Oberlin's commitments to abolitionism, women's rights, and social transformation. Scholars generally agree that the community's growing conservatism after the departure of Mahan as president in 1850 was directly related to its diminishing interest in Christian perfection. W.C.K.

OKE, JANETTE LORENE STEEVES (b. Champion, Alberta, 18 February 1935). Evangelical Missionary Church of Canada author of best-selling Christian fiction. The sixth of nine children born to prairie farmers, Oke received her elementary education in a one-room school. She earned a tertiary diploma in 1957 at Mountain View Bible College (Didsbury, Alberta), where she met her future husband, Edward. For the next two decades, her primary roles were as wife and mother. Her husband served as a United Missionary Church pastor and educator—president of Mountain View Bible College, professor at Bethel College (Indiana), and dean of Rocky Mountain Bible College (Calgary, Alberta). Sensing a divine call to write, she began with *Love Comes Softly* (1979), a Christian romance set on the Canadian frontier. A profusion of works followed, including a series of children's books for Bethel Publishing, starting with *Spunky's Diary* (1982). Soon a celebrity, she received numerous publishing awards and an honorary doctor of humanities degree from Bethel College (1987). In 1991, *Publisher's Weekly* noted that she was the best-selling Canadian author of all time, and by 1997, total sales of her books exceeded 20 million copies, with translations in a dozen languages. T.P.E.

OLDHAM, WILLIAM F(itzjames) (b. Bangalore, India, 15 December 1854; d. Glendale, California, 27 March 1937). Methodist Episcopal Church (MEC) minister, missionary, and bishop. Converted in India under the ministry of D. O. Fox, an associate of **William Taylor**, Oldham was educated at Allegheny College (Pennsylvania) and Boston University (1879–1883). In 1885, **James Thoburn** chose Oldham to aid him in the establishment of Methodist missions in Singapore. Experiencing remarkable success, Oldham established English and Tamil churches and an Anglo-Chinese school. Returning to the United States, he served as an MEC minister in Pittsburgh (1890–1895) and a professor of missions at Ohio Wesleyan University (1895–1900). From 1900 to 1904, Oldham served as an assistant corresponding secretary of the Missionary Society of the MEC. He served as a missionary bishop in Asia (1904–1912) and South America (1916–1928). He was corresponding secretary of the Board of Foreign Missions of the MEC (1912–1916). Although initially critical of the holiness movement, Oldham experienced full salvation in Malaysia while serving as bishop of Asia and became one of the most influential MEC advocates of holiness experience in the first four decades of the 20th century. Under his leadership, the South American Methodist missions maintained especially close ties to the holiness movement. Following his retirement as bishop, Oldham frequently spoke in holiness settings, while serving on the board of Chicago Evangelistic Institute (1928–1937; see **Vennard College**). Among his most notable books were an account of the Methodist missions in Asia (1914) and biographies of Isabella Thoburn (1902) and James Thoburn (1918). W.C.K.

OLT, G. RUSSELL (b. Dayton, Ohio, 10 November 1895; d. Anderson, Indiana, 28 June 1958). **Church of God (Anderson)** (CG[A]) minister and educator. Russell Olt joined Anderson College as its first dean in 1925 and continued in that position for 33 years. He was the architect of Anderson's curriculum and, in partnership with **John Morrison**, laid the foundation for that institution's academic credibility. A churchman, social reformer, and internationalist, Olt pastored a congregation in Cincinnati, Ohio, for 25 years while academic dean at Anderson. A man of action and causes rather than a writer, he was an advocate of labor's right to organize and of civil rights. Olt chaired numerous committees and agencies on a range of social causes, including a church commission responsible for relocating displaced persons after World War II. His commitments brought him into contact with people and groups with whom many holiness people did not fraternize, including various groups and projects sponsored by the National Council of Churches. Olt refused to heed the potential for controversy latent in his connections, because he genuinely respected justice over considerations of personal popularity or convenience. M.D.S.

OMS INTERNATIONAL (OMS). A nondenominational missionary agency, OMS International was founded as the Oriental Missionary Society in 1901 by **Charles** and **Lettie Burd Cowman**, **E. A. Kilbourne**, and **Jugi Nakada**. Although it was never officially a ministry of the International Apostolic Holiness Union (IAHU; see **Pilgrim Holiness Church**), the OMS's early publicity and support came from the IAHU and from *God's Revivalist*. **God's Bible School**'s Cincinnati campus served as American headquarters for the mission into the 1920s. Likewise, OMS's theology remained consistent with the fourfold gospel of the IAHU and its founder **Martin Wells Knapp**. Beginning as a Bible school in Tokyo, the OMS gradually adopted a mission strategy known as "The Great Village Campaign," which, according to

Charles Cowman, distributed millions of gospel tracts and Bibles and, by 1923, had an estimated 7,000 converts. Under the leadership of John Thomas and William Heslop, the mission's greatest success came in Korea, which became the primary mission field for the OMS. In 1921, OMS headquarters was moved from Tokyo to Seoul. A Korean Bible school, later Seoul Theological Seminary, emerged as the largest graduate Wesleyan theological seminary in the world. In 1941, the **Korea Evangelical Holiness Church**, now the world's largest distinctly holiness denomination, was established as a self-supporting denomination with 30,000 members and 185 preachers.

In 1925, the OMS established the Cowman Bible Institute in Shanghai, marking the official beginning of the OMS presence in China. In 1929, this presence was augmented with the absorption of the South China Holiness Mission, headquartered in Canton, which had been founded by Elbridge and Minnie Munroe in 1903. In the early 1940s, as mission fields were being closed in Asia, the OMS expanded its ministries into India, where the Allahabad Bible Institute was opened in 1943; Mexico; Colombia, where El Seminaro Biblico de Colombia was opened in 1944; and Brazil, where the OMS agreed to support the ministry of Congregational pastor and holiness proponent Jonathas Thomas de Aquino. As of 1999, the OMS consisted of 450 missionaries in partnership with 3,530 churches, with membership exceeding one million. Its presidents have included Charles E. Cowman (1901–1924), E. A. Kilbourne (1924–1928), Lettie Burd Cowman (1928–1949), Eugene A. Erny (1949–1969), and **Wesley L. Duewel** (1969–1982). As of 1999, the president was J. B. Crouse. W.C.K.

ORR, CHARLES EBERT (b. Ohio, 5 May 1861; d. Guthrie, Oklahoma, 22 September 1933). **Church of God (Anderson)** (CG[A]) and **Church of God (Guthrie, Oklahoma)** (CG[Guthrie]) minister, evangelist, author, and editor. A teacher in Tampico, Indiana, Orr was converted in 1889 and joined the Church of God Reformation movement in 1891. After selling their home, Charles and his wife, Sadie, invested their life's savings in spreading the CG(A) message throughout the Midwest. Charles served as pastor of the Federalsburg, Maryland, CG(A) (1898–1912) and was a contributing editor of the *Gospel Trumpet* (1903–1913). A mystic and poet deeply committed to the radical asceticism of **D. S. Warner** and the early Church of God movement, in 1903, Orr published *Christian Conduct*, an early sign that cultural compromises on neckties and the wearing of jewelry were disrupting the CG(A) movement. In 1910, Orr's growing concern with changing social mores in the movement, such as racial segregation, led him to found a periodical, the *Herald of Truth*. Orr was the primary leader of the CG(A) dissidents who eventually united as the CG (Guthrie). In 1915, a repentant Orr severed his ties with the *Herald of Truth* and resumed writing for the *Gospel Trumpet*. He remained officially active in the CG(A) until 1926. In 1928, he became pastor of a CG(A) congregation in Hammond, Louisiana, and established a second periodical, the *Path of Light*. In 1932, increased association with CG (Guthrie) supporters resulted in the merger of Orr's paper with *Faith and Victory* (Guthrie). Among Orr's most significant works are an interpretation of the Christian church in history, *The Gospel Day, or the Light of Christianity* (1904), and a series of devotional works, including *The Hidden Life* (1908) and *How to Live a Holy Life* (1912). Many of his works are still in print. W.C.K.

ORWIG, WILLIAM (b. near Orwigsburg, Pennsylvania, 1810; d. 29 May 1889). Pioneer churchman and holiness advocate of the Evangelical Association (EA). William Orwig was converted at age 16 and began to preach two years later. At age 22, he was made presiding elder of the Eastern Conference of the EA. Four years later, he was elected by the General Conference to the office of book agent and editor, with headquarters in New Berlin, Pennsylvania. He became sole editor of the denominational organ, *Der Christliche Botschafter*, in 1839, and he was elected to a four-year term as bishop in 1859. As a literary figure, Orwig wrote the earliest catechism for the church and the earliest history of the denomination, *Geschichte der Evangelische Gemeinschaft*, as well as a classic volume of pastoral theology. Orwig strongly defended the denominational holiness doctrine against its detractors in an apology published in 1859. His concern for missions and education led to the development of his denomination's first general mission society and its first educational enterprise, Union Seminary in New Berlin, Pennsylvania. J.S.O.

OSBORN, WILLIAM BRAMWELL (b. Hillsdale, New York, 22 March 1832; d. Tunnelton, West Virginia, 4 September 1902). Businessman, Methodist Episcopal Church minister, presiding elder, missionary, evangelist, founder of Ocean Grove and other **camp meeting** resorts, and a founding member of the National Holiness Association (see **Christian Holiness Partnership**). The son of minister Elbert Osborn, William Osborn decided to enter the business world for financial reasons, and by the time he was in his early 20s, he owned a wholesale marble business in Philadelphia and prospered. While studying in Hackettstown, New Jersey, Osborn had been converted under the ministry of William P. Corbit. A few years later, while attending a New Jersey camp meeting, he felt called to the ministry and, in 1857, accepted his first Methodist parish in Imlayston, New Jersey. He served several other New Jersey parishes, including South Amboy and Cape May.

It is not known when Osborn experienced **entire sanctification**, but he quickly became an outstanding proponent of this doctrine. While attending a camp meeting at Red Bank, New Jersey, in the summer of 1866, **John A. Wood** shared with Osborn the idea of holding a camp meeting for the specific purpose of promoting the doctrine of Christian holiness. Osborn became so engrossed with the thought that in April 1867, he traveled to New York City to consult with **John S. Inskip**. Four months later, the first National Camp Meeting for the Promotion of Holiness convened at Vineland, New Jersey. The success of the Vineland encampment greatly encouraged Osborn, and he soon began the process of establishing a permanent holiness camp meeting at the seashore in New Jersey. Many of his holiness friends joined him in the venture, and Ocean Grove later became the most popular Christian resort on the East Coast.

In 1875, following the deaths of his wife and son, he joined Bishop **William Taylor**'s missionary work in India, serving as a district superintendent. There, in 1879, he married another missionary, Lucy Reed Drake. She had been sanctified in 1865 and had spent her life in evangelistic Christian service, including missionary work with **Charles Cullis**. She and William did extensive evangelistic work, founding an Indian encampment called the Lanowli Camp Meeting Association. The Osborns left India and traveled with John and Martha Inskip to Australia. There William established the Australian Ocean Grove. In 1883, the Osborns established two camp meetings: Ocean Park, near Portland, Oregon; and Wesley Park, at Niagara Falls, New York. At the latter place, the Osborns established a missionary conference, and at the first session, William conceived the idea for a missionary training school. Lucy Osborn soon believed God had called her to establish such a school, so she started one in their cottage at Wesley Park. She had 22 students the first year. Three years later, her first student was called to the mission field, and William P. Byers sailed for India in 1887. Others quickly followed. In 1889, through the help of Bishop William Taylor, the school moved to Brooklyn, New York, where it became known as Union Missionary Training Institute. In 1891, the school expanded, buying a farm near Hackettstown, New Jersey. William Osborn founded a camp meeting there, too.

In the summer of 1902, William left to preach at a camp meeting near Tunnelton, West Virginia. At the encampment, he received a telegram urging him to return home because his daughter was very ill. While attempting to cross the tracks in a thick fog at the train station, he was struck by a locomotive and died about one week later. Lucy Reed Osborn continued to lead the Union Missionary Training Institute. By the time she became "principal emeritus" in 1917, the school could boast that 250 of its trained missionaries were serving under 27 mission boards in 26 countries. K.O.B.

– P –

PAGE, ISAAC E. (b. Nottingham, England, 16 January 1839; d. 27 August 1926). British Wesleyan minister. Converted in 1855, Page immediately became a local preacher and was accepted for the ministry at 20. In 1872, he was one of the founders of the *King's Highway*, the first British journal devoted to scriptural holiness. In all his circuits, he established holiness conventions and was a founding preacher at the national **Southport Methodist Holiness Convention**. He wrote little but built an outstanding holiness library. He remained in close contact with the American holiness movement through **George Hughes**. A man of broad vision who considered the Wesleyan way to be the more truly scriptural but nevertheless reported **Keswick** meetings alongside distinctively Wesleyan gatherings, he was editor of the connexional *Local Preachers' Magazine* for 14 years. W.P.

PAINE, STEPHEN WILLIAM (b. Grand Rapids, Michigan, 28 October 1908; d. Houghton, New York, 1992). **Wesleyan Methodist Church** (WMC) and **Wesleyan Church** (WC) educator. Following his education at Wheaton (Illinois) College and the University of Illinois, Paine was appointed instructor in classics at Houghton (New York) College in 1933. In 1934, he was named dean of the college and professor of Greek. He served as president of Houghton College (1937–1972). During his administration, the college became the most respected evangelical college in the East. One of the primary founders of the National Association of Evangelicals (NAE), Paine served as

NAE president (1948–1949) and was on the NAE-sponsored committee that led to the publication of the New International Version of the Bible. A friend and early supporter of evangelist Billy Graham, Paine vigorously defended Graham from the attacks on him by fundamentalist separatists. An active leader in the WMC, Paine served for 30 years on the general board of administration of the WMC and WC. He was the author of four books, including his best-known work, *Beginning Greek: A Functional Approach* (1961). In 1987, Houghton College published a biography of Paine by his daughter Miriam Paine Lemecio, *Deo Volente: A Biography of Stephen W. Paine*. W.C.K.

PALMER, PHOEBE WORRALL (b. New York City, 18 December 1807; d. New York City, 2 November 1874). Methodist Episcopal Church (MEC) holiness advocate, author, revivalist, practical theologian, and editor. Phoebe Worrall Palmer ranks as one of the most significant American Protestant women of the 19th century. Convinced that holiness or sanctification as an act of consecration subsequent to conversion was an essential aspect of genuine Christianity, Palmer promoted her own teachings on the subject through an influential and well-attended prayer meeting/fellowship group in her home, the Tuesday Meeting for the Promotion of Holiness, which she led from 1840 until her death; popular books, including *The Way of Holiness* (1843), *Entire Devotion to God* (1845), and *Faith and Its Effects* (1848); extensive revival tours to churches and **camp meetings** in the United States, Canada, and Great Britain; and a decade (1864–1874) as editor of the *Guide to Holiness*, one of the nation's most widely circulated religious monthlies. These efforts made Palmer a major catalyst behind the concern for holiness in mid-19th-century Methodism. Her influence also affected the holiness revival that energized associations and sects with Methodist roots during the final third of the century and that fostered the spread of **Keswick** and other "higher Christian life" teachings among Protestants more generally. Although she became most well known among North American Methodists, Palmer's importance was both transdenominational and transatlantic.

The core content of Palmer's work drew from a traditional Methodist emphasis on holiness or "perfect love" as the goal of Christian spirituality, modified and simplified in light of her own experiences and understanding of the Bible. For Palmer, holiness involved an ongoing consecration to God after conversion that brought with it an awareness of being constantly saved or kept from all sin. She offered a "shorter way" to attain this spiritual state and presented holiness as the expected norm for Christian living rather than its culmination. Palmer's "way of holiness" involves three elements: "entire consecration," the renunciation of worldly desires and the surrender of every aspect of one's life to God; faith, which was for Palmer an absolute trust in the biblical promises that God would accept and sanctify those who had laid themselves "upon the altar"; and the need to bear testimony or tell others of holiness. Although disputed by some Methodist clergy, Palmer's teachings made sanctification understandable and accessible to ordinary laypeople and furthered the trend toward lay activism among Protestants during the second half of the 19th century. Palmer's ideas appealed to the spiritual earnestness of Victorian evangelicals, as well as to the struggle, especially among mid-century Methodists, to balance a growing social respectability with a denominational heritage of intense religious commitment.

Palmer's holiness downplayed the role of emotion, a hallmark of early Methodist spirituality but increasingly problematic for the urban children and grandchildren of the movement. Her understanding of consecration included traditional strictures against fashionable dress, dancing, the theater, and frivolous conversation, but it did not involve a rejection of wealth or social position per se. In addition, while Palmer's teachings were directed to all Christians, they were particularly effective in offering spiritual empowerment to middle-class women.

In many ways, the underlying motifs in Palmer's writings reflected the experiences of her own life. Phoebe Worrall was the fourth of 16 children born to English immigrant Henry Worrall and his American-born wife, Dorothea. The Worrall home on Manhattan's Lower West Side combined an atmosphere of comfortable affluence and thoroughgoing piety shaped by the influences of both British and American Methodism. Phoebe married New York City physician **Walter Clark Palmer** in 1827. The Palmers had six children, three of whom died in infancy; two daughters, Sarah and Phoebe, and a son, Walter Clark, Jr., survived. Palmer experienced sanctification on 26 July 1837, her "Day of Days," when, after prolonged spiritual struggles, she embraced the way of holiness she would later recommend to others.

By 1840, Palmer had assumed leadership of the Tuesday Meeting and had launched her public career. In addition to writing books and articles, during the next three decades Palmer became increasingly famous as a revivalist at Methodist camp meetings and churches. She also engaged in tract distribution and poor relief in New York City. Palmer spearheaded efforts to found the Five Points Mission, an outreach mission that was most effective in its care of children in one of the city's poorest areas, begun in 1850 and sponsored by the Ladies Home Missionary Society of the MEC. Assisted by Walter, Palmer made numerous speaking tours in New England, Upstate New York, and Canada during the 1850s. The enthusiastic responses to her messages of salvation and sanctification at Canadian camp meetings during the summer of 1857, culminating in an October revival in Hamilton, Canada West (Ontario), were early manifestations of the revival of 1857–1858. Palmer's activities in that revival also influenced her book, *The Promise of the Father; or, a Neglected Specialty of the Last Days* (1859), in which she argued for an egalitarian piety that affirmed women's rights to speak in religious assemblies and to share fully with men all other responsibilities of Christian lay work. The book also reflected Palmer's increasing emphasis on the role of the Holy Spirit in empowering and sanctifying Christians and her use of language that evoked the early church's experience at Pentecost.

The Palmers followed the spread of the 1857–1858 revival to Great Britain, where from 1859 to 1863 they brought the message of salvation and sanctification to overflowing crowds. Back in the United States, during the late 1860s, Palmer extended her revival ministry to the Midwest and even California. Ill health curtailed her travels from 1871 until her death. K.T.L.

PALMER, WALTER CLARK (b. New York City, 6 February 1804; d. New York City, 20 July 1883). Methodist Episcopal Church (MEC) lay leader, lay preacher, homeopathic physician, and, with his wife, Phoebe, editor of the *Guide to Holiness*. Raised in a family of earnest Methodists, Walter Palmer received his medical degree from the College of Physicians and Surgeons of New York. Although he was often overshadowed by his famous wife, Phoebe, it was Walter's support, both emotional and financial, that enabled Phoebe to extend her influence through itinerant preaching and extensive publication. In 1863, Walter and **Phoebe Palmer** purchased the *Guide to Holiness* and another holiness paper, the *Beauty of Holiness*, and combined them. The success of his medical practice allowed Walter to retire early, and from 1859 onward he traveled with Phoebe as a preaching team until her death in 1874. In 1876, Walter married Phoebe's sister, **Sarah Worrall**

Lankford, and the two continued to run the Tuesday Meeting for the Promotion of Holiness, which Sarah had founded, and to edit the *Guide to Holiness*. D.H.S.

PAMP, CHARLES RAYMOND (b. Athens, Michigan, 27 October 1909; d. Tampa, Florida, 26 February 1951). Native American Lower Light Missionary Association minister, evangelist, Bible school president, and founder and organizer of Native American missions and **camp meetings**. A full-blooded Pottawatamie, Pamp often went by his Indian name, Chief Charles Pam-to-pee. His father had been converted at a Methodist camp meeting, and the family regularly attended services at the Methodist Mission House on the Nattawaseppe Indian Reservation, near Athens, Michigan. Pamp experienced racial discrimination, and by the time he finished high school, it had embittered him.

A gifted athlete, Pamp received many scholarship offers to play college football. Instead, he became a professional athlete soon after graduating high school. He played on various baseball, basketball, and football teams. He wasted most of his money on alcohol, which ruined his promising sports career and almost ended his life.

Pamp's family continually prayed for him, and on 21 March 1937, he gave his life to Christ under the ministry of the Reverend T. W. Willingham. Shortly afterward, he claimed the call to preach and began to conduct revival services in various churches. He also experienced **entire sanctification** and was known for the rest of his life as an uncompromising holiness preacher.

Along with his brothers, Elliott and Warren, Charles Pamp held his ministerial credentials with the Lower Light Mission Association in Michigan. However, he gained considerable fame throughout the holiness movement as an evangelist, and his great passion was for his own people. He preached in church revivals and camp meetings in many states and assisted in the founding of various ministries for Native Americans. In 1941, he helped to start the Six Nations Indian Holiness Camp Meeting on the Onondaga Indian Reservation near Syracuse, New York, and served as president for seven years. In 1945, he helped to organize the Indian Mission Home and Camp Meeting near Athens, Michigan. A 40-acre farm was purchased as the site of the encampment and as a home for needy Native American children. The organization is now known as All Tribes Missionary Council, and it conducts mission outreach in Michigan, South Dakota, and Canada. In 1946, Pamp was called to the presidency of the newly established Brainerd

Indian School near Hot Springs, South Dakota. Since 1968, the school has been affiliated with the **Wesleyan Church**.

Pamp preached on numerous Indian reservations and from 1947 to 1951 traveled as a part of the "GI's of the Cross Caravan," sponsored by **God's Bible School**. His trailer was marked, "All Indian GI's of the Cross." At the time of his death, he was holding revival services in Florida and laying plans for an evangelistic tour to the Native Americans of Alaska. K.O.B.

PATTY, SANDRA FAYE (SANDI) (b. Oklahoma City, Oklahoma, 12 July 1956). Gospel singer. Sandi Patty was born into a family of **Church of God (Anderson)** (CG[A]) ministers who were very fine musicians. She received a degree in music from Anderson College in 1979, after which she toured with the **Bill Gaither** Trio and the Imperials. Her brilliant soprano voice quickly launched her career as a solo recording artist, and, in 1982, she received the first of several Dove Awards, including Gospel Artist of the Year. She has also received several Grammies. Known for her stirring rendition of the "Star Spangled Banner," which gave her a national audience, in the 1980s and early 1990s, Patty frequently performed at various Republican Party functions, where her identification with the family, Christianity, American musical standards, and patriotism has found a ready acceptance. M.D.S.

PAUL, JOHN HAYWOOD (b. Rapids Parish, Louisiana, 23 September 1877; d. Fort Wayne, Indiana, 31 December 1967). Methodist Episcopal Church and Methodist Church minister, editor, evangelist, and educator. Raised in an impoverished family, Paul was forced to leave school at the age of 12 to help support his family. Although primarily self-educated, he was enrolled for a time in the extension program of the University of Chicago and attended classes at Meridian (Mississippi) College, where he served on the faculty (1909–1913). Converted in 1896, Paul served pastorates in Texas, Mississippi, Kentucky, and South Carolina. He was city editor for the *Pentecostal Herald* in Louisville, Kentucky (1904–1908), and editor of the *Way of Faith* in Columbia, South Carolina (1913–1915, 1922–1923). A longtime associate of **Henry Clay Morrison**, he served as vice president of **Asbury College** (1916–1922), professor at **Asbury Theological Seminary** (1941–1946), a member of the Seminary board (1941–1962), and an associate editor of the *Pentecostal Herald* (1941–1967). Paul also was president of **Taylor University** (1922–1931), a professor at Chicago

Evangelistic Institute (1932–1933; see **Vennard College**), and president of John Fletcher College (Iowa; 1933–1936).

An evangelist of note, Paul was also a prolific writer for such holiness periodicals as the *Pentecostal Herald, Way of Faith, Heart and Life,* and the *Christian Witness.* Among his most notable books were *The Way of Power* (1918), *What Is the New Theology?* (1921), *Main Street in Jericho* (1937), a critique of **E. Stanley Jones's** widely discussed *Christ's Alternative to Communism,* and an interpretation of the book of Revelation, *The Climax of the Bible* (n.d.). Although Paul was an unapologetic defender of traditional Wesleyan teaching and experience, especially during the troubling decade of the 1920s, he was remembered as a warmhearted Wesleyan who avoided personal vendettas while insisting that the essence of the Wesleyan message was heart purity and perfect love. W.C.K.

PEABODY, NETTIE (b. Minden, Louisiana, 1873; d. Brownfield, Texas, 28 August 1971). Methodist Episcopal Church and Methodist Church (MC) educator. Arriving at the **God's Bible School** (GBS) **Camp Meeting** in June 1901, Peabody remained as a student for the fall term. In 1902, she joined the GBS faculty and taught theology and Bible until ill health forced her to retire in 1965. She was one of the most beloved teachers in the history of the school, who remained a loyal member of the MC even after GBS had become closely identified with the **Inter-Church Holiness Convention**. She was a frequent contributor to *God's Revivalist* and wrote *The Glory of the Son of God* (1960). W.C.K.

PECK, GEORGE (b. Otsego County, New York, 8 August 1797; d. Scranton, Pennsylvania, 20 May 1876). Methodist Epsicopal Church (MEC) minister, presiding elder, editor, and author. One of four brothers to enter the ministry of the MEC, another being bishop **Jesse T. Peck**, George Peck united with the MEC in 1812 and entered the ministry in the Genesee Conference in 1816. A pioneer circuit rider in western New York, he was a charter member of the Oneida Conference in 1829 and the Wyoming (New York) Conference in 1832. He served as a presiding elder (1834–1835). A studious pastor, Peck served as principal of the Oneida Conference seminary at Cazenovia (1835–1839), editor of the *Methodist Quarterly Review* (1840–1848), and editor of the *Christian Advocate* (New York; 1848–1852). Following successful pastorates at Wilkes-Barre and Scranton, Pennsylvania (1852–1857), Peck was a presiding elder of the Wyoming, Binghamton, and Lackawanna Districts (1857–1872).

Peck's experience of **entire sanctification** while fording the Susquehanna River on 1 October 1839 naturally propelled him into a leadership role in the emerging holiness revival. In 1840, in response to controversies concerning the experience of full salvation, generated, in part, by the antinomian perfectionism of **John H. Noyes** and the **Oberlin perfectionism** of **Asa Mahan** and **Charles G. Finney**, Peck delivered a series of lectures in New York City defending the Wesleyan understanding of full salvation. Published as *The Scriptural Doctrine of Christian Perfection* (1842) and substantially revised in 1848, Peck's work, which went through at least eight editions in the 19th century and remains in print, is one of the most important defenses of the Wesleyan understanding of Christian perfection.

A proponent of a more educated Methodist ministry, Peck was one of the creators of the course of study for MEC ministers. He was the author of histories of the Wyoming and Genesee Conferences of the MEC and an autobiography, *The Life and Times of Rev. George Peck* (1874). Two of his sons became MEC ministers. His daughter, Mary Peck, was the wife of prominent MEC minister and holiness movement critic T. J. Crane. Their son, Stephen Crane, was an important American literary figure. Papers documenting Peck's career are located at Syracuse University. W.C.K.

PECK, JESSE T(ruesdale) (b. Otsego County, New York, 11 April 1811; d. Syracuse, New York, 17 May 1883). Methodist Episcopal Church (MEC) minister, educator, bishop, and author. Licensed to preach in 1829, Peck was admitted into the Oneida Conference in 1832. While a student at Cazenovia (New York) Seminary, where his brother, **George Peck,** was principal, he served as an itinerant minister in the Oneida Conference until 1837. He was principal of the high school that became Gouverneur Seminary (1837–1840) and Troy Conference Academy in Poultney, Vermont (1841–1848). He served as president of Dickinson College (Pennsylvania; 1848–1852). He was pastor of the Foundry Church in Washington, D.C. (1852–1854), and an editor for the MEC tract society (1854–1856). Peck then served as pastor of the Greene Street MEC congregation in New York City (1856–1858). Transferring to California in 1858, he served influential pastorates in San Francisco and Sacramento (1858–1866), while serving on the board of trustees of the University of the Pacific and as president of the California Bible Society. Returning to New York, Peck served pastorates in Peekskill, Albany, and Syracuse (1866–1872). As an MEC bishop (1872–1883), he presided over 83 annual conferences including those in Germany, Denmark, and Sweden. One of the principal founders of Syracuse University, Peck left his estate of $50,000 to that university. An important champion of the Wesleyan experience of full salvation, Peck was the author of an important explication of its meaning, *The Central Idea of Christianity* (1857), which went through several editions and revisions during his lifetime and remains in print. A precursor of the social gospel, Peck's *History of the Great Republic* (1869) celebrated the American democratic experiment as the culmination of human civilization, with Methodism as the principal backbone of that glorious experiment. Papers documenting Peck's life are located at Syracuse University. W.C.K.

PENIEL MISSIONS. The first Peniel Mission was founded in Los Angeles, California, in 1886 by T. P. Ferguson (1853–1920), an Oberlin College graduate and Presbyterian minister, and his wife, Manie Payne Ferguson (b. 1850), who was author of the famous gospel hymn, "Blessed Quietness." The two had experienced **entire sanctification** in 1880 through the ministry of the California and Arizona Holiness Association (see **Holiness Church**). Drawing much of their support from the thriving holiness community in southern California (**Phineas Bresee** was for a time active with the Peniel Missions) and through their widely circulated periodical the *Peniel Herald*, the Fergusons established a chain of missions from San Diego to Alaska. Other missions were opened in Hawaii, India, and Egypt. Typical of most rescue missions, Peniel Missions fed the hungry, provided shelter and later drug and alcohol counseling, operated a home for unwed mothers in Sacramento, sought the conversion of sinners, and provided regular religious instruction. Among the most notable converts of the Peniel Missions was **Haldor Lillenas**. The membership in North America never exceeded the 703 that it reported in 1906. Shortly after her husband's death, Manie Payne Ferguson wrote a biography of him, *T. P. Ferguson: The Love Slave of Jesus Christ and His People and Founder of the Peniel Mission*. Following Manie's own death, leadership was provided by Ella S. Melody and later Gene Moyer. In 1949, the Peniel work in Egypt became part of **World Gospel Mission** (WGM). In 1957, the WGM assumed direction of the remaining West Coast missions, which continue to be known as Peniel Missions. W.C.K.

PENTECOSTAL CHURCH OF THE NAZARENE (PCN). *See* CHURCH OF THE NAZARENE.

PENTECOSTAL LEAGUE OF PRAYER. *See* HARRIS, R(ICHARD) READER.

PEOPLE'S METHODIST CHURCH (PMC). Founded on the campus of the People's Bible School, Greensboro, North Carolina, in 1938. Initially known as the People's Christian Movement, the PMC's stated purposes included the evangelization of the masses and preaching opportunities for students at the school who were increasingly being denied access to Methodist pulpits. It was renamed the People's Methodist Church in 1948. Its name reflected the populist style of its founder, former Methodist Episcopal Church, South, evangelist **Jim H. Green**, who advocated simple church structures while expressing reservations as the church moved toward an increased denominational structure in the late 1940s. Green served as general superintendent (1938–1951) and was editor of the movement's periodical, the *People's Herald*. By 1942, the church had 15 congregations, had established the Avon Park (Florida) **Camp Meeting**, and had sent its first foreign missionary to China. By 1952, the church had 26 congregations. Virgil L. Mitchell, pastor of the Asheville, North Carolina, church, was named general superintendent in 1951. He was followed by J. N. Anderson in 1958. At the church's 1962 conference, it voted to merge with the **Evangelical Methodist Church**. At the time of its merger, the church had 23 congregations and 1,200 members, primarily in North Carolina and Virginia. W.C.K.

PEPPER, E(leuthera) I. D. (b. Philadelphia, Pennsylvania, 27 November 1832; d. Gainesville, Florida, 9 March 1908). Methodist Episcopal Church (MEC) minister, evangelist, editor, and member of the National Holiness Association (NHA; see **Christian Holiness Partnership**). Raised in an MEC home, Pepper was converted early in life and experienced **entire sanctification** after reading **Phoebe Palmer**'s *The Way of Holiness*. He began preaching in 1852 and served as a pastor in the Philadelphia Annual Conference until 1884. Pepper joined the NHA in the early 1870s. A skilled evangelist, he was the preacher who led **Joseph H. Smith** into the experience of full salvation in 1874. Pepper followed **John S. Inskip** as editor of the *Christian Standard*, holding that position until his death. He was one of the leaders of the famed Friday meeting for the promotion of holiness in Philadelphia and, in 1900, was elected president of the Philadelphia Holiness Association. With John Thompson, he edited the widely read *Holiness Bible Texts* (1896). K.O.B.

PICKETT, L(eander) L(ycurgus) (b. Burnsville, Mississippi, 1859; d. Middlesboro, Kentucky, 9 May 1928). Methodist Episcopal Church, South (MECS), minister, evangelist, and reformer. Raised in Arkansas and Texas, L. L. Pickett began preaching in MECS and Baptist churches in 1877. Convinced of the validity of Methodist baptismal practices, he entered the ministry of the MECS, serving as a pastor from 1880 to 1885. A passionate controversialist who loved theological debate, Pickett was refused appointment in the Texas Conference in 1885 when he refused to follow the local custom of performing baptism by immersion. Entering an evangelistic ministry, he established the Pickett Publishing Company in the late 1880s and served as director of the Oliver Gospel Mission, Columbia, South Carolina (1891–1893). Noted as a songwriter and editor, Pickett was the editor of one of the earliest and most significant series of gospel songbooks, *Tears and Triumphs* (1894–1910). Under the influence of **A. B. Simpson**, Pickett embraced premillennialism in 1896. An influential figure in the spread of premillennialism throughout the holiness movement, he was the author of several widely read premillennial works, including *Our Lord Cometh* (1896), *The Blessed Hope* (1901), and *The Renewed Earth* (1903). A polished holiness apologist noted for his skill in public debate, Pickett also wrote *A Plea for the Holiness Movement* (1896). He was also noted for his role in the Pickett–Smith Debate, which was published in 1897. Deeply committed to temperance, sabbatarianism, and anti-Catholicism, he was a Prohibition Party candidate for gov-ernor of Kentucky. **PICKETT, LUDIE CAR-RINGTON DAY** (b. Louisiana, 31 March 1867; d. Wilmore, Kentucky, 1 March 1953). Methodist Episcopal Church, South (MECS), reformer. A schoolteacher who shared in the ministry of her husband, **L. L. Pickett**, Ludie Pickett served as president of the Kentucky Woman's Christian Temperance Union (1923–1947). A son, Deets Pickett, was a nationally known temperance reformer, while another son, J. Waskom Pickett, was a missionary to India and bishop in the Methodist Church. W.C.K.

PIERCE, LOVICK (b. Martins County, North Carolina, 24 March 1785; d. Sparta, Georgia, 9 November 1879). Methodist Episcopal Church (MEC) and Methodist Episcopal Church, South (MECS), minister. Converted under MEC preaching in 1803, Pierce entered the ministry in South Carolina in 1804. In 1809, he married Ann Foster, the daughter of a wealthy Green County, Georgia, planter. He served as a presiding elder (1809–1812) and an army chaplain during the War of 1812. Following medical school, Pierce was a physician in Greensboro, Georgia (1816–1823). Returning to the Methodist itinerancy in 1823, he served various circuits in Georgia. In 1830, he became a charter member of the Georgia Conference of the MEC. Despite the fact that he was a wealthy planter and slave owner, Pierce worked diligently to maintain unity in the MEC, even as slavery increasingly proved to be a divisive issue. Although one of the principal organizers of the MECS, Pierce attempted to maintain fraternal relations in the antebellum era and continued to work for unity following the war. Ironically lionized in late-19th-century Georgia Methodism as a progressive who never testified to full salvation, Pierce was, in fact, an organizer of special holiness prayer meetings who claimed that he had experienced full salvation in 1843. He was the author of *A Miscellaneous Essay on Entire Sanctification* (1878). W.C.K.

PILGRIM HOLINESS CHURCH (PHC). A holiness denomination. The International Holiness Union and Prayer League (later the International Apostolic Holiness Union [IAHU]) was organized in 1897 in Cincinnati, Ohio, by **Martin Wells Knapp**, **Seth Cook Rees**, and **C. W. Ruth**. The league was designed originally as an evangelistic association, not unlike hundreds of other holiness associations. However, because of its nationally known leadership, the newly organized group quickly became the rallying point for many other similar associations. Most of these already were organizing new holiness churches rather than affiliating with, or continuing existing affiliations with, the established denominations.

By 1897, Knapp had already established one of the more influential nondenominational centers for Wesleyan/Holiness promotion at Cincinnati. Support from the 25,000 or more subscribers to his *God's Revivalist* and profits from his widely circulated holiness books supported **God's Bible School** (GBS) and his aggressive evangelism agenda. By the end of the first decade of the 20th century, the Cincinnati enterprise included overseas missions in Africa, China, Japan, and the Caribbean.

In 1900, the group's name was changed to the International Apostolic Holiness Union. Because of Knapp's leadership of both GBS and the IAHU until his death in 1901, it is often difficult to distinguish historically between the overlapping activities and interests of the two organizations. The mingled history of the IAHU and GBS continued for a decade after Knapp's death. In 1906, the U.S. Census Bureau reported that the Apostolic Holiness Union and Churches, as the denomination was then known, had 74 churches and 2,744 members.

Seth Cook Rees served as the first superintendent of the IAHU. Upon his resignation in 1905, he was succeeded by **George B. Kulp**, who continued to regard the GBS complex of ministries as the heart of the developing movement. As the union grew and began to establish overseas missions and educational institutions and the influence of the leaders of GBS diminished within the church, the lines between the two movements became more distinct, and eventually church and school had no official organizational ties. Nevertheless, GBS and *God's Revivalist* always enjoyed the support and loyalty of a significant number of the IAHU's membership.

In spite of its consistent growth, the church experienced an ever-pressing need to find the financial resources to support and advance its institutions and programs. This, along with the positive nature of its experiences in the early mergers that had brought it into being, created a continuing openness to further alliances. What seemed to many to be a very natural union—one with the PHC and the Pentecostal Church of the Nazarene (see **Church of the Nazarene**)—never developed. Attempts to appeal to their similarities were often muted by the significant difference in the sizes of the two bodies.

Membership grew as a result of the church's aggressive evangelism and several mergers and additions. In 1913, the IAHU changed its name to the International Apostolic Holiness Church, recognizing that its member fellowships, with their own buildings and pastors, were functioning as congregations rather than as the interdenominational evangelistic associations originally anticipated. From 1919 to 1925, five churches, two mission societies, and an indigenous church in Barbados merged with the church. In 1919, the midwestern sectors of the Holiness Christian Church (see **Evangelical Christian Church**) united with the church to create the International Holiness Church (InHC). The Pentecostal Rescue Mission, with churches throughout New York and in Pennsylvania, joined two years later. In 1922, the Pilgrim Church of California merged with the InHC to form the PHC, with Pilgrim Church founder Seth Cook Rees becoming general superintendent.

After the creation of the PHC, several smaller mergers added new congregations and mission churches. The World Wide Missionary Society, founded in 1921 by H. J. Olsen, with headquarters in Baltimore,

Maryland, became part of the church in 1923. A year later, the Bible Home and Foreign Missionary Society, founded in Attleboro, Massachusetts, joined the PHC. The Pentecostal Brethren in Christ, a small association of Ohio churches reaching back to the River Brethren (see **Brethren in Christ Church**) joined the PHC. The final addition during this period was the People's Mission of Colorado Springs, Colorado, with its Western Holiness College and Bible Training School, founded by William Lee, son of Daniel Lee, pioneer Methodist missionary to Oregon. **Paul W. Thomas**, Lee's successor, brought the group into the PHC in 1925. Thomas eventually became one of the denomination's general superintendents. In 1946, the **Holiness Church** of California, which had been founded in the 1870s and which operated a Bible Institute at El Monte (California) and overseas missions in Peru, joined the PHC. Ora Lehman's Africa Evangelistic Mission, with its 2,000 members, joined the church in 1962.

The doctrines and practices that the group eventually established reveal the eclectic nature of its origins. Its Articles of Religion drew heavily on those of the Methodist churches with which many of its members had been affiliated. It allowed infant baptism but placed greater emphasis on dedication of children and believer's baptism. At the same time, by insisting that spirit baptism was the most valid baptism of all, it deferred to the Quaker and **Salvation Army** ancestries of many of its members. The explicit affirmation of divine healing and a premillennial **eschatology** reflect the close relationship that both Knapp and Rees had with **A. B. Simpson**'s **Christian and Missionary Alliance** and the fourfold gospel he espoused. **John Wesley**, George Fox, and **Charles Finney** were all called on to support the church's ordination of women and their place in the councils of the church.

Typical of the holiness churches in general, Spirit leadership and guidance, corporate and individual, were strongly promoted. The influence of Methodism and the holiness **camp meeting** created a freedom in worship style, whether in preaching, testimony, prayer, or song. The altar rail was a center for conversion, sanctification, healing, and observation of the Lord's Supper. Kneeling was the usual but not exclusive posture for worship prayers. The disciplined lifestyle, which was common to all holiness churches, was radically promoted in protest against the prevailing popular culture.

In 1958, the Pilgrim General Conference approved a plan of merger with the Wesleyan Methodist Church (WMC). The latter body narrowly rejected the merger, but negotiations continued and were eventually successful. At the point of final merger in 1968, the PHC maintained five colleges: one liberal arts college, Owosso (Michigan) College (founded 1909), and four Bible colleges—Bartlesville (Oklahoma) College (1905); Eastern Pilgrim College (Pennsylvania, 1921); Frankfort (Indiana) Pilgrim College (1927); and Kernersville (North Carolina) Pilgrim College (1946), which also maintained a high school division.

A strong emphasis on overseas missions had resulted in growing and, by then, largely indigenous churches in Mexico and the Philippines. African mission centers were located in South Africa, Mozambique, Swaziland, and Zambia. There were churches in the Caribbean, and in Brazil, Guyana, Peru, and Suriname in South America. At the time of merger, the PHC reported 1,432 churches and 1,566 ordained ministers, a worldwide membership of 56,607, and a Sunday school enrollment of 160,104. The church's international headquarters and its Pilgrim Press were located in Indianapolis, Indiana. M.E.D.

PILLAR OF FIRE, INTERNATIONAL (POF). An international religious, educational, and benevolent organization that was formally incorporated in March 1902. Its key founders were **Alma Bridwell White**, a schoolteacher, and her husband, Kent White, a Methodist minister. The POF is firmly rooted within the Wesleyan Methodist tradition and emerged as an outgrowth of the holiness movement. Its founding name, Pentecostal Union, was changed to Pillar of Fire in 1916. Like other revivalist groups of its day, it was known for its lively and expressive worship. Through its early decades, the POF emphasized rescue and mission work. In 1908, it established its headquarters at Zarephath, New Jersey. The first overseas mission was established in London in 1911.

Christian education has always been central to the mission of the POF, which has primary and secondary schools in Zarephath, New Jersey; Cincinnati, Ohio; Denver, Colorado; and Los Angeles and Pacifica, California. It also operates Belleview College in Westminster, Colorado, and Zarephath (New Jersey) Christian College (formerly Zarephath Bible Institute). The POF received a license to operate radio station KPOF in Denver in 1928 and later extended its network to include WAKW in Cincinnati and WAWZ in Zarephath. WAWZ received the Station of the Year award from the National Religious Broadcasters in 1996. While once more than 40 mission homes were scattered throughout the United States, as of 1998, there were seven churches in the United States with a membership of approximately 1,000. Also, approximately 75,000 members lived in England, the Philippines, India, Malawi, Nigeria, and Liberia, where the church maintains missions that include churches, schools, orphanages, and medical clinics. R.W.C.

PRIMITIVE METHODIST CHURCH (PrMC). Founded by the champions of **camp meetings** and demonstrative worship in English Methodism in 1807. The first PrMC congregations in North America were composed of Cornish miners who settled in Wisconsin and Pennsylvania. In 1840, the American church was formally separated from the parent body. Although growth was modest, missions were begun in 1897 in Africa and in 1921 in Guatemala. Currently, the PrMC is divided into six districts, with most of its members still located in Wisconsin and Pennsylvania. In 1990, the church had nearly 10,000 members in more than 80 congregations. It publishes the *Primitive Methodist Journal* and has its headquarters in Wilkes-Barre, Pennsylvania. It actively supports **Taylor University** and is a member of the **Christian Holiness Partnership**. W.C.K.

PRUDENTIALS. Rules of conduct for individuals in holiness churches. These rules include prohibitions against the consumption of liquor, use of tobacco, dancing, and theatergoing. Since the advent of television and such distinctly evangelical forms of popular entertainment as films and evangelical-style rock concerts, many holiness churches have relaxed their prudential stands. For example, in 1951, the **Free Methodist Church** (FMC) modified its prudential stance as articulated in the church's discipline, arguing that such rules were culturally bound and needed periodic revisions. In response to the relaxing of the prudential code by some holiness churches, including the **Church of the Nazarene**, **Wesleyan Methodist Church**, FMC, and the **Church of God (Anderson)**, many holiness conservatives have separated from their former denominations and congregations and have affiliated with the **Inter-Church Holiness Convention**. W.C.K.

PURKISER, W(estlake) T(aylor) (b. Oakland, California, 28 April 1910; d. Pasadena, California, 18 July 1992). **Church of the Nazarene** (CN) minister, educator, and editor. Educated at Pasadena College, now Point Loma Nazarene University, and the University of Southern California (Ph.D., 1948), Purkiser served as a CN pastor (1930–1937); professor and later dean at Pasadena College (1937–1949); president of Pasadena College (1949–1957); professor of English Bible, Nazarene Theological Seminary (1957–1975); and editor of the *Herald of Holiness* (1960–1975).

A generalist in an age of increased academic specialization, Purkiser was a biblical scholar and theologian whose primary ministry was not to scholars but to students and theological novices. He was the editor and principal author of three widely used texts for college students, *Exploring the Old Testament* (1955), *Exploring Our Christian Faith* (1960; revised 1978), and *God, Man and Salvation: A Biblical Theology* (1977). In retirement, he wrote *Exploring Christian Holiness: Biblical Foundations* (1983). In 1975, he was named "Holiness Exponent of the Year" by the Christian Holiness Association (see **Christian Holiness Partnership**). W.C.K.

– R –

RAMSEYER, JOSEPH EICHER (b. near New Hamburg, Waterloo County, Ontario, 7 February 1869; d. Fort Wayne, Indiana, 25 January 1944). Evangelist, revivalist, and spiritual father of both the **Missionary Church Association** (MiCA) and Fort Wayne Bible Institute (FWBI). Reared in an Amish Mennonite family, Ramseyer was converted in 1885 after reading the biography of George Mueller. Three days of prayer in July 1891 led to his experience of **entire sanctification** near Elkton, Michigan; in 1892, he was ordained by the Defenseless Mennonites (Egly Amish). He pastored in Elkton, Michigan, and Archbold, Ohio, where his evangelistic work began, and in 1895 became the first superintendent of Bethany Bible Institute in Bluffton, Ohio, forerunner to FWBI. The influence of the **Christian and Missionary Alliance** (CMA) led to baptism by immersion in August 1896, then to his excommunication from the Defenseless Mennonites for undue emphasis on CMA teachings. In 1898, he joined Pennsylvania Mennonite revivalist A. E. Funk and others to organize the MiCA, which was largely composed of disaffected Defenseless Mennonites and the German branch of the CMA. He assumed the presidency of the association in 1900, holding the position for the remainder of his life. A key founder of FWBI in 1904 and an early superintendent (1904, 1911–1912), he became its first president in 1912, also for life. His leadership was more spiritual and promotional than administrative, for he traveled incessantly to hold special meetings. Honorary vice president of the CMA, he ministered ecumenically. A saintly mystic who sought to renew daily his deep experience of God, "Daddy" Ramseyer was loved and revered by those who knew him. His second wife, Macy Garth, founded the Sunshine Makers, a children's movement for Christian education and missions. T.P.E.

RAVENHILL, LEONARD (b. Leeds, England, 18 June 1907; d. Lindale, Texas, 27 November 1994). International Holiness Mission and Calvary Holiness Church (CHC) minister, evangelist, and author. Raised in a working-class Methodist family, Ravenhill was converted in 1921 and experienced **entire sanctification** under the ministry of **Maynard James** in 1929. While attending **Cliff College** (1930–1931), Ravenhill became one of a number of evangelistically inclined students known as "trekkers" who engaged in an itinerant evangelistic ministry throughout Great Britain. In 1934, he joined with Maynard James and **Jack Ford** in the organization of the CHC. He served as a CHC pastor and evangelist (1934–1951). He was a fiery evangelist, and his street preaching gained both opposition and notoriety during the 1940s and 1950s. Relocating to the United States, Ravenhill served on the staff of **Bethany Fellowship** (1958–1964) and as chaplain for David Wilkerson's Teen Challenge in New York City (1964–1966). Ravenhill's no-nonsense radicalism and open association with Pentecostals such as Wilkerson frequently angered Wesleyan traditionalists. But even as old doors closed, Ravenhill found new audiences among Pentecostals, Charismatics, and radical evangelicals. In fact, with Wilkerson, Ravenhill was one of the key figures in the emergence of the new youth-oriented, so-called Jesus People Movement of the late 1960s and early 1970s. His books, *Why Revival Tarries* (1959), *Tried and Transfigured* (1963), and *Sodom Had No Bible* (1971), are important documents in the creation of an alternative evangelicalism that turned a generation of often unchurched youth into evangelical activists. W.C.K.

READE, T(haddeus) C. (b. Steuben County, New York, 29 March 1846; d. Upland, Indiana, 25 July 1902). Methodist Episcopal Church (MEC) minister and president of **Taylor University** (1891–1902). A graduate of Ohio Wesleyan University, Reade served as a minister of MEC churches in Ohio before becoming president of Taylor University in 1891, the year after the North Indiana Conference of the MEC had transferred ownership of the college to the National Association of Local Preachers of the Methodist Church, which had changed the name of the institution from Fort Wayne College to Taylor University. Reade was directly involved in the relocation of the institution to Upland, Indiana. His primary contribution, however, was to create a deeply religious environment at the school while higher education in general was moving in a secular direction. Reade's most noteworthy single accomplishment was to draw attention to the life of the school's most famous student, **Sammy Morris** of Liberia. His biography of Morris had sold more than 200,000 copies by the 1920s. W.C.R.

REDFIELD, JOHN WESLEY (b. Clarendon, New Hampshire, 23 January 1810; d. Marengo, Illinois, 2 November 1863). Methodist Episcopal Church (MEC) and **Free Methodist Church** (FMC) evangelist. A physician, portrait painter, and abolitionist lecturer, in 1841, Redfield began an itinerant lay evangelistic career in New York City. In 1844, following an experience of **entire sanctification** through the ministry of **Walter** and **Phoebe Palmer**, he began accepting calls to preach in New Jersey and New England. He was a gifted preacher with an exceptional singing voice, and his evangelistic appeals proved especially successful with prisoners, students, the poor, and African Americans. Several of his most notable revivals occurred on college campuses, at Wesleyan University (1848), the University of Vermont (1855), and Lawrence University (Wisconsin; 1856). During the early 1850s, he experienced remarkable evangelistic success in such western New York cities and villages as Syracuse, where he organized an independent congregation, Albion, Bath, and Henrietta. In 1856, Redfield began a series of remarkable meetings in northern Illinois, Wisconsin, and St. Louis, Missouri. Although revivals accompanied his preaching in Green Bay, Fond du Lac, Appleton, and Waukesha, Wisconsin, his greatest success came in the northern Illinois communities of St. Charles, Marengo, Elgin, and Aurora, where his followers, known as "Redfieldites," were expelled from the MEC. Redfield is rightly understood as being, with **B. T. Roberts**, a cofounder of the FMC. It was his converts and supporters who had organized the first FMC congregation, an integrated congregation in St. Louis in 1859, and the first conference at St. Charles, Illinois, in 1860.

Although Redfield was an inspiring preacher and mystic who readily attested to divine visitations and guidance, his life was filled with suffering and personal tragedy. He suffered from bouts of depression, while an unfortunate early marriage ended in divorce. A second marriage, while more stable, seems to have been somewhat troubled. Equally troubling were the persistent charges that his ministry was divisive and encouraged fanaticism. Redfield was defended by B. T. Roberts and many of his converts who entered the ministry, but E. P. Hart (d. 1919), a convert of his Marengo, Illinois, meetings and later an FMC bishop, believed that Redfield's preaching did encourage fanaticism. In spite of his early death, many of the most radical features of Redfield's ministry continued to flourish in the FMC and the holiness movement well into the 20th century, especially through the ministry of Redfield's convert, **"Auntie" Coon**, and, in turn, her convert, **E. E. Shelhamer**. On Redfield's life, see the important biography by Joseph Goodwin Terrill, *The Life of the Rev. John Wesley Redfield* (1889). W.C.K.

REES, PAUL STROMBERG (b. Providence, Rhode Island, 4 September 1900; d. Boca Raton, Florida, 20 May 1991). **Pilgrim Holiness Church** and Evangelical Covenant pastor, author, and orator, and World Vision vice president. The son of **Seth Cook Rees**, Paul Rees began preaching at a downtown Los Angeles, California, mission in 1917. He was ordained in the Pilgrim Church in 1921 and served several pastorates in California and Detroit. In 1938, Rees became pastor of the First Covenant Church in Minneapolis, Minnesota, and transferred his ordination to the Evangelical Covenant Church in 1945. After an extremely successful pastorate, which included the development of writing and radio ministries, Rees left First Covenant Church in 1958 to become vice president at large of World Vision International, a Christian service ministry. In this capacity, he traveled extensively on preaching tours, visiting more than 60 countries, and organized international pastors' conferences and **Keswick** conventions. He also served as editor of *World Vision Magazine* (1964–1972).

Rees was active and visible in the national and world Christian communities. Though his only earned degree was a B.A. from the University of Southern California, he received many honorary doctorates as well as preaching and leadership awards. In his later years, he was at the forefront of an evangelical witness for ecumenism and social justice. He attended numerous meetings of the World Council of Churches (WCC) as an observer and attempted to forge closer links between the WCC and evangelical Christianity.

Rees wrote 14 books and thousands of articles, pamphlets, and sermons and served as a contributing editor to a number of periodicals, including the *Asbury Herald*, *Christianity Today*, and *God's Revivalist*. He was perhaps most noted for his powerful, clear, and eloquent preaching, which recalled a former era of religious oratory. J.L.W.

REES, SETH COOK (b. Westfield, Indiana, 6 August 1854; d. Pasadena, California, 22 May 1933). Society of Friends, **Christian and Missionary Alliance** (CMA), International Apostolic Holiness Union (IAHU), **Metropolitan Church Association** (MCA), Pentecostal Church of the Nazarene (PCN; see **Church of the Nazarene**), and **Pilgrim Holiness Church** (PHC) minister, evangelist, administrator, and author. **REES, HULDA ANN JOHNSON** (b. Randolph County, Indiana, 15 October 1855; d. Randolph County, Indiana, 3 June 1898). Society of Friends and CMA minister and evangelist. Following her conversion in 1871, Hulda Ann Johnson began preaching in Quaker meetings in Indiana, where she meet Seth C. Rees, a Quaker preacher who had been converted in 1873. Following their marriage in 1876, the two continued preaching and, in 1883, experienced **entire sanctification**. They served as Quaker pastors in Smithfield, Ohio (1884–1888); Adrian, Michigan (1888–1890); and Providence, Rhode Island (1890–1893); and as joint pastors of the nondenominational Church of Emmanuel in Providence (1893–1896). They entered full-time evangelistic work in 1896, but their joint ministry was tragically cut short by Hulda's death in 1898. Shortly after her death, their son, Byron, edited a volume of her sermons that included a short biography of his mother, *Hulda: The Pentecostal Prophetess*.

In 1897, Seth C. Rees joined **Martin Wells Knapp** in the organization of the IAHU, later the PHC. Rees served as president of the IAHU (1897–1905). Noted as the "earth-quaker" for his demonstrative and radical preaching, Rees attracted national attention and front-page coverage in the local press in 1901 for his leadership of two revivals in Chicago and Boston. The revivals, which were conducted under the auspices of the IAHU and MCA, were the most spectacular of Rees's career. In 1901, he established his first "rest cottage" in Chicago, Illinois. In the next decade, Rees would establish 10 such homes for unwed mothers and prostitutes across the country, as well as a short-lived periodical, the *Full Gospel and Rescue Journal* (1905–1909). Joining the PCN in 1905, Rees served as pastor of the University Church, Pasadena, California (1912–1917).

Noted for his uncompromising premillennialism and attacks on divorce and remarriage, Rees was for all practical purposes expelled from the PCN in 1917, when his congregation was disbanded. Organizing an independent congregation, the Pilgrim Tabernacle, Rees served as its pastor (1917–1925). In 1922, Rees led the Pilgrim Tabernacle, which included about 400 members, into the IAHU. Rees served as general superintendent of the PHC (1926–1933). Although remembered as an uncompromising holiness radical deeply rooted in the fourfold gospel he had learned from **A. B. Simpson** and as one of the great holiness orators, Rees was also a very effective communicator through the written word. Among his most notable books are *The Ideal Pentecostal Church* (1897), *The Holy War* (1904), and *Miracles in the Slums* (1905). A biography of Rees by his son, **Paul Rees**, *Seth Cook Rees: Warrior-Saint*, was published in 1934. W.C.K.

REID, ISAIAH (b. Salem, Indiana, 16 April 1836; d. Hutchinson, Kansas, 3 October 1911). Presbyterian, Iowa Holiness Association, and Pentecostal Church of the Nazarene (see **Church of the Nazarene**) minister, evangelist, and editor. Following his education at Auburn (New York) Theological Seminary, Reid became pastor of a Presbyterian congregation in Nevada, Iowa (1865–1875). After a year as pastor of a Presbyterian congregation in Albion, Iowa, he returned to Nevada and resumed his former pastorate. Following an experience of **entire sanctification**, Reid organized an independent holiness congregation where he served as pastor (1878–1890). He was the founding editor of the *Highway*, a holiness periodical he published from the late 1870s until it was merged with the *Christian Witness* in the early 1890s. He continued to serve as western editor of the *Christian Witness* until his death. Reid was the principal organizer of the Iowa Holiness Association and served as its president (1879–1911). He held a faculty appointment at Deets Pacific Bible College, now Point Loma Nazarene University (1906–1910), and was on the faculty of Kansas Holiness College in Hutchinson, Kansas, at the time of his death. Deeply committed to postmillennialism, Reid was one of the most articulate critics of the rising tide of premillennialism and faith healing that engulfed the early 20th-century holiness movement. Among his most notable books are *Holiness Bible Reading* (1883), *The Holy Way* (1892), and *How They Grow* (1894). W.C.K.

REYNOLDS, HIRAM FARNHAM (b. Lyons, Illinois, 12 May 1854; d. Haverhill, Massachusetts, 13 July 1938). Methodist Episcopal Church (MEC) pastor and evangelist, and **Church of the Nazarene** (CN) general superintendent and missions executive. Raised in rural Illinois near Chicago, Reynolds was converted in New England, attended Montpelier Methodist Seminary, and served churches in the Vermont Conference. Bishop John Hurst ordained him an elder in 1886. In 1892, he became president of the Vermont Holiness Association and entered full-time evangelism. He united with the Association of Pentecostal Churches of America in 1895. As home and foreign missions secretary (1897–1907), he oversaw the sending of missionaries to India (1898) and Cape Verde. He was the second general superintendent elected for the Pentecostal Church of the Nazarene (see CN) when mergers created that body in 1907 and 1908, and he was senior general superintendent from 1915 until his retirement in 1932. He was also the church's missions executive (1907–1922; 1925–1927). He used his dual role to focus the new denomination's priorities and energies around overseas missions, for which he was an ardent advocate and able publicist. He traveled abroad on several occasions, and, in 1913 and 1914, he visited Nazarene churches and missions in Japan, China, India, Africa, Cape Verde, and the British Isles. He laid foundations critical to the denomination's expansion into an international body with more than half of its membership today outside North America. R.S.I.

REZA, H(onorato) T. (b. Alahuixtlan, Guerrero, Mexico, 27 October 1912). **Church of the Nazarene** (CN) preacher, church executive, and educator. A graduate of Pasadena College and the University of Mexico, Reza contributed to CN growth in Central and South America. Ordained in 1939, he was pastor of various churches in Mexico and the United States. In the early 1940s, he was dean of his denomination's Spanish Bible College (Los Angeles) and professor at Pasadena College. From 1946 to 1981, he was executive director of the CN's International Publications Board in Kansas City, Missouri, overseeing the publication of Spanish, French, and Portuguese materials, including curricula, magazines (such as *El Heraldo de Santidad*), hymnals, and theological texts. For 23 years he was the preacher on *La Hora Nazarena* radio broadcast heard on nearly 550 stations in Latin America and the United States. In 1980, he became founding president of Seminario Nazareno Mexicano (Mexico City). He was a liaison between Cuban Nazarenes and the wider denomination from the 1960s to the 1980s. R.S.I.

RIDOUT, GEORGE W(hitefield) (b. St. John's, Newfoundland, 1 April 1870; d. Philadelphia, Pennsylvania, 19 March 1954). Methodist Episcopal Church (MEC) and Methodist Church minister, educator, evangelist, and author. Entering the ministry in the New Jersey Conference of the MEC in 1895, Ridout quickly established a reputation as an effective evangelist and forceful defender of traditional Wesleyan doctrine and experience. In 1913, Ridout joined the faculty of **Taylor**

University. In 1922, he was named professor of evangelism and practical theology at **Asbury College**. Credited with first proposing that Asbury College establish a full-fledged divinity school, Ridout served on the faculty of both the College and **Asbury Theological Seminary** (1922–1928). A lifelong disciple of the missionary methods of bishop **William Taylor**, Ridout embarked on a two-year around-the-world missionary tour in 1928. Deeply gratified by the success of his trip, Ridout returned to Brazil and Argentina in the fall of 1930. The widely attended meetings, held in Methodist, Presbyterian, and Congregational churches, resulted in one of the most significant spiritual awakenings in South America. Although formally retiring in 1939, Ridout continued to preach and write until the time of his death. As a frequent contributor to Methodist and holiness periodicals, such as the *Christian Advocate, God's Revivalist,* and the *Pentecostal Herald*, of which he was a corresponding editor from 1920 to 1954, Ridout was both a forceful defender of holiness experience and a fierce critic of theological liberalism. Among his most notable books are *The Beauty of Holiness and Maxims of the Holy Life* (1920s), *The Present Crisis of Methodism* (1921), and *Dr. Fosdick Answered* (1920s). Along with **Henry Clay Morrison** and **Andrew Johnson**, Ridout created the synthesis of holiness experience and fundamentalist theology that would characterize Asbury College and Asbury Theological Seminary for much of the 20th century. W.C.K.

RIGGLE, H(erbert) M(cClellan) (b. Cochran's Falls, Pennsylvania, 18 February 1872; d. Rochester, Indiana, 9 October 1952). **Church of God (Anderson)** (CG[A]) minister, evangelist, and author. Raised in a community deeply influenced by the asceticism and piety of the **Free Methodist Church**, the **Wesleyan Methodist Church**, and the Mennonite Brethren in Christ (see **United Missionary Church**), Riggle was naturally drawn to the vision of Christian unity and radical nonconformity to the world of the early CG(A). He was converted in 1891 and experienced **entire sanctification** in 1893. In January 1893, he married Minnie Shelhamer, a preacher who was a cousin of FMC evangelist **E. E. Shelhamer**. Forming the Riggle Evangelistic Company, the young couple spread the CG(A) message throughout the Midwest. Although Riggle held brief pastorates in Maryland, Pennsylvania, Indiana, Oklahoma, and Ohio, his primary skill was that of an evangelist who was especially adept at organizing new CG(A) congregations. From 1920 to 1923, the Riggles served as missionaries to Syria.

Riggle served as the treasurer of the CG(A) mission board (1930–1934) and president of the Gospel Trumpet Company (1908–1930). In 1903, Riggle completed **D. S. Warner's** final manuscript, *The Cleansing of the Sanctuary*, for publication. Among his other books are *Two Works of Grace* (1899), *Man, His Past and His Present* (1904), and an autobiography, *Pioneer Evangelism* (1924). W.C.K.

ROBERTS, BENJAMIN TITUS (b. Chautauqua County, New York, 25 July 1823; d. Cattaraugus County, New York, 27 February 1893). Principal founder of the **Free Methodist Church** (FMC). **ROBERTS, ELLEN LOIS STOWE** (b. Windsor, New York, 4 March 1825; d. North Chili, New York, 28 January 1908). Methodist Epsicopal Church (MEC) and FMC reformer and editor. Raised on New York State's western frontier, B. T. Roberts early became an abolitionist. Some years after his father, Titus Roberts, was converted in a "burned-over district" revival and became a Methodist lay preacher, Benjamin was himself converted at age 21, partly through Presbyterian influence.

Following his conversion, Roberts gave up the study of law and was licensed as a Methodist exhorter in 1845. After two terms at the Genesee Wesleyan Seminary, he attended Wesleyan University in Middletown, Connecticut, graduating in 1848. At Wesleyan, Roberts was influenced by President Stephen Olin and by the Methodist lay evangelist **John Wesley Redfield**, who conducted a stirring revival in Middletown. Also, while at Wesleyan, Roberts met Ellen Stowe of New York City, niece of Methodist book agent George Lane, and, in 1849, the two were married.

During several Methodist pastorates, Roberts became increasingly concerned with the spiritual state of the MEC. A series of articles he wrote for the *Northern Independent* brought him into conflict with leaders in the Genesee Conference where he was serving. Roberts protested what he termed "New School Methodism" and called for spiritual renewal, doctrinal fidelity to Methodist distinctives, and free, rather than rented, pews. The articles exacerbated a growing conflict between "Nazarites," who called for revival and reform, and the "Buffalo Regency," composed largely of city pastors, several of whom were Freemasons. Because of his writings, Roberts was tried and expelled from the conference (and thus the denomination) in 1858, along with several others.

Partly in protest against these actions, a series of laypeople's conventions led to the organization of the Free Methodist Church at Pekin,

New York, in August 1860. The new denomination vowed "to maintain the Bible standard of Christianity, and to preach the Gospel to the poor." Roberts was appointed general superintendent, a position he held until his death in 1893. The laymen's conventions also prompted the founding of the *Earnest Christian* magazine, which Roberts started in 1860 and edited until his death.

In the interim between his expulsion from the MEC and the organization of the FMC, Roberts conducted revival meetings, working at times with John Wesley Redfield. In 1859, he organized a "free church" in St. Louis, Missouri, partly in protest against slaveholding. Thus, when the FMC was organized in 1860, "Free Methodist" meant freedom of the Spirit, free pews, and freedom from slavery.

Benjamin and Ellen Roberts based their ministry in Buffalo, New York, but later moved to Rochester and founded Chili Seminary (now Roberts Wesleyan College) in 1866 at nearby North Chili. While B.T. traveled extensively for the growing denomination, Ellen carried on a ministry among the poor in Buffalo and, after 1866, worked tirelessly in the day-to-day interests of the seminary, assisting also with the *Earnest Christian.* Seven children were born to the Robertses, some of whom died young. Their fourth child, Benson Howard, served as principal of Chili Seminary (1876–1879) and as joint principal with his capable wife, Emma Sellew Roberts (1881–1906).

During wide-ranging travels as general superintendent, Roberts presided over annual conferences, held revivals, participated in interdenominational gatherings seeking broader Christian unity, and published several books. In 1872, he issued a booklet, *The Right of Women to Preach the Gospel. Fishers of Men* (1876), a manual on evangelism and pastoral work, was followed by *Why Another Sect* (1879), written in response to MEC Bishop Matthew Simpson's account of Free Methodism in his *Cyclopedia of Methodism: First Lessons on Money* (1886), a discussion of economic policy and manual on stewardship, shows that Roberts had read economist Richard T. Ely, later influential in the Social Gospel movement. *Ordaining Women* (1891), a spirited defense of women's ministry, was prompted by the refusal of the 1890 FMC General Conference to adopt Roberts's view that no one should be "refused ordination on account of sex, or race, or condition."

Roberts also published hymnbooks for the denomination in 1879 and 1883 and served as editor of the *Free Methodist* from 1886 to 1890, a heavy responsibility that probably hastened his death.

Doctrinally Roberts was Wesleyan, committed to scriptural authority, and an advocate of **entire sanctification**. Both B.T. and Ellen were influenced spiritually by **Phoebe Palmer**. As a young woman in New York City, Ellen had attended class meetings held by the Palmers.

Despite strict membership rules and a ban on instrumental music, the FMC grew steadily during B. T. Roberts's lifetime. At his death, the denomination counted 24,000 members in 29 annual conferences, had started several colleges, and sponsored mission work in India, Portuguese East Africa, South Africa, and the Dominican Republic.

Surviving her husband, Ellen Roberts contributed frequently to the *Free Methodist* and continued her active interest in FMC foreign missions, serving as first president of the Woman's Missionary Society (1864). Following her death in 1908, the denomination issued a collection of her writings. (Biography: Benson Howard Roberts, *Benjamin Titus Roberts: Late General Superintendent of the Free Methodist Church, a Biography by His Son* [1900].) H.A.S.

ROBERTS, JAMES P. (b. Greenville, Texas, 27 November 1867; d. Pilot Point, Texas, 2 January 1937). Nazarene minister and social worker. Roberts's social conscience was awakened by a sermon by **Seth Rees** and, with an unusual vision he experienced, he was inspired to establish Rest Cottage, a home for unwed mothers, which opened in Pilot Point, Texas, in 1903. It became a ministry of the Holiness Association of Texas in 1905 and later was supported by the southern districts of the **Church of the Nazarene**. Roberts led the ministry until his death, and more than 4,000 girls and women were assisted in his lifetime. He was known as a friend to the poor, African Americans, and any whom society branded social outcasts. A brother and a nephew, John F. Roberts and Geren Roberts, supervised Rest Cottage until it closed in the 1970s. R.S.I.

ROBINSON, REUBEN A. (Bud) (b. White County, Tennessee, 27 January 1860; d. Pasadena, California, 2 November 1942). Methodist Episcopal Church, South (MECS), Methodist Episcopal Church (MEC), and **Church of the Nazarene** (CN) minister, evangelist, and author. "Uncle Buddie," as he was affectionately known, was raised in Texas, converted in 1880, and experienced **entire sanctification** under the ministry of **W. B. Godbey** in 1886. Entering the ministry shortly after his conversion, Robinson served a number of isolated circuits in the MECS. Although experiencing some success, his lack of education, stuttering, and occasional epileptic seizures greatly hindered his ministry. He was expelled from the MECS for his holiness views. An early attempt to establish an itinerant evangelistic ministry brought few invitations to hold services until **H. C. Morrison** began promoting Robinson in 1898. Supported by Morrison and provided with a home by **A. M. Hills**, Robinson gained national attention as the central figure in the **Metropolitan Church Association**–sponsored 1901 Chicago revival. He was a remarkable storyteller who turned his speech impediment into an asset, and his optimistic autobiographical message that God loved even a worthless, thieving Texas cowboy left a deep impression on all who heard him. In 1908, Robinson joined the Pentecostal Church of the Nazarene (see CN). He traveled two million miles, preached an estimated 33,000 sermons, saw an estimated 100,000 people saved at his meetings, and spent $85,000 providing educations for young people. In spite of the fact that he never held a church office, Robinson contributed more to the rapid growth of the CN than any other person. He was a frequent contributor to H. C. Morrison's *Pentecostal Herald* and wrote a regular column in the *Herald of Holiness*, "Good Samaritan Chats." Among his most important books are *A Pitcher of Cream* (1906), *Honey in the Rock* (1913), and an early autobiography, *Sunshine and Smiles* (1903). Shortly after his death, his son-in-law, George Wise, wrote a short biography, *Rev. Bud Robinson* (1946). W.C.K.

ROOT, HELEN I(sabel) (b. Port Byron, New York, 13 April 1873; d. Winona Lake, Indiana, 3 November 1945). Congregational and **Free Methodist Church** (FMC) missionary, pastor, and editor. Root was educated at Cornell University, where she was converted through the influence of student volunteer movement leader John R. Mott (1865–1955). She was a Congregational missionary to Ceylon for seven years. Experiencing **entire sanctification** as a result of the influence of Ella Clark, wife of FMC bishop William Clark, Root joined the FMC, serving as pastor in Corinth, New York. From 1917 to 1922, she was an FMC missionary in India. She served as a traveling secretary for the Woman's Missionary Society (WMS) of the FMC; pastor of FMC congregations in Glen Ellyn and Aurora, Illinois (1923–1927); and a general secretary for the WMS (1927–1941). She was editor of the *Missionary Tidings* (1931–1943) and, at the time of her death, was book review editor for the Free Methodist Publishing House. While serving as editor of the *Missionary Tidings*, she taught theology at the Olive Branch Mission Training School. She also wrote biographies of pioneer FMC missionaries Grace Barnes and Clara Leffingwell. W.C.K.

ROSE, DELBERT R(oy) (b. Corunna, Michigan, 17 September 1912). Evangelical Church, Evangelical United Brethren, and United Methodist Church minister, evangelist, and educator. Educated at Cleveland Bible Institute (now Malone College), John Fletcher College, Garrett Biblical Institute, Union Theological Seminary (New York), and Iowa State University, Rose taught at **Kletzing College** (1946–1947), Western Evangelical Seminary (1947–1952), **Asbury Theological Seminary** (1952–1974), and **Wesley Biblical Seminary** (1975–1985). In retirement, he continued to teach at Wesley Biblical Seminary and in mission schools sponsored by the Oriental Missionary Society (see **OMS International**) and **World Gospel Mission**. His Iowa State University Ph.D. dissertation, "The Theology of Joseph H. Smith" (1952), was published as *The Theology of Christian Experience* (1965) and *Vital Holiness: A Theology of Christian Experience* (1975). A prolific author, Rose has written essays appearing in *Christian Witness,* the *Herald,* the *Asbury Seminarian,* and two important anthologies of holiness thought, *Insight into Holiness* (1963) and *The Word and the Doctrine* (1965). While serving as historian for the National Holiness Association (1951–1972; see **Christian Holiness Partnership**), Rose was responsible for collecting a significant body of material that documented the 19th- and 20th-century holiness revival. A noted evangelist, Rose was a frequent **camp meeting** and revival preacher. He was a charter member of the **Wesleyan Theological Society** (WTS) and served as its president (1972–1973). In 2000, Rose and his wife, Susan Schultz Rose, longtime librarian at Asbury Theological Seminary, were jointly awarded the Lifetime Achievement Award by the WTS. W.C.K.

RUTH, C(hristian) W(isner) (b. Bucks County, Pennsylvania, 1 September 1865; d. Wilmore, Kentucky, 27 May 1941). Holiness Christian Church (HCC; see **Evangelical Holiness Church**) and **Church of the Nazarene** (CN) evangelist and superintendent. Irenic and ecumenical, Ruth was raised in the Evangelical Association but joined the HCC and was its presiding elder (general leader) in the mid-1890s. After 1896, he traveled from his home in Indianapolis as a full-time evangelist for the National Holiness Association (NHA; see **Christian Holiness Partnership**), except for a brief time in pastoral roles. A crucial revival he conducted in Los Angeles led Ruth to serve briefly as First Church of the Nazarene's associate pastor (1901–1903) and, more important, as assistant general superintendent (1901–1907) of the expanding Nazarene movement. The latter role well complemented

Ruth's evangelistic itinerary. Convinced that holiness churches should unite, he pursued the contacts that resulted in the mergers creating the Pentecostal Church of the Nazarene (see CN) in 1907–1908. From 1908 to 1918, he was a vice president of the NHA. In 1910, he was an organizer of a key NHA auxiliary, the National Holiness Missionary Society (later **World Gospel Mission**), and was its president from 1925 to 1941. He lived in Pasadena, California, in his last years. R.S.I.

– S –

SACRAMENTS. The religious ceremonies that serve as either the conduits of divine grace or symbols of a significant spiritual reality. Holiness churches such as the **Wesleyan Church**, **Free Methodist Church**, and the **Church of the Nazarene**, which see themselves as drawing direct inspiration from **John Wesley**, recognize two sacraments, baptism and the Lord's Supper. Other holiness bodies, such as the **Salvation Army** and holiness-related members of the Society of Friends (see **Evangelical Friends International**), find little spiritual value in such external rites. A third group of holiness bodies, especially the **Brethren in Christ**, prefer the term *ordinance* to *sacrament*. By *ordinance* they mean rites that do not convey grace in their own right but are commanded by God. Such bodies, including the **Church of God (Anderson)**, frequently identify the washing of the saints' feet, as described in John 13, as an ordinance binding on all Christians. W.C.K.

SALVATION ARMY (SA). An international evangelical Protestant denomination whose doctrines are based on Wesleyan holiness teaching and a commitment to world evangelism and that conducts a program of temporal relief and welfare services. The SA developed from the East London Christian Mission, founded in 1865 by **William Booth** (1829–1912) and his wife, **Catherine** (1829–1890), who were successful evangelists trained in Wesleyan doctrine, as well as effective and attractive speakers. In 1878, the leaders of the Christian Mission renamed it the Salvation Army, adding military trappings partly based on biblical teaching about the reality of spiritual warfare. The severe military-style discipline to which converts were expected to submit, in the form of the "Articles of War" and a proliferation of "Orders and Regulations," reflected scriptural principles of personal holiness, self-sacrifice, and evangelism. SA leaders also recognized the contemporary appeal of military elements such as uniforms, parades, flags, and brass bands, which also provided an effective means of outdoor evangelism. The military structure also lent itself to William Booth's autocratic leadership style and allowed for efficient deployment of ministry personnel and the proper outfitting of impoverished converts whose shabby dress excluded them from regular Sunday church services of the day.

The SA spread rapidly throughout Great Britain and then overseas. The first country outside of Britain to be "invaded" was the United States, on which the SA officially "opened fire" in March 1880. By 1888, the SA had spread throughout the British Empire and to France, Switzerland, Germany, Italy, the Netherlands, and Scandinavia. The Booths and their associates were convinced that they were carrying the gospel to people who had been overlooked by other Christian programs; this belief gave them a sense of urgency and zeal.

Constantly faced with the terrible effects of urban poverty, early in their ministry the Booths began to offer small-scale practical relief. The superior organizational structure of the SA and its capacity to attract large numbers of converts and extensive publicity enabled its early leaders to expand their social welfare program. By the time that it had come to the public's attention, the SA was no longer simply an evangelistic crusade; it had developed a combined ministry, which was well expressed by a later SA motto, "Heart to God, hand to man." The motivation for the SA social welfare program was twofold: the commands of Christ, in passages such as Matthew 7:12 and 25:34–40, and the belief that the availability of temporal relief would encourage people to listen to the gospel. The SA developed a host of services, which were characterized by efficient delivery, immediate practicality, and flexible response to need. These services became increasingly diverse and sophisticated. Programs for the marginalized, disadvantaged, and disabled were developed, many of which continue in some form to the present day. Canteen programs for military personnel in the two world wars played a crucial role in securing the SA a permanent place of respect and affection in the public mind, especially in the United States. A few services, such as hospitals for unwed mothers, were reduced or abandoned as changing social standards rendered them obsolete. The SA is the largest Protestant welfare agency in the world, and national opinion polls in the United States show it to be the most popular charity in the country.

The Booths and their early followers were eager to use almost any means to the great end of evangelism and social uplift, among them

popular music forms, and the SA has been quick to adopt technological innovations such as bicycles, magic lanterns, motion pictures,
sound recordings, automobiles, radio, television, the Internet, and e-
mail. Salvationists are expected to abstain from alcohol and tobacco
in all forms. With few exceptions, they adopt a frugal and unobtru-
sive lifestyle and are willing to accept a degree of personal discipline
that has become more and more exceptional with the passing years.
Largely because of the influence of Quaker teachings on Catherine
Booth, the SA does not practice sacramental observances, such as
baptism and communion. Women are given equal opportunity for
ministry and leadership in the SA. Of the 14 generals (international
leaders) of the SA, two have been single women, as have been a
number of national and territorial leaders. As a denomination, the
SA is committed to Wesleyan holiness. The experience of **entire
sanctification** forms an important part of the SA's pastoral ministry
in its congregational units (called "corps"). In 1947, the SA in the
United States established an annual refresher course in the doctrine
and experience of holiness, named the Brengle Institute after
Samuel Logan Brengle. As of 1996, the SA operated in 103 countries and territories, offering its programs and services in 160 different languages. It had 17,389 officers (clergy) and 858,694 soldiers
(adult lay members), with 3,645 active officers and 83,690 soldiers in
the United States. E.H.M.

SANDERS, CHERYL J. (b. Washington, D.C., 1953). **Church of God
(Anderson)** (CG[A]) minister. Cheryl Sanders received a B.A. degree
from Swarthmore College in 1974, and M.Div. (1980) and Th.D.
(1985) degrees from Harvard Divinity School. Sanders has served the
Third Street Church of God, Washington, D.C., as associate pastor
(1986–1997) and senior pastor (1997–). She has taught at Howard
University since 1984 and, as of 1998, was professor of Christian ethics.
She has been a visiting professor at Harvard Divinity School (1988),
Wesley Theological Seminary (1996), and Lutheran Theological Seminary (1996). Her published works include *Living the Intersection:
Womanism and Afrocentrism in Theology* (1995) and *Saints in Exile:
The Holiness Experience in African American Religion and Culture*
(1996). She has been active in **Wesleyan/Holiness Women Clergy**
conferences. B.L.C.

SCHMUL, HAROLD E. (b. Erie, Pennsylvania, 26 January 1921;
d. Salem, Ohio, 26 June 1998). Conservative holiness minister, publisher,

and convention organizer. Converted in October 1935, Schmul began pastoring in the **Wesleyan Methodist Church** in 1944. In 1951, a conversation with **H. Robb French** concerning the need for revival precipitated the call for an interdenominational holiness convention. The first such convention (later called the **Inter-Church Holiness Convention** [IHC]) was conducted from 31 December 1951 through 1 January 1952, with French and **R. G. Flexon** as speakers. Schmul agreed to organize the event, a task he performed until 1997. As general secretary of the IHC, Schmul led local conventions around the world as well as the annual general convention, which has been located at Dayton, Ohio, since 1975. In 1953, Schmul also began to serve the entire Wesleyan tradition by establishing Schmul Publishing Company, which specializes in reprints of Wesleyan classics. While involved in these roles, Schmul was also an active pastor, ministering for more than 30 years at Salem (Ohio) Pilgrim Church. An advocate of "**sweet radical holiness**," Schmul exercised a moderating influence on the diverse membership of the conservative holiness movement through the unifying nature of the IHC, and he kept conservatives connected with their heritage through his publishing endeavors. W.T.

SCOTT, ORANGE (b. Brookfield, Vermont, 13 February 1800; d. Newark, New Jersey, 31 July 1847). Abolitionist and founder of the **Wesleyan Methodist Church** (WMC). From a very poor family, Scott received only 13 months of formal elementary education. In September 1820, he was converted at a **camp meeting** near Barre, Vermont, and joined the Methodist Episcopal Church (MEC). Almost immediately, he became a class leader and was licensed as an exhorter. In 1821, he started itinerating as a Methodist preacher. The following year, he was received into the New England Conference on trial. Three years later, he was appointed pastor of a prominent church in Charlestown, Massachusetts. Soon thereafter, he was made a presiding elder, supervising the pastors of the Springfield District.

Scott became convinced of the evils of slavery and of the need to work for abolition, and he wrote and spoke frequently on the topic. He also sent William Lloyd Garrison's antislavery newspaper, the *Liberator*, to 100 New England Conference preachers. As a result, the majority of conference members became abolitionists, and Scott was elected to head the New England delegation to the 1836 General Conference in Cincinnati, Ohio. His vocal support of abolitionism at the Cincinnati meeting thrust him into national prominence in the MEC.

Scott's abolitionist activities led to his removal from his leadership position in the district, and he became a traveling lecturer and fundraiser for the American Anti-Slavery Society. He urged abolitionists to become politically active in the Liberty Party, thus placing himself in opposition to Garrison. Seeing the increasing implacability of the Methodist hierarchy on the abolition issue, by the early 1840s, he gave up on the possibility of significant reform within the MEC. He and several other abolitionists, including **Luther Lee** and **Lucius C. Matlack**, seceded from the MEC in 1842 and, in 1843, organized the Wesleyan Methodist Connection (later WMC). For the next four years, Scott worked indefatigably for the success of the new group. His special concern was the development of a viable newspaper and book concern. The importance of his efforts on behalf of the Wesleyan Methodist Connection is evident in an early derisive name given to the Wesleyan Methodists: "Scottites." Scott's unexpected death from tuberculosis in 1847 was a severe loss to the young denomination. D.M.S.

SCRIPTURE MEDITATION EVANGELISTIC ASSOCIATION (SMEA). Founded by Claude Lee Lane (d. 1977) and his wife, Lois. In 1951, while working for the Mansfield Tire and Rubber Company, Claude Lane, who had graduated from Cleveland Bible Institute, now Malone College, was called to pastor a church in Shelby, Ohio. Relocating to Bath, New York, in 1954, Claude Lane established a new church, now affiliated with the **Christian and Missionary Alliance** and began a series of radio meditations on WWHG in Hornell, New York. In response to the success of the program, the Lanes founded the SMEA. In 1957, they relocated their ministry to Transfer, Pennsylvania, where an old public school was turned into the S.M.E.A. Bible Institute, after 1977 the C. L. Lane Bible Institute, and a nondenominational church was founded. Expanding their radio ministry, the Lanes began mission work among Native Americans at Pine Ridge, South Dakota, in 1958, which has evolved into a mission station and children's home at Wanblee, South Dakota. Graduates from the C. L. Lane Bible Institute serve churches in more than 12 states. It currently has fewer than 100 students. Catherine Rexford is president. As of 1999, Lois Lane was still a classroom teacher. W.C.K. and R.M.J.

SHARPE, GEORGE (b. Lanarkshire, Scotland, 17 April 1865; d. Glasgow, Scotland, 26 March 1948). Congregational and **Church of the Nazarene** (CN) minister. Converted in 1882, employment took Sharpe to New York in 1886. Joining the MEC, he pastored churches in the Northern New York Conference. In holiness services conducted in one of his churches by a **Salvation Army** officer, he experienced **entire sanctification**. Vacationing in Scotland in 1901, he accepted an invitation to become minister of Ardrossan Congregational Church on the west coast and, in 1905, became the pastor of Parkhead Congregational Church in Glasgow. His strong emphasis on Wesleyan holiness met with growing opposition from some of his deacons and, in 1906, he was dismissed from the pastorate. Some 80 members of the congregation joined their pastor to form the Parkhead Pentecostal Church. A holiness Bible school was begun at Parkhead in 1908, other holiness churches were founded, and the new denomination was named the Pentecostal Church of Scotland. In 1915, it united with the Pentecostal Church of the Nazarene (see CN). A diligent pastor, a visionary leader, an able administrator, and an impassioned preacher of scriptural holiness, Sharpe was the recognized "father" of the holiness movement in 20th-century Scotland. H.M.

SHAW, S(olomon) B(enjamin) (b. Crown Point, Indiana, 11 June 1854; d. Phoenix, Arizona, 19 November 1941). **Wesleyan Methodist Church** (WMC), **Free Methodist Church** (FMC), Primitive Holiness Mission, and **Christian and Missionary Alliance** (CMA) minister, editor, evangelist, and publisher. Converted in 1876 under the ministry of **Sarah Cooke**, Shaw served as a WMC and FMC minister in Michigan, president of the Michigan Holiness Association (1880s–1890s), and editor of the *Michigan Holiness Record* (1883–1890).

In 1890, frustrated by the denominational rivalry of holiness adherents, Shaw organized the Primitive Holiness Mission, a quasi-denomination in Dutton, Michigan. In spite of the fact that the Primitive Holiness Mission was a failure, Shaw gained a significant national following when he published *Touching Incidents and Remarkable Answers to Prayer* in 1893. The work, which went through many editions and remains in print, resulted in the establishment of the S. B. Shaw Publishing Company. Relocating to Chicago, Illinois, in the late 1890s, Shaw expanded his publishing ministry while emerging as an important leader in the national holiness movement. In 1901, Shaw, who had played a role in a national holiness assembly that had met in Chicago in 1885, was the convener of a second General Holiness Assembly and served as editor of its proceedings.

In 1907, Shaw returned to Grand Rapids, Michigan, where he continued his evangelistic and publishing ministry. In 1919, Shaw was named head of the Grand Rapids branch of the CMA. In the early 1920s, he retired to southern California, although he continued to hold evangelistic meetings into the 1930s. A passionate holiness ecumenist, Shaw made repeated attempts to organize a "national interdenominational association" that had greater cohesion and organizational unity then the National Holiness Association (see **Christian Holiness Partnership**). Deeply disappointed with the failure of the 1901 General Holiness Assembly to create such a national body, Shaw gradually withdrew from active leadership in the holiness movement. Among his most important books are *God's Financial Plan* (1897), *Dying Testimonies of Saved and Unsaved* (1898), and *The Great Revival in Wales* (1905). W.C.K.

SHELHAMER, E(lmer) E(llsworth) (b. near Mateer, Pennsylvania, 16 December 1869; d. Joplin, Missouri, 21 January 1947). **Free Methodist Church** (FMC) revivalist, author, and publisher. **SHELHAMER, MINNIE BALDWIN** (b. near Euclid, Ohio, 30 June 1867; d. Atlanta, Georgia, 28 March 1902). FMC evangelist. **SHELHAMER, JULIA ARNOLD**, FMC educator and evangelist. (b. Sycamore, Illinois, 1880; d. Nicholasville, Kentucky, 2 June 1981). Converted at 16, E. E. Shelhamer early felt called to preach. He studied three years at Wheaton Academy where he became acquainted with and joined the FMC, partly through the influence of **Harriet Arvilla ("Auntie") Coon**.

Shelhamer was sanctified wholly under the ministry of **Vivian A. Dake** and soon joined Dake's Pentecostal Bands (PB). As a PB leader, he held revivals and helped to found a number of FMC churches, mainly in Pennsylvania and Illinois. At 22, he was divinely healed of tuberculosis. Tall, decisive, and striking in appearance, Shelhamer was viewed by many as Dake's natural successor when Dake died in 1892, but this role was filled by Thomas Nelson. When the PB became independent of the FMC in 1895, Shelhamer remained with the denomination, becoming an ordained FMC minister. His wife, Minnie (Baldwin), also a former PB worker, was a noted evangelist and street preacher, especially recognized for her prison ministry. The Shelhamers planted churches, pastored, and engaged in evangelistic campaigns. They opened FMC work in Georgia and Florida, laying the basis for what became the Georgia–Florida Conference and the Florida Spanish Mission.

After Minnie Shelhamer died, E. E. Shelhamer married Julia Arnold (1903). Together they continued the evangelistic work and published many books and pamphlets, which had broad circulation. E. E. Shelhamer traveled widely, holding evangelistic meetings in South America, Africa, Australia, Asia, and Europe. He taught divine healing as well as conversion and sanctification. For several years, the Shelhamers based their ministry at **God's Bible School**. Among the books Shelhamer wrote or edited were *Life and Labors of Auntie Coon* (1905), *Heart Talks to Ministers and Christian Workers* (which included selections by **John Wesley**, **H. C. Morrison**, and Richard Baxter), and *Finney on Revival* (published in various editions). One of his most widely circulated pamphlets was *Five Reasons Why I Do Not Seek the Gift of Tongues*. His autobiography was published as *The Ups and Downs of a Pioneer Preacher* (1915), later as *60 Years of Thorns and Roses*, and after his death as *A Spartan Evangel: Life Story of E. E. Shelhamer* (1951). Always committed to radical holiness, Shelhamer autographed his books and photos: "Yours for a *clean,* rather than a *big* work."

After Shelhamer's death, **Paul S. Rees**, to whom Shelhamer had been something of a mentor, paid tribute to him as a "gracious senior preacher" who had shown great interest in "younger ministers" and whose "fraternal interest in ministers overleaped all sectarian barriers." Julia Shelhamer survived her husband by more than four decades, dying at the age of 101. She taught at Kingswood (Kentucky) College, Frankfort Pilgrim College, and God's Bible School. Following her husband's death, she founded the Shelhamer Memorial Mission in Washington, D.C., which she operated with her sister until 1960. She later served as a fund-raiser for the FMC and continued to preach until ill health forced her into retirement in the mid-1970s. E. E. Shelhamer's daughter, Esther, married Gilbert James, influential professor of the church and society at **Asbury Theological Seminary** in the 1960s and 1970s. H.A.S.

SHILLING, HENRY (b. New Bethlehem, Pennsylvania, 9 July 1902; d. Brookville, Pennsylvania, 17 August 1998). Methodist Church minister, publisher, and educator. Henry Shilling was converted in a tent meeting at the age of 12 and joined the Methodist Episcopal Church. He experienced **entire sanctification** at **God's Bible School** from which he graduated in 1925. Enrolling at **Asbury College** (1928), he became convinced that the Wesleyan idea of Christian perfection was not only theologically correct but also philosophically sound. He furthered his education at Grove City College, Westminster College,

Western Seminary, Thiel College, and Burton College. Licensed to preach in June 1925, he ministered in the Erie Conference (Pennsylvania) for 15 years. He established the Fountain Press in 1935 and edited the *Fountain*, a holiness weekly. He also founded Transylvania Bible School (Freeport, Pennsylvania, 1938). While pastoring at the West Middlesex (Pennsylvania) Methodist Church, he opened the 1936 presidential campaign of Governor Alfred Landon, who had been born in the church's parsonage. Covering the campaign was writer H. L. Mencken. Shilling stated that he was going to preach an old-fashioned evangelistic sermon and dared Mencken to attend the service, which he did. Some believe that after the encounter with Shilling, Mencken developed a milder tone in his writings and improved his lifestyle. Shilling was the author of eight books published by Fountain Press, including *Seven Years of Faith, 1938–1945* (n.d.), *The Gift of the Gods: A Study of the Historical Development of the Doctrine of Eternal Security* (1951), *The Second Seven Years of Faith, 1945–1952* (1953), *From Horses to Jets: An Autobiography* (1976), and *Revised Religion* (n.d.). J.M.

SIERRA CASTRO, WILFRIDO (b. Rioverde, Esmeraldas, Ecuador, 9 August 1909; d. Esmeraldas, Ecuador, 16 February 1969). **United Missionary Church** lay evangelist with La Iglesia Evangélica Misionera Ecuatoriana. A hardworking farmer in poverty-stricken Rioverde, he became the first evangelical Christian in his community. His radical devotion, holiness, and sacrificial love astounded those who knew him, then drew international attention through the writings of Moritz Thomsen, his bitterly agnostic friend and neighbor (1966–1968). Sierra emerged as a central figure in the Peace Corps classic *Living Poor* (1969). Thomsen later wrote, "[W]ithout shoes, without teeth, dressed in rags . . . his poverty stood out in that town of poor people. . . . He loved God. . . . he opened his Bible a dozen times a day. . . . [H]e studied the holy words, his whole face radiant. . . . I tried to save his body. He tried to save my soul." His holy life speaks for earnest unsung believers in Latin America. His testimony lives on in rural congregations that his disciples helped to form. Thomsen, whose poignantly humorous, deeply acerbic works won critical acclaim, experienced a joyous deathbed conversion in Guayaquil, Ecuador (1991). P.A.E. and T.P.E.

SIMPSON, A(lbert) B(enjamin) (b. Prince Edward Island, 15 December 1843; d. New York City, 29 October 1919). Presbyterian minister and founder of the **Christian and Missionary Alliance** (CMA). Following his education at Knox College, Toronto, Simpson entered the Presbyterian ministry, serving congregations in Hamilton, Ontario (1865–1873); Louisville, Kentucky (1873–1879); and New York City (1879–1881). In 1874, after reading **W. E. Boardman**'s *The Higher Christian Life*, Simpson experienced **entire sanctification**. In 1881, Simpson founded a periodical, the *Gospel in All Lands*, to promote mission among the poor of New York City and around the world. Although Simpson's mission among New York City poor bore fruit, his congregation's failure to provide a welcoming atmosphere for them and his own failing health led him to separate from the Presbyterian church in 1881. During the summer of 1881, Simpson experienced divine healing under the ministry of **Charles Cullis**, at the Old Orchard Beach (Maine) **Camp Meeting**, causing him to refocus his ministry.

In 1882, he founded an independent congregation in Manhattan, which became known as the Gospel Tabernacle; a new periodical, later known as the *Alliance Witness*; a home for faith healing; and a missionary training school, now Nyack College. In 1887, following the suggestion of Methodist W. E. Blackstone (1841–1935), Simpson organized his movement into two branches: "the Christian Alliance," to direct North American work, and "the Evangelical Missionary Alliance," to direct foreign missions. In 1897, these were united into the CMA. Although remembered as a passionate champion of missions and experiential piety, Simpson was an important theological innovator whose memorable reformulation of basic Christian teaching is aptly captured in his phrase "the fourfold gospel." As Simpson taught, the ministry of Jesus consisted in the four acts of Jesus as savior, sanctifer, healer, and coming king.

As the first historian of the CMA, George Pardington, noted, Simpson brilliantly united the primary emphases of the most dynamic Protestant movements of the late 19th century, the gospel evangelism of **Charles G. Finney** and D. L. Moody, the holiness movement, the divine healing movement, and the growing interest in the Second Coming of Jesus. Rejecting both the Wesleyan teaching that the sinful nature is eradicated in sanctification and the **Keswick** notion that the sinful nature is suppressed, Simpson, drawing on the Catholic mystical tradition of Madame Guyon (1648–1717) and Francis Fénelon (1651–1715), insisted that the point of sanctification was the life of Christ in the believer. This is most clearly expressed in his book *Wholly Sanctified* (1890). He was the author of more than 100 books, many of which went through several revisions and numerous editions. Among his most important books are *The Gospel of Healing* (1886), *The Four-fold Gospel* (1887), *The Love Life of the Lord* (1890), and *The Gospel of the Kingdom* (1887). W.C.K.

SIMS, A(lbert) (b. Townsend, Gloucestershire, England, 26 September 1851; d. Toronto, Ontario, 21 August 1935). Primitive Methodist and **Free Methodist Church** (FMC) minister, evangelist, editor, publisher, and author. Converted in 1869, Sims entered the ministry of the Primitive Methodist Church in 1874. In that year he was sent as a missionary to Canada, where he rapidly emerged as a church leader. In 1879, following his experience of **entire sanctification** at an FMC **camp meeting** at Tonawanda, New York, Sims entered the ministry of the FMC. The virtual father of the FMC in Canada, Sims frequently served as conference secretary and chair of the Canadian Conference. Beginning in 1883, he served for more than 40 years as a traveling district elder.

Sims was a frequent contributor to such holiness periodicals as the *Earnest Christian,* the *Free Methodist,* and *God's Revivalist* while also editing two holiness periodicals, the *Radical Christian* (1880s–1890s) and the *Lamp of Life* (1901–1910s). Sims established his own publishing company in Otterville, Ontario, in the 1880s, which he relocated to Toronto in the early 20th century. Influenced by **A. B. Simpson**, Sims was a passionate champion of faith healing and premillennialism. The author of an estimated 50 books and 100 tracts whose circulation exceeded three million copies, Sims was Canada's most prolific holiness author. He was deeply committed to the conservative cultural heritage of the FMC, writing in opposition to such popular entertainments as dancing and roller skating, as well as church entertainments, fashionable dress, and the use of tobacco. His most widely read books include *Bible Salvation and Popular Religion Contrasted* (1886), *Helps to Bible Study* (1890), and *Behold the Bridegroom Cometh* (1896). Sims was a respected Canadian evangelical leader. His funeral, which was conducted by Oswald J. Smith at Toronto's famed Peoples' Church, was attended by approximately 1,500 people. W.C.K.

SLOAT, L. RUSSELL (b. Elkhart County, Indiana, 3 September 1909; d. Goshen, Indiana, 1 August 1997). Missionary statesman who served with **Mennonite Brethren in Christ/United Missionary Church/Missionary Church** missions in Nigeria. A graduate of Fort Wayne Bible Institute (1932), Sloat served a brief pastorate in Dayton, Ohio, before settling in Salka, Nigeria, in 1935 to begin nine years of solitary pioneer evangelism among 80,000 Kamberis. He learned their language and traveled thousands of miles on foot and by bicycle. Initially few responded to his ministry, but a later mass movement swept thousands of Kamberis into the UMiC of Nigeria, today the largest church body in the International Fellowship of Missionary Churches. During furloughs, Sloat completed a missionary medical course in New York City and earned two degrees from Goshen College (1945, 1949) and an M.S. in education from Indiana University (1958). In 1946, he married Evelyn Kress, a fellow United Missionary Society missionary in Nigeria, and began 17 years as field superintendent. He later became principal of Igbetti Teachers Training School, then of the UMiC Theological College of Ilorin, before retiring in 1986. P.A.E. and T.P.E.

SMITH, A. J. (b. 1887; d. 1960). Missionary, educator, and writer. Smith went to China as a **Church of the Nazarene** missionary in 1920. He was born again in 1927 and returned to the United States later that year. He pastored, promoted missions, served as a district superintendent, and was involved in evangelistic work until he became president, first of Intercession City (Florida) Biblical College (1939–1946) and then of Kingswood College, near Morristown, Tennessee. He associated with the People's Christian Movement (later the **People's Methodist Church**) and was dean of People's Bible School at Greensboro, North Carolina (1947–1949). In 1949, he led the first Western expedition after World War II to Mount Ararat. The following year he returned to Intercession City, Florida, as president of the renamed Southern Wesleyan Biblical College. He returned to Greensboro in 1952, where he continued to preach and write until his death. Although Smith was a pioneer in the modern search for Noah's ark and published two books on that subject, he is primarily remembered for his zeal in calling the holiness movement back to Wesleyan doctrine. He came under heavy criticism for claiming that all born-again Christians have the Holy Spirit. In *Bible Holiness* (1953), Smith contended that the experience of the disciples at Pentecost was the new birth and was not the occasion of their **entire sanctification**, as the modern holiness movement had taught. The Fundamental Wesleyan Society, formed in 1979, is a continuation of his influence. V.R.

SMITH, AMANDA BERRY (b. Long Green, Maryland, 23 January 1837; d. Sebring, Florida, 25 February 1915). African Methodist Episcopal (AME) evangelist, singer, and missionary. A former slave and laundress, Smith was converted in 1856 and experienced **entire sanctification** in 1868 under the ministry of **John S. Inskip**. She was an active participant in the Palmers' Tuesday Meeting (see **Phoebe Palmer**). In spite of the fact that her emphasis on entire sanctification was controversial in the AME church, Smith's beautiful singing voice and simple but forceful preaching made her one of the nation's primary 19th-century **camp meeting** preachers. In 1875, she joined the Woman's Christian Temperance Union (WCTU) and remained an important leader in the temperance movement for the rest of her life. In 1878, she was invited to Great Britain, where she spoke at the **Keswick** Convention and at a series of WCTU-sponsored meetings in England and Scotland. She served as missionary to India (1879–1881) and Liberia (1882–1889).

In India, although creating controversy because of her gender, race, and holiness emphasis, Smith attracted considerable attention and numerous converts, especially among indigenous Indians. In Africa, although she did find considerable satisfaction in her work with **William Taylor**, she was frustrated by native customs and the lack of interest in temperance.

Returning to North America in 1890, Smith resumed her career as a camp meeting preacher and evangelist. With the exception of an extended speaking tour of England (1893–1894), she remained in North America. In 1895, she began raising funds for an orphanage for African American children. In 1899, she opened the Amanda Smith Orphan Home and Industrial School in Harvey, Illinois. She operated the home until ill health forced her to retire in 1912. Her retirement was spent in Sebring, Florida, at the holiness retirement community that had recently been established by Ohio businessman George Sebring, who had experienced entire sanctification under Smith's preaching. She was the author of *Autobiography: The Story of the Lord's Dealings with Mrs. Amanda Smith, the Colored Evangelist* (1893). W.C.K.

SMITH, FREDERICK G. (b. near Lacota, Michigan, 12 November 1880; d. Anderson, Indiana, 24 April 1947). **Church of God (Anderson)** (CG[A]) minister. Smith was born to devout Methodist parents who taught the importance of conversion and sanctification. In 1883, they joined the CG(A) movement and made their home an important meeting place for evangelists and colporteurs. Bright and eager, Smith quickly attracted notice in such company. Two of his books, *The Revelation Explained* (1906) and *What the Bible Teaches* (1914), which popularized a church-historical interpretation of the apocalyptic books of the Bible, raised him to prominence, and, at age 36, he became third editor of the *Gospel Trumpet*. In the 1920s, opponents began disputing Smith's power and moved to deny him reelection. In 1930, he lost the editorship and took a pastorate in Akron, Ohio. In 1946, he accepted an invitation from the Gospel Trumpet Company to return as president. M.D.S.

SMITH, HANNAH WHITALL (b. Philadelphia, Pennsylvania, 7 February 1832; d. Oxford, England, 1 May 1911). Author, evangelist, and feminist reformer. **SMITH, ROBERT PEARSALL** (b. Philadelphia, 1827; d. Friday's Hill, England, 17 April 1899). Minister, evangelist, and businessman. Both Hannah and Robert were birthright Quakers. She was born into a wealthy family, owners of a glass manufacturing company. Robert's family looked back to their ancestor James Logan, personal secretary to William Penn. Hannah and Robert were married on 15 June 1851. Both experienced evangelical conversion under the influence of the Plymouth Brethren in the Revival of 1858. The following year, they resigned their memberships in the Philadelphia Yearly Meeting of Friends. Both professed the experience of **entire sanctification** through the ministry of the National Holiness Association (see **Christian Holiness Partnership**) and eventually moved into holiness evangelism. Although Hannah was inclined to join the Methodist Episcopal Church, she never did. Years later, she rejoined the Friends. Robert became a Presbyterian.

In 1873, Robert Smith went to Egypt to recover his health. A stopover with some English friends changed the course of his future and the future of the holiness movement. English evangelical leaders, especially those associated with the Mildmay Conference, were taken by his enthusiastic witness to complete consecration and cleansing of the heart by faith. He quickly found himself in the middle of a series of revival efforts that, within two years, embraced not only Great Britain but most of Europe as well. The revival finally climaxed in a pan-European meeting of 10,000 pastors and laypersons at Brighton, England, in July 1875.

By 1874, Hannah was fully involved in the meetings, but not before she had promised the sponsoring committee not to promote her restitutionist doctrine (a form of universalism). At meetings for the Promotion of Christian Holiness, held on the Broadlands estate of Lord and Lady Mount Temple, she spoke to crowds of 5,000 laypersons and pastors whose churches had traditionally rejected women's preaching. Lady Mount Temple gave her the title of "Angel of the Churches." B. B. Warfield, although one of the strongest critics of the Smiths, called the meetings one of the greatest bursts of Christian activity since the Apostles.

Robert and Hannah Smith's holiness revivalism gave birth to the annual conventions for the promotion of holiness at **Keswick**, strengthened the work of the Methodist and Evangelical missions in Germany, and infused new life into the inner city missions and the German pietist fellowship movement within the established Evangelical Lutheran Church. The German independent holiness movement and many of the early Pentecostal movements of Europe also grew out of these revivals.

Shortly after the Brighton Convention, the Smiths' sponsoring committee, hearing rumors of Robert's use of sexual imagery to describe Christian experience, abruptly dismissed him. The trauma of the event shattered his fragile psyche, and, in spite of the support of holiness leaders in the United States, he lost his ministry and, eventually, his Christian faith. Hannah, however, quickly reestablished her own ministry in other areas of Christian work. She became a leader in the Woman's Christian Temperance Union (WCTU). She was one of the founders of the WCTU in Pennsylvania and was influential in the election of Frances Willard as national president of the WCTU. Hannah was Willard's lifelong friend and adviser. She served as the WCTU's national evangelistic secretary and played a crucial role in the creation of the Woman's International Temperance Union after the family had taken up permanent residence in England in 1888. She actively supported the women's suffrage movement in both England and the United States and was a frequent speaker in both countries on behalf of numerous humanitarian and educational reforms. Hannah's effectiveness in advancing all of these causes was built on her worldwide reputation as the author of numerous books of practical Christian living. Her most widely read work, *The Christian's Secret of a Happy Life*, went through 30 editions to become one of the best-selling Christian books of the 19th century. It remains one of the contemporary classics of Christian devotion. M.E.D.

SMITH, JENNIE (b. Vienna, Ohio, 18 August 1842; d. Washington, D.C., 3 September 1924). Methodist Episcopal Church and Woman's Christian Temperance Union (WCTU) evangelist, author, and temperance lecturer. The daughter of an Ohio dry goods merchant, Smith suffered chronic health problems and was unable to walk from 1862 to 1878. Shortly after reading **Asa Mahan**'s *Baptism of the Holy Spirit*, she experienced **entire sanctification** in 1871. Although still unable to walk, she began an itinerant evangelistic ministry in the early 1870s. In 1874, she was a founding member of the Ohio Woman's Crusade, which eventually became the WCTU. In 1876, in part to support herself and her invalid mother, she published an account of her physical sufferings and spiritual triumphs, *Valley of Baca*. In 1878, following the prayers of **Charles Cullis** and her many friends and with the aid of prominent homeopathic physician John C. Morgan, she regained the use of her legs. Becoming a full-time WCTU evangelist, Smith served as national superintendent of the Railroad Department of the WCTU (1880s–1924). Although remembered for her ministry to newsboys, firefighters, and police, Smith was rightly remembered as the "railroad evangelist," who, besides her work with the WCTU, was a leader in the National Railroad YMCA. Among her other books were *From Baca to Beulah* (1880); *Ramblings in Beulah Land,* 2 vols. (1886, 1887); and *Incidents and Experiences of a Railroad Evangelist* (1920). W.C.K.

SMITH, JOSEPH HENRY (b. Philadelphia, Pennsylvania, 4 June 1855; d. Redlands, California, 8 April 1946). Methodist Episcopal Church (MEC) minister, pastor, evangelist, and Bible school professor; president of the National Holiness Association (NHA; see **Christian Holiness Partnership**); and author. Converted on 29 January 1874, Smith experienced **entire sanctification** five weeks later. Believing that God had called him to preach, he began to speak in area churches; a year later, he and his young wife, Sallie, volunteered to serve as home missionaries in Georgia. In 1881, the Smiths moved back to Pennsylvania, and the next year Joseph joined the Philadelphia Annual Conference of the MEC. Five years later, that body granted him a supernumerary relationship, which freed him from required pastoral appointments and allowed him to enter full-time evangelism.

Smith quickly gained a reputation as a revival preacher and Bible expositor, and churches, conventions, and **camp meetings** repeatedly called for his services. He taught as he preached, a practice that made him popular. In 1883, he joined the National Association for the Promotion of Holiness and served with many of the early leaders at the National Camp Meetings. He considered the camp meeting to be the "unit and center" of the holiness movement and excelled as a holiness camp meeting preacher. Most of his summers were spent at camp meetings and by 1939, he claimed to have spent 10 solid years (night and day) on campgrounds.

By 1890, Smith had also begun to write for several holiness periodicals. During the next 50 years, he published thousands of articles and at least seven books. His last book, *Things of the Spirit*, appeared in 1940. In 1897, Smith inaugurated the "School of the Prophets" at the Mountain Lake Park Camp Meeting in Maryland, and this "itinerant institute on evangelism" soon became a famous and important part of his work. In 1901, the Philadelphia Annual Conference appointed him "conference evangelist," a position he held until retirement in 1923. In 1925, Smith accepted the presidency of the NHA and served for three years. From 1928 until his death, he was referred to as the honorary president of the association. K.O.B.

SMITH, TIMOTHY L. (b. Central, South Carolina, 13 April 1924; d. West Palm Beach, Florida, 19 January 1997). **Church of the Nazarene** (CN) scholar and pastor. Trained in American history at the University of Virginia and Harvard University, Smith taught at Eastern Nazarene College, East Texas State College, the University of Minnesota, and Johns Hopkins University. He inherited strong interests in urban history and social reform from his mentor, Arthur Schlesinger, Sr. Specializing in American religious history, Smith wrote pioneering essays exploring how race and ethnicity have shaped American religion. He also examined religion's relationship to higher education. His best-known books are *Revivalism and Social Reform* (1957) and *Called unto Holiness* (1962). In the former, he argued that revivalism often initiates social change by expanding visions and creating energies that promote social reform. While scholars debated its thesis, evangelicals used it as a resource to rediscover their commitment to social ministries. In the second book, a study of Nazarene origins, Smith emphasized the two holiness traditions (urban and rural) embraced by the CN as sources of both strength and ongoing tension. In 1990, Smith served as president of the American Society of Church History. Smith is highly regarded as a mentor to the succeeding generation of evangelical scholars. R.S.I.

SMITH, WILLIAM MARTIN (b. Erie County, Pennsylvania, 28 February 1872; d. Westfield, Indiana, 2 April 1964). Friends minister, author, editor, and educator. Smith was converted at age four and became a member of the Friends in 1896. He attended Cleveland Bible Institute (now Malone College) and later taught there and at Fort Wayne Bible College. In 1911, he moved to Westfield, Indiana, where he became superintendent of Union High School, a Friends institution, and started an undergraduate school, Union Bible Seminary, which primarily served Friends until the 1980s when it became interdenominational. Smith served as superintendent of the latter institution (now Union Bible College) until his death. He also served Friends and the holiness movement in general through writing several books and booklets and editing the *Gospel Minister*, which he founded in 1913 as the *Friends Minister*. His writings strongly opposed modernism and promoted premillennialism and the Wesleyan doctrine of **entire sanctification**. W.T.

SNIDER, WILLIAM (b. Marion, Indiana, 11 September 1949). **Bible Methodist Connection of Churches** minister, evangelist, educator, and bookseller. Following his education at Hobe Sound (Florida) Bible College and Aldersgate School of Religion in Salem, Ohio, Snider served as a pastor in North Carolina and Alabama (1972–1992). During these years, he established a significant ministry selling rare holiness books. He has served on the faculty of Christ College in Friendsville, Tennessee, and is currently rare books librarian and director of the practical ministry program at Hobe Sound Bible College. W.C.K.

SNYDER, HOWARD A(lbert) (b. Santo Domingo, Dominican Republic, 9 February 1940). **Free Methodist Church** (FMC) minister, missionary, and educator. Snyder was educated at Spring Arbor (Michigan) College, Greenville (Illinois) College (B.A., 1962), **Asbury Theological Seminary**, and the University of Notre Dame (Ph.D., 1983). He has served as an FMC minister in Detroit, Michigan (1966–1968); a missionary in Saõ Paulo, Brazil (1968–1975); executive director of Light and Life Men (1975–1980); and an FMC pastor in Chicago, Illinois (1980–1989). He has taught at United Theological Seminary, Dayton, Ohio (1989–1996), and Asbury Theological Seminary (1996–present). A conscious heir to the long-standing FMC tradition of significant ethical reflection associated with **B. T. Roberts**, **Mary Alice Tenney**, and his own mentor, Gilbert James, and drawing on the insights of his University of Notre Dame professor John Howard Yoder, Snyder has long urged Wesleyans to affirm a radical believer's church ecclesiology while working for racial, economic, and environmental justice. Among his most important books are *The Problem of Wineskins*

(1975), *The Radical Wesley and the Pattern of Church Renewal* (1980), *Liberating the Church* (1983), *Signs of the Spirit* (1989), and *Earth Currents* (1995). W.C.K.

SOUTHPORT METHODIST HOLINESS CONVENTION. Began as a Wesleyan Methodist expression of the fresh stimulus to the holiness and higher Christian life movements that emerged in Great Britain in the last quarter of the 19th century. Established in 1885, it has continued as an annual gathering, with the exception of some years during times of war. Many leading figures have been associated with the convention over the years, not all of whom have been expositors of the distinctively Wesleyan position. There have always been strong links to **Cliff College**. The trustees own the land and property used in Southport, a resort town on the Lancashire coast. W.P.

SPRUNGER, J(ohn) A. (b. Canton Bern, Switzerland, 12 August 1852; d. Birmingham, Ohio, 28 September 1911). Mennonite business and ministry entrepreneur. As a child, J. A. Sprunger moved with his family to the area near Bern, Indiana. After the death of his second child, he put extensive business interests aside to concentrate on ministry. Despite his limited formal education, he was an able businessman, evangelist, Bible teacher, and writer in both German and English. He returned to his European homeland to preach, and, impressed with the deaconess ministries he found there, he decided to plant the deaconess model in the United States. With his business interests in the hands of others, Sprunger organized the Light and Hope Missionary Society in 1893. His home at Bern became a deaconess home, an orphanage, a school, and a church. Among his later ministries were maternity hospitals in Chicago, Cleveland, and Detroit; The Light and Hope Bible School, which sent missionaries to Africa, India, China, and Turkey; a rescue mission; and the Light and Hope Publishing Company. He published at least seven books in German and English and taught at Bible institutes in Ohio and Indiana. He was one of the speakers at the Bible conference in 1898 that resulted in the organization of the **Missionary Church Association** (now the **Missionary Church**). W.J.G.

STALKER, CHARLES H(enry) (b. Westfield, Indiana, 1 October 1875; d. Youngstown, Ohio, 18 January 1963). Society of Friends evangelist. Charles H. Stalker was recorded as a Friends minister in 1892. In 1900, during meetings at the Metropolitan Holiness Church (see **Metropolitan Church Association**), funds were raised to send Stalker and Byron J. Rees on a missionary tour around the world, a feat Stalker duplicated on two other occasions. His first two global missionary adventures were recounted in a widely circulated book, *Twice around the World with the Holy Ghost* (1906). In all, Stalker made 35 missionary trips to England, where he was instrumental in establishing a small holiness denomination, the Independent Holiness Movement. In North America, Stalker made more than 50 transcontinental evangelistic trips. Although only infrequently speaking to Friends gatherings, Stalker was noted for emphasizing such Quaker distinctives as personal spiritual discernment and immediate divine guidance. His wife, **Catherine Stephenson Stalker,** was a prominent Friends minister and rescue mission worker. W.C.K.

STALKER, CATHERINE STEPHENSON (b. Pennsylvania, 6 June 1873; d. Youngstown, Ohio, 5 June 1962). Society of Friends minister and rescue mission worker. A graduate of Adrian (Michigan) College, Catherine Stalker had experienced **entire sanctification** under the ministry of **Seth C. Rees** in 1906. She served on the staff of **God's Bible School**. In 1914, she was recorded as a Friends minister. She served for years on the Missionary Board of the Ohio Yearly Meeting and on the board of the Friends Rescue Mission in Columbus, Ohio. Her husband, **Charles H. Stalker,** was a prominent holiness evangelist. W.C.K.

STANDARD CHURCH OF AMERICA. Organized by **Ralph C. Horner** in 1919 after Horner had been removed as bishop of the **Holiness Movement Church** (HMC). Its doctrine follows that of the HMC. Like the HMC, it is primarily a Canadian body, although it has conferences in New York and Egypt. It operates Brookville (Ontario) Bible College. In 1974, **Charles E. Jones** estimated that it had 2,000 members. In 1990, it had more than 40 ordained ministers, with G. H. MacGarvey serving as general superintendent. W.C.K.

STANDLEY, M(eredith) G. (b. Washington State, 1877; d. Miami, Florida, 13 May 1962). **Pilgrim Holiness Church** (PHC) evangelist and president of **God's Bible School** (GBS). **STANDLEY, BESSIE QUEEN** (d. Miami, Florida, 11 April 1960). Editor of *God's Revivalist* (1902–1950). Raised in a prominent Cincinnati, Ohio, family, Bessie Queen was converted in services conducted by **Martin Wells Knapp** in the late 1890s. Forced by her parents to choose between themselves and the holiness people, she went to live with the Knapps and served as an editorial assistant with *God's Revivalist*. She assumed the position of editor at the time of Knapp's death in 1901 and became a member of the GBS board of trustees. In 1902, she married **M. G. Standley**, pastor of the church at GBS and a professor at the school. Until 1950, the Standleys administered the extended ministries of the Bible school, which, besides the school and the widely read periodical, included several Cincinnati area rescue missions and a home for unwed mothers. In 1906, M. G. Standley was named to the board of trustees, becoming president in 1910.

The Standleys' tenure at GBS was marked by repeated controversy, ending with their ouster in 1950. Among their difficulties was a prolonged struggle with Knapp's son, John Franklin Knapp, for control of the institution. More troubling were hints of financial irregularity that first surfaced in controversies over the use of mission funds in 1906 and resurfaced in the 1940s when the Standleys were unable to account for large amounts of funds that were being raised by the school's supporters. In 1949, M. G. Standley wrote an autobiography and defense of his administration, *My Life as I Have Lived It for God and Others*. An important figure in the early PHC, M. G. Standley served on the General Council of the PHC (1906–1930) and for several years was a member of the PHC Board of Foreign Missions. After his ouster from GBS, M. G. Standley continued to preach in PHC churches, health permitting. W.C.K.

STANGER, FRANK BATEMAN (b. Cedarville, New Jersey, 31 August 1914; d. Lexington, Kentucky, 17 April 1986). Methodist Church and United Methodist Church pastor, seminary president, and churchman. Frank Bateman Stanger came from a long line of Methodists in southern New Jersey and displayed an early interest in ministry, entering **Asbury College** at age 15. He pursued theological education at **Asbury Theological Seminary**, Princeton Theological Seminary (Th.B.), and Temple University (S.T.M., S.T.D.). He was ordained deacon in 1936 in the New Jersey Conference of the Methodist Episcopal Church. His first pastorate was a mission charge in High Bridge, Kentucky. From 1935 to 1959, he served seven churches in the New Jersey Conference and was active on the conference level. After declining several other offers to join the faculty of the Asbury institutions, in 1959, he accepted the position of executive vice president of the seminary. **Henry Clay Morrison** had made known his desire that Stanger would one day head the seminary, and, in 1962, Stanger assumed its presidency. During his 20-year tenure, the seminary enrollment tripled, faculty size doubled, and physical facilities and assets increased greatly. Stanger, who also served on the faculty, was known for his pastoral approach to administration and his concern for academic respectability. He had an abiding interest in spiritual formation and the church's healing ministry, and he helped to pioneer seminary curricula in these areas. Always concerned for the seminary's relationship to Methodism and the church, he was active on denominational levels and served numerous times as a delegate to General and Jurisdictional Conferences, the World Methodist Conference, and other conferences.

Stanger wrote six books, of which the most famous are *A Workman That Needeth Not to Be Ashamed* (1958) and *God's Healing Community* (1985), as well as articles and editorials in the fields of healing and spirituality. J.L.W.

STANLEY, SUSIE C. (b. Ashland, Kentucky, 3 May 1948). **Church of God (Anderson)** minister. Susie Stanley graduated from Towson (Maryland) State University in 1977 and received a Ph.D. in American Religion and Culture from Iliff School of Theology/University of Denver in 1987. She served as professor of church history and women's studies at Western Evangelical Seminary in Portland, Oregon (1983–1995), and, in 1995, became professor of historical theology at Messiah College in Pennsylvania. Stanley was president of the **Wesleyan Theological Society** in 1993, and she founded and convened the first three **Wesleyan/Holiness Women Clergy** Conferences in the 1990s. In 1993, she represented the holiness movement at the Fifth World Conference on Faith and Order of the World Council of Churches. She has lectured frequently on Christian college and university campuses, especially on the subjects of social holiness and women in ministry. She is the author of *Feminist Pillar of Fire: The Life of Alma White* (1993). B.L.C.

STEELE, DANIEL (b. Windham, New York, 5 October 1824; d. Milton, Massachusetts, 2 September 1914). Methodist minister, pastor, evangelist, New Testament scholar, theologian, college and seminary professor, and author. Steele's conversion was gradual, and he could only tell the year that it happened—1842. He graduated with honors from Wesleyan University in 1848 and joined the New England Annual Conference of the Methodist Epsicopal Church in 1849. On 8 August 1850, he married Harriet Binney, daughter of Methodist theologian Amos Binney. For the next 12 years, the Steeles served several churches in Massachusetts. Beginning his scholastic career in 1862, Steele taught for 10 years at Genesee College and Syracuse University, where he served as acting vice president and acting chancellor. From 1872 to 1889, he served churches in the Boston area and then for several years taught New Testament Greek, exegesis, and theology at Boston University. He also taught for 14 years at the New England Deaconess Training School.

On November 17, 1870, Steele professed the experience of **entire sanctification** and quickly became known as a holiness preacher. Beginning in 1871, he wrote hundreds of articles on holiness subjects for various periodicals. He served on the editorial staffs of two holiness periodicals. His books include: *Love Enthroned* (1875), *Milestone Papers* (1878), *Half Hours with St. John's Epistles* (1901), *Half Hours with St. Paul* (1901), *Defense of Christian Perfection* (1886), *Jesus Exultant* (1899), and *Steele's Answers* (1912). He also issued *Binney's Theological Compendium Improved* (1915) and wrote two volumes for *Whedon's Commentary*. Steele advocated a postmillennial view of **eschatology**. His book, *Antinomianism Revived* (1887), later issued as *A Substitute for Holiness* (1889), rebuked the doctrines of Calvinism and premillennialism as they were preached in the Bible and Prophecy Conference movement.

Steele's holiness ministry began shortly after his sanctification experience, and he often preached at National Holiness Association Camps (see **Christian Holiness Partnership**), as well as independent holiness camps. K.O.B.

STEPHENSON, THOMAS BOWMAN (b. Newcastle-upon-Tyne, England, 22 December 1839; d. London, 14 July 1912). British Wesleyan minister. Stephenson was one of a small circle of young preachers, stirred by **William Arthur** and the Oxford and Brighton conventions, who helped to restore Wesley's holiness theology in the late 1860s and 1870s. For many years, he either presided over or spoke at the annual Wesleyan Conference Holiness Meeting. He is much better known, however, as founder of what became the National Children's Home and Orphanage in 1869, an arm of the Methodist Church. He also worked to create an order of deaconesses and was the first warden of the Wesleyan Sisters, thus uniting his faith with a deeply effective and practical social conscience. W.P.

STOKES, ELWOOD HAINES (b. Medford, New Jersey, 10 October 1815; d. Ocean Grove, New Jersey, 16 July 1897). Methodist Episcopal

Church (MEC) minister, pastor, gospel songwriter, author, and president of the Ocean Grove **Camp Meeting** Association. Although raised a Quaker, in 1834, Stokes was converted under the preaching of Charles Pitman and joined the MEC. In 1843, Stokes received his license to preach and soon was serving a pastoral appointment in the New Jersey Annual Conference. While serving as presiding elder (district superintendent) of the New Brunswick District, Stokes helped to establish a Christian seaside resort in New Jersey called Ocean Grove. He was elected president of the Ocean Grove Camp Meeting Association in its first year, 1869, and held that position for the next 28 years. In 1875, he received a full-time appointment to work at Ocean Grove, and under his leadership it became the premier holiness camp meeting and Methodist resort on the East Coast. At the height of its popularity, the Ocean Grove complex drew hundreds of thousands over the summer. Following Stokes's death, friends erected a large bronze memorial statue of him that stands between the auditorium and the ocean at Ocean Grove. K.O.B.

STONE, MARY (b. Kiukiang, Kiangsi, China, 1 May 1873; d. Pasadena, California, 29 December 1954). Medical doctor and founder of the Bethel Mission of China. Shih Maiyu (later Mary Stone) was the daughter of a Chinese Methodist pastor who was educated at Methodist mission schools in China, the University of Michigan, and Johns Hopkins University. Stone and her friend, Ida Khan, were the first women medical doctors in China. She served as the head of the Elizabeth Skelton Danforth Hospital in Kiukiang (1902–1920). In 1920, Stone and American missionary Jennie Hughes (d. 1951) founded the Bethel Mission of China. The original mission included an orphanage, schools, a hospital, and a nursing school. Among the notable features of the nursing program was Stone's religious instruction. By 1937, the nursing program had become the largest in China. In 1938, the mission established a branch in Hong Kong. Although its program has been reduced in size, the mission currently supports work in Hong Kong, Taiwan, and Indonesia from its North American headquarters in Pasadena, California. Its second-generation leaders have been Betty Hu and Alice Lan. W.C.K.

SURBROOK, WALTER L(ewis) (b. Croswell, Michigan, 4 March 1891; d. Kernersville, North Carolina, 20 March 1988). **Pilgrim Holiness Church** (PHC) and **Wesleyan Church** minister, evangelist, and educator. Following his conversion in 1913, Surbrook was educated at Owosso (Michigan) College, Kingswood (Kentucky) College, and the University of Southern California. He served as president of Kingswood College (1927–1930), general superintendent of the PHC (1932–1946), founding president of Pilgrim Bible College in Kernersville, North Carolina (1946–1948); president of Owosso College (1948–1955); an itinerant evangelist and pastor of the First Pilgrim Holiness Church in Troy, North Carolina (1955–1963); and dean of theology at Southern Pilgrim College in Kernersville, North Carolina (1963–1971). Surbrook was one of the most gifted evangelistic preachers of the 20th-century holiness movement, whose services were accompanied by deep emotion and numerous conversions. He wrote *Striking Signs of the Second Coming* (1931). W.C.K.

SWEET RADICAL HOLINESS. A term embraced by the mid-20th-century proponents of strict adherence to traditional holiness behavioral standards. It appears that **Church of the Nazarene** radicals, many of whom became members of the **Bible Missionary Church**, used the term *sweet radical* more than their radical counterparts in other denominations, such as the **Wesleyan Methodist Church** and **Pilgrim Holiness Church**. However, the term was widespread among the radical constituents of most holiness fellowships during the 1950s and 1960s. It has been criticized as an oxymoron; however, its usage signifies an attempt by radicals such as **H. Robb French** to maintain a balance between love and holiness, mercy and judgment, and charity and austerity.

As the radical come-out groups associated with the **Inter-Church Holiness Convention** (IHC) matured, most of them abandoned self-identification as sweet radicals in favor of the less socially stigmatizing term *conservative*, so that they became known as the Conservative Holiness Movement. Dissidents from the IHC, particularly those associated with the *Voice of the Nazarene* (see **W. L. King**), have continued to embrace the term *sweet radical holiness*, leading even further to its disuse by other, more moderate holiness people. In addition, the use of the word *radical* to mean "antiestablishment" in conjunction with the cultural changes of the 1960s undoubtedly cast the term into disfavor among many holiness people. However, the primary reason for the abandonment of the term appears to be an ironic change within the inner logic of the radical movement. Its replacement with the term *conservative* has coincided with (and may itself serve as a subtle indication of) the quest for upward social mobility among the radical, or conservative, holiness people, a quest that was the central object of many early radical protests. W.T.

– T –

TAYLOR, A. WINGROVE (b. Nevis, Virgin Islands, 1923). **Pilgrim Holiness Church** (PHC) and **Wesleyan Church** (WC) minister, evangelist, and administrator. Taylor was educated at **God's Bible School** (GBS) (Th.B., 1952) and Indiana Wesleyan University (M.A., 1981). He served as a PHC pastor, Port-of-Spain, Trinidad (1953–1964); PHC district superintendent (1962–1964); president of Caribbean Wesleyan College (1964–1974); and general superintendent, Caribbean Conference, WC (1974–1994). Although Taylor established his reputation as one of the great holiness evangelists of the 20th century, he has made equally significant contributions as one of the primary advocates of evangelical ecumenism in the Caribbean. He served as president of the Caribbean Evangelical Theological Association (1973–1989) and has been an officer in the Evangelical Association of the Caribbean since 1977. He has been director of Lighthouse Literature, formerly Choice Books Caribbean, since 1990. He was chairman of Wycliffe Bible Translators Caribbean (1993–1998) and has been a member of the board of GBS since 1970. W.C.K.

TAYLOR, B(ushrod) S(hedden) (b. Poultney, Vermont, 26 November 1849; d. Marcy, New York, 8 October 1935). Methodist Episcopal Church (MEC) minister, missionary, and evangelist. Educated at Fort Edward Institute in Washington County, New York, and at Wesleyan University in Middletown, Connecticut (class of 1874), Taylor began his ministry in the Nebraska Conference of the MEC in 1875. In 1876, Taylor experienced **entire sanctification** at a National Holiness Association (see **Christian Holiness Partnership**) **camp meeting** at Bennett, Nebraska. Taylor served as a pastor in the Troy (New York) Conference of the MEC (1877–1881) and as a missionary to Aspinwall, Colombia, now Panama, under **William Taylor** (1881–1882). Returning to the Troy Conference, Taylor organized a series of holiness conferences throughout the conference, including a five-week one at Glens Falls, New York, which resulted in numerous testimonies to full salvation. Returning to Aspinwall, he served as a missionary (1884–1885). For the next half century, Taylor was a holiness evangelist and author. He was a master of the nonliteral interpretation of the Bible that characterized the late-19th-century holiness movement. He was convinced that the testimonies of the saints and personal spiritual experience illuminated the Bible text. His most significant books include *Full Salvation* (1886), *Holy Fire* (1887), *The Gibeonites* (1896), and *Bible Readings and Spiritual Essays*, 3 vols. (1886–1900). W.C.K.

TAYLOR, RICHARD S(helley) (b. Cornelius, Oregon, 30 March 1912). **Church of the Nazarene** minister, educator, and author. Taylor was educated at Cascade (Oregon) College, George Fox College, Pasadena College (now Point Loma Nazarene University), and Boston University. He served as a pastor in Washington (1931–1941), Oregon (1941–1949), Massachusetts (1949–1951), and Australia (1954–1960). He has taught at Cascade College (1944–1946) and Nazarene Theological Seminary (1961–1977) and served as president of the Nazarene Bible College in Sydney, Australia (1952–1960). Taylor is one of the most prolific holiness writers of the 20th century, with articles appearing in the *Herald of Holiness*, *Preacher's Magazine*, *God's Revivalist*, and the *Wesleyan Theological Journal*. His most significant books include *The Right Conception of Sin* (1939; revised 1945), *The Disciplined Life* (1962), *Exploring Christian Holiness: Theological Foundations* (1985), *Some Holiness Cornerstones* (1992), and *The Scandal of Pre-Forgiveness* (1993). Taylor's ministry has been characterized by vigorous polemics against Calvinism and extended defenses of the traditional doctrinal formulations of the holiness movement. He served as president of the **Wesleyan Theological Society** (1968–1969). W.C.K.

TAYLOR, WILLIAM (b. Rockbridge County, Virginia, 2 May 1821; d. Palo Alto, California, 18 May 1902). Methodist Episcopal Church (MEC) minister, missionary, author, and bishop. Converted in 1841 and experiencing **entire sanctification** in 1848, Taylor served as an MEC minister in Virginia (1845–1849) and a missionary to California (1849–1856). After an itinerant ministry in the United States and Canada (1856–1861), Taylor served a series of itinerant ministries that included England, Australia, and South America (1862–1866); South Africa, the West Indies, Australia, and Ceylon (1866–1870); India (1870–1875); South America (1877–1884); and, after being elected a missionary bishop, Africa (1884–1896). Convinced of the universal validity of the itinerant style of church planting and nurture that he had learned on the American frontier, Taylor sought to duplicate this style of mission around the world. Although he angered denominational officials, Taylor's so-called Pauline Missionary Method produced converts around the world and entered the popular mythology of the holiness movement and much of evangelical Christianity. During his lifetime, Taylor was a legendary figure who supported himself by the wide sales of the books he wrote about his worldwide adventures. **Taylor University** is named for him. Especially significant were his books *Seven Years Street Preaching in San Francisco* (1856), *Four Years Campaign in India* (1875), *Pauline Missionary Methods* (1879), and *Ten Years Self-Supporting Missions in India* (1875). He also edited several periodicals including the *African News* (1889–1894) and *Illustrated Africa* (1891–1896). W.C.K.

TAYLOR UNIVERSITY. An educational institution with roots in mid-19th-century Methodism. Beginning in 1846 as the Indiana Methodist College for Women, Taylor College became coeducational in 1855. The North Indiana Conference of the Methodist Episcopal Church operated the college until 1890, when it deeded the school to the National Association of Local Preachers of Methodism, which governed the college until the 1920s. Since then, the institution has been under the control of an independent board of trustees. From the late 19th to the mid–20th centuries, the college, which was named after **William Taylor**, was only loosely connected with the Methodist Church but closely related to the holiness wing of that denomination. During this period, the college attracted young men and women who were preparing for careers in Christian ministry or the helping professions, and it was closely related to the Prohibition movement. After the institution dropped its Methodist affiliation in 1922, an increasing number of students from the smaller holiness denominations, such as the **Christian and Missionary Alliance**, began to enroll. The college's statement of faith included a sanctification proviso, and the college received the endorsement of several holiness organizations and hosted national holiness conventions. The Holiness League was one of the major student organizations. After 1945, following a national trend away from emphasizing denominational distinctives, the college began to decrease its holiness orientation and increasingly to identify with the transdenominational evangelical movement. Today its students come from a broad range of "low-church" evangelical groups (especially Methodist, Baptist, independent, and the many small evangelical denominations). W.C.R.

TENNEY, MARY ALICE (b. Nora Springs, Iowa, 1889; d. Greenville, Illinois, 24 March 1971). **Free Methodist Church** (FMC) educator. Mary Alice Tenney was raised in an Iowa Congregationalist home that was deeply rooted in the radical spiritual heritage of **Charles G. Finney** and Oberlin College. She was educated at Drake University, Greenville (Illinois) College (1914), the University of Southern California (M.A., 1919), the University of Minnesota, and the University of Wisconsin (Ph.D., 1939). She served on the faculties of Los Angeles Pacific College (1915–1917) and Greenville College (1921–1955), where she was chair of the Division of Language, Literature and Fine Arts (1930–1955). She was a role model for two generations of young FMC women who admired her independence of spirit and passion to enlarge the world of her students. In 1948, her grateful students funded a sabbatical in England that resulted in her book *Blueprint for a Christian World* (1953), which she revised for lay audiences as *Living in Two Worlds* (1959).

Although it is largely unknown today, Tenney was one of the principal catalysts for the recovery of the evangelical social vision in the 1950s and 1960s. Following **E. Stanley Jones** and her own roots in the ethically activistic perfectionism of Charles G. Finney (see **Oberlin perfectionism**), Tenney insisted that the essence of a vital Christianity was a life of radical discipleship lived in conformity with the ethical teachings of Jesus. Fittingly, she was suspicious of what she believed to be the excessive emotionalism and lack of ethical vigor in much holiness preaching. W.C.K.

THOBURN, J(ames) M(ills) (b. Clairsville, Ohio, 7 March 1836; d. Meadville, Pennsylvania, 28 November 1922). Methodist Episcopal Church (MEC) missionary, bishop, and author. Thoburn was educated at Allegheny College (Pennsylvania), where he was converted in 1852. Entering the Pittsburgh Conference of the MEC, he served as a minister (1857–1859). In 1859, Thoburn became an MEC missionary to India. In 1868, he experienced **entire sanctification**. Empowered by his new religious experience, he invited controversial MEC missionary **William Taylor** to establish self-supporting missions in India. With Thoburn's support, Taylor established a series of flourishing churches in India's largest cities. From 1874 to 1887, Thoburn was the pastor of a large church planted by Taylor in Calcutta. Elected a bishop in 1888, he initiated the expansion of Methodism into Burma, Malaysia, and the Philippines. He remained in office until ill health forced him to retire in 1908. He was the founder and first editor of the *Lucknow Witness*, later the *Indian Witness*. Among his most important books are a discussion of mission theory in *The Church at Pentecost* (1899); an autobiographical work, *My Missionary Apprenticeship* (1884); and a biography of his sister, Isabella Thoburn, who also served as a missionary in India, *Life of Isabella Thoburn* (1903). A standard holiness account of Thoburn's life, *Thoburn—Called of God* (1918), was written by bishop **W. F. Oldham**. W.C.K.

THOMAS, DAVID (b. Carmarthen, Wales, 29 September 1860; d. Wellingborough, England, 16 June 1930). Leaving his Welsh home in 1880, Thomas began work in London, and, in 1884, he opened his own clothing business, which prospered. Converted at the age of 30, he sought the experience of **entire sanctification** some months later under the preaching of American holiness preacher **G. D. Watson**. He joined **Reader Harris**'s Pentecostal League at its beginning in 1891; in 1906, he founded the Holiness Mission in Battersea, London, to promote scriptural holiness through an established organization. The mission's monthly magazine, *Holiness Mission Journal*, was begun in 1908. A godly and prayerful layman, Thomas never preached, but he encouraged many young men to enter the holiness ministry. The Holiness Mission extended its work to South Africa in 1914, and, in 1920, it was renamed the International Holiness Mission (IHM). Always seeking new ways to promote the preaching and experience of entire sanctification, Thomas inaugurated the annual Easter Convention at Battersea, which for nearly 40 years was the most important holiness gathering in the south of England. In 1952, the IHM merged with the **Church of the Nazarene**. H.M.

THOMAS, PAUL WESTPHAL (b. Stockton, California, 28 September 1894; d. Baywood Park, California, 1 March 1972). People's Mission Church, **Pilgrim Holiness Church** (PHC), and **Wesleyan Church** minister, administrator, and editor. The son of **Salvation Army** officers, Thomas spent part of his youth as a member of John Alexander Dowie's Zion, Illinois, community. In 1912, while a student at the Western Holiness College and Bible Training School in Colorado Springs, he was converted. He experienced **entire sanctification** in 1913. In 1919, he was named superintendent of the People's Mission Church. Deeply impressed with the mission work of the PHC in the West Indies, Thomas worked for the union of the People's Mission Church with the PHC, which occurred in 1925. He was president of

Colorado Springs Training School (1925–1930). He served as general secretary for the PHC (1930–1934), personal secretary to PHC General Superintendent **Seth C. Rees** (1930–1933), PHC missionary secretary (1934–1946), editor of the *Pilgrim Holiness Advocate* (1946–1962), and a general superintendent of the PHC (1962–1966). In retirement, Thomas organized the denominational archives and began work on a denominational history that was posthumously published as *Days of Our Pilgrimage: The History of the Pilgrim Holiness Church* (1976). A deeply committed holiness ecumenist, Thomas worked for the 1968 union of the PHC with the **Wesleyan Methodist Church** and received an honorary degree from Olivet Nazarene College (1962). W.C.K.

TILLMAN, CHARLES D(avis) (b. Tallassee, Alabama, 20 March 1861; d. Atlanta, Georgia, 2 September 1943). Methodist Episcopal Church, South (MECS), evangelist, publisher, and gospel songwriter. The son of an MECS evangelist, Charles Tillman was converted in 1886 while working as a traveling organ salesman in the southeastern states. Noted for his charming personality and tenor voice, Tillman gained considerable fame for his singing during the large revival campaigns of famed evangelist Sam Jones (1847–1906). He also served as the song leader for such noted evangelists as J.B. Culpepper and Arthur Moore (1888–1974). Beginning in 1888, Tillman, who had formed his own publishing company, began publishing songbooks containing popular gospel songs. His last book, *Day School Singer* (1927), was widely used in the public schools of the South. He was the author of more than 100 gospel songs, including such staples of the holiness movement as "My Mother's Bible," "Save One Soul for Jesus," "Life's Railroad to Heaven," and "The Old Time Power." Among his most significant contributions to gospel music were his arrangements of the songs he heard among African Americans, such as his widely sung "Old Time Religion." W.C.K.

TINDALL, WILLIAM H. (b. Rochdale, Lancashire, 18 December 1838; d. Weybridge, Surrey, 21 August 1908). British Wesleyan minister. William H. Tindall maintained a powerfully effective ministry, which included being the associate of **Hugh Price Hughes** at the height of the extension of central missions in London. He was the founder of the **Southport Methodist Holiness Convention** and for 21 years presided over its sessions. An effective preacher, he helped to make the holiness influence evident in mainline Methodism in the late 1920s and early 1930s when only **Cliff College** was prominent as a witness. W.P.

TREFFRY, RICHARD (b. Cornwall, England, December 1771; d. London, 19 September 1842). Methodist minister and author. Born into a Wesleyan Methodist family, Richard Treffry entered the ranks of Wesley's preachers in 1792 and, in 46 years of active ministry, served in 26 circuits. Although lacking in formal education, Treffry was a disciplined reader and widely recognized throughout his ministry as an able preacher and scholar. He achieved fame as an author of six biographies, numerous religious tracts, and an exposition of Christian holiness, *A Treatise on Christian Perfection*. Widely recognized by his colleagues as a preacher of power and persuasion and an able administrator, he was elected conference president in 1833. From 1838 to 1841, he served as house governor of Methodism's first theological school at Hoxton in London. H.M.

TROXEL, CECIL WARREN (b. El Paso, Illinois, 1 April 1879; d. Oskaloosa, Iowa, 9 June 1944). Methodist Episcopal Church (MEC) and **Free Methodist Church** (FMC) missionary. Converted while a student in Iva Durham's (see **Iva Durham Vennard**) Sunday school class at the MEC in Normal, Illinois, Troxel experienced **entire sanctification** in 1899, as a result of the preaching of **H. C. Morrison** at the Bloomington (Illinois) **Camp Meeting**. In response to publicity surrounding the Boxer Rebellion, Troxel volunteered as a missionary to China, serving with the South Chih Mission (1901–1909). In 1905, he married fellow missionary Ellen Armour. In 1909, as a result of the inroads of Pentecostalism, the Troxels and several supporters separated from the South Chih Mission. Granted mission territory by an ecumenical consensus in the Lintsing region, in 1910 the Troxel mission became the initial mission field for the National Holiness Missionary Society (NHMS), which was established by the National Holiness Association (see **Christian Holiness Partnership**). Under Troxel's leadership, a mission compound, including a Bible school, was established in Nankwantago. A skilled administrator and evangelist, Troxel expanded the NHMS work throughout North China. In 1932, he opened the Tientsin Bible Seminary at the port city of Tientsin. Imprisoned by the Japanese during World War II, Troxel was released in 1943. He received an honorary degree from **Asbury College** in 1944. In 1948, the NHMS published a biography of Troxel written by his wife and daughter (Mrs. John J. Trachsel), *Cecil Troxel: The Man and His Work*. W.C.K.

TSUTADA, DAVID T. (b. Singapore, 19 March 1906; d. Tokyo, 25 July 1971). Japan Holiness Church pastor and founder of the **Immanuel General Mission** (IGM). The recipient of a Rhodes scholarship, Tsutada was educated at the University of London and at the Oriental Missionary Society (see **OMS International**)—sponsored Bible Training Institute, Tokyo. He was converted in 1928 while in London and, through contact with **A. Paget Wilkes**, came to the attention of **Jugi Nakada**, who recruited him for his OMS-related work. Although closely related to Nakada, Tsutada remained an OMS loyalist when Nakada's supporters separated from the parent body. A successful pastor, Tsutada was the principal leader of the Revival League, a spiritual renewal movement among OMS-related pastors (1938–1942). Following imprisonment during World War II, Tsutada, who had grown suspicious of what he believed was the holiness movement's departure from Primitive Methodism, organized his followers into the IGM. At the time of his death, his movement had grown to more than 7,000 members. From 1945 to 1971, he served as president of the Bible school he had organized. Although some of his critics considered him dictatorial, Tsutada, who was hailed as the "John Wesley of Japan," was respected for his deep piety and commitment to evangelism. He served as director of the 1967 Billy Graham Tokyo Crusade and was president of several interdenominational evangelistic organizations. W.C.K.

TURNER, GEORGE A(llen) (b. Willsboro, New York, 28 August 1908; d. Greenville, Illinois, 7 January 1998). **Free Methodist Church** (FMC) minister and educator. Following his conversion in 1922 and experience of **entire sanctification** in 1923, Turner was educated at Chili Seminary (now Roberts Wesleyan College), Greenville (Illinois) College, Biblical Seminary in New York, and Harvard University. He served as pastor of Congregational Christian churches and FMC congregations in South Dakota, Massachusetts, and Ohio. Turner taught at Wessington Springs (South Dakota) College (1936–1938) and **Asbury Theological Seminary** (1945–1979). He was one of the most influential evangelical leaders of his generation, and his Ph.D. dissertation, published as *The More Excellent Way* (1952), revised and published as *The Vision That Transforms* (1964), was justly hailed as one of the most important defenses of the scriptural validity of traditional holiness soteriology of his generation. Consistent with his heritage in New York's famed "burned-over district," Turner, in part as a result of the influence of **Mary Alice Tenney**, was deeply concerned with ethical implications of Wesleyan doctrine. A fervent champion of civil rights for African Americans, Turner took a leading role in the integration of Asbury Theological Seminary and the community of Wilmore, Kentucky. He was the principal founder and first chair of Wilmore's Council on Human Relations. He was a frequent contributor to such publications as the *Free Methodist, Herald, Asbury Seminarian,* and the *Wesleyan Theological Journal.* In retirement, he completed his final work, a sympathetic study of believer's churches, *Churches of the Reformation: A Study of Origins* (1994). W.C.K.

– U –

UNITED HOLY CHURCH OF AMERICA, INC. (UHC). Founded as the Holy Church of Virginia and North Carolina as a result of holiness preaching in 1884 among members of an African Methodist Episcopal church in Method, North Carolina. In 1894, the first Convocation, or national meeting, was held in Durham, North Carolina, with L. M. Mason being elected president. Under the leadership of W. H. Fulford (1901–1916), the church experienced rapid growth. In 1916, the name was changed to United Holy Church, and Henry L. Fisher (1874–1947) was elected president, later bishop. Although in theory a Pentecostal denomination, under Fisher's leadership, the church adopted a Wesleyan soteriology and even placed **E. P. Ellyson**'s *Theological Compend* (1908) in its required reading course. Following Fisher, the church continues to insist that while speaking in tongues may be considered evidence of the **baptism of the Holy Spirit**, it is not the only evidence. In the North, the UHC maintained especially close ties to the **Christian and Missionary Alliance** (CMA). Among the most important early UHC leaders with CMA ties were J. W. Houston (d. 1937), the UHC's most fervent champion of premillennialism; E. B. Nichols (d. 1937), the UHC's great champion of foreign missions; and E. B. Lyons (d. 1962), the UHC's best-known champion of divine healing. Today the UHC has about 50,000 members and supports missions in the West Indies, Liberia, and England. W.C.K.

UNITED MISSIONARY CHURCH (UMiC). Established in 1883 when the followers of progressive Mennonite evangelists **Daniel Brenneman** and Solomon Eby (1834–1931), who through a series of mergers had formed the Evangelical United Mennonites in 1879, merged with the followers of John Swank to form the Mennonite Brethren in Christ (MBIC). The new church supported revival meetings, Sunday schools, **camp meetings**, and the preaching of women. Its largest district was in Pennsylvania. In 1947, the MBIC changed its name to the United Missionary Church. In 1952, the Pennsylvania Conference separated from the UMiC, forming the Bible Fellowship Church in 1959. In the Midwest, the dominant early leader of the MBIC was Daniel Brenneman, while Soloman Eby was the dominant force in Ontario until he embraced Pentecostalism in the early 20th century. Among the most important second-generation leaders was **J. A. Huffman** who founded Bethel Publishing Company and the UMiC Missionary Society in 1921. In Nigeria, A. W. Banfield established the most significant missionary presence, while other fields were opened in Cyprus, Syria, Lebanon, Chile, Mexico, and Brazil.

During the 1940s, the Mennonite emphasis, including nonresistance, began to wane. Among the new leaders emerging were South Bend Gospel Center pastor Q. J. Everest (b. 1907), whose radio program, *Your Worship Hour*, was heard around the world, and Everek K. Storms, who served as editor of the *Gospel Banner* (1950–1969) and UMiC historian. Another important leader was Kenneth Geiger, who served as general superintendent of the UMiC (1955–1969). In 1969, when it merged with the **Missionary Church Association**, the UMiC had 211 churches with 11,871 members and operated Bethel College in Mishawaka, Indiana. T.P.E.

UPDEGRAFF, DAVID BRAINERD (b. Mount Pleasant, Ohio, 23 August 1830; d. Mount Pleasant, Ohio, 23 May 1894). Gurneyite Quaker minister. Although he experienced conversion in a Methodist revival in 1860, David Brainerd Updegraff remained loyal to the Gurneyite Quaker faith in which he was raised. The turning point of Updegraff's life came in 1869 when, under the preaching of **John S. Inskip**, he experienced immediate sanctification. Within two years, he became well known as a Quaker preacher and evangelist, traveling widely to bring revivalism based on Wesleyan holiness teachings to Gurneyite Quaker congregations across the Midwest, especially in Ohio, Indiana, and Iowa. He also became well known among non-Quaker holiness believers and regularly participated in holiness **camp meetings** at Mountain Lake Park (Maryland) and Vineland (New Jersey).

Updegraff was a central figure in transforming American Quakerism after the Civil War. Under his leadership, and that of his holiness allies, a majority of American Friends gave up most of the distinctives that had characterized them since the 17th century. Revivals and altar calls became common, and music became an integral part of worship. Pastors replaced silent meetings, and peculiarities of speech and dress disappeared. While influential, Updegraff also proved controversial. By 1879, he had repudiated the traditional Quaker peace testimony, drawing intense criticism from the more traditional Friends. He aroused even greater criticism in 1884 when he openly repudiated Quaker teachings on the spirituality of the sacraments and underwent water baptism. He was an outspoken advocate of toleration of the ordinances among Friends, a position that even most holiness Quakers could not accept. Updegraff was a frequent contributor to holiness periodicals, especially the *Quaker Christian Worker* (1871–1894), and he edited his own journal, the *Friends' Expositor* (1887–1893). Many of his writings and sermons were published before his death as *Old Corn* (1892). T.D.H.

UPHAM, THOMAS C. (b. Deerfield, New Hampshire, 30 January 1799; d. Kennebunkport, Maine, 2 April 1872). Congregational minister, holiness author, and educator. The son of a successful New England merchant and state congressman, Upham attended Dartmouth College, graduating at age 19. He also studied at Andover Theological Seminary under Moses Stuart and Leonard Woods. He served a Congregational pastorate in Rochester, New Hampshire, for two years (1823–1825) before his appointment as professor of mental and moral philosophy at Bowdoin College in Maine. During his 43-year tenure at Bowdoin, he produced 24 books. *Elements of Mental Philosophy*, a study of the fundamental laws of the mind according to the principles of Scottish commonsense realism, went through 57 editions between 1826 and 1899. Proceeding by a method of "eclecticism and deduction," as Upham states in his introduction, the volume divided the mental functions of the personality into intellect, sensibilities, and will and provided an encyclopedic survey of contemporary psychological knowledge. The *Treatise on the Will* and *Outlines of Imperfect and Disordered Mental Action* (1865) were further investigations of human volition and mental pathologies, respectively.

In 1838, at the suggestion of his wife, Phoebe Lord Upham, he attended one of **Phoebe Palmer**'s Tuesday Meetings for the Promotion of Holiness. He soon testified to a personal experience of **entire sanctification**. Subsequent to this spiritual crisis, Upham became an ardent supporter of Wesleyan holiness and "higher life" initiatives. He opened his home in Maine for meetings of the Palmer type, contributed to leading holiness periodicals, and published philosophical and theological works such as *Principles of the Interior or Hidden Life* (1843), *The Life of Faith* (1845), *Divine Union* (1852), and *Christ in the Soul* (1872). With **Charles Finney** and **Asa Mahan**, he is remembered as a significant Congregationalist ally in the cause of Christian perfection, warmly sympathetic to Wesleyan teaching on the **baptism of the Holy Spirit** and actively supportive of the holiness revival in its ecumenical and interdenominational dimensions. In the 20th century, Upham's *Interior Divine Guidance* appeared several times in reprint form and remains a classic work on discerning the will of God. *The Life of Faith* has also been reprinted.

Upham's two-volume *Life of Madame Guyon* was a product of his attempt to amalgamate the insights of Wesleyan perfectionism with the emphases of Catholic mysticism (suffering, acquiescence, indifference, inactivity). Perhaps this preoccupation with mysticism has been the most controversial feature of the Upham legacy. Protestant critics, including Phoebe Palmer, warned of the dangers of passivity and quietism. Benjamin Warfield launched a full-scale assault on Upham in his *Perfectionism* (1931). Catholic readers, such as Ronald Knox, have accused Upham of misreading and "Wesleyanizing" Madame Guyon. A humble, withdrawn man in his personal demeanor, Upham never assumed the posture of social crusader. Even so, he wrote on behalf of Christian pacifism, supported the antislavery cause, and opposed the liquor traffic. J.P.V.

– V –

VAN WORMER, H(arold) C(harles) (b. Mannsville, New York, 7 October 1898; d. Salem, Ohio, 16 January 1988). **Wesleyan Methodist Church** (WMC) and **Allegheny Wesleyan Methodist Connection** (AWMC) minister, evangelist, and administrator. A barber by trade, Van Wormer was educated at **Taylor University** and Houghton (New York) College. Beginning his ministry in the Rochester (New York) Conference of the WMC in the late 1920s, Van Wormer transferred to the Allegheny Conference in 1933, where he served as a pastor (1933–1938, 1940–1943) and evangelist (1938–1940). He was conference president (1943–1969) and founding president of the AWMC (1969–1973). Although formally retired, he continued to serve as a conference evangelist (1973–1980). As a conference leader, he was president of the Stoneboro Camp (1943–1974) and founder and editor of the *Conference Messenger*, later *Allegheny Wesleyan Methodist* (1943–1973). He served on the board of Houghton College (1948–1956). A defender of traditional WMC polity, behavior standards, and holiness teaching, Van Wormer vigorously opposed cultural and doctrinal changes that increasingly affected the WMC in the years following World War II. He was the primary leader in the separation of the Allegheny Conference from the WMC in 1966. Noted for the depth of his piety and his wide reading in Wesleyan theology, he authored *God's Absolute Standard: Entire Sanctification* (1980) and *Why I Do Not Have a Television Set* (n.d.). W.C.K.

VENNARD, IVA MAY DURHAM (b. Prairie City, Illinois, 27 December 1871; d. Chicago, Illinois, 12 September 1945). Methodist deaconess, evangelist, and founder of Epworth Evangelistic Institute (EEI) and Chicago Evangelistic Institute (CEI; see also **Vennard College**). Durham was converted at the age of 12 and joined the MEC shortly thereafter. Six years later, she claimed sanctification after attending first a holiness meeting in Decatur, Illinois, and then a revival preached by **Joseph H. Smith**. Following graduation from Illinois State Normal University in 1890, she taught before entering Wellesley College in 1892. In 1895, Durham entered the Deaconess Home in Buffalo, New York, and was assigned to conference evangelism. Three years later, she was appointed deaconess at large, traveling across the country promoting deaconess work and preaching revivals.

In 1902, Vennard founded EEI in St. Louis, a training school for deaconesses, evangelists, and missionaries. Two years later, she married architect Thomas Vennard. The Christian Witness Company, directed by **G. A. McLaughlin** and **H. F. Kletzing**, invited Vennard to begin a training school in Chicago, and, in the fall of 1910, she founded CEI, an interdenominational, coeducational, holiness training school. She remained its principal until her death in 1945.

In addition to her work in educational institutions, Vennard preached at churches and **camp meetings** throughout the country and around the globe; was a board member and treasurer of the National Holiness Missionary Society (later **World Gospel Mission**), an organization that she helped to create; belonged to the Association of

Women Preachers and served on its Executive Board; edited *Inasmuch* at EEI and *Heart and Life* at CEI; and wrote three books, including a book on Revelation, a book on holiness entitled *Heart Purity*, and a book of sermons entitled *Upper Room Messages*. Vennard received a local preacher's license from the Methodist Episcopal Church in 1920 and an honorary doctor of divinity degree from **Taylor University** in 1923. P.P.-L.

VENNARD COLLEGE. Founded by **Iva Durham Vennard** in 1910 in Chicago, as Chicago Evangelistic Institute (CEI). Initial support came from **H. F. Kletzing** and **G. A. McLaughlin** of the Christian Witness Company. From its beginning, it was a coeducational school committed to the training of holiness ministers, missionaries, church workers, and evangelists. A heavy emphasis was placed on practical ministry, with students operating their own settlement house and serving in such local ministries as the Olive Branch Mission, the West Side Pentecostal Mission, and a Chinese Sunday school. The school opened with 91 students. In spite of controversies surrounding the school's finances in the wake of Kletzing's sudden death in 1910, Vennard rapidly turned CEI into the central institution for training Methodist Episcopal Church (MEC) holiness loyalists in the Midwest. Among her most important supporters were **Joseph H. Smith**, who frequently taught and lived at the school when he was not engaged in evangelistic meetings, and MEC bishops **William F. Oldham** and Arthur F. Wesley, who established a cooperative holiness bookstore at the school in 1913.

From the beginning, the majority of CEI's students were women whose ministerial vocations were affirmed by Dr. Vennard and the largely female faculty that included Susanna Swartz, who taught at the school (1910–1940); Beatrice C. Beezley, who operated a rescue mission near the school; professor of theology Mary Ella Bowie; and Ruth Fogle. By the 1920s, CEI women graduates were filling a significant number of MEC pulpits in the Midwest. In spite of the popularity of Vennard's handpicked successor, popular holiness teacher **Harry E. Jessop**, the death of Vennard, the changing neighborhood surrounding the school, and a decline in enrollment resulted in a 1951 decision to relocate to the campus of **Kletzing College** in University Park, Iowa.

Led by loyal supporters, such as **Merne Harris**, president (1968–1988), and a dedicated body of the alumni of CEI and Kletzing College, it has continued to train pastors, missionaries, and evangelists. Although its enrollment did reach 300 in the 1970s, it had fewer than 100 students in 1994 when an attempt to merge the school with Circleville Bible College was defeated by alumni loyal to the CEI–Kletzing tradition. In the late 1990s, the school had fewer than 50 students. W.C.K.

VOICE OF THE NAZARENE ASSOCIATION OF CHURCHES. *See* KING, W(alter) L(ee).

– W –

WALKER, E(dward) F(ranklin) (b. Steubenville, Ohio, 20 January 1852; d. Glendora, California, 6 May 1918). Methodist Episcopal Church (MEC), Presbyterian and Pentecostal Church of the Nazarene (PCN; see **Church of the Nazarene**) minister and evangelist. Converted under the preaching of **John S. Inskip** in 1871, Walker experienced **entire sanctification** in 1873. He served as an MEC pastor in California while attending the University of the Pacific. Following graduation, he joined the Presbyterian Church. He served for a time as the pastor of the Third Congregational Church in San Francisco. After graduating from Western Theological Seminary in Pittsburgh, Pennsylvania, he served as pastor of Presbyterian churches in Evansville, Indiana; Parsons, Kansas; and Fort Collins, Colorado (1880s–1891). Making his home in Greenfield, Indiana, Walker served as an itinerant holiness evangelist (1891–1906). Relocating to southern California, he joined the PCN in 1908 and was elected a general superintendent in 1911. While general superintendent, he served short stints as president of Olivet Nazarene College (Illinois) and Pasadena College, now Point Loma Nazarene University. Although noted for his scholarly exegesis of Scripture, Walker was an uncompromising holiness radical whose services were often punctuated by such physical manifestations as shouting, jumping, and laughter. He was the author of the widely read book *Sanctify Them* (1899). W.C.K.

WARNER, DANIEL S. (b. Bristol, Ohio, 25 June 1842; d. Grand Junction, Michigan, 12 December 1895). **Church of God (Anderson)** founder, minister, writer, and reformer. A Union Army veteran of very limited service, Warner was converted in 1865. He registered at Oberlin College later that year and again in 1866, but he left to enter the ministry. In 1867, he was licensed by the General Eldership of the Churches of God, a group organized by John Winebrenner in 1830.

After initial service as a pastor–evangelist, Warner worked as a home missionary in Nebraska (1873–1875). Back in Ohio in 1877, after initially rejecting the holiness message, he experienced **entire sanctification**. As a consequence, he lost his ministerial license, but an Indiana splinter group of the General Eldership relicensed him in 1878. That year he became associate editor of the *Herald of Gospel Freedom*, which, in 1880, merged with another holiness journal, the *Pilgrim*, to become the *Gospel Trumpet*. Warner, part owner with Joseph C. Fisher, edited the *Trumpet* until his death. By 1880, he had also completed his first book, *Bible Proofs of a Second Work of Grace*.

In 1881, Warner withdrew from the Indiana State Holiness Association and the Northern Indiana Eldership. In both cases, the issue was Warner's emergent ecclesiology: He was convinced that denominations per se and what he termed the "sect system" were sinful and that the truly sanctified had no choice but to flee the entire system and join together in a new movement to be known simply as "the Church of God." Warner's new movement was characterized by a combination of believer's church ecclesiology, inherited from the General Eldership, and Wesleyan soteriology, drawn from the holiness movement. M.D.S.

WARNER, GEORGE (b. Southam, Warwickshire, England, 8 November 1829; d. Settle, Yorkshire, 14 April 1899). British Primitive Methodist minister. The first entirely connexionally supported evangelist of his church, George Warner had a vision to unite the call to salvation with the challenge of holiness. Part of his ministry was spent in Ireland, where he served as the general superintendent of the Primitive Methodist churches. Among his converts was famed evangelist Gipsy Smith. He published little but did leave several powerful manuscripts on the doctrine of **entire sanctification**. Perhaps more than anyone else, he assisted **Asa Mahan** when he settled in England, and he wrote the preface to Mahan's *Christian Perfection*. When Sir Henry Thompson performed surgery on Warner, he remarked on the state of Warner's knees. Warner told him that night after night after night on his knees praying and reading the Scriptures had produced a particularly painful problem. W.P.

WARREN, BARNEY E. (b. Lewiston, New York, 20 February 1867; d. Springfield, Ohio, 21 April 1951). **Church of God (Anderson) (CG[A])** minister and songwriter. At the age of 15, Barney E. Warren was converted by CG(A) evangelists in Michigan, where he had moved with his family. From a musical family, he attracted the attention of

D. S. Warner, who invited him to sing in the "evangelistic company" Warner was then forming. Organized into teams of from two to six people, these "Flying Messengers" were a standard form of evangelization in the early Church of God movement.

Warren's gospel songs were his chief contributions to the CG(A). Many of them, including "What a Mighty God" and "I Am a Child of God," have become standards within the denomination. Warren also edited such Gospel Trumpet Company hymnals and songbooks as *Melodies of Zion* (1926), *Select Hymns* (1911), and *Hymns and Spiritual Songs* (1930). M.D.S.

WATSON, G(eorge) D(ouglas) (b. Accomac County, Virginia, 26 March 1845; d. Santa Monica, California, 28 February 1924). Methodist Episcopal Church (MEC) and **Wesleyan Methodist Church** (WMC) minister, evangelist, and author. Watson was converted while a soldier in the Confederate Army in 1863. After attending Concord (New Hampshire) Bible Institute for a year, he entered the ministry of the MEC, serving pastorates in Delaware and Maryland (1867–1875). From 1875 to 1883, he served prominent MEC appointments in Indianapolis, Indiana; Newport, Kentucky; and Evansville, Indiana.

Experiencing **entire sanctification** in 1876, Watson emerged as a highly sought-after holiness evangelist. In 1883, he began a 40-year evangelistic career that would take him throughout the United States and to Canada, Great Britain, Jamaica, and Australia. Watson settled in Florida shortly after he embarked on his evangelistic career, where his speculation in real estate proved to be a financial disaster when, in 1894, an early freeze destroyed his orange grove, greatly reducing the value of the property in which he had speculated. About the same time, Watson's woes were exacerbated by charges of marital infidelity. In 1894, Watson voluntarily left the ministry of the MEC and publicly apologized for his behavior. His 1894 book, *The Secret of Spiritual Power*, deals freely with the issues of greed and spiritual restoration.

Joining the WMC in 1896, the contrite Watson, whose now fervent premillennialism played no small role in the holiness movement's embrace of the new **eschatological** theory, resumed his evangelistic career. A deeply mystical interpreter of holiness spirituality, Watson, especially after his personal crisis in 1894, was a master of the allegorical nonliteral interpretation of Scripture. Among his most important books are *A Holiness Manual* (1882), *Coals of Fire* (1886), *Love Abounding*

(1891), *Our Own God* (1904), *The Heavenly Life* (1904), and *Bridegroom Saints* (1913). Following his death, his widow wrote a biography, *The Life of the Rev. G. D. Watson* (1928). W.C.K.

WAUGH, THOMAS (b. Brampton, Cumberland, England, 3 September 1853; d. Colwyn Bay, Wales, 17 October 1932). British Wesleyan minister. Dramatically converted, Thomas Waugh prepared himself for admission to Headingley College (Seminary) in 1880. Convinced in 1881 of the need for holiness, he claimed the fullness of the Spirit at the **Keswick** convention. Accepting his call to evangelism, the Wesleyan Conference appointed him as a connexional evangelist and colleague of **Thomas Cook** in 1883. He traveled more than 250,000 miles and averaged 350 services a year. He published nine popular books, including his *Power of Pentecost*. A personal friend of C. H. Spurgeon and D. L. Moody, he emphasized power as opposed to the more classical Wesleyan emphasis on purity. While perhaps more in tune with the early Keswick message, he shared in very many distinctly Wesleyan holiness conventions. W.P.

WESLEY, JOHN (b. Epworth, England, 17 June 1703; d. London, 2 March 1791). Founder of the Methodist movement within the Church of England. Little is known about Wesley's earliest years. It is known that in 1709, a fire in the parsonage in which his family resided caused him to sense not only the gracious, providential activity of God but also the possibility that God had a special calling for this "brand plucked from the burning." Wesley studied at Charterhouse School (1713-1720) and then at Christ Church, Oxford, where he received his baccalaureate degree in 1724. The following year, he was ordained a deacon and, in 1728, a priest. He was installed as a fellow of Lincoln College, Oxford, in 1726, an honor that gave his father, Samuel, considerable joy.

Between August 1727 and November 1729, however, John Wesley actually spent much time away from the university in the parishes of Epworth and Wroot assisting his elderly father. Wesley was eventually called back to the university in 1729. In the meantime, his younger brother, Charles, had formed a small group of sincere and earnest believers at Oxford—a group that soon accepted John's leadership and that was referred to by its detractors as "The Holy Club" or "The Sacramentarians." In addition to the Wesleys, early members of this society included William Morgan and Robert Kirkham.

In 1735, George Whitefield joined the society. Also in 1735, John and Charles Wesley, along with Benjamin Ingham and Charles Delamotte, embarked on a missionary journey to the colony of Georgia. John later confessed to a friend that his chief motivation for undertaking this arduous task was to save his own soul. En route to Georgia, the ship, *The Simmonds*, was buffeted by powerful Atlantic storms. Wesley, who was quite fearful, even admitting his reluctance to die, marveled at the serenity of the Moravian community on board that calmly sang on in the midst of such terror. Shortly after arriving in America, Wesley was questioned pointedly by August Spangenberg, a Moravian leader, concerning his spiritual condition, and it was soon evident to the young Anglican missionary that he lacked the assurance that Christ had saved him.

When John Wesley returned to England in 1738, he continued his contacts with the Moravian community and helped to form a religious society at Fetter Lane in London with Peter Bohler, a young Moravian leader. Under Bohler's spiritual direction, on 24 May 1738, while at a meeting in Aldersgate Street, Wesley experienced the power, peace, happiness, and holiness for which he had so longed, as well as the assurance that his sins were forgiven and that he was, therefore, no longer a servant but a child of God.

Emboldened by his Aldersgate experience, Wesley continued to preach justification by grace through faith, with the result that, by 1739, many Anglican churches had closed their doors to him. A new avenue for ministry, however, was opened by George Whitefield, who persuaded the reluctant Wesley to preach outdoors in Bristol in April 1739. The response to Wesley's field preaching was so great that, in 1739, he established two chapels: the New Room in Bristol and the Foundry in London. In 1742, the third major center of what had come to be called "Methodism" was established further north at Newcastle-upon-Tyne.

During the 1740s, the institutional structure of Methodism began to take shape with the employment of John Cennick and Thomas Maxfield as lay preachers, the establishment of the class meeting as an important discipleship tool, and the institution of the first Methodist conference, which was held at the Foundry in June 1744. In these conferences, Wesley and those assembled invariably emphasized the three grand doctrines of Methodism: repentance ("the porch of religion"); justification by faith ("the door of religion"); and sanctification or holiness ("religion itself"). Ever concerned with the indigent and outcasts of 18th-century Britain, Wesley begged money for the poor, collected clothing on their behalf, established a medical dispensary, gave loans to those in need, visited the sick and dying, helped to provide housing for widows and orphans, supported education at the Kingswood School and elsewhere, preached against the dangers of riches, and wrote forcefully against the institution of American slavery.

One way in which Wesley sought "to spread Scriptural holiness across the land" was to underscore the importance of **entire sanctification** in his sermon "Christian Perfection" (1741) and his treatise *A Plain Account of Christian Perfection* (1766). These writings, as well as some key letters, clearly reveal that it was John Wesley himself, and not the 19th-century American holiness movement, who first employed the language of "secondness" and thereby affirmed that entire sanctification is always a second, distinct work of grace. In fact, of such importance was the teaching and realization of Christian perfection in this life that Wesley exclaimed in a letter in 1758, "Unless we have clean hearts before we die, it had been good we had never been born."

The elderly Wesley made provision for the continuance of Methodism in England after his death by signing the Deed of Declaration in 1784, which made the 100 preachers of the Methodist conference the legal heirs of Wesley, in America by ordaining Richard Whatcoat and Thomas Vasey as preachers, and by commissioning Thomas Coke to ordain Francis Asbury and others for ministry in the New World. By the time of his death, he had traveled more than 250,000 miles in ministry and delivered more than 50,000 sermons. There were nearly 75,000 Methodists in the United Kingdom. To the faithful who were with him when he died, he exclaimed a truth that had characterized his entire ministry: "The best of all is God is with us." K.J.C.

WESLEY BIBLICAL SEMINARY (WBS). Located in Jackson, Mississippi, and founded in 1974 by Dr. Ivan C. Howard, assisted by Drs. **Eldon Fuhrman** and **Delbert R. Rose**. Originally named Wesley Biblical Center, WBS is accredited by the Association of Theological Schools. It holds membership in the Evangelical Council for Financial Accountability, the National Association of Evangelicals, and the **Christian Holiness Partnership**. The seminary's transdenominational character is demonstrated by more than 10 denominations, including the **Congregational Methodist Church**, **Evangelical Methodist Church**, and Independent Methodist Church, which currently approve it for the training of their pastors. Its presidents have included Ivan Howard (1974–1977), Eldon Fuhrman (1977–1985), Howard Spann (1985–1995), and Ronald Smith (1998–present). In 2000, it had more than 100 students, of whom 27 percent were African American. Its trustee board is composed of men and women who are interracial, international, and interdenominational in background. It is Wesleyan–Arminian in doctrinal commitment. Its graduates are at work on six continents, serving in missions, educational institutions, and business enterprises. D.R.R.

WESLEYAN CHURCH (WC). Born of a merger between the **Pilgrim Holiness Church** (PHC) and the **Wesleyan Methodist Church** (WMC). Efforts begun in the 1920s finally bore fruit in 1968 when PHC and WMC representatives met in joint general conference to form the WC. The merger brought few significant changes from the statements of faith of the predecessor bodies. The new church required water baptism for full membership in place of the recommended, but optional, baptismal requirements of the former PHC. The new statement on the nature of Scripture adopted the "inerrancy" language of the former Wesleyan Methodists, replacing the old Methodist/Anglican "rule for faith and practice" understanding of the PHC. The explicit premillennial article in the PHC's manual was also changed in favor of a broader statement on the expectation of Christ's imminent return. The merged body retained the commitment to the ordination of women, which both bodies had supported historically. The new church also drafted a strong statement of opposition to any acceptance of the precepts and practices of the charismatic revival that was coming to the fore just as the church was being created.

The polity of the new church varied little from that of the merging bodies. Ultimate legislative authority lies with a quadrennial General Conference. Three general superintendents, elected by and responsible to the quadrennial General Conference, give overall administrative and spiritual supervision to the church. A General Board of Administration acts on behalf of the General Conference in the interim of its sessions. All district and general church deliberative bodies have equal clergy and lay representation. Pastors are placed by congregational call on final approval of their respective district conferences.

The burden of the support of educational institutions had been a strong impetus to merge, and, motivated by the consensus for educational reform, the WC undertook a drastic reorganization of its educational structure. The position of general secretary of education was created with responsibility for reduction in the number of denominational educational institutions in order to provide more adequate support and accreditation.

The result was a new denominationally supported system of four liberal arts colleges: Bartlesville (Oklahoma) Wesleyan College, Houghton (New York) College, Marion College (now Indiana Wesleyan University), and Central (South Carolina) College (now Southern Wesleyan University); two Bible colleges: Bethany Bible College (New Brunswick, Canada) and United Wesleyan College (Pennsylvania; eventually merged with Houghton College); and two continuing high school programs: Houghton (New York) Academy and Kernersville (North Carolina) Wesleyan Academy (control of which subsequently passed to a local Wesleyan church). The church also maintained Brainerd Training School (South Dakota) in connection with its Native American ministries.

The new church reaffirmed its relationship with **Asbury Theological Seminary** through the Wesleyan Seminary Foundation. It also gave denominational accreditation to other Wesleyan-oriented seminaries for the preparation of its ministers.

After merger, the Caribbean and Philippines missions were organized into indigenous General Conferences, paralleling the original North American General Conference. Together they constitute the Wesleyan World Fellowship. Other significant overseas mission centers are maintained in South America, Australia, the British Isles, Haiti, Honduras, Korea, Liberia, Mexico, New Guinea, Puerto Rico, Sierra Leone, South Africa, Suriname, and Zambia. Pioneer missions are supported in Eastern Europe, Asia, Costa Rica, Germany, Indonesia, and Sri Lanka. In Japan, the WC cooperates with the **Immanuel General Mission**. The denomination also maintains the Hephzibah Children's Home in Macon, Georgia, and serves as the organizational base for World Hope International, a relief agency.

Since its formation, the WC has experienced a steady constituent growth of about 3 percent per year. At its first quadrennial General Conference in 1972, the church reported a 10 percent increase in membership. Thirty years after merger, WC world membership was 248,579, with more than 370,000 constituent persons participating in the ministries of its 3,473 congregations.

The WC maintains its international offices at Indianapolis, Indiana. It is a member of the **Christian Holiness Partnership**, the National Association of Evangelicals, and the World Methodist Council. M.E.D.

WESLEYAN HOLINESS ASSOCIATION OF CHURCHES (WHAC).

Founded in 1959 by **Glenn Griffith** and his supporters, who were convinced that the **Bible Missionary Church**'s position that the so-called innocent party in a divorce was free to remarry violated the teachings of Scripture. The WHAC has three conferences—Ohio, Michigan, and Rocky Mountain—missions to Native Americans in Arizona; and foreign missions in the Philippines, Bolivia, the Dominican Republic, Haiti, Guatemala, New Guinea, and Honduras. It has more than 40 churches and 100 ministers. It operates Wesleyan Holiness Bible College in Point Pleasant, West Virginia, and, since 1961, has published the *Eleventh Hour Messenger*. W.C.K.

WESLEYAN/HOLINESS WOMEN CLERGY INTERNATIONAL (WHWC). An organization that supports women in ministry in holiness churches. The purpose of WHWC is "to equip and encourage divinely-called women in vocational ministry and professional leadership positions." The impetus for the organization arose from the realization that while many Wesleyan/Holiness churches ordained women from their beginnings, the current percentage of women clergy in holiness denominations, with the exception of the **Salvation Army** (SA), is lower than it has been in the past. The WHWC sponsored its first conference in 1994 and has subsequently met biannually, averaging 450 in attendance. Schools serve as sponsoring institutions by providing financial support so that students can attend.

The Planning Board consists of one representative from each of the seven denominations that provided initial funding: **Brethren in Christ**, **Church of God (Anderson)**, **Church of the Nazarene**, Evangelical Friends, **Free Methodist Church**, the SA, and **Wesleyan Church**. **Susie Stanley** has convened the group since its inception. WHWC incorporated as a nonprofit organization in 1996. It publishes a newsletter and pamphlets and sponsors a listserv to achieve its purposes. S.C.S.

WESLEYAN/HOLINESS STUDIES CENTER. Established at **Asbury Theological Seminary** through a grant from the Pew Charitable Trust in 1991. The center was the culmination of a three-year project directed by **Melvin E. Dieter**, "An Ascending Hope: Revivalism, Social Reconstruction and Mission in the American Wesleyan/Holiness Tradition." The project sponsored three conferences and provided funding for the research of William Kostlevy, which resulted in his book *Holiness Manuscripts: A Guide to Sources Documenting the Wesleyan Holiness Movement in the United States and Canada* (1994). The center publishes the *Wesleyan Holiness Studies Center Bulletin*. D. William Faupel is the director; William Kostlevy is associate director. W.C.K.

WESLEYAN METHODIST CHURCH (WMC). A denomination organized by Methodist Episcopal Church (MEC) abolitionists. The Wesleyan Methodist Connection of America was formed at Utica, New York, in 1843. **Orange Scott** chaired the founding conference of clergy and laypersons who believed that the refusal of the northern churches to support the immediate abolition of slavery was neither biblically nor morally tenable. A strong populist, antiepiscopal stance also marked the new movement. Scott's periodical, the *True Wesleyan*, first published in January 1843, soon became the official voice of the new church.

Luther Lee, La Roy Sunderland, Jotham Horton, and **Lucius Matlack** joined Scott as founding leaders of the new connection. Most of the clergy and laypersons who quickly joined the new group had been members of the MEC. The remainder represented former members of other denominations and of the growing Christian union movements of the time.

The leaders of the new denomination looked to the teachings of **John Wesley** for historical and theological support for their claim to be the "True Wesleyans." They tied the ultimate success of their reform cause to a faithful devotion to the Wesleyan doctrine of Christian perfection (see **entire sanctification**), and the denomination was one of the first to make the doctrine a particular article of faith within its discipline.

Up to the eve of the Civil War, Wesleyan "home missionaries" carried the new church's abolitionist crusade into Virginia and North Carolina. Lynchings and mob and legal action finally forced the last of the Wesleyan evangelists to leave just before the war began. The Wesleyans' commitment to the abolitionist cause was also evident in the involvement of members such as Daniel Worth and Laura Smith Haviland, who helped escaping slaves find their way along the Underground Railroad to freedom in Canada. Wesleyans also supported the ordination of women and other women's concerns of the period. Luther Lee preached the sermon at the first formal ordination of a woman to the Christian ministry in the United States, and the first women's rights convention was held in the Wesleyan Methodist Church in Seneca Falls, New York.

The end of the Civil War and the abolition of slavery threw the Wesleyan Methodists into a crisis of indecision about the future of the church. Luther Lee and many others believed that the church had fulfilled its central mission and returned to the MEC. Other leaders at the church's college at Adrian, Michigan, tried to convince the drastically reduced numbers who remained to join with the Methodist Protestants and the Congregationalists in a postwar union movement. The need for more adequate support for their educational ventures in large part energized this thrust. Control of Wheaton College, which had its beginnings in the Illinois Institute chartered by the Wesleyan Methodists in 1848, had already passed to the Congregationalists because of needed additional financial support. Similar circumstances threatened the Wesleyan's control of Adrian College, which they had founded. The denominational union efforts eventually failed, however. In the process, control of Adrian College passed to the Methodist Protestants along with most of the Wesleyan leaders who had been promoting the union movement. These early experiences encouraged the adoption of policies of strong denominational control over the church's affiliated colleges.

After a decade of indecision over denominational identity following the Civil War, a new generation of leaders, led by **Adam Crooks**, ultimately allied the future of the church with the holiness movement revivals that were sweeping the nation. The Christian perfectionism that had energized the early social reform movements now directed the spiritual energies of the church into the rising postwar holiness/deeper-life revival. Over the succeeding decades of the 19th century and beyond, this revivalist focus overwhelmed the perfectionist activism that had marked the church's founding. The latter became a muted, but never totally ignored, element of institutional memory.

The organizational structure of the church gradually changed as well. Recovery of the membership that the church had lost at the war's close came slowly. Its struggle to redefine its mission together with its loosely organized association of churches made it a less attractive church home for many of the revival converts than were some of the newer churches. It was not until the middle of the 20th century that it moved from its Baptist-like original connection of autonomous congregations to a pattern of centralization closer to the episcopal system of Methodism.

Recurrent moves were made to unite the WMC and **Free Methodist Church**. When these repeatedly failed, the WMC and the **Pilgrim Holiness Church** (PHC) initiated merger discussions. As early as 1922, they began informal talks that eventually led to formal union in 1968. Between 1948 and 1966, several other groups joined the WMC: portions of the **Hephzibah Faith Missionary Association**

(1948); the Missionary Bands of the World, with its eight congregations in the United States and extensive mission work in India and Jamaica (1958); and the **Alliance of Reformed Baptist Churches of Canada** (1966).

By 1968, the church had a powerful general conference, general superintendents, and general church organizations very similar to those of the PHC. At the time of the union, the WMC supported Houghton College (New York, founded 1884), Marion College (Indiana, 1911), Miltonvale College (Kansas, 1909), the Brainerd Indian Training School (South Dakota), and the Wesleyan Seminary Foundation, affiliated with **Asbury Theological Seminary**. Overseas mission congregations existed in Sierra Leone, India, South Africa, Rhodesia, Jamaica, Colombia, Haiti, Puerto Rico, Honduras, and New Guinea. An Australian conference was organized in 1947 and a Bible college established at Melbourne. In Japan, the church work was affiliated with the **Immanuel General Mission**, an indigenous Wesleyan church led by **David T. Tsutada**, to form the Immanuel–Wesleyan Federation. The church also maintained an orphanage at Macon, Georgia.

Conservative elements protested the movement toward a more centralized organization. They also were unhappy with the increasing willingness of many to modify or even reject the prudential rules of conduct and dress that had once been a hallmark of holiness churches, in deference to the growing impetus to broaden evangelistic opportunities in the post–World War II years. In the midst of the social and cultural unrest of the 1960s and under the shadow of the approaching merger, small groups separated and formed new organizations. The largest of these was the Original Allegheny Conference of the Wesleyan Methodist Connection of America, Inc. (see **Allegheny Wesleyan Methodist Connection**), centered largely in western Pennsylvania. In Ohio, Tennessee, and scattered areas in the Midwest, dissenting groups formed the **Bible Methodist Connection of Churches**. About 10 percent of the church's premerger constituency was lost to these new organizations.

At the time of the merger, the WMC around the world had 1,454 congregations, 2,301 ministers, and a worldwide membership of 62,559. The international offices of the church were at Marion, Indiana. M.E.D.

WESLEYAN QUADRILATERAL. A term used to describe the four loci of theological authority in the Wesleyan tradition. Although the

Wesleyan Quadrilateral draws its inspiration, at least in part, from the theological method of **John Wesley**, it was first articulated by American Methodist theologian Albert Outler, chair of the United Methodist commission that was authorized to formulate a new statement of faith in the wake of the Methodist Church and Evangelical and United Brethren merger of 1968. At the 1984 meeting of the **Wesleyan Theological Society**, Outler explained that the first and foremost component of the Wesleyan Quadrilateral was Scripture, which in turn was subject to interpretation that was informed by Christian Antiquity (tradition), critical reason, and the Christian experience of grace. In popular use, the quadrilateral located authority in four sources: Scripture, tradition, reason, and experience. Although many critics believe that the quadrilateral undermines the authority of Scripture, its use has become common among North American Christians, especially many in the holiness tradition. Likewise, the extent to which all four elements played a significant role in the theological method of the holiness movement remains contested. It appears that Scripture interpreted in the light of the experience of grace and reason has often formed a triad of authority. As a locus of theological authority, tradition has often been treated with considerable suspicion. W.C.K.

WESLEYAN TABERNACLE ASSOCIATION (WTA). Founded in 1936 as the International Holiness Tabernacle Association. It was renamed the Wesleyan Tabernacle Association in the 1960s. It functions as an accrediting agency for nondenominational evangelists and pastors. Initially many of its members were associated with independent holiness schools, such as Chicago Evangelistic Institute (see **Vennard College**) and **God's Bible School**, and with missionary agencies such as the Oriental Missionary Society (see **OMS International**), **World Gospel Mission**, and Kentucky Mountain Bible Institute (see **McConnell, Lela G.**) In recent years, most of its members seem to be associated with the **Inter-Church Holiness Convention**. In 1990, it had more than 200 evangelists, ministers, and song leaders as members and more than 20 supporting congregations. In recent years, its moderator has been Tom Reed, pastor of the influential Wesleyan Missionary Church in Chicago. W.C.K.

WESLEYAN THEOLOGICAL SOCIETY (WTS). Established in 1965 by scholars serving educational institutions in the holiness movement. Although it initially was an independent body, it has been a commission of the **Christian Holiness Partnership** since 1970. Its stated goals included stimulating scholarship among young theologians and pastors and publishing a journal. Its annual meeting is generally held on the campus of a holiness movement–related educational institution. The *Wesleyan Theological Journal* was established in 1966. The organization's first president and principal founder was **Leo G. Cox**, with Charles Carter as first editor of the journal. Since its inception, the WTS annual meetings have inspired significant theological debates, especially surrounding the holiness movement's continuity or lack of continuity with the thought of **John Wesley** and the movement's relation to Pentecostalism. Especially significant have been debates among **Donald W. Dayton, Timothy L. Smith**, and **Asbury Theological Seminary** professor Larry Wood and debates between Randy Maddox and Kenneth Collins. In 1999, the WTS had more than 600 members. W.C.K.

WEST, SAMUEL E. (b. Parkersburg, West Virginia, 18 January 1889; d. 15 April 1970). **Free Methodist Church** (FMC) and Reformed Free Methodist Church minister and publisher. West was called to the ministry in the FMC in 1910 and served several pastorates in Pennsylvania, Ohio, and West Virginia. In the late 1920s, he became a major voice of dissent in the denomination. In 1932, he joined with other dissenters to form the Reformed Free Methodist Church. West was elected overseer, a position he held until his retirement in 1955. R.M.J.

WHITE, ALMA B(ridwell) (b. Lewis County, Kentucky, 16 June 1862; d. Zarephath, New Jersey, 26 June 1946). Methodist Episcopal Church (MEC) and **Pillar of Fire** (POF) evangelist and bishop. Converted in 1878 under the preaching of **W. B. Godbey**, Alma Bridwell was educated at Millersburg (Kentucky) Female College and the University of Denver. After teaching school in Montana and Nevada (1885–1887), she married Methodist theological student Kent White. In 1893, in part through the influence of Denver pastor Finis Yoakum (1851–1920), she experienced **entire sanctification**. Later in 1893, she was one of the principal organizers of the Colorado Holiness Association. She served as a holiness evangelist (1894–1901). Increasingly frustrated with the conservative leadership of the National Holiness Association (see **Christian Holiness Partnership**), White, in part under the influence of the **Metropolitan Church Association** (MCA), separated from the MEC in 1901, organizing her followers into the Pentecostal Union, later the POF. She adopted the demonstrative worship and theological emphases of the MCA and worked closely with the MCA from 1901 to 1906. After breaking with the MCA, White established a permanent national headquarters near Bound Brook, New Jersey, now known as Zarephath. In 1918, she was consecrated a bishop by W. B. Godbey.

A flamboyant personality whom many considered autocratic, White was a supporter of women's rights and the Ku Klux Klan. Although the POF had only about 4,000 members at the time of her death, it owned extensive property, including the Alma Temple on the capitol square in Denver and significant holdings in New Jersey and other urban centers. Among White's most important books are an early autobiography, *Looking Back from Beulah* (1902; revised 1909); a five-volume autobiography, *Story of My Life* (1919–1923); *The Chosen People* (1910); *The New Testament Church*, 2 vols. (1911–1912); and *My Heart, My Husband* (1923). Her sons, Ray White (1892–1946) and Arthur K. White (1889–1981), played key roles in the POF, with Arthur succeeding his mother as bishop W.C.K.

WHITE, STEPHEN S(olomon) (b. Walnut Springs, Texas, 25 January 1890; d. Kankakee, Illinois, 21 March 1971). **Church of the Nazarene** (CN) minister, educator, and editor. Educated at Peniel (Texas) College, Drew University, Brown University, and the University of Chicago, White served as a pastor in Texas, Illinois, Massachusetts, and Ohio. Beginning in the 1920s, he taught philosophy, psychology, and theology at Eastern Nazarene College, Bethany-Peniel College (now Southern Nazarene University), Trevecca Nazarene College, Olivet Nazarene College, and Nazarene Theological Seminary (NTS; 1945–1960). While on the faculty of NTS, he served as editor of the *Herald of Holiness* (1948–1960). In retirement, he served as a lecturer at Olivet Nazarene College. He was a theological moderate whose thought had been shaped by his Drew University mentor, Olin Curtis (d. 1915), and the personalism of Borden P. Bowne (d. 1910). Among his most important books are *Essential Christian Belief* (1940), *Five Cardinal Elements in the Doctrine of Entire Sanctification* (1948), and *Eradication; Defined, Explained, Authenticated* (1954). W.C.K.

WHITESIDE, E(dward) D(rury) (b. St. John, New Brunswick, 4 May 1848; d. Pittsburgh, Pennsylvania, 8 August 1927). Methodist Episcopal Church and **Christian and Missionary Alliance** (CMA) minister and evangelist. Educated at the University of New Brunswick and Alliston College, Whiteside entered the Methodist ministry on Prince Edward Island in the early 1870s. In 1877, Whiteside, who was suffering chronic health problems, was forced to leave the ministry. In 1888, following a period of relative inactivity, he established an insurance agency in Pittsburgh, Pennsylvania. In 1889, after experiencing what he believed to be divine healing, he founded a rescue mission on Pittsburgh's near north side. In 1894, this mission, which became Northside Gospel Tabernacle, affiliated with the CMA. Whiteside remained its pastor until his death. By the end of the 1890s, Whiteside had established 15 CMA branches in western Pennsylvania. Under his leadership, that region emerged as one the principal centers of the CMA. Deeply concerned with the nurturing of church leaders, Whiteside trained a generation of CMA pastors and missionaries. In 1923, he established the Pittsburgh Training School. A close personal friend of holiness evangelist **G. D. Watson**, Whiteside was probably the most significant Wesleyan advocate of full salvation among first-generation CMA leaders. He signed the call for the 1901 General Holiness Assembly (see **S. B. Shaw**) and served as president of the Pittsburgh Holiness Association (1900s–1920s). W.C.K.

WILCOX, LESLIE D. (b. Silver Creek, New York, 12 July 1907; d. Easley, South Carolina, 2 December 1991). **Wesleyan Methodist Church** (WMC) and **Bible Methodist Connection of Churches** minister, administrator, and educator. Converted in a WMC revival in Ashville, New York, in 1924, Wilcox was educated at **God's Bible School** (GBS). Following his graduation, Wilcox served WMC pastorates in Pataskola, Dayton, and Olmstead Falls, Ohio (1927–1936). He served as president of the Ohio Conference of the WMC (1936–1948) and pastor of the Vine Street WMC, Cincinnati (1948–1950); First WMC, Central, South Carolina (1950–1954); and the Belmont WMC, Dayton, Ohio (1954–1955). Although self-educated, Wilcox established a reputation as a Greek scholar and theologian that resulted in his appointment as dean and professor of theology at GBS, where he served on the faculty (1955–1963, 1966–1981).

As a leader of the conservative faction of the WMC, Wilcox vigorously defended the church's traditional cultural conservatism in matters of dress and entertainment during the 1950s and 1960s. More than any other person, he was responsible for the identification of GBS with the **Inter-Church Holiness Convention** (IHC)-related Conservative Holiness Movement. In 1969, Wilcox joined other WMC dissenters in the Bible Methodist Connection of Ohio, serving briefly as connectional chair. As one the most thoughtful leaders of the Conservative

Holiness Movement, Wilcox was author of that movement's most important theological text, *Be Ye Holy* (1965; revised 1977). The work included a careful exposition of holiness teaching, a sketch of the historical development of the holiness movement that emphasized the IHC constituency, and an important introduction to the movement's literature. In retirement, Wilcox completed his magnum opus, *Profiles in Theology* (1983–1985), a two-volume selection of the classic theological literature of Methodism and the holiness tradition, with a third volume containing Wilcox's own lectures on the classic themes of theology. W.C.K.

WILEY, H(enry) ORTON (b. Marquette, Nebraska, 15 November 1877; d. Pasadena, California, 27 August 1961). United Brethren in Christ and **Church of the Nazarene** (CN) minister, educator, and theologian. Following his experience of **entire sanctification** under the ministry of **C. W. Ruth** in 1901, Wiley became active in the CN, serving as pastor of the CN congregation in Berkeley, California (1906–1910). He was educated at the University of the Pacific (A.B., 1910) and the Pacific School of Religion (S.T.M., 1916; S.T.D., 1929). He served on the faculty of Deets Pacific College, later Pasadena College and now Point Loma Nazarene University (1910–1913), president of the same school (1913–1916, 1926–1929, 1933–1949), and president of Northwest Nazarene College (1916–1926). He also was editor of the *Herald of Holiness* (1928–1936).

Although a skilled administrator who turned Northwest Nazarene College and Pasadena College into thriving educational institutions, Wiley is remembered primarily for his three-volume systematic theology, *Christian Theology* (1941). Authorized in 1919 and written while he was burdened with heavy administrative responsibilities, *Christian Theology* was rightly hailed as the definitive systematic expression of the early-20th-century holiness movement. In spite of the fact that Wiley's thought is deeply rooted in the classic 19th-century Methodist theologians, such as William Burt Pope (1822–1903) and John Miley (1813–1895), *Christian Theology* is a distinctly early-20th-century synthesis of holiness experiential theology and the personalism commonly associated with liberal Methodism. It is an experiential, optimistic, and existential construction of the Christian faith that insists that the life of holiness is deeply ethical. Fittingly for a work inspired by the optimism of Wesleyan soteriology and personalist anthropology, Wiley's theology evidences little sign of interaction with the less optimistic theologies of such contemporaries as Karl Barth, Emil Brunner, and Reinhold Niebuhr. Although **H. Ray Dunning**'s *Grace, Faith and Holiness* (1988) has replaced *Christian Theology* as the official CN theology, Wiley's work continues to be read by serious students of Wesleyan theology. W.C.K.

WILKES, A(lphaeus) PAGET (b. Titchwell, England, January 1871; d. Chandlers Ford, England, 5 October 1934). Church of England and Japanese Evangelistic Band (JEB) missionary and author. The son of an Anglican cleric, Wilkes was educated at Lincoln College in Oxford. In 1897, he became a missionary to Japan with the Church Missionary Society. While in Japan, he experienced **entire sanctification**, in part through the influence of reading **Samuel Logan Brengle**. In 1903, with Barclay F. Buxton (1860–1940), he founded the JEB, an interdenominational agency that managed holiness conventions and trained indigenous church leaders from its headquarters in Kobe. Besides his work in organizing and directing holiness conventions, Wilkes was a popular author whose books were read around the world. Among his most important books are *The Dynamic Faith* (1922), *Dynamic Service* (1924), *The Dynamic of Redemption* (1928), and *The Dynamic Life* (1931). He was the author of the popular hymn "Jesus, Jesus, Jesus, Sweetest Name on Earth." In 1983, the JEB celebrated its 80th anniversary. W.C.K.

WILLIAMS, CLARA TEAR (b. near Paynesville, Ohio, 22 September 1858; d. Houghton, New York, 1 July 1937). **Wesleyan Methodist Church** (WMC) minister and evangelist. Raised in a pious Methodist home, Clara Tear was converted in 1871 and experienced **entire sanctification** in 1875. After teaching school for several years, she joined **Mary DePew** in a series of notable revival meetings in Indiana and Michigan in 1882 and 1883. From 1888 to 1894, she served as a remarkably successful evangelist in the Lockport and Allegheny Conferences of the WMC. She served as the pastor of the Middlefield, Ohio, WMC (1894–1895). In 1895, she married William H. Williams (1855–1934). Together the Williamses served as pastors in several Allegheny Conference churches, including Youngstown and Massillon, Ohio, and Pine Grove and Indiana, Pennsylvania (1895–1915). In 1915, they moved to Houghton, New York, where William was a janitor for Houghton College while Clara continued to preach in area churches. Along with her friends Mary DePew and Bertha Grange, Clara Tear Williams played a decisive role in transforming the WMC from a denomination largely committed to social reforms, such as anti-Masonry, to a deeply committed holiness denomination. W.C.K.

WILLIAMS, ROY T(ilman) (b. Milam, Texas, 14 February 1883; d. Tuscambia, Missouri, 25 March 1946). Methodist Episcopal Church, South, and **Church of the Nazarene** (CN) minister, evangelist, and administrator. Following his education at Texas Holiness University and the University of Chicago, Williams served as president of Bell City (Louisiana) College (1906–1908) and taught at Texas Holiness University (1908–1911), where he also served as president (1911–1913). From 1913 to 1918, his skill and growing popularity as an evangelistic preacher made him a nationally known figure in the Pentecostal Church of the Nazarene (see CN). He was elected a general superintendent in 1918, holding that position until his death. Williams, who had been deeply influenced by the homiletical style of his teacher **A. M. Hills**, was a gifted preacher who was noted for his carefully crafted sermons and moving evangelistic messages. Along with **John Wesley Goodwin** and **J. B. Chapman**, Williams, a truly skillful administrator, guided the CN during a period of remarkable growth. He was the author of *Sanctification: The Experience and the Ethics* (1928). W.C.K.

WILLING, JENNIE FOWLER (b. Burford, Ontario, 22 January 1834; d. New York City, 6 October 1916). Organizer in home and foreign missionary work, temperance, and education; author; evangelist; and founder of New York Evangelistic Training School and Settlement House. Jennie Fowler was converted in childhood and, in 1853, married William Crossgrove Willing, who became a minister in the Genesee Conference of the Methodist Episcopal Church (MEC). In 1860, the Willings transferred to the Rock River Conference and served there until 1889. In 1869, Jennie was elected one of three corresponding secretaries of the newly formed Woman's Foreign Missionary Society of the MEC, serving in that capacity for 14 years. In 1873, she was licensed to preach in the Joliet District of the MEC and became professor of English language and literature at Illinois Wesleyan University. The following year, she helped to found two organizations, the Women's Educational Association and the Illinois Woman's Christian Temperance Union (WCTU), and served as president of both. She was the first editor of *Woman's Temperance*, later known as *Our Union*. In 1884, she was appointed general organizer of the Women's Home Missionary Society; two years later, she became the organization's secretary for the Bureau for Spanish Work and oversaw its work in New Mexico and Arizona. In addition, she served as one of the organization's vice presidents.

Jennie's and William's shared commitment to city mission work prompted them in 1889 to change conferences so they could serve inner-city churches in New York City. From 1895 until her death, she was listed as a WCTU evangelist and held the position of secretary of the Department of Evangelistic Institutes and Training for the WCTU. Under the umbrella of this department, she founded the New York Evangelistic Training School and Settlement House in 1895. She wrote a monthly column for the *Guide to Holiness* and, in 1898, was named a corresponding editor of the journal. She wrote 17 books and pamphlets and more than 200 journal articles. P.P.-L.

WIMBERLY, CHARLES FRANKLIN (b. Jefferson County, Illinois, 19 November 1866; d. Columbia, South Carolina, 10 July 1946). Methodist Episcopal Church, South (MECS), minister, evangelist, and author. Following his education at Ewing College, Southern Illinois Normal School, Kansas Normal School, and Vanderbilt University, Wimberly entered the ministry in the MECS, serving in the Missouri Conference (1895–1905). In 1905, he accepted the position of office editor of the *Pentecostal Herald* in Louisville, Kentucky. He was pastor of the Lindsay Memorial MECS, Louisville (1906–1911), and an MECS pastor in Madisonville, Franklin, and Glasgow, Kentucky (1911–1920). Relocating to South Carolina, he dedicated the remaining years of his ministry to evangelism and writing. He served on the board of **Asbury College** and was a corresponding editor for the *Pentecostal Herald*. An ardent premillennialist and critic of the social gospel, Wimberly, who was a delegate to the 1918 World Prophetic Conference in Toronto, took special delight in attacking what he considered to be the naïveté of the notion of the universal "brotherhood" of man. He was the author of more than 30 books, including *New Clothes for the Old Man* (1909), *Behold the Morning* (1916), *Brotherhood* (1917), and *The Wrath of God and Other Sermons* (1930). W.C.K.

WINCHESTER, OLIVE MAY (b. Monson, Maine, 22 November 1880; d. 15 February 1947). **Church of the Nazarene** (CN) religion scholar and dean. A Winchester Rifle Company heir, Olive Winchester graduated from Radcliffe College (1902) before breaking gender barriers as the first woman admitted to and graduated from the B.D. program at the University of Glasgow and the first woman ordained in Scotland (1912), under the auspices of the Pentecostal Church of Scotland. She played a minor role in the merger of that body with the CN. She earned other degrees at Pacific School of Religion (S.T.M.) and Drew University (Th.D.). Winchester taught at Eastern Nazarene College; Northwest Nazarene College (1917–1935), where she was simultaneously vice president and academic dean (1922–1935); and Pasadena College. She published three books in New Testament studies and wrote frequently for Nazarene periodicals. Her *Crisis Experiences in the Greek New Testament* stood in the linguistic-exegetical tradition of Methodist theologian **Daniel Steele**. R.S.I.

WITMER, SAFARA (b. Allen County, Indiana, 31 January 1899; d. Fort Wayne, Indiana, 11 September 1962). Educator and leader of the Bible college movement. Witmer was born into a Swiss Mennonite family who followed **Joseph Ramseyer** from the Defenseless Mennonite tradition into the **Missionary Church Association**. In 1904, Ramseyer and others established what became Fort Wayne Bible College, the institution in which Witmer was to serve most of his adult life as professor (1924–1932), dean (1935–1943), and president (1945–1958). Witmer became the intellectual leader of the college and led its change in status from a two-year diploma-granting institution to a four-year degree-granting Bible college. Furthermore, he worked actively as one of the early leaders of the American Association of Bible Institutes and Colleges, which was founded in 1947 to promote academic development, and he was selected as that organization's first full-time executive secretary. An able internal critic of and external spokesman for the Bible college movement (see his well-crafted *The Bible College Story: Education with Dimension* [1962]), by the late 1950s he was generally recognized as the leading authority on the Bible college–type of education. W.C.R.

WITNESS OF THE SPIRIT. A Christian experience of internal peace. One of the most distinctive and controversial teachings of the holiness movement has been its insistence that the subjective assurance of salvation and **entire sanctification** are present realities that are experienced by most Christians. As **John Wesley** wrote in his definitive sermon, "The Witness of the Spirit," "the testimony of the spirit is an inward impression on the soul, whereby the Spirit of God directly witnesses to my spirit that I am a child of God . . . and I, even I, am reconciled to God." Wesley's emphasis was continued by his early disciples, such as Adam Clarke, and continued to find expression in such holiness movement theologians as **A. M. Hills**, **H. Orton Wiley**, **J. Kenneth Grider**, and **H. Ray Dunning**. Critics of Methodism and the holiness movement have long insisted that to place a central emphasis on a subjective religious experience, such as the witness of the spirit, leads to eccentricity and fanaticism. In fairness to the holiness movement and Methodism, beginning with Wesley and continuing through J. Kenneth Grider, all advocates of the experience have insisted that it not only entails a subjective dimension but also includes such objective elements as living in obedience to Scripture, especially the teachings of Jesus. In recent years, many Wesleyan scholars, most notably Rob Staples, have questioned the common Wesleyan teaching that the experience of the witness of the spirit applies to the experience of entire sanctification while Wesleyan scholars rooted in process theology, such as Michael Lodahl, have found considerable value in the experiential elements of this traditional holiness doctrine. For a tradition that has placed such a high premium on the sense of immediate guidance of the Holy Spirit, Staples's work implies a radical departure from not only the holiness movement but Methodism as well. W.C.K.

WOMEN'S COMMONWEALTH. The product of the religious experience of Martha McWhirter (1827–1906), a Methodist Episcopal Church, South, laywomen from Belton, Texas, who experienced **entire sanctification** in 1866. McWhirter gradually emerged as the leader of a group of entirely sanctified women who taught that such women should separate from their unregenerate husbands. In 1879, they began to live communally. For a time, they supported themselves by taking in laundry and later operated a hotel. By the 1880s, about 50 people, including several men, were living communally. In 1899, the community relocated to Washington, D.C., eventually acquiring a farm in Montgomery County, Maryland, where the last members of the community died in the 1930s. W.C.K.

WOOD, A(rthur) SKEVINGTON (b. Ashbourne, Derbyshire, England, 21 January 1916; d. Sheffield, Yorkshire, 28 January 1993). British Methodist minister, author, teacher, world evangelist, tutor, and principal of **Cliff College**. A. Skevington Wood was an outstanding scholar and preacher and probably the leading representative of the Evangelical Wesleyan wing of British Methodism during the last 20 years of his ministry. He wrote several exceptional works including, in Wesley studies, *The Burning Heart* (1967) and *The Inextinguishable*

Blaze (1960), and major work on Martin Luther and lesser-known evangelical leaders of the 18th century, as well as sermonic and devotional writings. He was appointed principal of Cliff College. He was one of the few Wesleyans invited to preach at the **Keswick** Convention in the late 20th century and was widely accepted in broader evangelical circles. He served as president of British Christian Endeavour; vice president of several mission agencies; and president and cofounder, with Herbert McGonigle and William Parkes, of the Wesley Fellowship, a lesser but similar body to the **Wesleyan Theological Society**. W.P.

WOOD, J(ohn) A(llen) (b. Fishkill, New York, 28 June 1828; d. South Pasadena, California, 7 July 1905). Methodist Episcopal Church (MEC) minister, pastor, evangelist, author, and one of the founders of the National **Camp Meeting** Association for the Promotion of Christian Holiness. Converted at age 10, Wood joined the MEC three years later. By 19, he felt called to the ministry and decided to begin his ministerial training by living and studying with the Reverend William Hill, a disciple of **Phoebe Palmer**. In July 1849, Wood received his first MEC appointment, a small parish in Brookline, Vermont. Four years later, he transferred to the Wyoming (New York) Annual Conference, where he became an ordained elder in 1854. He spent the next twelve years serving churches in New York and Pennsylvania.

Although he became very familiar with the doctrine of **entire sanctification** under Hill's teaching, Wood could not seem to discover the way of the holy life. Consequently, he developed certain prejudices against the doctrine of sanctification and held special animosity toward those persons who "lost their strength," or fell under the power of the Holy Spirit in public services.

In May 1858, Wood was appointed pastor of the Court Street MEC in Binghamton, New York. Numerous members of this congregation professed entire sanctification, and their testimonies greatly influenced Wood. He attended the District Camp Meeting in September and, on the last day of the meeting, he experienced a powerful spiritual manifestation during public worship. He, who had criticized others for falling during public services, lay for three hours on the camp meeting platform, exclaiming, "Precious Jesus! Precious Jesus!"

The new experience forever changed Wood's life, and from that time forth, he was known as a holiness preacher. Two years later, he published *Perfect Love*, a book about the doctrine of entire sanctification, which was probably one of the most influential holiness books of the

19th century and made Wood financially independent. The book has gone through many editions and remains in print.

In the summer of 1866, Wood suggested to some friends the possibility of conducting a camp meeting for the promotion of Christian holiness. Wood's friend, **William B. Osborn**, took the idea to **John S. Inskip** in New York City, and they laid plans for the initial encampment. In the summer of 1867, Wood, Osborn, Inskip, and several other Methodist ministers conducted the first National Holiness Camp Meeting at Vineland, New Jersey. So successful was this camp meeting that the leaders planned another for the summer of 1868. They also formed a loosely framed organization to manage these meetings, the National Camp Meeting Association for the Promotion of Holiness.

Evidence suggests that Wood first conceived the idea for a holiness camp meeting. He preached at the first two encampments and served on the organizing committees of both camps. He became a charter member of the new holiness association and took an active role in its work. By the time of his retirement many years later, Wood claimed to have attended more than 60 national camp meetings.

Ill health forced Wood from the pastorate for a few years, and, starting in 1867, he began to preach as an itinerant holiness revivalist. His work took him to churches and camp meetings in many states, and he joined Inskip and **William McDonald** in their world tour of holiness revivalism in 1880. Wood often preached in large city churches, and his ministry touched the lives of such notables as President Ulysses S. Grant and his family and Chief Justice Salmon P. Chase. Wood also continued to write, publishing *Purity and Maturity* (1876) and *Christian Perfection as Taught by John Wesley* (1885). In 1886, Wood retired to South Pasadena, California, where he continued to hold revivals and published three more books: *Sunset Echoes* (1904), *Autobiography of Rev. J. A. Wood* (1904), and *Mistakes Respecting Christian Holiness* (1905). K.O.B.

WORLD GOSPEL MISSION (WGM). Founded in 1910 as the Missionary Bureau of the National Holiness Association (see **Christian Holiness Partnership**). Long headquartered at Chicago Evangelistic Institute (see **Vennard College**), its first executive officer was Beatrice Beezley (1910–1932), who founded its official publication, the *Call to Prayer,* in 1919. Beginning in 1910, it sponsored the work of **Cecil Troxel** and Woodford Taylor in China. In 1929, Clara Ford, later joined by Willis Hotchkiss, began work in Kenya. In 1937, Anna McGhie and

Annie L. Greiner founded a Bible school, now South India Biblical Seminary, in India. In 1940, WGM had 46 missionaries serving in its three fields. Under the leadership of George R. Warner (1934–1967), the National Holiness Missionary Society (its name after 1946) relocated to Marion, Indiana, in 1952 and, in 1954, changed its name to World Gospel Mission. More substantively, missions were opened in Bolivia (1943), later expanding into Argentina, Honduras (1943), Mexico (1950), Lebanon (1955), Haiti (1965), and Brazil (1966). The programs of the **Peniel Missions** also became part of WGM. Expansion continued under Hollis F. Abbot (1967–1979) and especially in Paraguay (1986), Tanzania (1984), Uganda (1992), and Eastern Europe under Thomas Hermiz, executive officer since 1979. The most successful field has been in Kenya, where the WGM-related Africa Gospel Church has more than 150,000 members and operates Kenya Highlands Bible College. Another significant field is in South America, where WGM missionaries founded Bolivian Evangelical University in 1982. WGM receives the support of the **Evangelical Methodist Church**, the **Churches of Christ in Christian Union**, and the **Congregational Methodist Church**. W.C.K.

WYNKOOP, MILDRED OLIVE BANGS (b. Seattle, Washington, 9 September 1905; d. Lenexa, Kansas, 21 May 1997). **Church of Nazarene** theologian. A devoted student of **H. Orton Wiley**, Mildred Bangs Wynkoop graduated from Pasadena College. She was ordained in 1934 and was an evangelist before earning advanced degrees in theology. She taught theology at Western Evangelical Seminary (1956–1961), Trevecca Nazarene College (1966–1976), and Nazarene Theological Seminary (1976–1979). She was founding president of Japan Nazarene Theological Seminary (1963–1966). She became president of the **Wesleyan Theological Society** in 1973. Her early writings were shaped by the anti-Reformed polemics common to the holiness theology of her youth, but she eventually broke free of that mold and grew critical of "holiness scholasticism" (a term she borrowed from John A. Knight). Many readers found her later writings a liberating antidote to the rigid Aristotelianism that dominated theological structures, and Wiley's underlying personalism became central to her later work, clearly expressed in *A Theology of Love* (1972). Her other significant works include *Foundations of Wesleyan–Arminian Theology* (1967), *John Wesley: Christian Revolutionary* (1970), and *The Trevecca Story* (1976). R.S.I.

– Y –

YAMAMURO, GUNPEI (b. Okayama, Japan, 1 September 1872; d. Tokyo, 13 March 1940). First native officer of the **Salvation Army** (SA) in Japan. Yamamuro helped to transform the SA into an indigenous expression of the Wesleyan holiness mission, uniquely adapted to the needs of Japan's emerging industrialized society. Concern for the spiritual welfare of the lower classes led him to dedicate his life to God for the salvation of the poor. Yamamuro employed his gifts as a writer, preacher, and administrator in the process of adapting the SA's mission and message to the cultural idiom of Japan. One of Yamamuro's literary works stands above others in terms of widespread influence and appeal in this regard. *Heimin no Fukuin* (Common People's Gospel [1899]), became a classic in Japanese literature, selling three million copies. Under Yamamuro's leadership, the evangelistic impact of the SA was felt, but not without a distinct social holiness emphasis. By adapting both its message and social service outreach to the Japanese cultural and social contexts, the SA in pre–World War II Japan enjoyed a period of growth and effectiveness, largely due to the influence of this "Salvationist Samurai." R.D.R.

YEAKEL, REUBEN (b. Montgomery County, Pennsylvania, 3 August 1827; d. 5 March 1904). Denominational editor, historian, and bishop of the Evangelical Association (EA). Converted in 1847, Yeakel began preaching in his native Pennsylvania. He entered the EA ministry in 1853 and became corresponding secretary of the General Mission Society (1859–1863), then editor. In 1879, he was elected bishop and served two terms until 1889. A prominent member of the National Holiness Association (NHA; see **Christian Holiness Partnership**), Yeakel was active in the promotion of holiness **camp meetings** in his denomination. He became director of the EA's first seminary, Union Biblical Institute (Naperville, Illinois). His history of the EA was the most extensive history of the denomination in the 19th century. J.S.O.

YOCUM, DALE (Morris) (b. Missouri, 19 October 1919; d. Overland Park, Kansas, 10 May 1987). **Church of God (Holiness)** (CG[H]) minister, educator, missionary, and evangelist. Yocum was educated at Kansas City College and Bible School (KCCBS), Northeast Missouri State Teachers College, Massachusetts Institute of Technology (MIT), and the University of Kansas (Ed.D., 1957). He served on the faculty and as dean (1940s–1969) and then president of KCCBS (1969–1971); as a missionary to South Korea and Jamaica (1971–1980); as a teacher at Holiness Theological Seminary in Seoul, Korea; and as director of Friends of Mission. Partly because of his training at MIT, Yocum was always fascinated with science and for many years wrote a regular science column for the Sunday school curriculum of the CG(H). He played an important role in the alignment of the CG(H) with the **Inter-Church Holiness Convention** (IHC). One of the most respected IHC-related scholars, he was the author of some of the most important books written from the IHC perspective, including *The Holy Way* (1976) and *Creeds in Contrast: A Study of Calvinism and Arminianism* (1986). W.C.K.

YORK, ALVIN (b. Pall Mall, Tennessee, 13 December 1887; d. Nashville, Tennessee, 2 September 1964). **Churches of Christ in Christian Union** (CCCU) speaker and fund-raiser. Following his conversion in 1915, York was influenced by Rev. W. W. Loveless, a member of the CCCU who conducted a revival meeting in the Pall Mall area that resulted in the formation of a CCCU congregation. York was elected elder and song leader of the church and became known as the "singing elder." With the start of World War I, York was drafted but, having no desire to kill another human being, registered as a conscientious objector. His appeal was rejected, and York found himself deep in the Argonne Forest of France. Practically single-handedly, he killed 25 of the enemy and captured 132. York was decorated by six nations and received the Congressional Medal of Honor.

Returning home, York refused hundreds of thousands of dollars in endorsements and returned to the mountains of Tennessee. He became a public speaker and traveled across the nation raising money to help people in his home county. His efforts are still in evidence. York Institute in Jamestown (Tennessee) was started thanks to York and his efforts. Roads were improved, and a Bible school was started. York remained faithful to God his whole life. Several books and a 1941 movie (*Sergeant York*, starring Gary Cooper) have been produced about York and his life; he is remembered for his love of God, country, and church. W.E.H.

– Z –

ZOOK, JOHN R(oel) (b. Whiteside County, Illinois, 4 November 1857; d. near West Milton, Ohio, 6 November 1919). **Brethren in Christ**

(BIC) minister and evangelist. The principal leader in the BIC adoption of holiness teaching, Zook was converted in 1874. Following education at Northern Indiana Normal School, later Valparaiso University (1879–1881), he served as a schoolteacher in Olge County, Illinois (1882–1890). After operating the family farm (1890–1896), he was called to the ministry and took charge of a rescue mission in Des Moines, Iowa. With several coworkers, Zook managed the mission until his death. Through contacts with the Hephzibah Faith Mission (see **Hephzibah Faith Missionary Association**) and the Iowa Holiness Association, Zook embraced a Wesleyan understanding of **entire sanctification** as a second distinct religious experience. More than any other person, Zook was responsible for the BIC's 1910 affirmation of holiness teaching. Zook's view on entire sanctification received classic expression in two *Gospel Visitor* articles that were later published as *Holiness and Empowerment* (n.d.). Zook was also a fervent advocate of faith healing and premillennial **eschatology**. A respected preacher, Zook was the most successful BIC evangelist of the first two decades of the 20th century. W.C.K.

Bibliography

A large and growing body of literature on the history of the holiness movement exists, from which the contents of this bibliography have been selected. Individuals in search of primary source materials will want to consult Charles Edwin Jones, *A Guide to the Study of the Holiness Movement* (Scarecrow Press, 1974), and William Kostlevy, *Holiness Manuscripts: A Guide to Sources Documenting the Wesleyan Holiness Movement in the United States and Canada* (Scarecrow Press, 1994).

An excellent listing of representative holiness movement texts appears in Leslie D. Wilcox, *Be Ye Holy* (Salem, Ohio: Schmul, 1977). A second source of representative texts of the holiness movement is found in a series of 44 books in the Garland Higher Life Series that were selected by Donald W. Dayton and published in the 1980s. Surprisingly, many holiness movement books have been reprinted by a number of publishers; especially noteworthy are reprints by the Schmul Publishing Company (P.O. Box 716, Salem, Ohio 44460).

REPOSITORIES

Archives of the United Church of Canada, Victoria University, 73 Queen's Park Crescent, Toronto, Ontario M5S 1K7
B. L. Fisher Library, Asbury Theological Seminary, Wilmore, Ky. 40390
Brethren in Christ Archives, Messiah College, Grantham, Pa. 17027
Church of God (Anderson) Archives, Anderson University, Anderson, Ind. 46012
Duke University, William R. Perkins Library, Manuscript Collections, Durham, N.C. 27706
General Commission of Archives and History, United Methodist Church, Drew University, Madison, N.J. 07940
Marston Memorial Historical Center, Free Methodist Church Headquarters, P.O. Box 535002, Indianapolis, Ind. 46253
Nazarene Archives, 6401 The Paseo, Kansas City, Mo. 64131
Salvation Army Archives, P.O. Box 269, Alexandria, Va. 22313
Salvation Army Heritage Center, 2130 Bayview Ave., Toronto, Ontario M4N 3K6
Wesleyan Church Archives, Wesleyan Church International Center, P.O. Box 50434, Indianapolis, Ind. 46250

GENERAL REFERENCE WORKS

Brown, Kenneth O. *Holy Ground: The Camp Meeting Family Tree.* Hazelton, Pa.: Holiness Archives, 1997.

Bundy, David D. *Keswick: A Bibliographic Introduction to the Higher Life Movement.* Wilmore, Ky.: B. L. Fisher Library, 1975.

Dayton, Donald W. *The American Holiness Movement: A Bibliographic Introduction.* Wilmore, Ky.: B. L. Fisher Library, 1971.

Dupree, Sherry Sherrod. *African-American Holiness Pentecostal Movement: An Annotated Bibliography.* New York: Garland, 1995.

Eltscher, Susan M. *Women in the Wesleyan and United Methodist Traditions.* Madison, N.J.: General Commission of Archives and History, United Methodist Church, 1991.

Harmon, Nolan B, ed. *Encyclopedia of World Methodism,* 2 vols. Nashville: United Methodist Publishing House, 1974.

Jones, Charles Edwin. *Black Holiness: A Guide to the Study of Black Participation in the Wesleyan Perfectionist and Glossolalic Pentecostal Movements.* Metuchen, N.J.: Scarecrow, 1987.

———. *A Guide to the Study of the Holiness Movement.* Metuchen, N.J.: Scarecrow, 1974.

Kostlevy, William. *Holiness Manuscripts: A Guide to Sources Documenting the Wesleyan Holiness Movement in the United States and Canada.* Metuchen, N.J.: Scarecrow, 1994.

———. "Historiography of the Holiness Movement." In William Kostlevy, *Holiness Manuscripts,* pp. 1–40.

Rowe, Kenneth E. *Methodist Union Catalog, Pre-1976 Imprints,* 7 vols. to date (A–I). Metuchen, N.J.: Scarecrow, 1975–.

Stanley, Susie C., comp. *Wesleyan/Holiness Women Clergy: A Preliminary Bibliography.* Portland, OR: Compiler, 1994.

Turner, Kristen. *A Guide to Resources on Women in the United Methodist Archives.* Madison, N.J.: General Commission on Archives and History, United Methodist Church, 1995.

Yrigoyen, Charles, Jr., and Susan E. Warrick. *Historical Dictionary of Methodism.* Lanham, Md.: Scarecrow, 1996.

COLLECTED EDITIONS OF HOLINESS TESTIMONIES

Garrison, S. Olin. *Forty Witnesses Covering the Whole Range of Christian Experience.* New York: Hunt & Eaton, 1888.

Holiness Doctrine and Experience. Kansas City, 1951.

Lawson, James G. *Deeper Experiences of Famous Christians*. Chicago: Glad Tidings, 1911.

Palmer, Phoebe. *Pioneer Experiences; or the Gift of Power Received by Faith*. New York: Palmer, 1868.

Riches of Grace, or the Blessing of Perfect Love. Brooklyn, N.Y.: Fox, 1853.

Smith, Bernie. *Flames of Living Fire: Testimonies to the Experience of Entire Sanctification*. Salem, Ohio: Schmul, 1984.

COLLECTED EDITIONS OF HOLINESS AND CAMP MEETING SERMONS

The Double Cure; or Echoes from National Camp-Meetings. Boston: Christian Witness, 1887.

Hughes, George. *Days of Power in the Forest Temple: A Review of the Wonderful Work of God at Fourteen National Camp-Meetings from 1867–1873*. Boston: Bent, 1873.

McLean, Alexander, ed. *Penuel; or Face to Face with God*. New York: Palmer, 1869.

The Nazarene Pulpit: A Collection of Sermons by Well Known Preachers. Kansas City, Mo.: Nazarene Publishing, 1925.

The Pentecostal Pulpit. Louisville, Ky.: Pentecostal Publishing Company, n.d.

Thornton, Wallace, Jr. *Sons of Thunder: Camp Meeting Sermons by Post–World War II Holiness Revivalists*. Salem, Ohio: Schmul, 1999.

Twentieth Century Holiness Sermons. Louisville, Ky.: Pentecostal Publishing Company, n.d.

Wallace, Adam, ed. *A Modern Pentecost; Embracing a Record of Sixteen National Camp-Meetings for the Promotion of Holiness*. Philadelphia: Methodist Home Journal Publishing, 1873.

COLLECTED EDITIONS OF HOLINESS WRITINGS

Anderson, T. M, ed. *Our Holy Faith*. Kansas City, Mo.: Beacon Hill, 1965.

Dieter, Melvin E., ed. *Great Holiness Classics, Vol. 4: The Nineteenth Century Holiness Movement*. Kansas City, Mo.: Beacon Hill, 1998.

Harper, A. F., ed. *Great Holiness Classics, Vol. 6: Holiness Teaching Today*. Kansas City, Mo.: Beacon Hill, 1987.

Holiness Miscellany. Philadelphia: National Holiness Association, 1882.

Taylor, Richard S., ed. *Great Holiness Classics, Vol. 3: Leading Wesleyan Thinkers*. Kansas City, Mo.: Beacon Hill, 1985.

Wilcox, Leslie D., ed. *Profiles in Wesleyan Theology*, 3 vols. Salem, Ohio: Schmul, 1983.

SYSTEMATIC THEOLOGY IN THE HOLINESS TRADITION

Bowie, Mary Ella. *An Introduction to Systematic Theology.* Chicago: Chicago Evangelistic Institute, 1942.
Byrum, Russell R. *Christian Theology.* Anderson, Ind.: Gospel Trumpet, 1925.
Callen, Barry. *God as Loving Grace: The Biblical Revealed Nature of God.* Nappanee, Ind.: Evangel Publishing, 1996.
Carter, Charles W., ed. *Contemporary Wesleyan Theology: Biblical, Systematic, Practical,* 2 vols. Grand Rapids: Zondervan, 1983.
Dunning, H. Ray. *Grace, Faith and Holiness; A Wesleyan Systematic Theology.* Kansas City, Mo.: Beacon Hill, 1988.
Finney, Charles G. *Lectures on Systematic Theology: Embracing Lectures on Moral Government.* Oberlin, Ohio: Fitch, 1846.
———. *Lectures on Systematic Theology: Embracing Moral Government,* 2 vols., ed. and rev. George Redford. London: Tegg, 1851.
Godbey, W. B. *Bible Theology.* Cincinnati: God's Revivalist Office, 1911.
Gray, Albert F. *Christian Theology,* 2 vols. Anderson, Ind.: Warner, 1944–1946.
Grider, J. Kenneth. *A Wesleyan–Holiness Theology.* Kansas City, Mo.: Beacon Hill, 1994.
Hills, A. M. *Fundamental Christian Theology: A Systematic Theology.* Pasadena, Calif.: Kinne, 1931.
Jones, Kenneth E. *Theology of Holiness and Love.* Lanham, Md.: University Press of America, 1996.
Lee, Luther. *Elements of Theology.* Syracuse, N.Y.: Lee, 1856.
Livermore, Paul. *God Our Salvation: Christian Theology from a Wesleyan Perspective.* Indianapolis: Light and Life Press, 1995.
Lowrey, Asbury. *Positive Theology: Being a Series of Dissertations on the Fundamental Doctrines of the Bible.* Cincinnati: Methodist Book Concern, 1853.
Ralston, Thomas Neeley. *Elements of Divinity.* Nashville: Methodist Episcopal Church, South, 1871.
Wiley, H. Orton. *Christian Theology,* 3 vols. Kansas City, Mo.: Nazarene Publishing, 1940–1943.

THE THIRTEEN MOST IMPORTANT HOLINESS TEXTS

Boardman, W. E. *The Higher Christian Life.* Boston: Hoyt, 1858.
Butler, C. W. *A Holiness Manifesto.* Louisville: Pentecostal Publishing Company, n.d.
Chambers, Oswald. *My Utmost for His Highest.* London: Simpkin Marshall, 1927.
Cook, Thomas. *New Testament Holiness.* London: Epworth, 1902.
Cowman, Mrs. Charles E. *Streams in the Desert.* Los Angeles: Oriental Missionary Society, 1925.

Hills, A. M. *Holiness and Power for the Church and the Ministry*. Cincinnati: Revivalist Office, 1897.

Jessop, Harry E. *Foundations of Doctrine in Scripture and Experience*. Chicago: Chicago Evangelistic Institute, 1938.

Mahan, Asa. *The Baptism of the Holy Spirit*. New York: Palmer, 1870.

———. *Scriptural Doctrine of Christian Perfection*. Boston: King, 1839.

Palmer, Phoebe. *The Way of Holiness, with Notes by the Way*. New York: Piercy & Reed, 1843.

Robinson, Bud. *A Pitcher of Cream*. Louisville: Pentecostal Publishing, 1906.

Upham, Thomas C. *The Life of Faith*. Boston: Waite, Pierce, 1845.

Wood, J. A. *Perfect Love*. Chicago: Christian Witness, 1880.

GENERAL INTERPRETATIONS

Bebbington, David W. "The Holiness Movements in British and Canadian Methodism in the Late Nineteenth Century." *Proceedings of the Wesley Historical Society* 50 (October 1996): 203–28.

Brasher, Larry. *The Sanctified South: John Lakin Brasher and the Holiness Movement*. Champaign: University of Illinois Press, 1994.

Brown, Joanne Elizabeth Carlson. "Jennie Fowler Willing (1834–1916), Methodist Church Woman and Reformer." Ph.D. diss., Boston University, 1983.

Brown, Kenneth O. *Inskip, McDonald, Fowler: Wholly and Forever Thine: Early Leadership in the National Camp Meeting Association for the Promotion of Holiness*. Hazelton, Pa.: Holiness Archives, 1999.

Bundy, David. "Between the Reveil and Pentecostalism: The American Wesleyan/Holiness Traditions in Belgium and the Netherlands." *Asbury Theological Journal* 51 (August 1996): 105–14.

Cho, David. "The Old Princeton Presbyterian Response to the Holiness Movement in the Late Nineteenth and Early Twentieth Centuries in America." Ph.D. diss., Westminister Theological Seminary, 1994.

Cooley, Steven D. "Applying the Vagueness of Language: Poetic Strategies and Camp Meeting Piety in the Mid–Nineteenth Century." *Church History* 63 (December 1994): 570–86.

———. "Manna and the Manual; Sacramental Constructions of the Victorian Camp Meeting during the Mid–Nineteenth Century." *Religion and American Culture* 6 (Summer 1996): 131–60.

———. "The Possibilities of Grace: Poetic Discourse and Reflection in Methodist/Holiness Revivalism." Ph.D. diss., University of Chicago, 1991.

Coppedge, Allan. "Entire Sanctification in Early American Methodism, 1812–1835." *Wesleyan Theological Journal* 13 (Spring 1978): 34–50.

Dayton, Donald W. *Discovering an Evangelical Heritage*. New York: Harper & Row, 1976.

————. "Good News to the Poor: The Methodist Experience after Wesley." In *The Portion of the Poor: Good News to the Poor in the Wesleyan Tradition*, ed. M. Douglas Meeks. Nashville: Abingdon, 1997.

————. *Theological Roots of Pentecostalism*. Metuchen, N.J.: Scarecrow, 1987.

Dayton, Lucille Sider, and Donald W. Dayton. "Your Daughters Shall Prophesy: Feminism and the Holiness Movement." *Methodist History* 14 (1976): 67–92.

Dieter, Melvin E. *The Holiness Revival of the Nineteenth Century*. Lanham, Md.: Scarecrow, 1996.

————. "Wesleyan–Holiness Aspects of Pentecostal Origins as Mediated through the Nineteenth-Century Holiness Revival." In *Aspects of Pentecostal-Charismatic Origins*, ed. Vinson Synan. Plainfield, N.J.: Logos International, 1975.

Dunlap, E. Dale. "Tuesday Meetings, Camp Meetings and Cabinet Meetings: A Perspective on the Holiness Movement in the Methodist Church in the Nineteenth Century." *Methodist History* 13 (April 1975): 85–106.

Gaddis, Merle E. "Christian Perfection in America." Ph.D. diss., University of Chicago, 1929.

Jones, Charles E. "Disinherited or Rural? A Historical Case Study in Urban Holiness Religion." *Missouri Historical Review* 66 (April 1972): 395–412.

————. "The Inverted Shadow of Phoebe Palmer." *Wesleyan Theological Journal* 31 (Fall 1996): 120–31.

————. *Perfectionist Persuasion: The Holiness Movement and American Methodism 1867–1936*. Metuchen, N.J.: Scarecrow, 1974.

Oldstone-Moore, Christopher. *Hugh Price Hughes: Founder of a New Methodism, Conscience of a New Nonconformity*. Cardiff: University of Wales Press, 1999.

Raser, Harold E. *Phoebe Palmer: Her Life and Thought*. Lewiston, N.Y.: Mellen, 1987.

Rose, Delbert R. *Vital Holiness: A Theology of Christian Experience: Interpreting the Wesleyan Message*. Salem, Ohio: Schmul, 2000.

Schneider, A. Gregory. "A Conflict in Associations: The National Camp Meeting Association for the Promotion of Holiness Versus the Methodist Episcopal Church." *Church History* 66 (June 1997): 268–83.

————. "Objective Selves versus Empowered Selves: The Conflict over Holiness in the Post–Civil War Methodist Episcopal Church." *Methodist History* 32 (July 1994): 237–49.

Simmons, Dale. "Phoebe Palmer—Enjoli Woman or Enigma? Review of the Recent Scholarship on Phoebe Palmer." *Wesleyan/Holiness Studies Center Bulletin* 4 (Summer 1996): 1, 4.

Smith, Timothy L. "Holiness and Radicalism in Nineteenth-Century America." In *Sanctification and Liberation: Liberation Theologies in the Light of the Wesleyan Tradition*, ed. Theodore Runyan. Nashville: Abingdon, 1979.

Turley, Briane K. *A Wheel within a Wheel: Southern Methodism and the Georgia Holiness Association*. Macon, Ga.: Mercer University Press, 1999.

Ward, Patricia. "Madame Guyon in America." *Church History* 67 (September 1998): 484–98.

Warfield, B. B. *Perfectionism*, 2 vols. New York: Oxford University Press, 1929.

White, Charles Edward. *The Beauty of Holiness: Phoebe Palmer as Theologian, Revivalist, Feminist and Humanitarian*. Grand Rapids: Francis Asbury Press, 1986.

Whiteley, Marilyn Färdig. "Sailing the Shore: The Canadian Holiness Tradition." In *Aspects of the Canadian Evangelical Experience,* ed. G. A. Rawlyk. Montreal: McGill-Queen's University, 1997.

ANTEBELLUM PERFECTIONISM

Bundy, David. "Thomas Cogswell Upham and the Establishment of a Tradition of Ethical Reflection." *Encounter* 59 (1998): 23–40.

Cross, Whitney R. *The Burned-Over District: The Social and Intellectual History of Enthusiastic Religion in Western New York, 1800–1850*. Ithaca, N.Y.: Cornell University Press, 1950.

Finney, Charles G. *The Memoirs of Charles G. Finney: The Completely Restored Text*. Garth M. Rosell and Richard A. G. Dupuis, eds. Grand Rapids, Mich.: Zondervan, 1989.

Fletcher, Robert S. *A History of Oberlin College from Its Foundations through the Civil War*. Oberlin, Ohio: Oberlin College, 1943.

Goodman, Paul. *Of One Blood: Abolitionists and the Origins of Racial Equality*. Berkeley: University of California Press, 1998.

Hambrick-Stowe, Charles. *Charles G. Finney and the American Spirit*. Grand Rapids, Mich.: Eerdmans, 1996.

Johnson, James E. "The Life of Charles G. Finney." Ph.D. diss., Syracuse University, 1959.

Kaufman, Paul L. *Logical Luther Lee and the Methodist War against Secret Societies*. Lanham, Md.: Scarecrow, 2000.

Kostlevy, William. "Luther Lee and Methodist Abolitionism." *Methodist History* 20 (1982): 90–103.

Kraditor, Aileen. *Means and Ends in American Abolitionism: Garrison and His Critics on Strategy and Tactics*. New York: Pantheon, 1969.

Lee, James W. "The Development of Theology at Oberlin." Ph.D. diss., Drew University, 1952.

Madden, Edward H., and James Hamilton. *Freedom and Grace: The Life of Asa Mahan*. Metuchen, N.J.: Scarecrow, 1982.

Mathews, Donald G. "Orange Scott: The Methodist Evangelist as Revolutionary." In *The Antislavery Vanguard: New Essays on Abolitionists*, ed. Martin Duberman. Princeton, N.J.: Princeton University Press, 1965.

Smith, Timothy L. "Charles G. Finney's Synthesis of Wesleyan and Covenant Theology." *Wesleyan Theological Journal* 13 (Spring 1978): 92–113.

————. *Revivalism and Social Reform: American Protestantism on the Eve of the Civil War*. Nashville: Abingdon, 1957.

Strong, Douglas M. *Perfectionist Politics: Abolitionism and the Religious Tensions of American Democracy*. Syracuse, N.Y.: Syracuse University Press, 1999.

Thomas, John L. "Romantic Reform in America." *American Quarterly Review* 17 (1965): 656–81.

Thomas, Robert David. *The Man Who Would Be Perfect: John Humphrey Noyes and the Utopian Impulse*. Philadelphia: Temple University Press, 1977.

Tyler, Alice Felt. *Freedom's Ferment: Phases of American Social History from the Colonial Period to the Outbreak of the Civil War*. Minneapolis: University of Minnesota Press, 1944.

Zikmund, Barbara. "Asa Mahan and Oberlin Perfectionism." Ph.D. diss., Duke University, 1969.

ALLIANCE OF REFORMED BAPTISTS

Rawlyk, George A. "The Holiness Movement and the Canadian Maritime Baptists." In *Amazing Grace: Evangelicalism in Australia, Britain, Canada and the United States*, ed. George A. Rawlyk and Mark A. Noll. Grand Rapids, Mich.: Baker Books, 1993.

BRETHREN IN CHRIST CHURCH

Alderfer, Owen H. "The Mind of the Brethren in Christ." Ph.D. diss., Claremont Graduate School, 1964.

Climenhaga, A. W. *History of the Brethren in Christ Church*. Nappanee, Ind.: E. V. Publishing, 1942.

Hawbaker, John B. "Preaching Holiness at the Roxbury Holiness Camp Meeting. *Brethren in Christ History and Life* 10 (April 1987): 3–47.

Keefer, Luke L., Jr. "The Three Streams in Our Heritage." *Brethren in Christ History and Life* 19 (April 1996): 3–25.

Sider, E. Morris. *Holiness Unto the Lord: The Story of the Roxbury Holiness Camp Meeting*. Nappanee, Ind.: Evangel, 1985.

————. *Nine Portraits: Brethren in Christ Biographical Sketches*. Nappanee, Ind.: Evangel, 1978.

Wittlinger, Carlton O. *Quest for Piety and Obedience: The Story of the Brethren in Christ*. Nappanee, Ind.: Evangel, 1978.

CHRISTIAN AND MISSIONARY ALLIANCE

Hartzfeld, David F., and Charles Nienkirchen, eds. *Birth of a Vision*. Beaverlodge, Ala.: Buena Book Service, 1986.

McGraw, Gerald Earl. "The Doctrine of Sanctification in the Published Writings of Albert Benjamin Simpson." Ph.D. diss., New York University, 1986.

Niklaus, Robert L., John S. Sawin, and Samuel J. Stoesz. *All For Jesus: God at Work in the Christian and Missionary Alliance over One Hundred Years*. Camp Hill, Pa.: Christian Publications, 1986.

Reid, Darrell R. "Toward a Fourfold Gospel: A. B. Simpson, John Salmon and the Christian and Missionary Alliance in Canada." In *Aspects of Canadian Evangelical Experience,* ed. G. A. Rawlyk. Montreal: McGill-Queen's University, 1997.

Reynolds, Lindsay. *Rebuilt: The Redevelopment of the Christian and Missionary Alliance in Canada: 1919–1983*. Willowdale, Ontario: Christian and Missionary Alliance in Canada, 1992.

CHURCH OF GOD (ANDERSON)

Brown, Charles Ewing. *When the Trumpet Sounded: A History of the Church of God Reformation Movement*. Anderson, Ind.: Warner, 1951.

Callen, Barry, ed. *Following the Light: Teachings, Testimonies, Trials and Triumphs of the Church of God Movement*. Anderson, Ind.: Warner, 2000.

Clear, Val. *Where the Saints Have Trod: A Social History of the Church of God Reformation Movement*. Chesterfield, Ind.: Midwest, 1977.

Smith, John W. *The Quest for Holiness and Unity: A Centennial History of the Church of God (Anderson, Indiana)*. Anderson, Ind.: Warner, 1980.

Strege, Merle D. *Tell Me Another Tale: Further Reflections on the Church of God*. Anderson, Ind.: Warner, 1993.

———. *Tell Me the Tale: Historical Reflections on the Church of God*. Anderson, Ind.: Warner, 1991.

Willowby, Richard L. *Family Reunion: A Century of Camp Meetings*. Anderson, Ind.: Warner, 1986.

CHURCH OF GOD (HOLINESS)

Cowen, Clarence Eugene. *A History of the Church of God (Holiness)*. Overland Park, Kans.: Herald & Banner, 1949.

CHURCH OF THE NAZARENE

Bangs, Carl. *Phineas F. Bresee: His Life in Methodism, the Holiness Movement and the Church of the Nazarene*. Kansas City, Mo.: Beacon Hill, 1995.

Baucom, Larry Mark. "The Reaction of the Church of the Nazarene to Historical Critical Bible Study." Ph.D. diss., Florida State University, 1995.

Cameron, James R. *Eastern Nazarene College: The First Fifty Years*. Kansas City, Mo.: Nazarene Publishing, 1968.

Cunningham, Floyd T. "The Early History of the Church of the Nazarene in the Philippines." *Philippine Studies* 41 (First Quarter 1993): 51–75.

———. "Mission Policy and National Leadership in the Church of the Nazarene in India, 1898–1960." *Indian Church History* 125 (June 1991): 17–48.

———. "Mission Policy and National Leadership in the Church of the Nazarene in Japan." *Wesleyan Theological Journal* 28 (Spring–Fall 1993): 128–64.

Emptage, Ronald R. "The Laymen's Holiness Association of America: The Development of a Wesleyan-Fundamentalist Sect." Ph.D. diss., University of Michigan, 1991.

Frankiel, Sandra Sizer. *California's Spiritual Frontiers: Religious Alternatives in Anglo-Protestantism*. Berkeley: University of California Press, 1988.

Gresham, L. Paul. *Waves against Gibralter: A Memoir of Dr. A. M. Hills, 1848–1935*. Bethany, Okla.: Southern Nazarene University, 1992.

Griffin, Jeffrey Peter. "Yours in His Service: H. Orton Wiley as an Evangelical Theologian and Educator." Ph.D. diss., University of New Mexico, 1998.

Ingersol, R. Stanley. "Burden of Dissent: Mary Lee Cagle and the Southern Holiness Movement." Ph.D. diss., Duke University, 1989.

———. "Christian Baptism and the Early Nazarenes: The Sources That Shaped a Pluralistic Baptismal Tradition." *Wesleyan Theological Journal* 25 (Fall 1990): 24–38.

———. "The Ministry of Mary Lee Cagle: A Study in Women's History and Religion." *Wesleyan Theological Journal* 28 (Spring–Fall 1993): 176–98.

———. *Nazarene Women and Religion: Sources on Clergy and Lay Women in the Church of the Nazarene*. Kansas City, Mo.: Nazarene Archives, 2000.

Kirkemo, Ronald B. *For Zion's Sake; a History of Pasadena/Point Loma College*. San Diego: Point Loma, 1992.

Laird, Rebecca. *Ordained Women in the Church of the Nazarene: The First Generation*. Kansas City, Mo.: Beacon Hill, 1993.

Purkiser, W. T. *Called Unto Holiness: The Story of the Nazarenes: The Second Twenty-Five Years*. Kansas City, Mo.: Nazarene Publishing, 1983.

Raser, Harold E. *More Preachers and Better Preachers: The First Fifty Years of Nazarene Theological Seminary*. Kansas City, Mo.: Nazarene Publishing, 1995.

Reed, Harold. "The Growth of a Contemporary Sect-Type Institution as Reflected in the Development of the Church of the Nazarene." Ph.D. diss., University of Southern California, 1943.

Smith, Timothy L. *Called Unto Holiness: The Story of the Nazarenes: The Formative Years*. Kansas City, Mo.: Nazarene Publishing, 1962.
White, J. Timothy. "Hiram F. Reynolds: Prime Mover of Nazarene Mission Education." Ph.D. diss., University of Kansas, 1996.

CHURCHES OF CHRIST IN CHRISTIAN UNION

Brown, Kenneth O., and P. Lewis Brevard. *From Out of the Past: A History of the Churches of Christ in Christian Union*. Circleville, Ohio: Circle, 1980.

EVANGELICAL ASSOCIATION

Corbin, J. Wesley. "Christian Perfection in the Evangelical Association through 1875." *Methodist History* 7 (January 1969): 28–44.
Schwab, Ralph Kendall. *The History of the Doctrine of Christian Perfection in the Evangelical Association*. Menasha, Wis.: Banta, 1922.

FREE METHODIST CHURCH

Hogue, Wilson T. *History of the Free Methodist Church of North America*, 2 vols. Chicago: Free Methodist Publishing, 1915.
Kostlevy, William. "Culture, Class and Gender in the Progressive Era: The Social Thought of the Free Methodist Church during the Age of Gladden, Strong and Rauschenbusch." In *Perspectives on the Social Gospel: Papers from the Inaugural Social Gospel Conference at Colgate Rochester Divinity School,* ed. Christopher Evans. Lewiston, N.Y.: Mellen, 1999.
Revell, James Alan. "The Nazirites: Burned-Over District Methodism and the Buffalo Middle Class." Ph.D. diss., State University of New York at Buffalo, 1993.
Snyder, Howard A. "Formative Influences on B. T. Roberts, Abolitionism, Revivalism, Perfectionism." *Wesleyan Theological Journal* 34 (Spring 1999): 177–99.
———. "To Preach the Gospel to the Poor: Missional Self-Understanding in Early Free Methodism, 1860–1890." *Wesleyan Theological Journal* 31 (Spring 1996): 7–39.

KOREA EVANGELICAL HOLINESS CHURCH

Hong, Paul. "Spreading the Holiness Fire: A History of the OMS Korea Holiness Church, 1904–1957." Ph.D. diss., Fuller Theological Seminary, 1996.

Park, Myung Soo. "Roots of the Evangelical Holiness Church with Special Reference to Holiness." M.A. thesis, Boston University, School of Theology, 1992.

GOSPEL WORKERS CHURCH

Hobbs, Helen G. "What She Could: Women in the Gospel Workers Church, 1902–1951." In *Changing Roles of Women within the Christian Church in Canada,* ed. Elizabeth Gillan Muir and Marilyn Färdig Whiteley. Toronto: University of Toronto Press, 1995.

Hobbs, R. Gerald. "Stepchildren of John Wesley: The Gospel Workers Church in Canada." *Canadian Methodist Historical Society Papers* 8 (1991): 174–88.

KESWICK

Bundy, David. "Keswick and the Experience of Evangelical Piety." In *Modern Christian Revivals,* ed. Edith L. Blumhofer and Randall Balmer. Champaign: University of Illinois, 1993.

METROPOLITAN CHURCH ASSOCIATION

Kostlevy, William. "Nor Silver, nor Gold: The Burning Bush Movement and the Communitarian Holiness Vision." Ph.D. diss., University of Notre Dame, 1996.

PENTECOSTAL LEAGUE OF PRAYER

Randall, Ian M. "The Pentecostal League of Prayer: A British Holiness Movement." *Wesleyan Theological Journal* 33 (Spring 1998): 185–200.

PILGRIM HOLINESS CHURCH

Hynson, Leon O. "Called to Be Pilgrims." *Methodist History* 33 (July 1995): 207–25.

Thomas, Paul Westphal, and Paul William Thomas. *The Days of Our Pilgrimage: The History of the Pilgrim Holiness Church.* Marion, Ind.: Wesley Press, 1976.

PILLAR OF FIRE

Stanley, Susie Cunningham. *Feminist Pillar of Fire: The Life of Alma White*. Cleveland: Pilgrim Press, 1993.

SALVATION ARMY

Green, Roger J. *Catherine Booth: A Biography of the Cofounder of the Salvation Army*. Grand Rapids, Mich.: Baker Book House, 1996.

Horridge, Glenn K. *The Salvation Army: Origins and Early Days, 1865–1900*. Godalming, Surrey: Ammonite Books, 1993.

McKinley, Edward H. *Marching to Glory: The History of the Salvation Army in the United States, 1880–1992*. Grand Rapids, Mich.: Eerdmans, 1995.

———. *Somebody's Brother: A History of the Salvation Army's Men's Social Service Department, 1891–1985*. Lewiston, N.Y.: Mellen, 1986.

Merritt, John G., ed. *Historical Dictionary of the Salvation Army*. Lanham, Md.: Scarecrow, anticipated 2001 publication.

Murdoch, Norman H. *Origins of the Salvation Army*. Knoxville: University of Tennessee Press, 1994.

———. "Salvation Army Disturbances in Liverpool England, 1879–1887." *Journal of Social History* 25 (Spring 1992): 575–93.

Rightmire, R. David. *Sacraments and the Salvation Army: Pneumatological Foundations*. Metuchen, N.J.: Scarecrow, 1990.

Spence, Clark C. *The Salvation Army Farm Colonies*. Tucson: University of Arizona Press, 1985.

Taiz, Lillian. "Applying the Devil's Works in a Holy Cause: Working-Class Popular Culture and the Salvation Army in the United States." *Religion and American Culture* 7 (Summer 1997): 195–224.

Winston, Diane H. *Red Hot and Righteous: The Urban Religion of the Salvation Army*. Cambridge, Mass.: Harvard University Press, 1999.

SOCIETY OF FRIENDS

Hamm, Thomas. *The Transformation of American Quakerism: Orthodox Friends, 1800–1907*. Bloomington: University of Indiana Press, 1988.

Oliver, John. "J. Walter Malone: The *American Friend* and an Evangelical Friends Social Agenda." *Quaker History* 80 (Fall 1991): 63–84.

Spencer, Carole D. "The American Holiness Movement: Why Did It Capture Nineteenth Century Friends?" *Quaker Religious Thought* (January 1998): 19–30.

———. "Evangelicalism, Feminism and Social Reform: The Quaker Woman Minister and the Holiness Revival." *Quaker History* 80 (Spring 1991): 24–48.

UNITED BRETHREN IN CHRIST

Elliott, Daryl M. "Entire Sanctification and the Church of the United Brethren in Christ." *Methodist History* 24 (July 1987): 203–21.
O'Malley, J. Steven. *Early German–American Evangelicalism Pietist Sources of Discipleship and Sanctification.* Lanham, Md.: Scarecrow, 1995.

UNITED HOLY CHURCH

Turner, William Clair, Jr. "The United Holy Church of America: A Study in Black Holiness–Pentecostalism." Ph.D. diss., Duke University, 1984.

UNITED METHODIST CHURCH

Spann, Glenn. "Evangelicalism in Modern American Methodism: Theological Conservatism in the 'Great Deep' of the Church, 1900–1980." Ph.D. diss., Johns Hopkins University, 1994.

WESLEYAN CHURCH

Caldwell, Wayne, ed. *Revivalists and Reformers: A History of the Wesleyan Church.* Indianapolis: Wesley Press, 1992.

CAMP MEETINGS

Jones, Charles Edwin. *Perfectionist Persuasion: The Holiness Movement and American Methodism, 1867–1936.* Metuchen, N.J.: Scarecrow, 1974, pp. 16–46.
Kostlevy, William. "Christian Perfection in Pennsylvania Dutch Country: The 1868 Manheim Camp Meeting of the National Holiness Association." *Chronicle: Journal of the Historical Society of the Central Pennsylvania Conference of the United Methodist Church* 9 (Spring 1998): 25–35.
Leyh, George, Jr. "Beulah Land on the Jersey Shore: Ocean Grove Camp Meeting, 1869–1919." Ph.D. diss., Temple University, 1997.

Messenger, Troy Wayne. *Recreation and Religion in God's Square Mile*. Minneapolis: University of Minnesota Press, 1999. (A study of Ocean Grove, New
Jersey.)

Uminowicz, Glenn. "Recreation in Christian America: Ocean Grove and Asbury
Park, New Jersey, 1869–1914." In *Hard at Play: Leisure in America, 1840–
1940*, ed. Kathryn Grover. Amherst: University of Massachusetts Press;
Rochester, N.Y.: Strong Museum, 1992.

EDUCATION

Dieter, Melvin E. "Holiness Churches." *Theological Education in the Evangelical
Tradition*, ed. D.G. Hart and R. Albert Mohler, Jr. Grand Rapids, Mich.: 1996.

Kisker, Scott. "The Claude Thompson Controversy at Asbury Theological Seminary." *Wesleyan Theological Journal* 33 (Fall 1998): 230–48.

Ringenberg, Roger. "A History of Jamaica Theological Seminary, 1960–1992."
Ph.D. diss., Trinity Evangelical Divinity School, 1992.

Ringenberg, William C. *Taylor University: The First 150 Years*. Grand Rapids,
Mich.: Eerdmans, 1996.

MISSIONS

Bays, Daniel H. "The Early Days of the Oriental Missionary Society: Foreign
Missionaries and Native Evangelists in Japan." *Fides et Historia* 29
(Winter/Spring 1997): 15–27.

Brown, Earl Kent. "Isabella Thoburn." *Methodist History* 22 (July 1984): 179–91.

Bundy, David. "Bishop William Taylor and Methodist Mission: A Study of Nineteenth Century Social History." *Methodist History* 27, 28 (July, October 1989):
197–210, 3–21.

———. "The Theology of the Kingdom of God in the Theology of E. Stanley
Jones." *Wesleyan Theological Journal* 23 (Spring–Fall 1988): 58–80.

THEOLOGY AND DOCTRINE

Bassett, Paul. "A Study in the Theology of the Early Holiness Movement."
Methodist History 13 (April 1975): 61–84.

Bassett, Paul M., and William M. Greathouse. *Exploring Christian Holiness: The
Historical Development*. Kansas City, Mo.: Beacon Hill, 1985.

Dayton, Donald W. "Millennial Views and Social Reform in Nineteenth Century
America." In *The Coming Kingdom: Essays on American Millennialism and*

Eschatology, ed. M. Darrol Bryant and Donald W. Dayton. Barrytown, N.Y.: International Religious Foundation, 1983.

Dayton, Donald W., and Lucille S. Dayton. "A Historical Survey of Christian Attitudes toward War and Peace in the American Holiness Tradition." In *Perfect Love and War: A Dialog on Christian Holiness and the Issues of War and Peace,* ed. Paul Hostetler. Nappanee, Ind.: Evangel Press, 1974.

Dieter, Melvin E. "The Concept of the Church in the Nineteenth Century Holiness Revival." In *The Church: Wesleyan Theological Perspectives,* ed. Melvin E. Dieter and Daniel N. Berg. Anderson, Ind.: Warner, 1985.

———. "The Development of Holiness Theology in the Nineteenth Century." *Wesleyan Theological Journal* 20 (Spring 1985): 61–77.

Langford, Thomas A. *Practical Divinity: Theology in the Wesleyan Tradition,* 2 vols. Nashville: Abingdon, 1998–1999.

Lindsay, Leroy. "Radical Remedy: The Eradication of Sin and Related Terminology in Wesleyan–Holiness Thought." Ph.D. diss., Drew University, 1996.

Numbers, Ronald. "Creation, Evolution and Holy Ghost Religion: Holiness and Pentecostal Responses to Darwin." *Religion and American Culture* 2 (Summer 1992): 127–58.

Peters, John L. *Christian Perfection in American Methodism.* Nashville: Abingdon, 1956.

Reed, Rodney. "Toward the Integrity of Social and Personal Ethics in the Holiness Movement." Ph.D. diss., Drew University, 1995.

Thornton, Wallace, Jr. *Radical Righteousness: Personal Ethics and the Development of the Holiness Movement.* Salem, Ohio: Schmul, 1998.

Wilcox, Leslie D. *Be Ye Holy: A Study of the Teaching of Scripture Relative to Entire Sanctification and the Literature of the Holiness Movement.* Salem, Ohio: Schmul, 1977.

Wood, Laurence W. *Pentecostal Grace.* Wilmore, Ky.: Francis Asbury Press, 1980.

WORSHIP

Jones, Charles Edwin. *Perfectionist Persuasion: The Holiness Movement and American Methodism 1867–1936.* Metuchen, N.J.: Scarecrow, 1974, pp. 35–46.

Reed, Rodney L. "Worship, Relevance and the Preferential Option for the Poor in the Holiness Movement." *Wesleyan Theological Journal* 32 (Fall 1997): 80–104.

Wilhoit, Mel R. "American Holiness Hymnody: Some Questions of Methodology." *Wesleyan Theological Journal* 25 (Fall 1990): 39–63.

About the Editors

William C. Kostlevy holds degrees from Asbury College, Marquette University, Bethany Theological Seminary, and the University of Notre Dame (Ph.D.). He is archivist and special collections librarian at Asbury Theological Seminary. His published articles have appeared in *Methodist History*, the *Wesleyan Theological Journal*, *Brethren Life and Thought*, and the *Wisconsin Magazine of History*. He is the author and compiler of *Holiness Manuscripts: A Guide to Sources Documenting the Wesleyan Holiness Movement in the United States and Canada* (Scarecrow Press, 1994). He is secretary-treasurer of the Wesleyan Theological Society and a fellow of the Center for the Study of Anabaptist and Pietist Groups at Elizabethtown College in Pennsylvania.

Gari-Anne Patzwald holds degrees from the State University of New York at Geneseo, the University of Wisconsin, and Lexington Theological Seminary. She is an independent scholar, editor, and indexer. Her book reviews have appeared in *Library Journal* and *American Reference Books Annual*. She has been an abstractor for *America: History and Life* and *Historical Abstracts*. She has presented several conference papers and is currently writing a book on the Megiddo Mission of Rochester, New York.